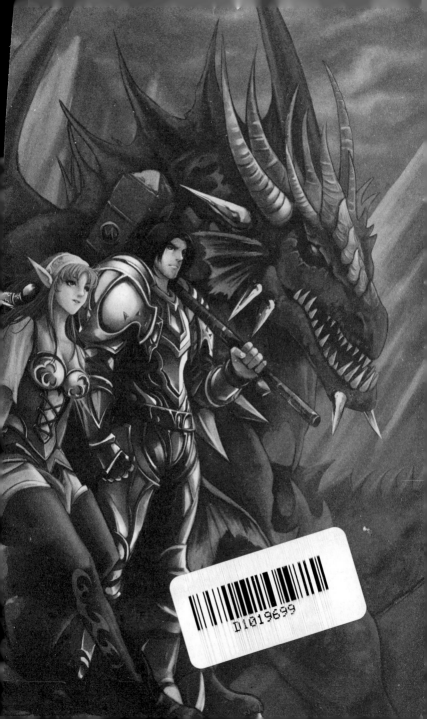

World Of Warcraft: Shadow Wing Vol. 1
Story by: Richard A. Knaak
Art by: Jae-Hwan Kim

Retouch Artist, Layout & Lettering - Michael Paolilli
Creative Consultant - Michael Paolilli
Cover Designer - Louis Csontos
Cover Artist - Jae-Hwan Kim
Cover Art Retouch - Michael Paolilli

Editors - Troy Lewter and Paul Morrissey
Editorial Translator - Janice Kwon
Print Production Manager - Lucas Rivera
Managing Editor - Vy Nguyen
Senior Designer - Louis Csontos
Art Director - Al-Insan Lashley
Director of Sales and Manufacturing - Allyson De Simone
Associate Publisher - Marco F. Pavia
President and C.O.O. - John Parker
C.E.O. and Chief Creative Officer - Stu Levy

BLIZZARD ENTERTAINMENT
Senior Vice President, Creative Development - Chris Metzen
Director, Creative Development - Jeff Donais
Lead Developer, Licensed Products - Mike Hummel
Publishing Lead, Creative Development - Micky Neilson
Story Developer - James Waugh
Art Director - Glenn Rane
Director, Global Business
Development and Licensing - Cory Jones
Associate Licensing Manager - Jason Bischoff
Historian - Evelyn Fredericksen
Additional Development - Samwise Didier, Cameron Dayton and
Tommy Newcomer

A  Manga

TOKYOPOP and ⬤ are trademarks or registered trademarks of TOKYOPOP Inc.

TOKYOPOP Inc.
5900 Wilshire Blvd. Suite 2000
Los Angeles, CA 90036

E-mail: info@TOKYOPOP.com
Come visit us online at www.TOKYOPOP.com

ISBN: 978-1-4278-1026-7

First TOKYOPOP printing: June 2010
10 9 8 7 6 5 4 3 2 1
Printed in the USA

WORLD OF WARCRAFT®
SHADOW WING™

VOLUME ONE
THE DRAGON'S OF OUTLAND

STORY BY
RICHARD A. KNAAK

ART BY
JAE-HWAN KIM

HAMBURG // LONDON // LOS ANGELES // TOKYO

WORLD OF WARCRAFT

SHADOW WING

CHAPTER ONE

HERE THERE BE DEMONS

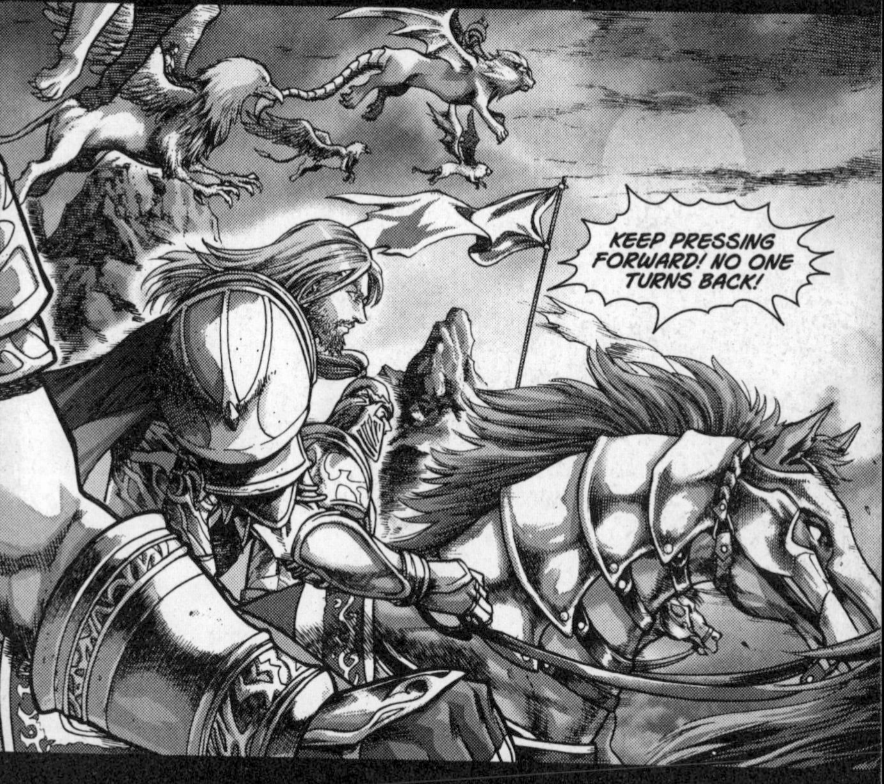
KEEP PRESSING FORWARD! NO ONE TURNS BACK!

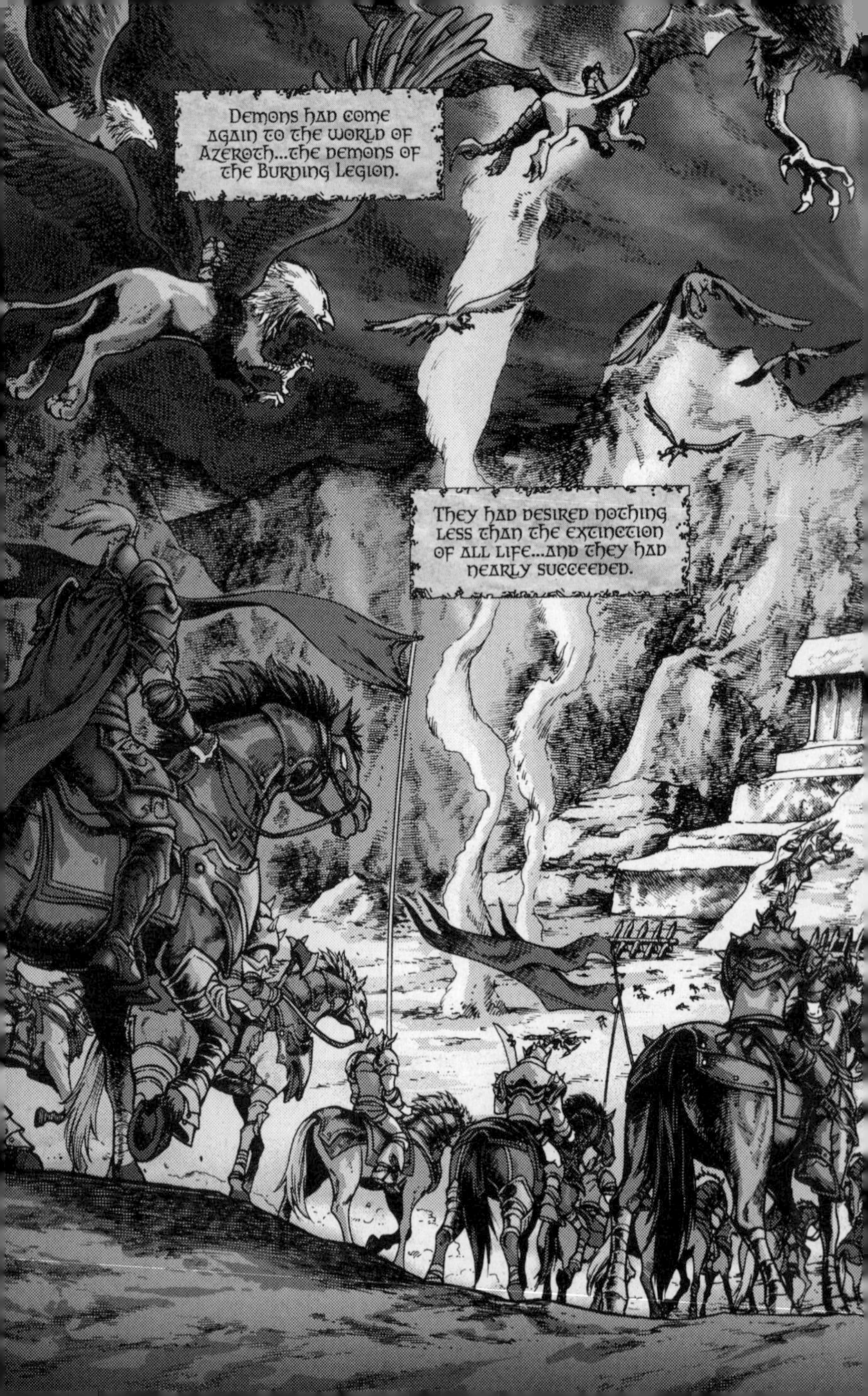
Demons had come again to the world of Azeroth...the demons of the Burning Legion.
They had desired nothing less than the extinction of all life...and they had nearly succeeded.

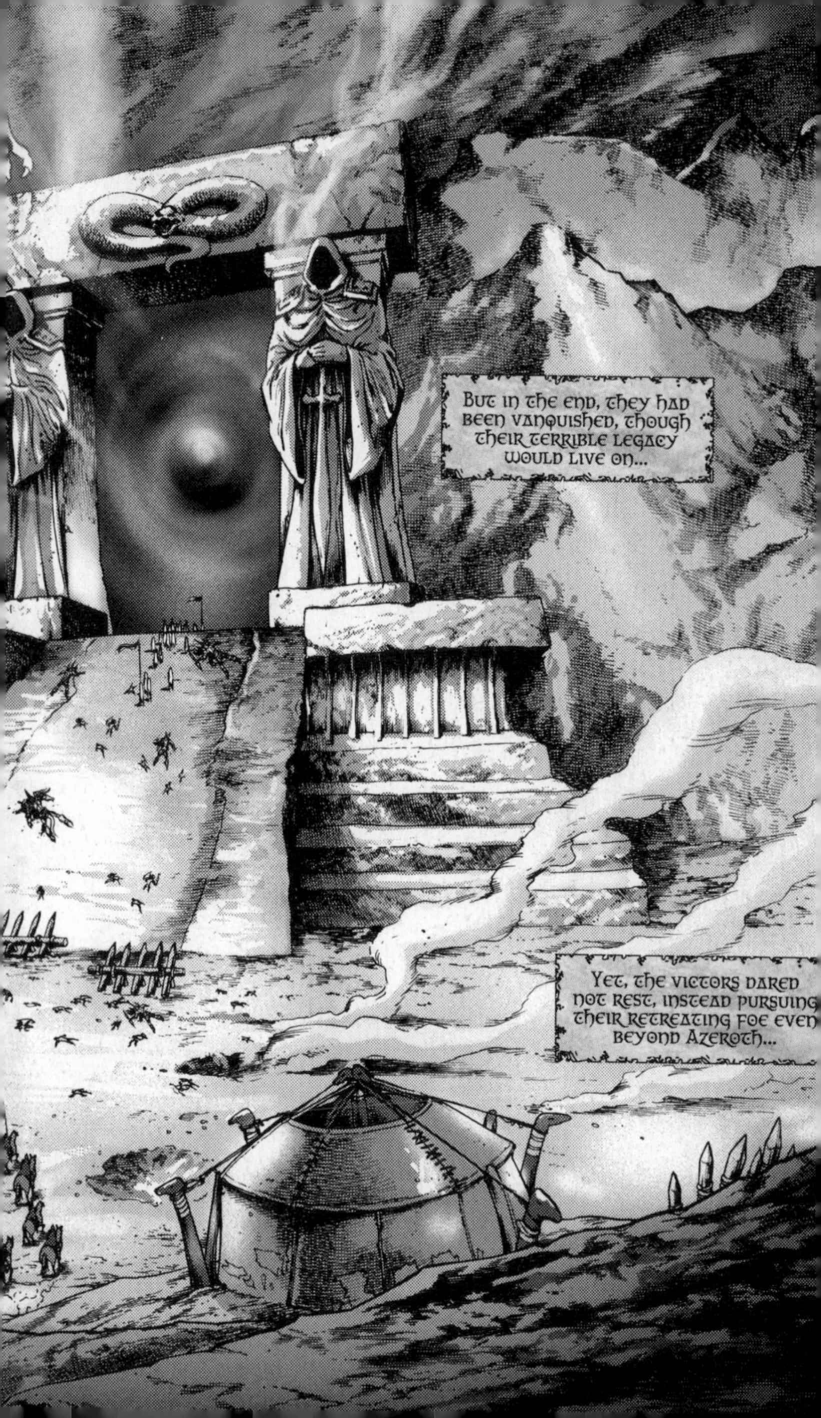
But in the end, they had been vanquished, though their terrible legacy would live on...
Yet, the victors dared not rest, instead pursuing their retreating foe even beyond Azeroth...

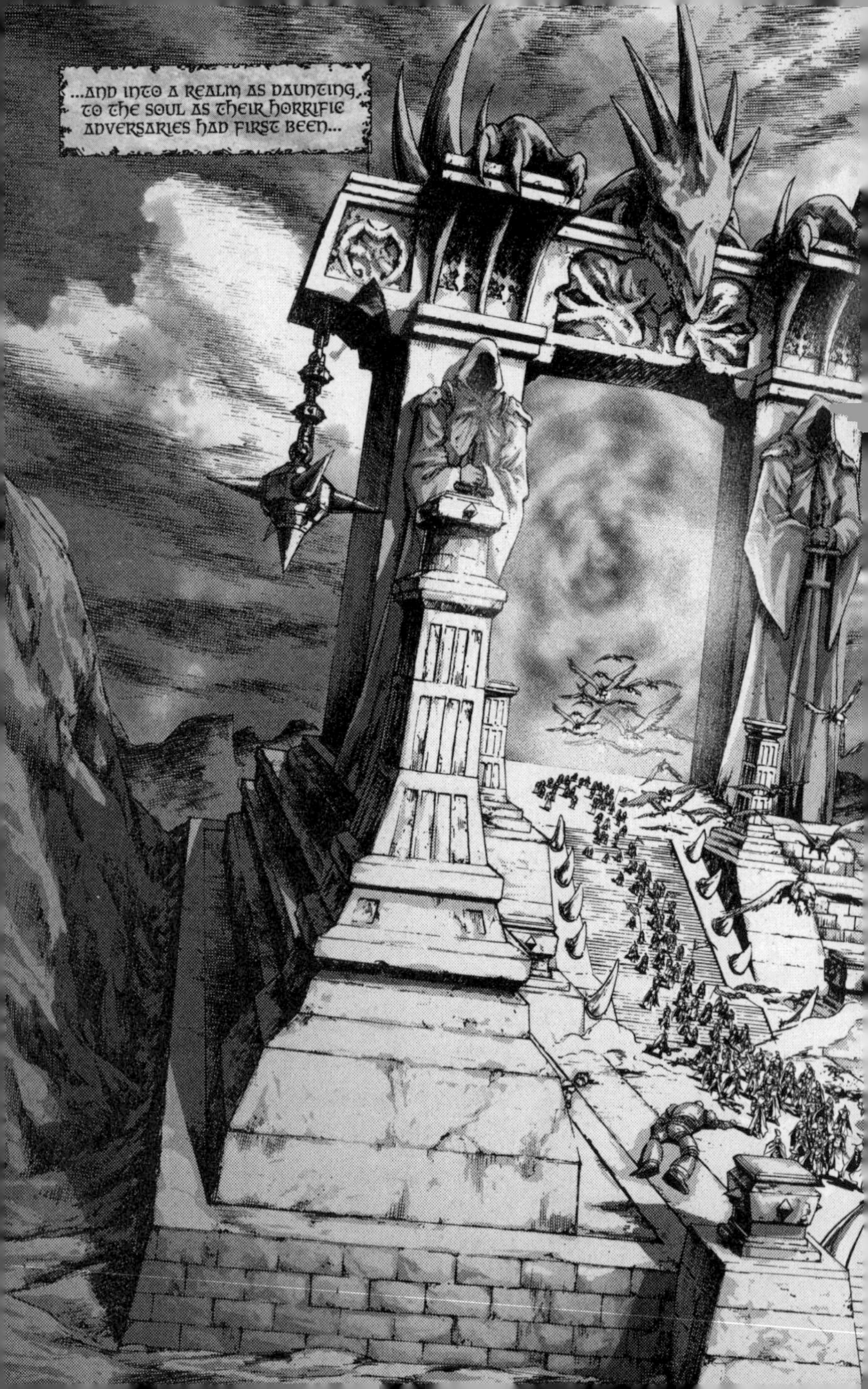
...AND INTO A REALM AS DAUNTING TO THE SOUL AS THEIR HORRIFIC ADVERSARIES HAD FIRST BEEN...

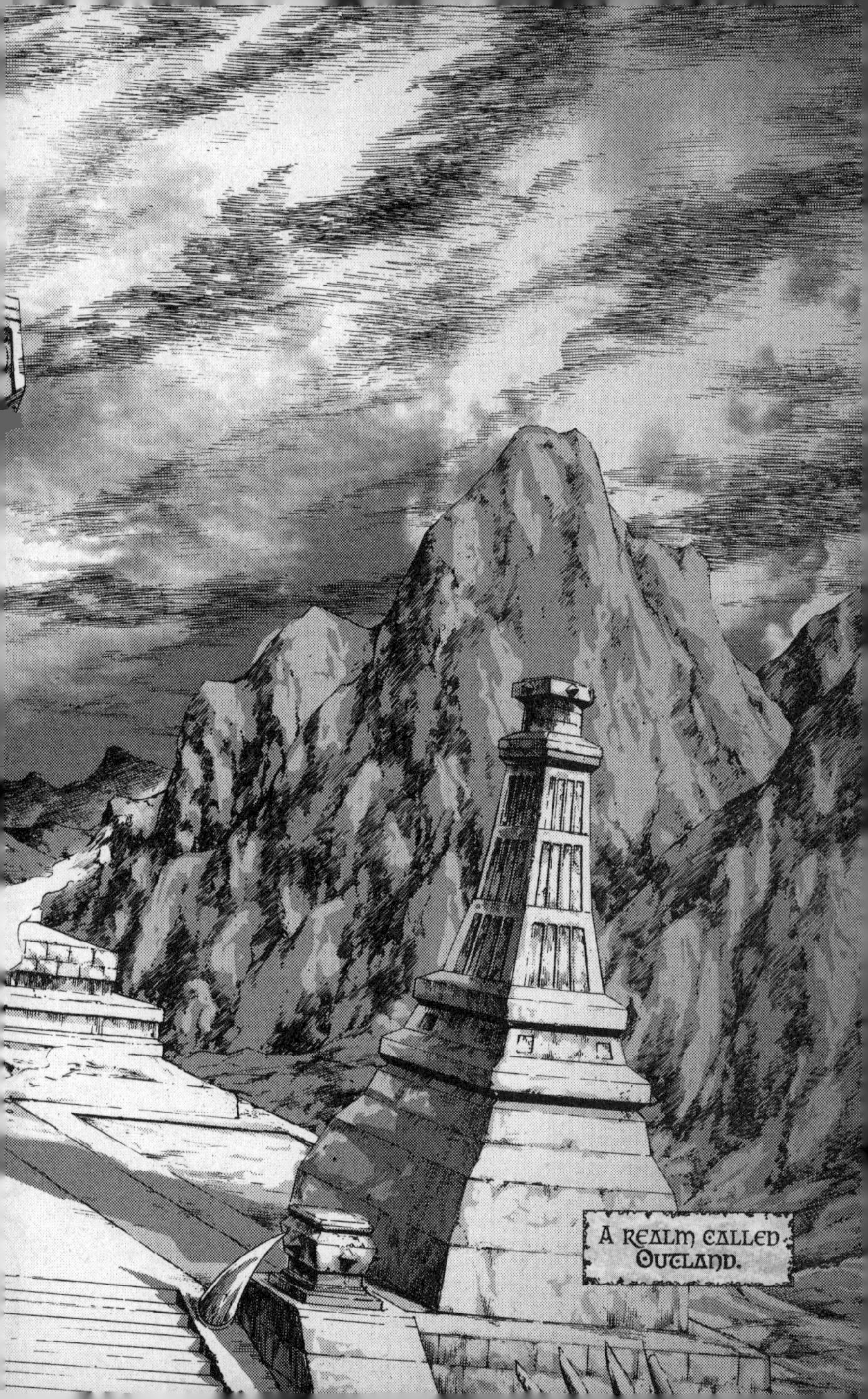
A REALM CALLED OUTLAND.

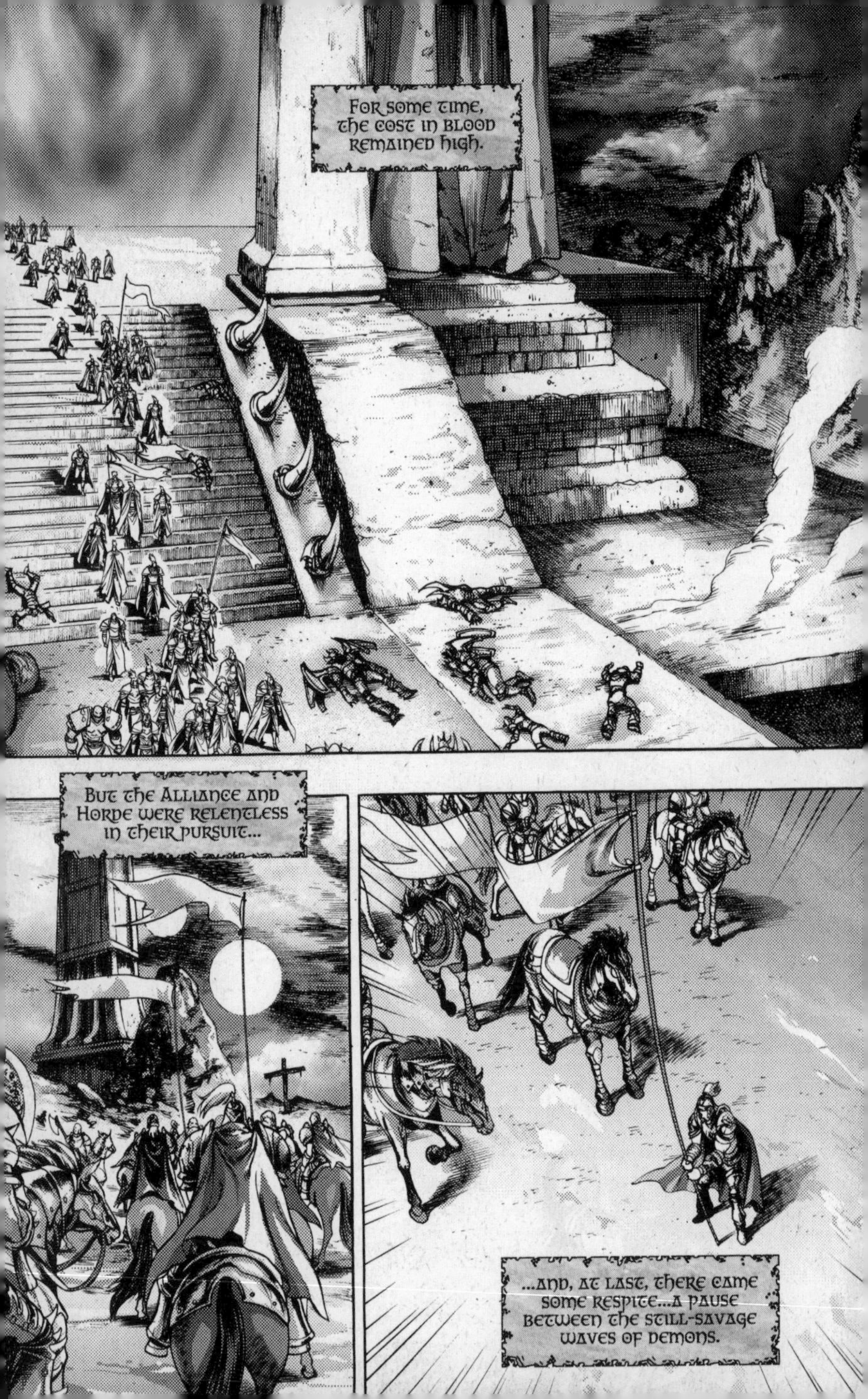
For some time, the cost in blood remained high.
But the Alliance and Horde were relentless in their pursuit...
...and, at last, there came some respite...a pause between the still-savage waves of demons.

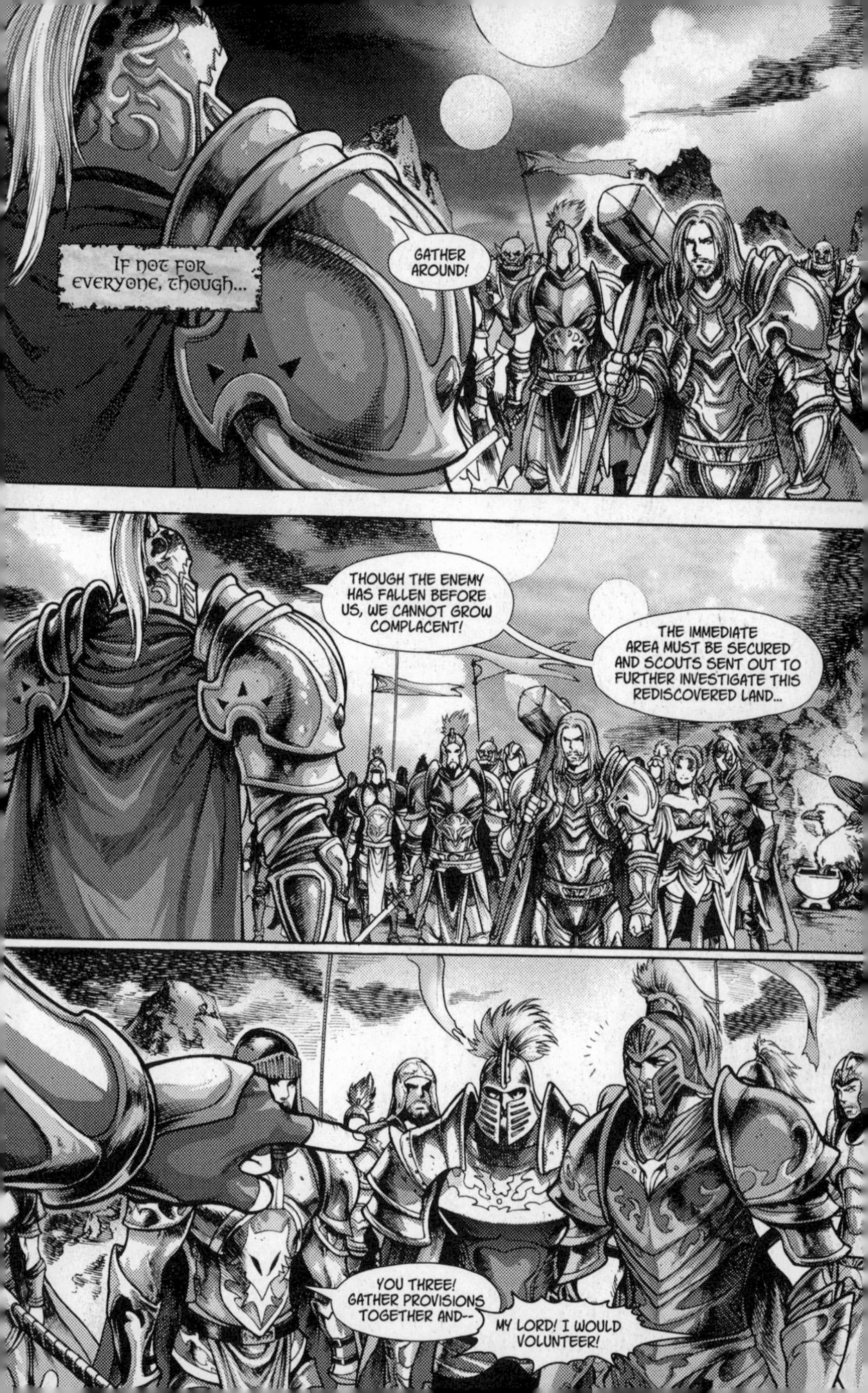
If not for everyone, though...
GATHER AROUND!
THOUGH THE ENEMY HAS FALLEN BEFORE US, WE CANNOT GROW COMPLACENT!
THE IMMEDIATE AREA MUST BE SECURED AND SCOUTS SENT OUT TO FURTHER INVESTIGATE THIS REDISCOVERED LAND...
YOU THREE! GATHER PROVISIONS TOGETHER AND--
MY LORD! I WOULD VOLUNTEER!

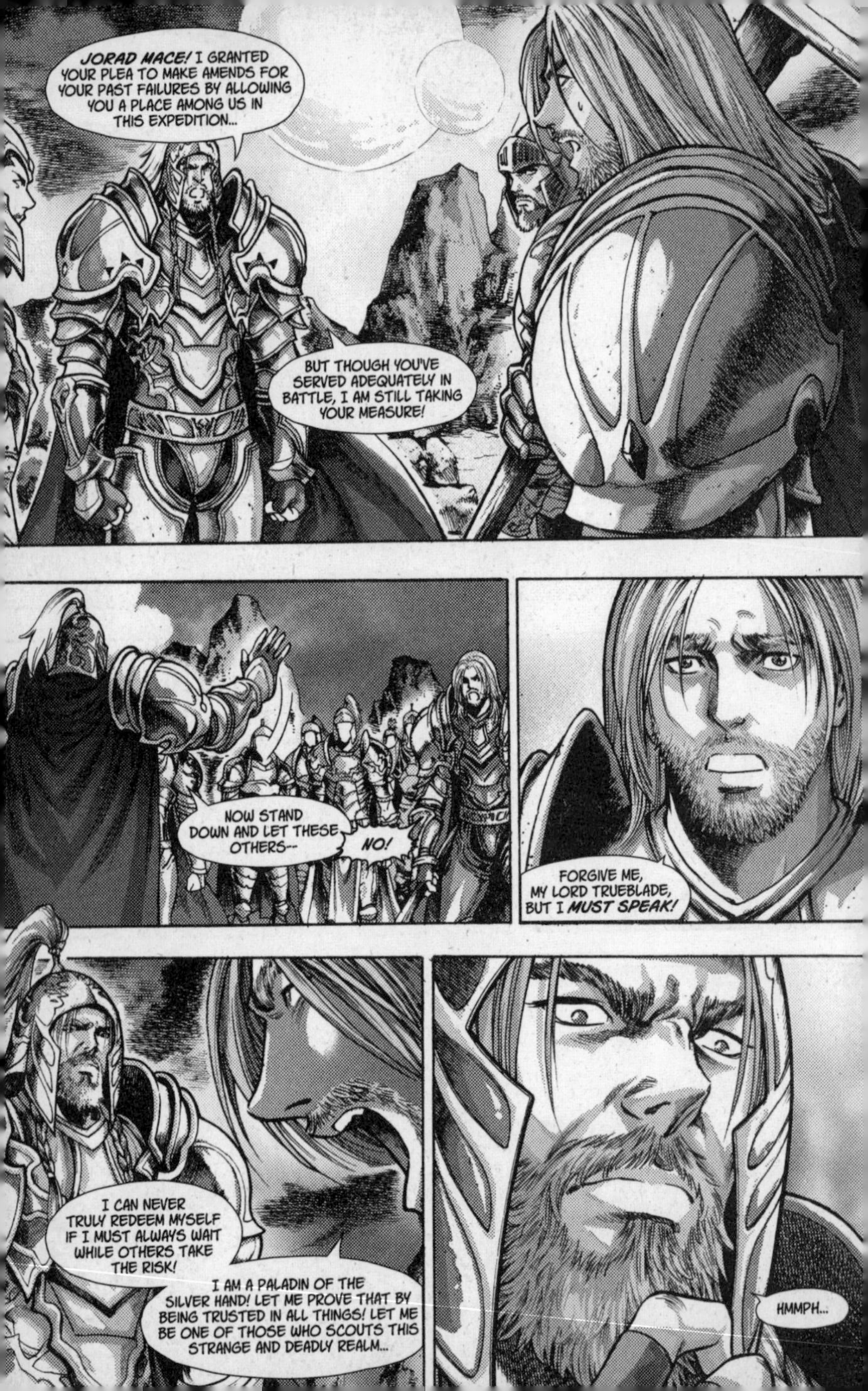
JORAD MACE! I GRANTED YOUR PLEA TO MAKE AMENDS FOR YOUR PAST FAILURES BY ALLOWING YOU A PLACE AMONG US IN THIS EXPEDITION...
BUT THOUGH YOU'VE SERVED ADEQUATELY IN BATTLE, I AM STILL TAKING YOUR MEASURE!
NOW STAND DOWN AND LET THESE OTHERS--
NO!
FORGIVE ME, MY LORD TRUEBLADE, BUT I MUST SPEAK!
I CAN NEVER TRULY REDEEM MYSELF IF I MUST ALWAYS WAIT WHILE OTHERS TAKE THE RISK!
I AM A PALADIN OF THE SILVER HAND! LET ME PROVE THAT BY BEING TRUSTED IN ALL THINGS! LET ME BE ONE OF THOSE WHO SCOUTS THIS STRANGE AND DEADLY REALM...
HMMPH...

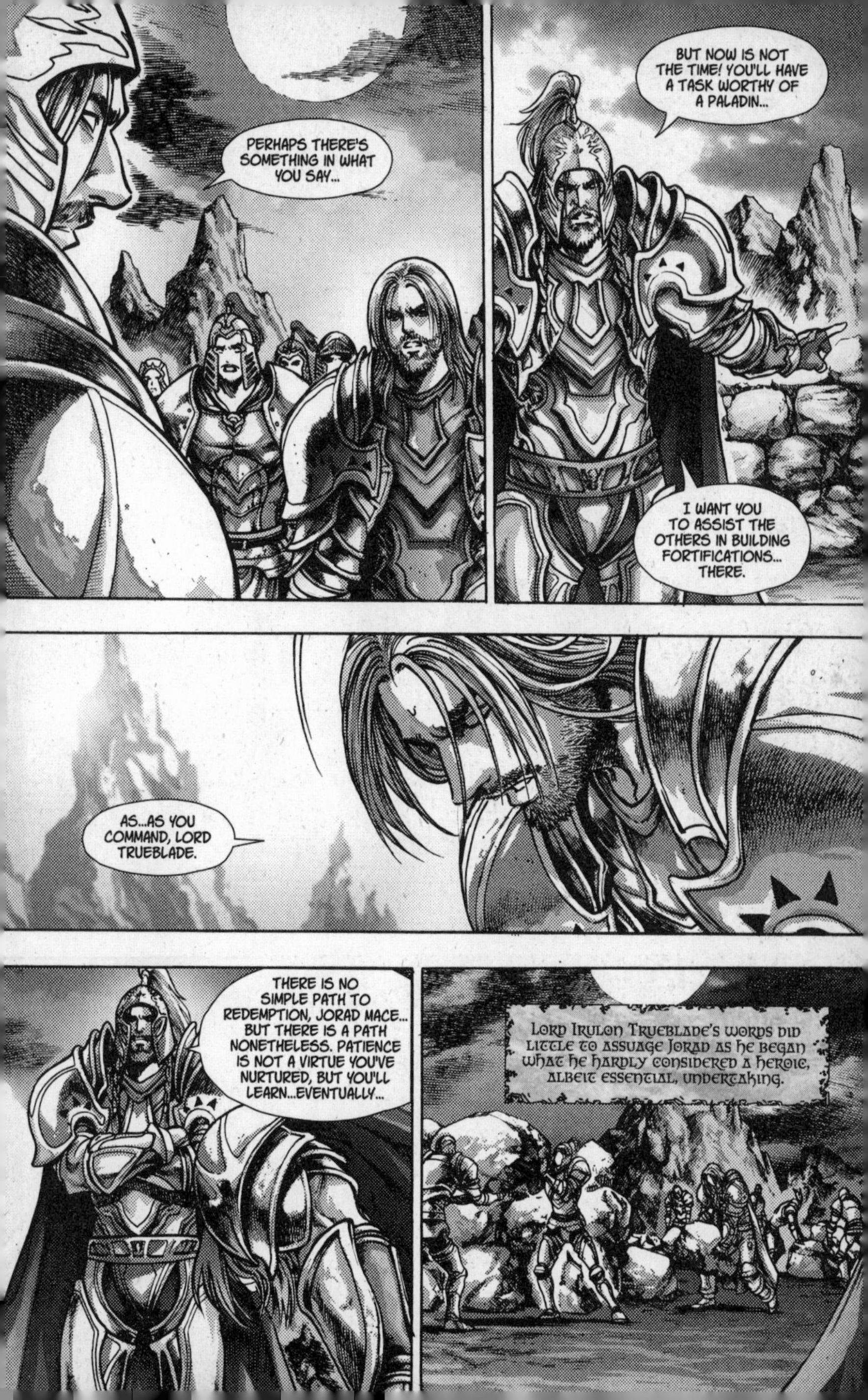
PERHAPS THERE'S SOMETHING IN WHAT YOU SAY...
BUT NOW IS NOT THE TIME! YOU'LL HAVE A TASK WORTHY OF A PALADIN...
I WANT YOU TO ASSIST THE OTHERS IN BUILDING FORTIFICATIONS... THERE.
AS...AS YOU COMMAND, LORD TRUEBLADE.
THERE IS NO SIMPLE PATH TO REDEMPTION, JORAD MACE... BUT THERE IS A PATH NONETHELESS. PATIENCE IS NOT A VIRTUE YOU'VE NURTURED, BUT YOU'LL LEARN...EVENTUALLY...
Lord Irulon Trueblade's words did little to assuage Jorad as he began what he hardly considered a heroic, albeit essential, undertaking.

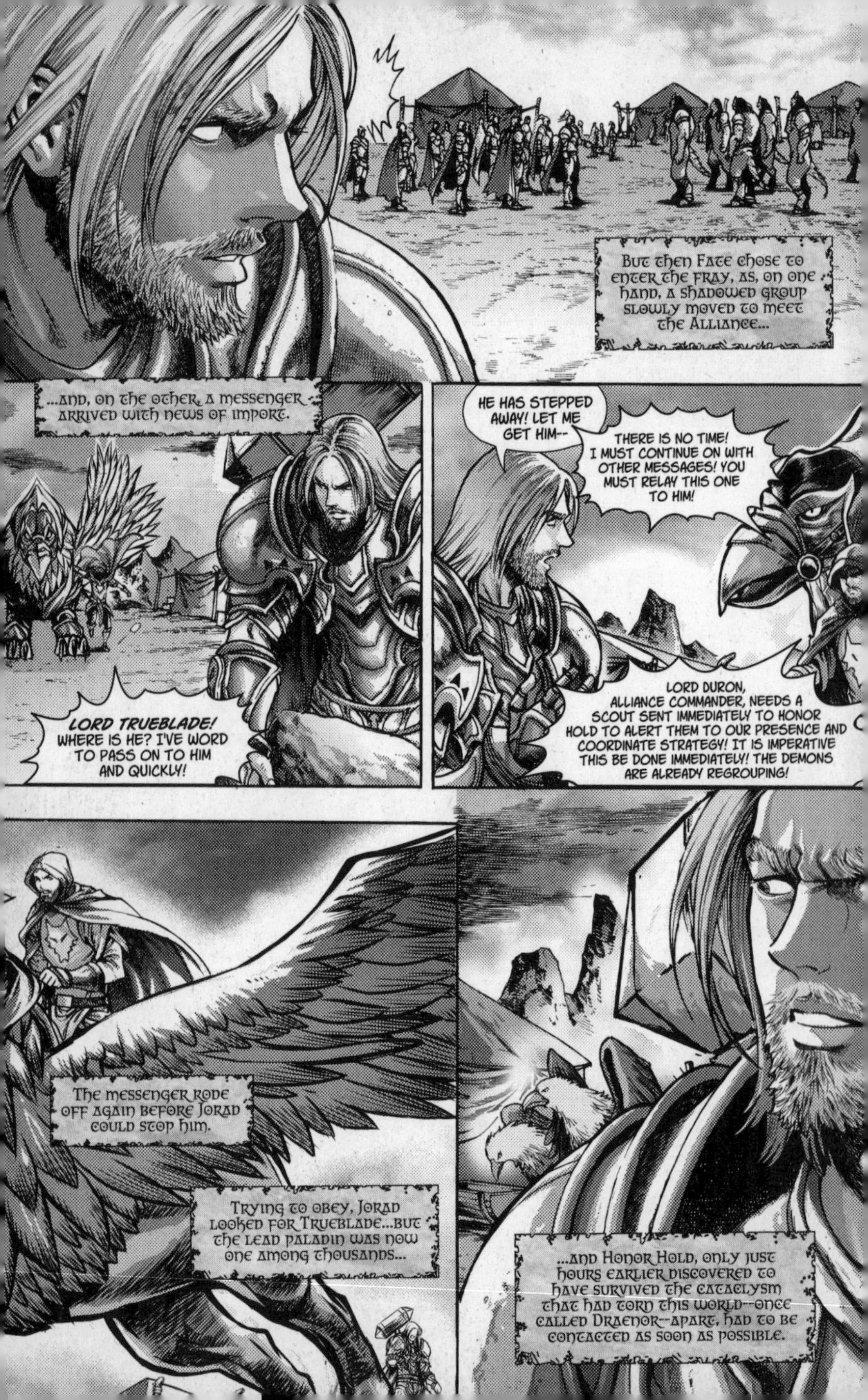
But then Fate chose to enter the fray, as, on one hand, a shadowed group slowly moved to meet the Alliance...
...and, on the other, a messenger arrived with news of import.
LORD TRUEBLADE! WHERE IS HE? I'VE WORD TO PASS ON TO HIM AND QUICKLY!
HE HAS STEPPED AWAY! LET ME GET HIM--
THERE IS NO TIME! I MUST CONTINUE ON WITH OTHER MESSAGES! YOU MUST RELAY THIS ONE TO HIM!
LORD DURON, ALLIANCE COMMANDER, NEEDS A SCOUT SENT IMMEDIATELY TO HONOR HOLD TO ALERT THEM TO OUR PRESENCE AND COORDINATE STRATEGY! IT IS IMPERATIVE THIS BE DONE IMMEDIATELY! THE DEMONS ARE ALREADY REGROUPING!
The messenger rode off again before Jorad could stop him.
Trying to obey, Jorad looked for Trueblade...but the lead paladin was now one among thousands...
...and Honor Hold, only just hours earlier discovered to have survived the cataclysm that had torn this world--once called Draenor--apart, had to be contacted as soon as possible.

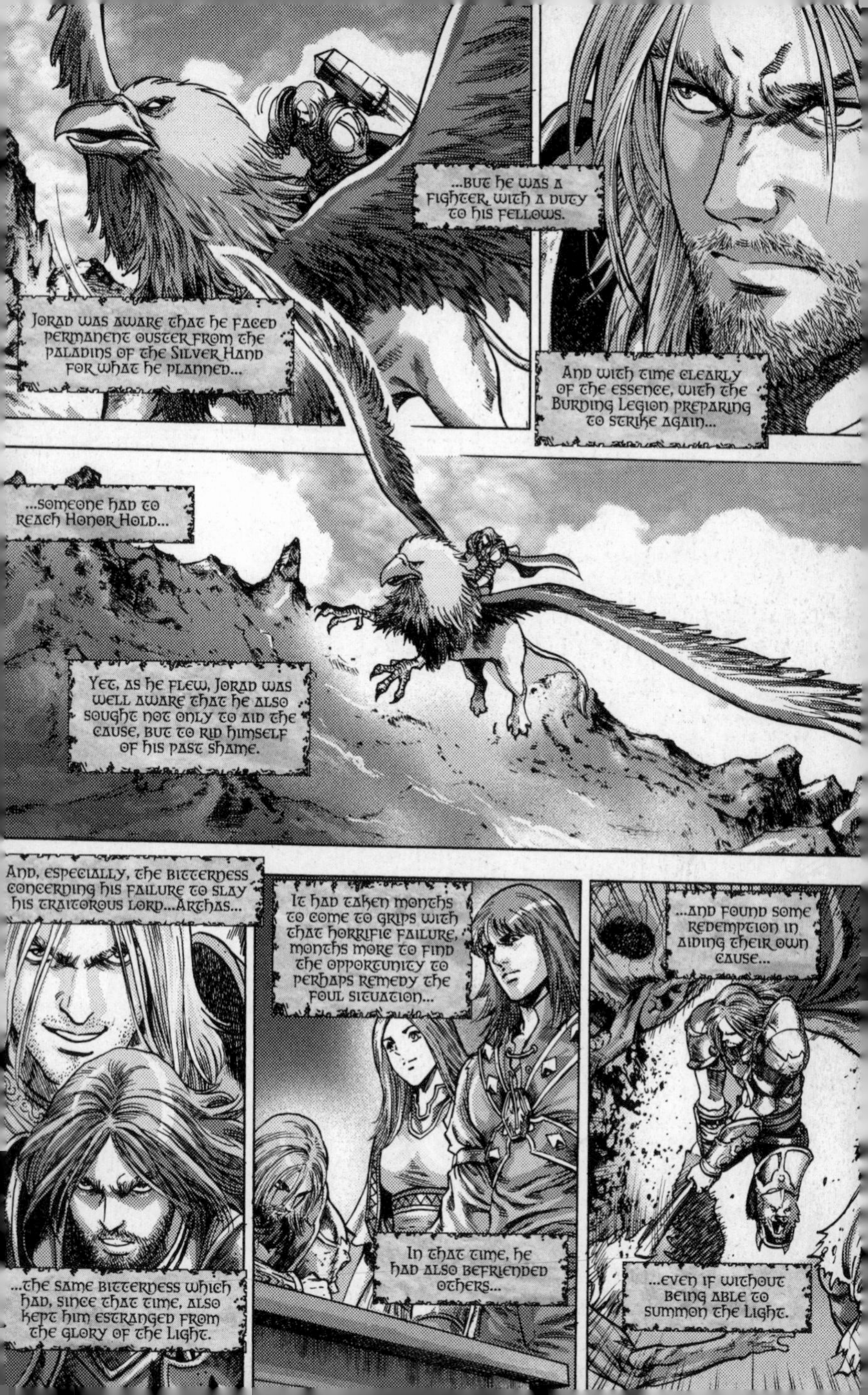
Jorad was aware that he faced permanent ouster from the paladins of the Silver Hand for what he planned...
...but he was a fighter, with a duty to his fellows.
And with time clearly of the essence, with the Burning Legion preparing to strike again...
...someone had to reach Honor Hold...
Yet, as he flew, Jorad was well aware that he also sought not only to aid the cause, but to rid himself of his past shame.
And, especially, the bitterness concerning his failure to slay his traitorous lord...Arthas...
...the same bitterness which had, since that time, also kept him estranged from the glory of the Light.
It had taken months to come to grips with that horrific failure, months more to find the opportunity to perhaps remedy the foul situation...
In that time, he had also befriended others...
...and found some redemption in aiding their own cause...
...even if without being able to summon the Light.

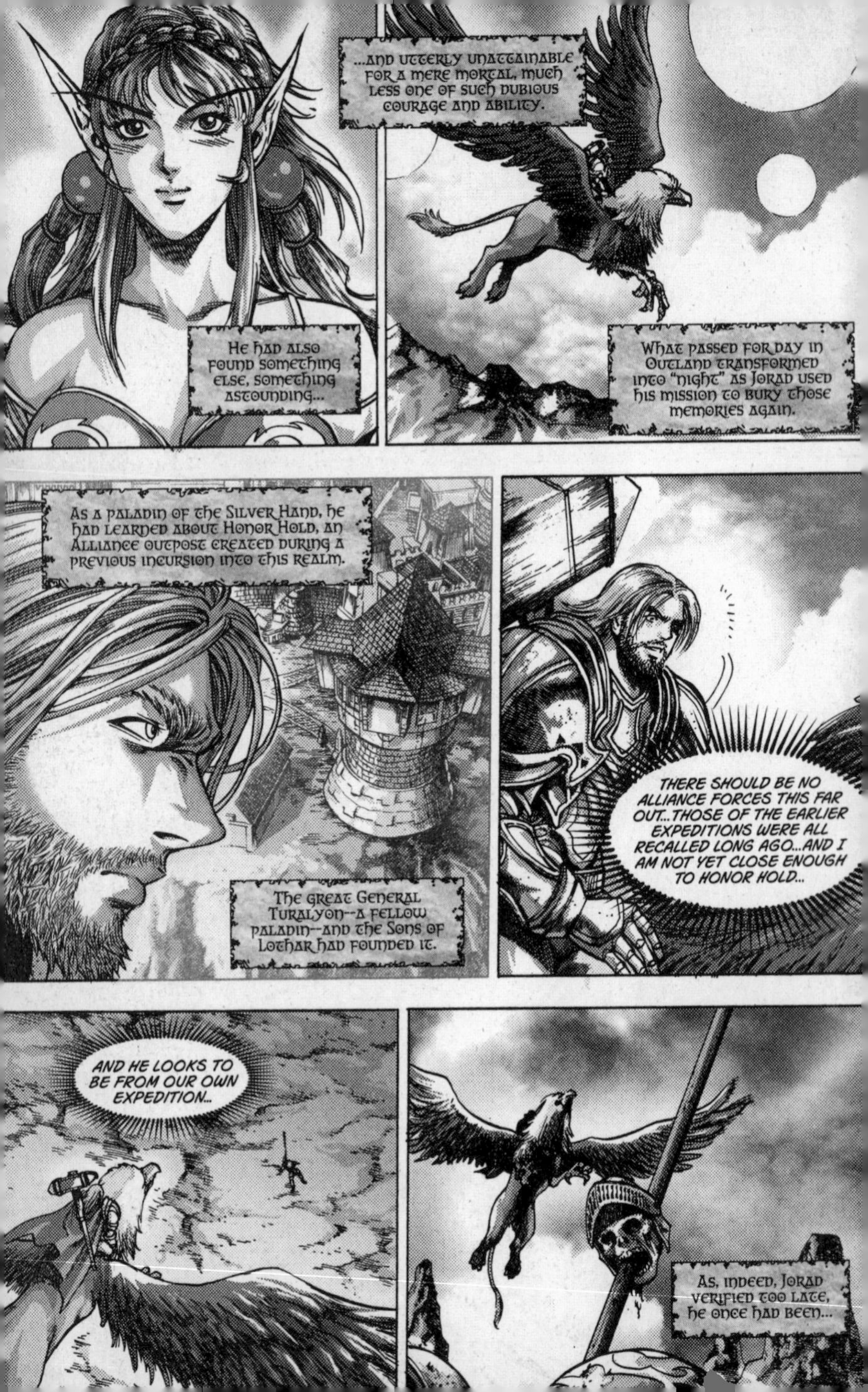

...AND UTTERLY UNATTAINABLE FOR A MERE MORTAL, MUCH LESS ONE OF SUCH DUBIOUS COURAGE AND ABILITY.
He had also found something else, something astounding...
What passed for day in Outland transformed into "night" as Jorad used his mission to bury those memories again.
As a paladin of the Silver Hand, he had learned about Honor Hold, an Alliance outpost created during a previous incursion into this realm.
The great General Turalyon--a fellow paladin--and the Sons of Lothar had founded it.
THERE SHOULD BE NO ALLIANCE FORCES THIS FAR OUT...THOSE OF THE EARLIER EXPEDITIONS WERE ALL RECALLED LONG AGO...AND I AM NOT YET CLOSE ENOUGH TO HONOR HOLD...
AND HE LOOKS TO BE FROM OUR OWN EXPEDITION...
As, indeed, Jorad verified too late, he once had been...

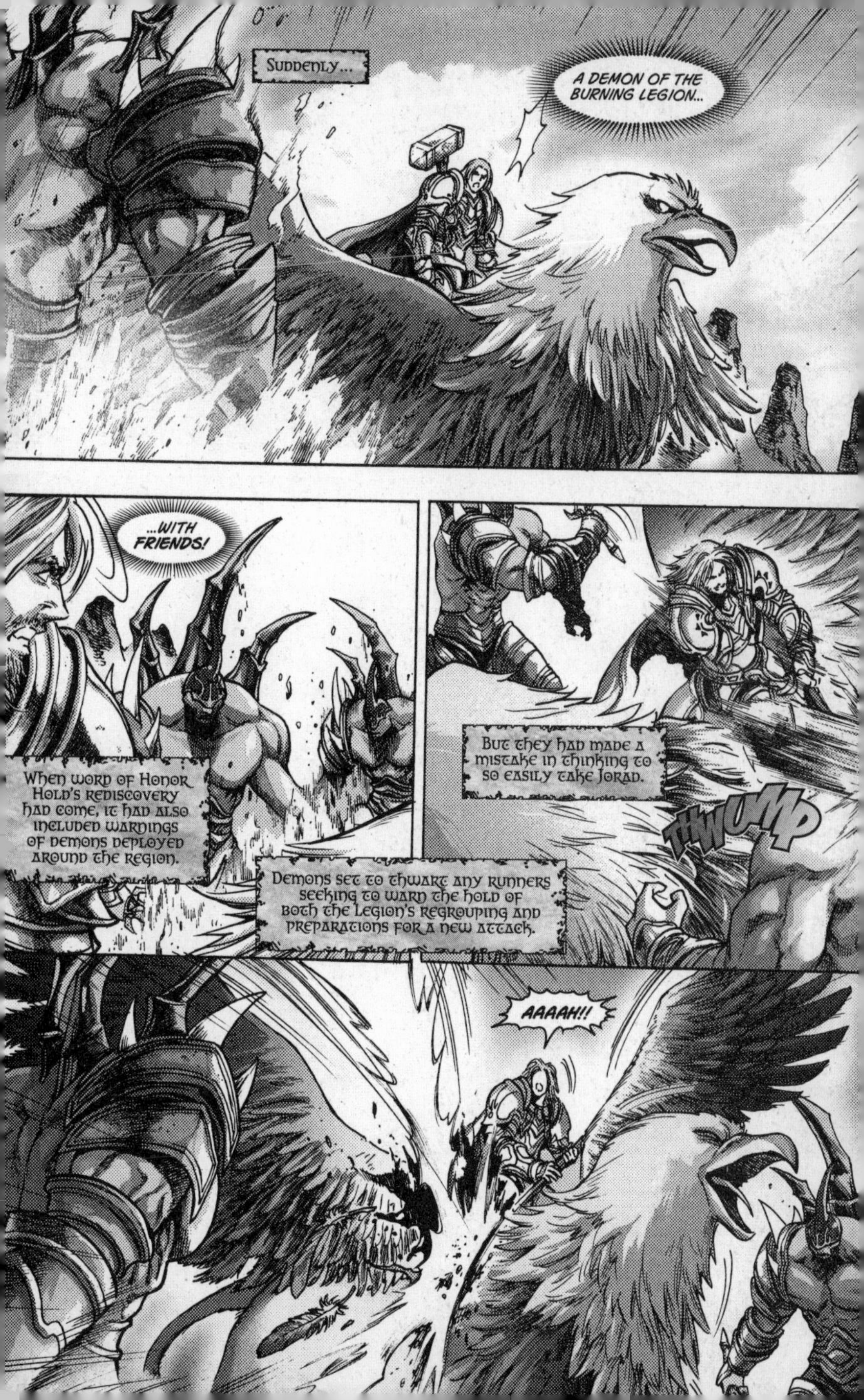
Suddenly...
A demon of the Burning Legion...
...With friends!
When word of Honor Hold's rediscovery had come, it had also included warnings of demons deployed around the region.
Demons set to thwart any runners seeking to warn the hold of both the Legion's regrouping and preparations for a new attack.
But they had made a mistake in thinking to so easily take Jorad.
THWUMP
AAAAH!!

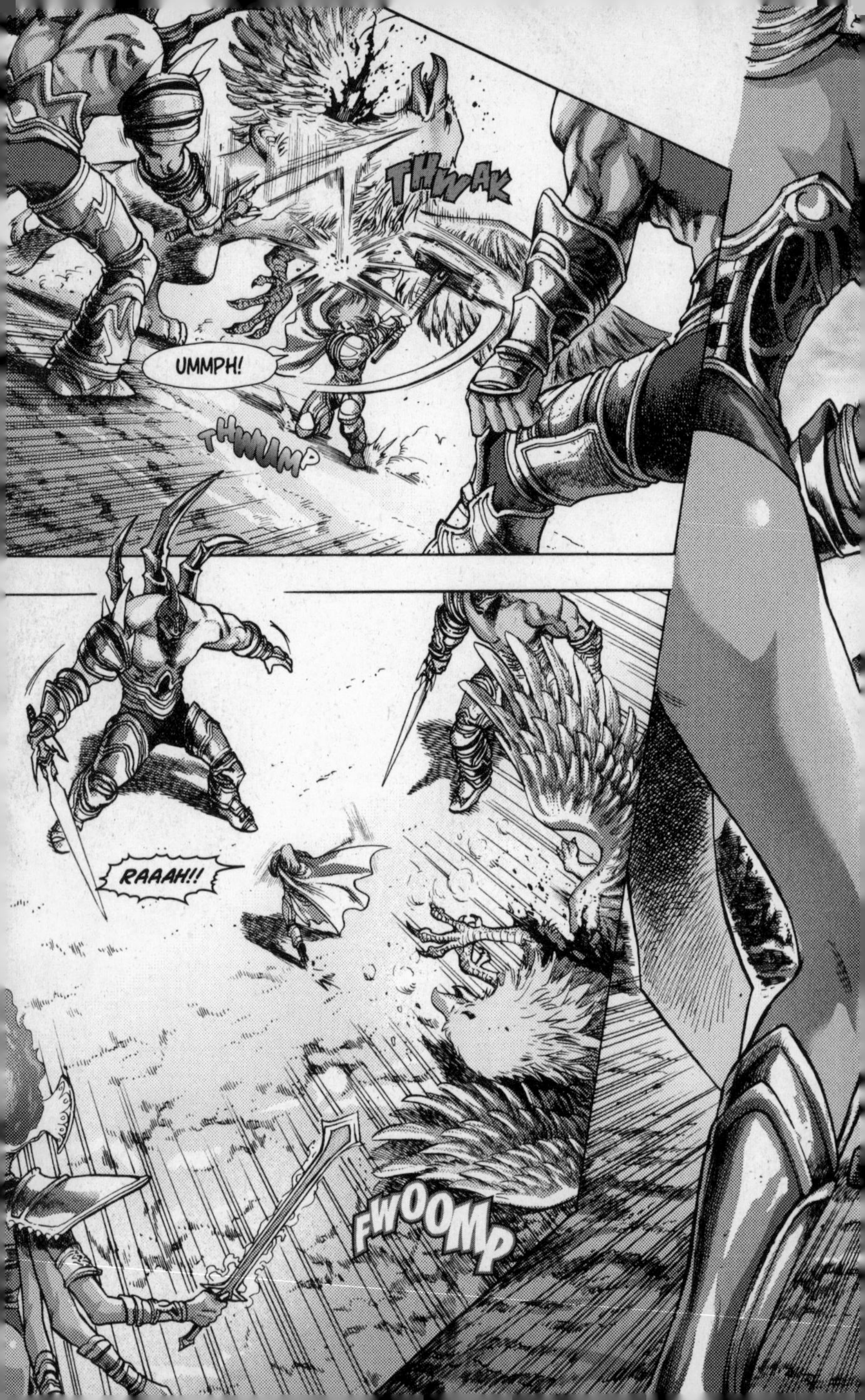

THWAK
UMMPH!
THWUMP
RAAAH!!
FWOOMP

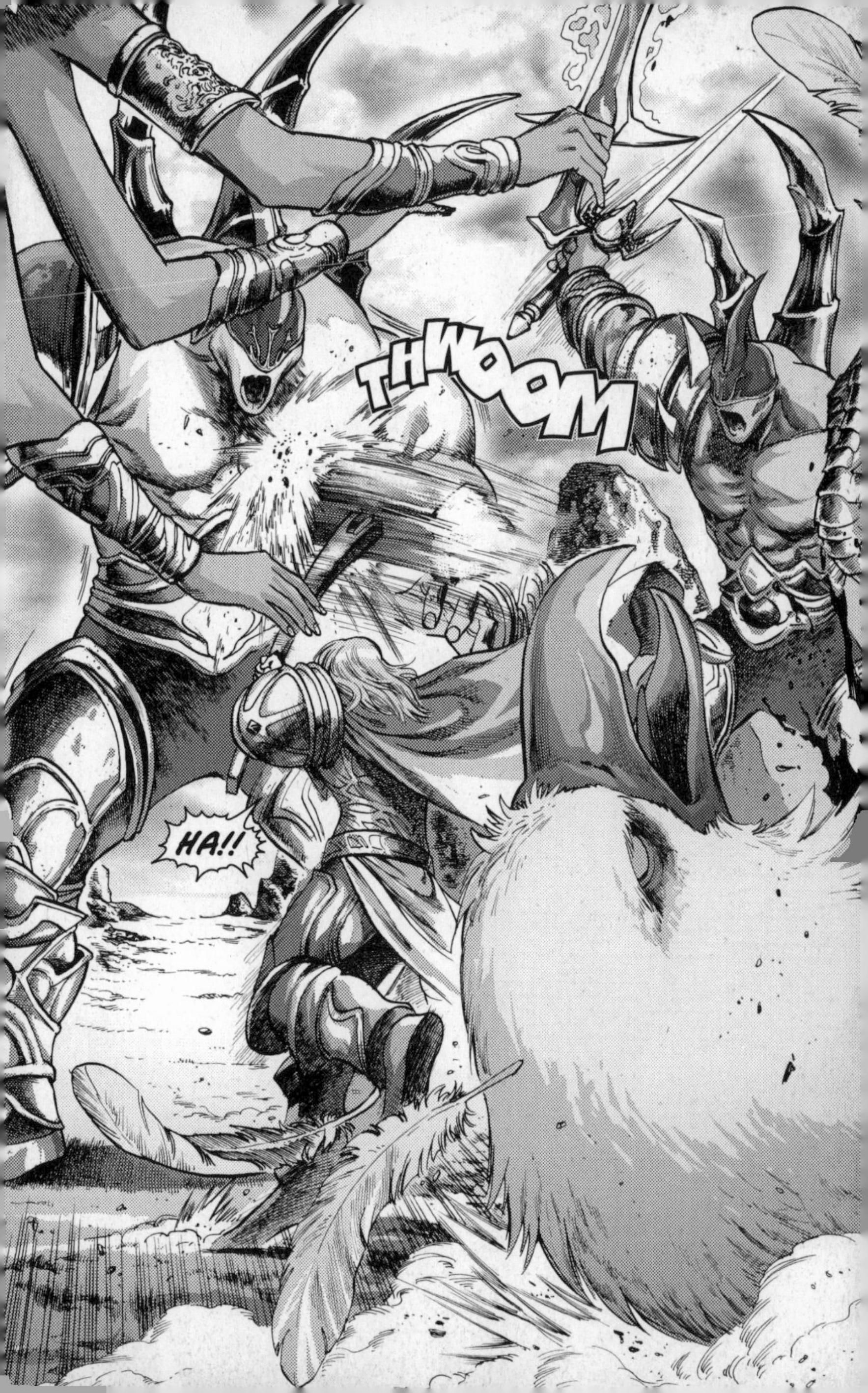
THWOOM
HA!!

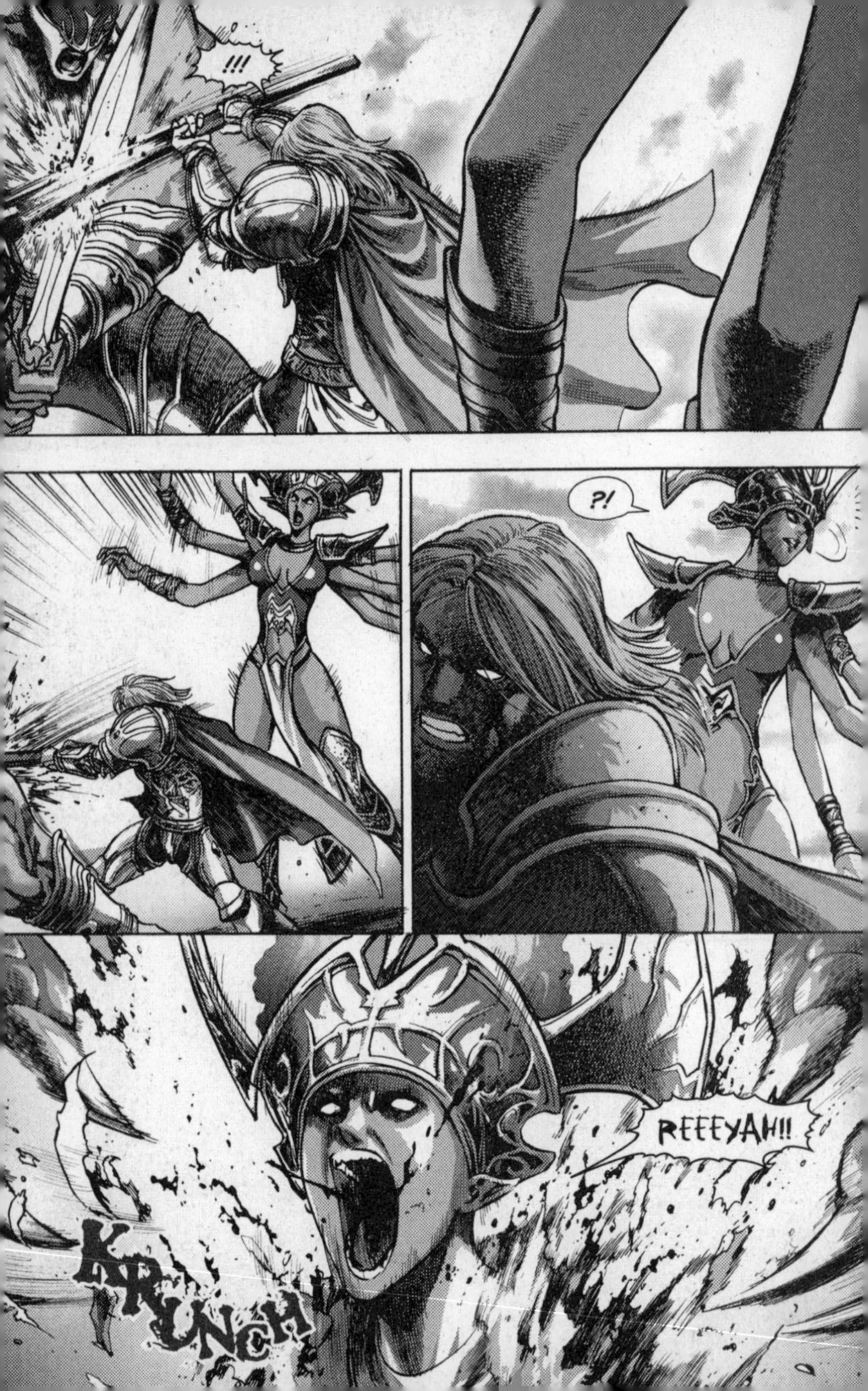
!!!
?!
REEEYAH!!
KRUNCH

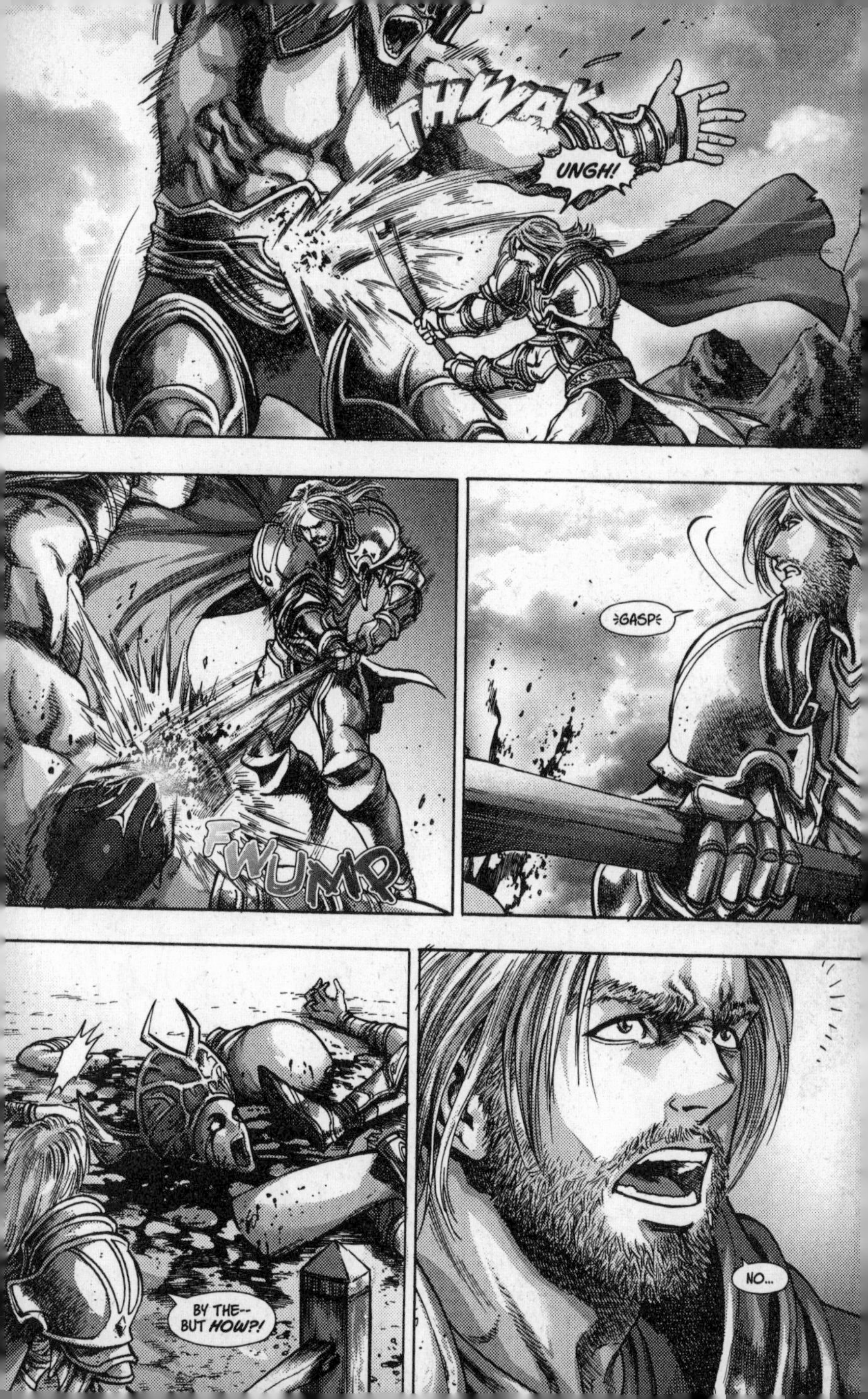
THWAK
UNGH!
FWUMP
GASP
BY THE-- BUT HOW?!
NO...

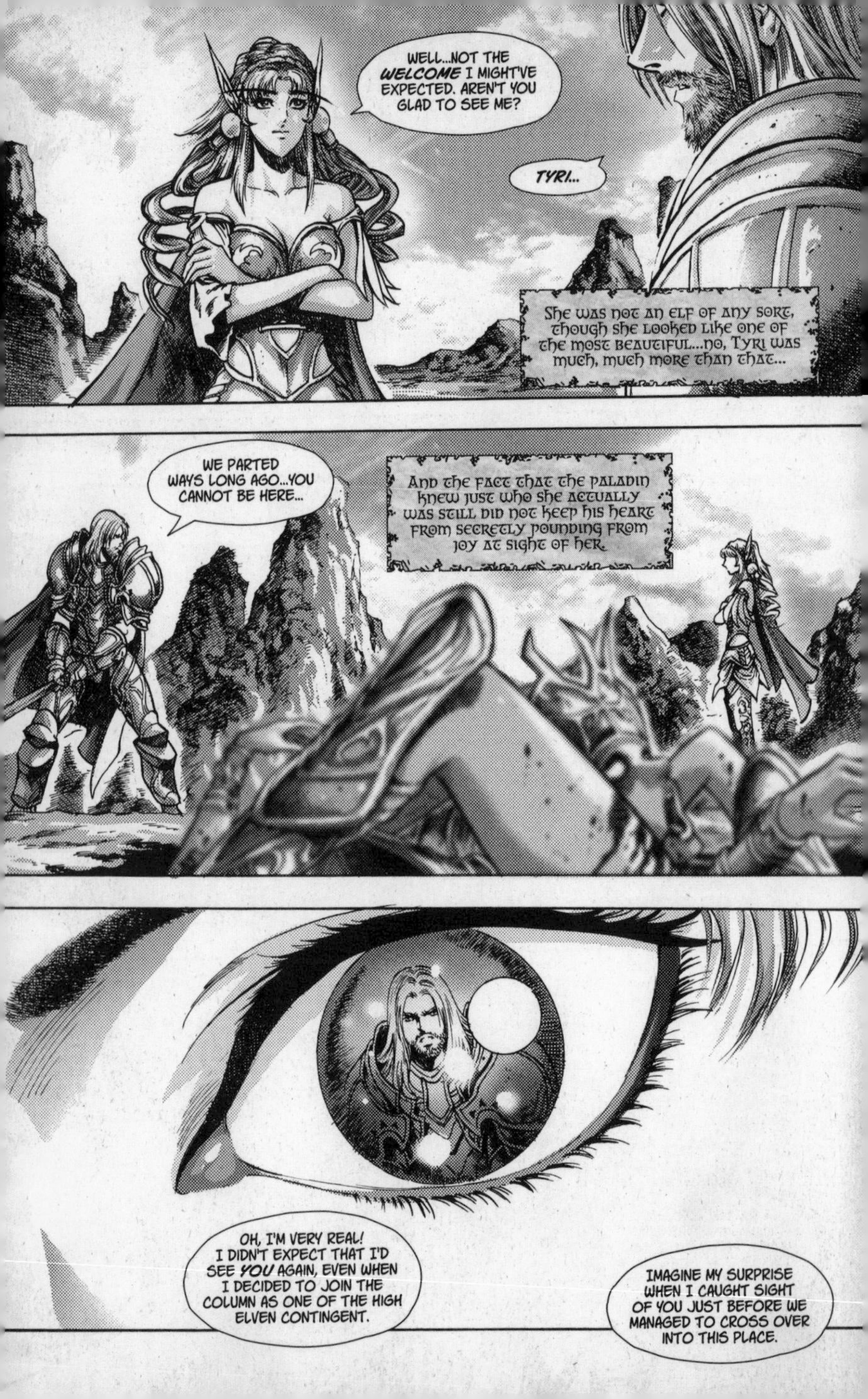
WELL...NOT THE WELCOME I MIGHT'VE EXPECTED. AREN'T YOU GLAD TO SEE ME?
TYRI...
She was not an elf of any sort, though she looked like one of the most beautiful...no, Tyri was much, much more than that...
WE PARTED WAYS LONG AGO...YOU CANNOT BE HERE...
And the fact that the paladin knew just who she actually was still did not keep his heart from secretly pounding from joy at sight of her.
OH, I'M VERY REAL! I DIDN'T EXPECT THAT I'D SEE YOU AGAIN, EVEN WHEN I DECIDED TO JOIN THE COLUMN AS ONE OF THE HIGH ELVEN CONTINGENT.
IMAGINE MY SURPRISE WHEN I CAUGHT SIGHT OF YOU JUST BEFORE WE MANAGED TO CROSS OVER INTO THIS PLACE.

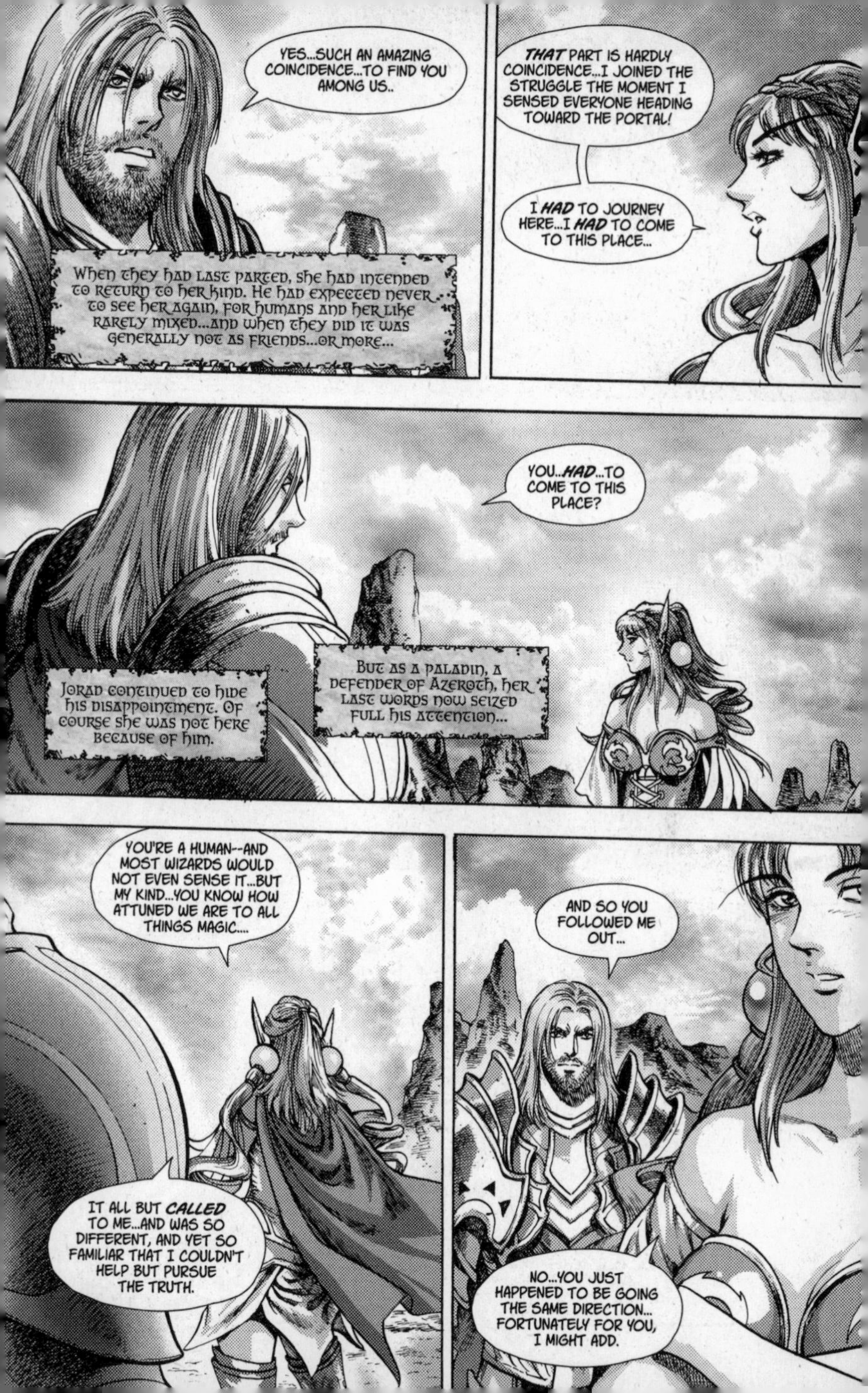

YES...SUCH AN AMAZING COINCIDENCE...TO FIND YOU AMONG US..
When they had last parted, she had intended to return to her kind. He had expected never to see her again, for humans and her like rarely mixed...and when they did it was generally not as friends...or more...
THAT PART IS HARDLY COINCIDENCE...I JOINED THE STRUGGLE THE MOMENT I SENSED EVERYONE HEADING TOWARD THE PORTAL!
I HAD TO JOURNEY HERE...I HAD TO COME TO THIS PLACE...
YOU...HAD...TO COME TO THIS PLACE?
Jorad continued to hide his disappointment. Of course she was not here because of him.
But as a paladin, a defender of Azeroth, her last words now seized full his attention...
YOU'RE A HUMAN--AND MOST WIZARDS WOULD NOT EVEN SENSE IT...BUT MY KIND...YOU KNOW HOW ATTUNED WE ARE TO ALL THINGS MAGIC....
IT ALL BUT CALLED TO ME...AND WAS SO DIFFERENT, AND YET SO FAMILIAR THAT I COULDN'T HELP BUT PURSUE THE TRUTH.
AND SO YOU FOLLOWED ME OUT...
NO...YOU JUST HAPPENED TO BE GOING THE SAME DIRECTION... FORTUNATELY FOR YOU, I MIGHT ADD.

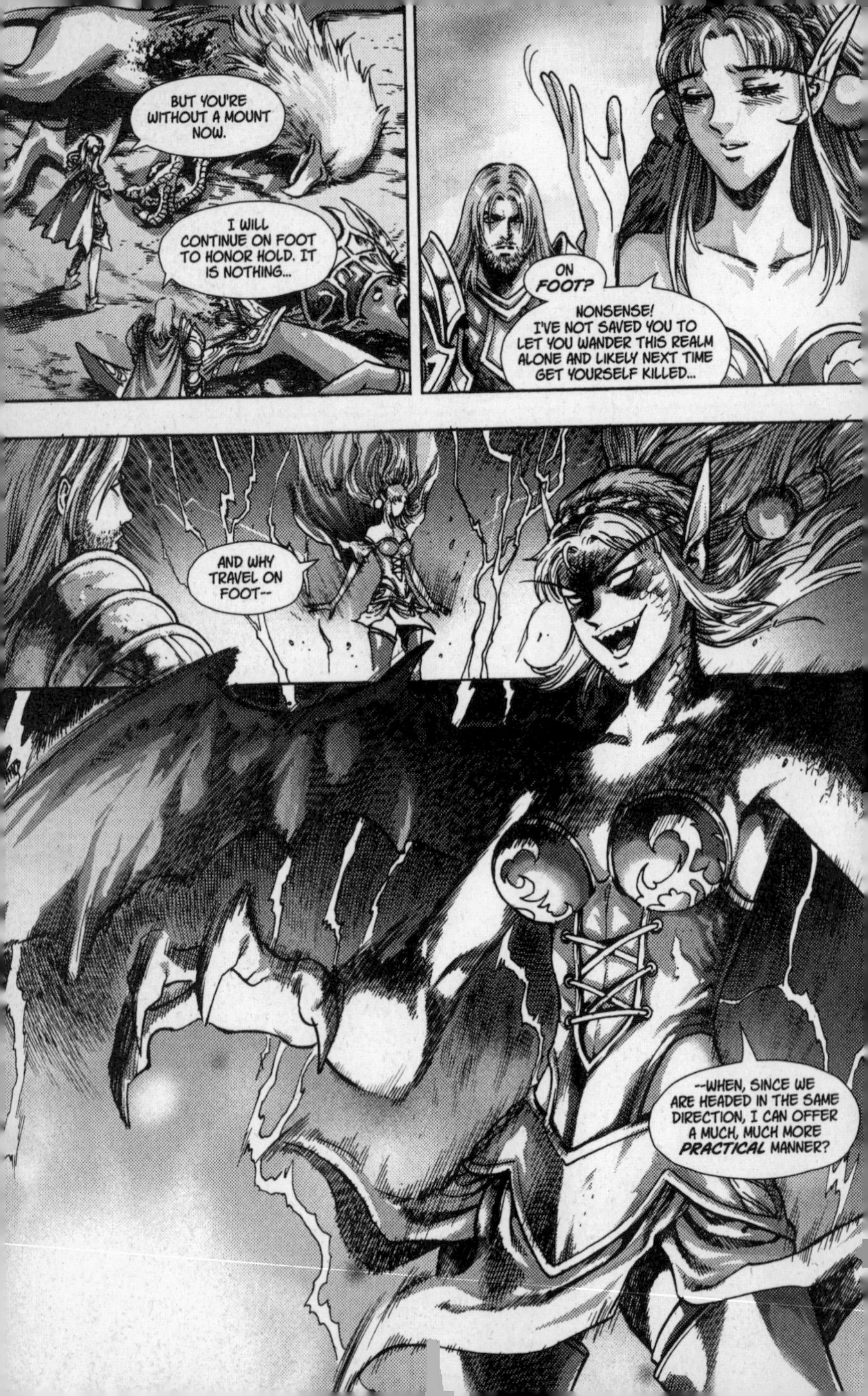
BUT YOU'RE WITHOUT A MOUNT NOW.
I WILL CONTINUE ON FOOT TO HONOR HOLD. IT IS NOTHING...
ON *FOOT?*
NONSENSE! I'VE NOT SAVED YOU TO LET YOU WANDER THIS REALM ALONE AND LIKELY NEXT TIME GET YOURSELF KILLED...
AND WHY TRAVEL ON FOOT--
--WHEN, SINCE WE ARE HEADED IN THE SAME DIRECTION, I CAN OFFER A MUCH, MUCH MORE *PRACTICAL* MANNER?

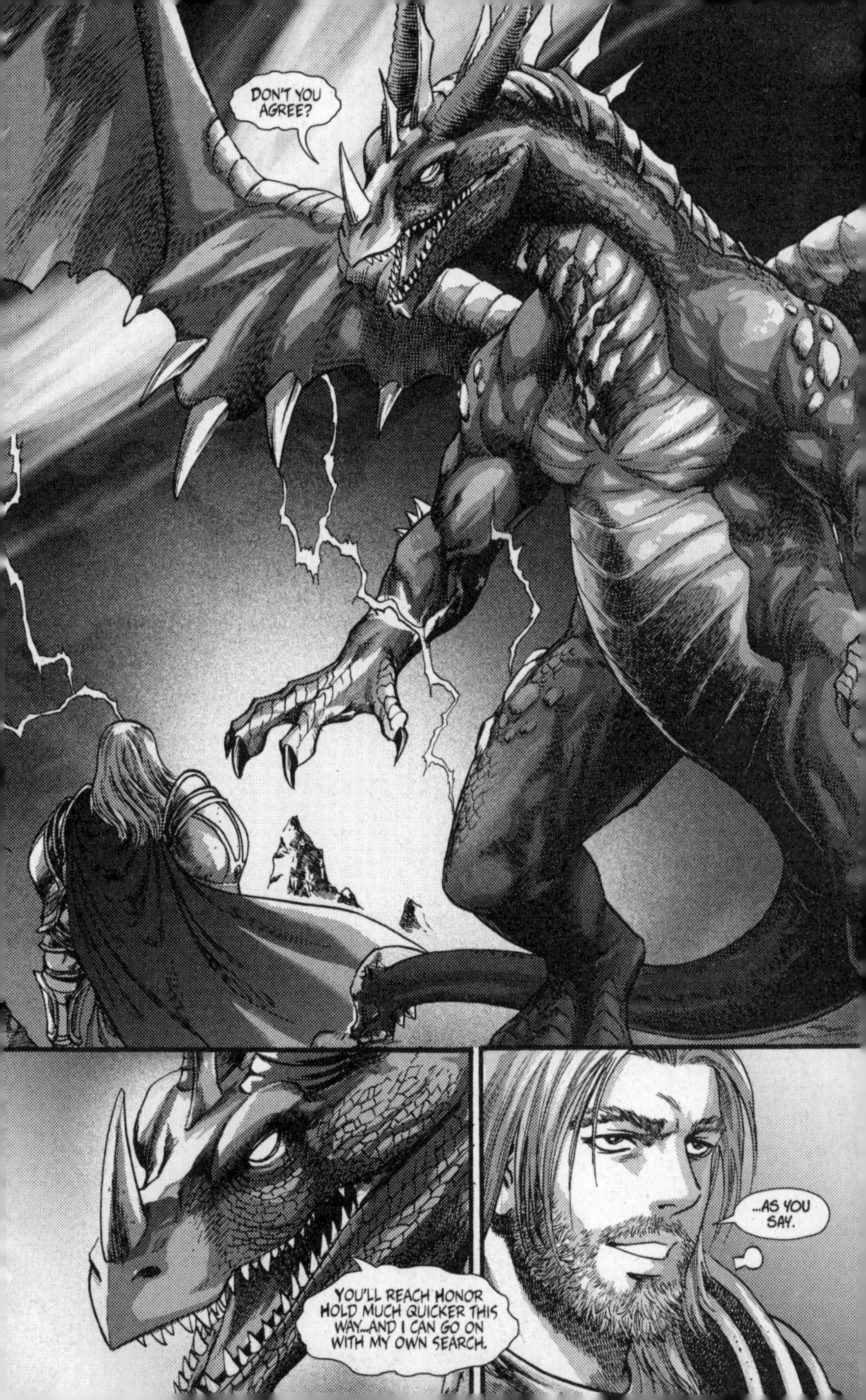
DON'T YOU AGREE?
YOU'LL REACH HONOR HOLD MUCH QUICKER THIS WAY...AND I CAN GO ON WITH MY OWN SEARCH.
...AS YOU SAY.

AS I SAY, YES...

NOW HOLD TIGHT!

THE SENSATION OF FLYING BY DRAGON THRILLED JORAD EVEN MORE THAN FLYING BY MERE GRYPHON...

...BUT REMINDED HIM ONCE AGAIN AT THE STRIKING DIFFERENCES BETWEEN TYRI AND HIM.

SHE WAS A BLUE DRAGON, ONE OF THOSE WHO SERVED MALYGOS, THE ASPECT OF MAGIC. HER LIFE WAS MEASURED IN MILLENNIA, NOT YEARS.

TYRI--OR TYRYGOSA, AS SHE WAS TRULY KNOWN--HAD BEEN FATED TO CHOOSE AS HER MATE ANOTHER BLUE...KALEEGOS...

BUT KALEEGOS--KALEE--HAD CHOSEN TO STAY WITH ANVEENA, WHO, DESPITE HER SEEMINGLY VERY HUMAN GUISE, HAD PROVEN TO BE MORE ASTOUNDING A BEING THAN EVEN THE DRAGONS...

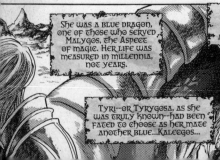

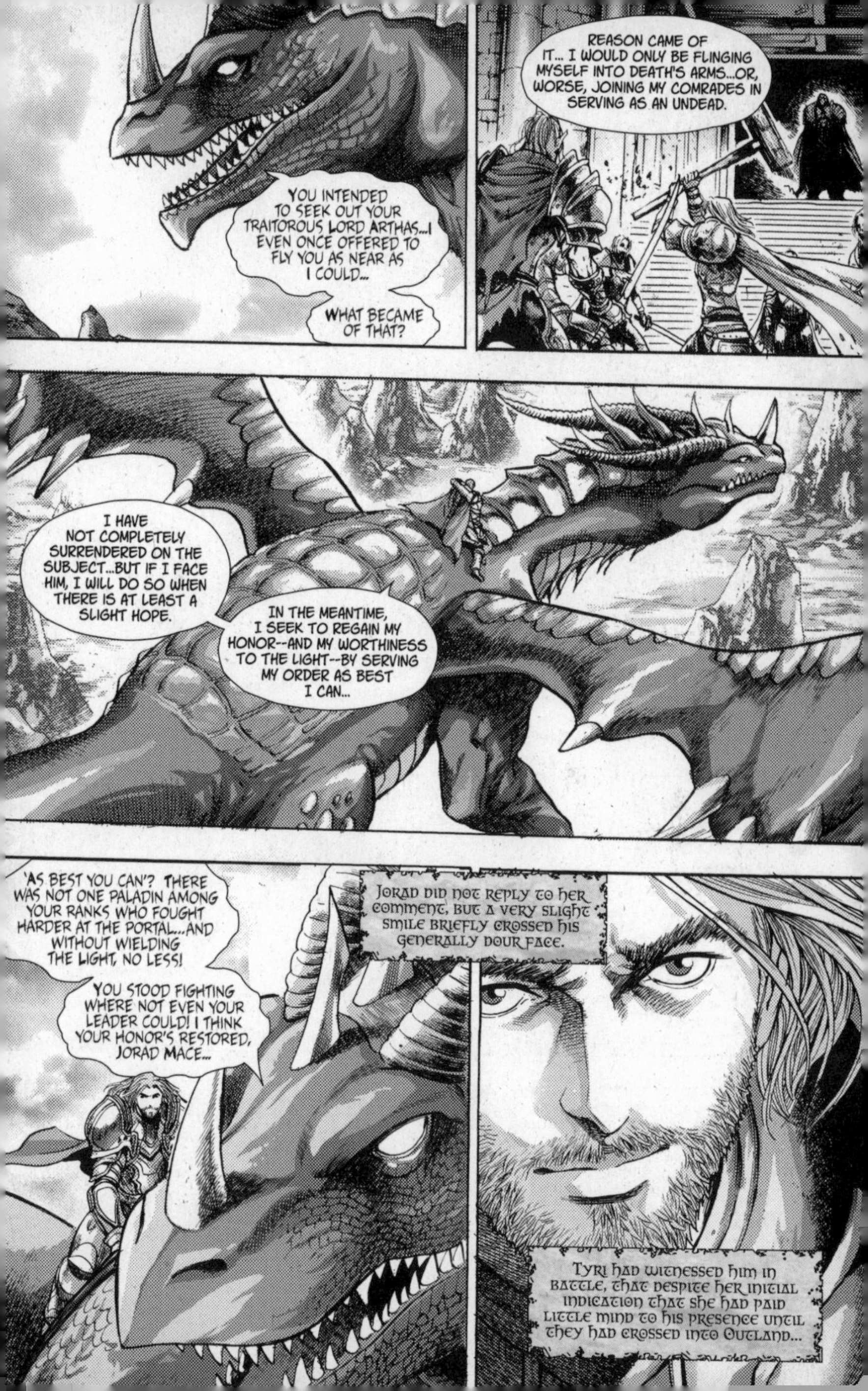

YOU INTENDED TO SEEK OUT YOUR TRAITOROUS LORD ARTHAS...I EVEN ONCE OFFERED TO FLY YOU AS NEAR AS I COULD...
WHAT BECAME OF THAT?
REASON CAME OF IT... I WOULD ONLY BE FLINGING MYSELF INTO DEATH'S ARMS...OR, WORSE, JOINING MY COMRADES IN SERVING AS AN UNDEAD.
I HAVE NOT COMPLETELY SURRENDERED ON THE SUBJECT...BUT IF I FACE HIM, I WILL DO SO WHEN THERE IS AT LEAST A SLIGHT HOPE.
IN THE MEANTIME, I SEEK TO REGAIN MY HONOR--AND MY WORTHINESS TO THE LIGHT--BY SERVING MY ORDER AS BEST I CAN...
'AS BEST YOU CAN'? THERE WAS NOT ONE PALADIN AMONG YOUR RANKS WHO FOUGHT HARDER AT THE PORTAL...AND WITHOUT WIELDING THE LIGHT, NO LESS!
YOU STOOD FIGHTING WHERE NOT EVEN YOUR LEADER COULD! I THINK YOUR HONOR'S RESTORED, JORAD MACE...
Jorad did not reply to her comment, but a very slight smile briefly crossed his generally dour face.
Tyri had witnessed him in battle, that despite her initial indication that she had paid little mind to his presence until they had crossed into Outland...

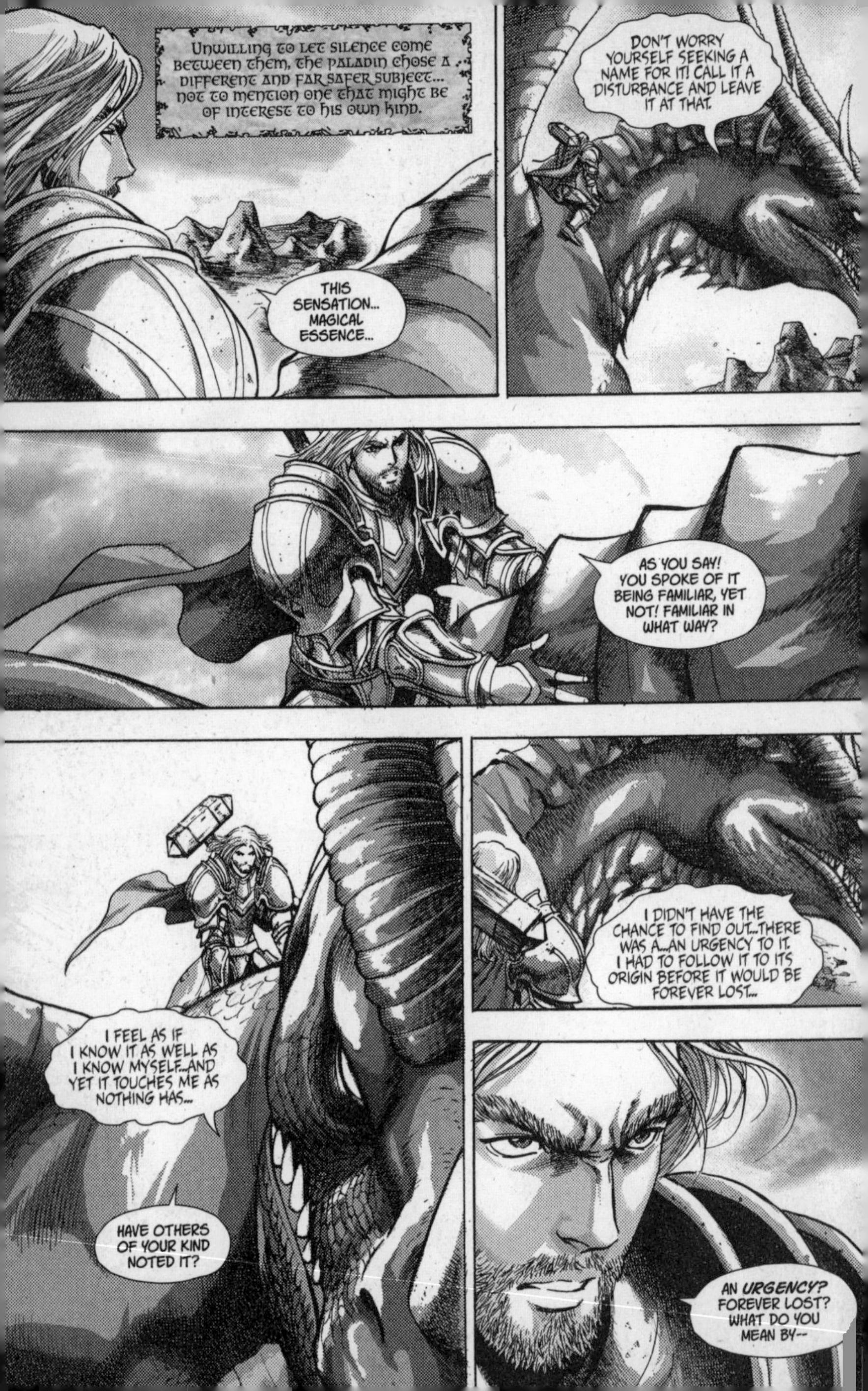
Unwilling to let silence come between them, the paladin chose a different and far safer subject... not to mention one that might be of interest to his own kind.
THIS SENSATION... MAGICAL ESSENCE...
DON'T WORRY YOURSELF SEEKING A NAME FOR IT! CALL IT A DISTURBANCE AND LEAVE IT AT THAT.
AS YOU SAY! YOU SPOKE OF IT BEING FAMILIAR, YET NOT! FAMILIAR IN WHAT WAY?
I FEEL AS IF I KNOW IT AS WELL AS I KNOW MYSELF...AND YET IT TOUCHES ME AS NOTHING HAS...
HAVE OTHERS OF YOUR KIND NOTED IT?
I DIDN'T HAVE THE CHANCE TO FIND OUT...THERE WAS A...AN URGENCY TO IT. I HAD TO FOLLOW IT TO ITS ORIGIN BEFORE IT WOULD BE FOREVER LOST...
AN *URGENCY?* FOREVER LOST? WHAT DO YOU MEAN BY--

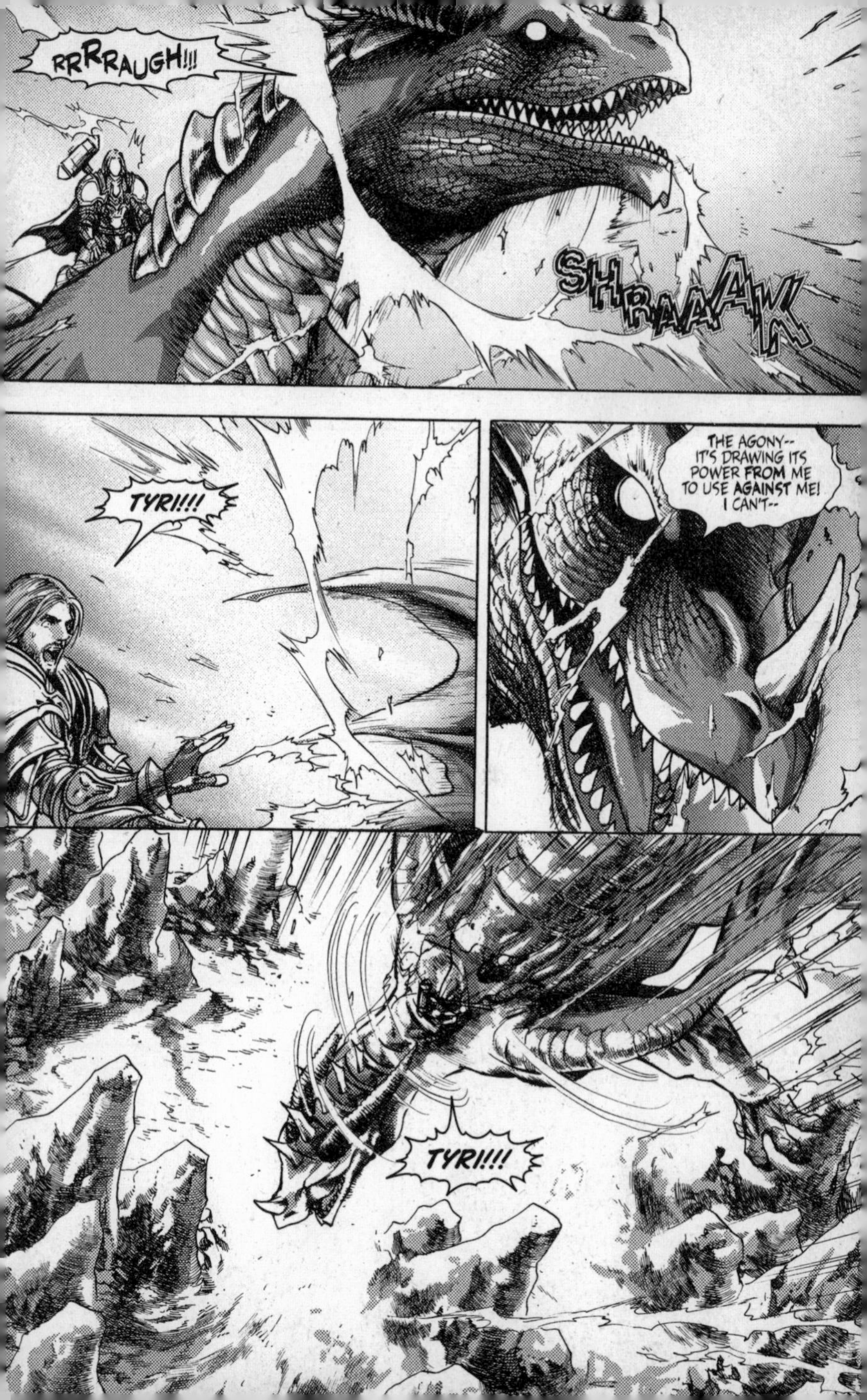
RRRRAUGH!!!
SHRAAAAK
TYRI!!!!
THE AGONY-- IT'S DRAWING ITS POWER FROM ME TO USE AGAINST ME! I CAN'T--
TYRI!!!!

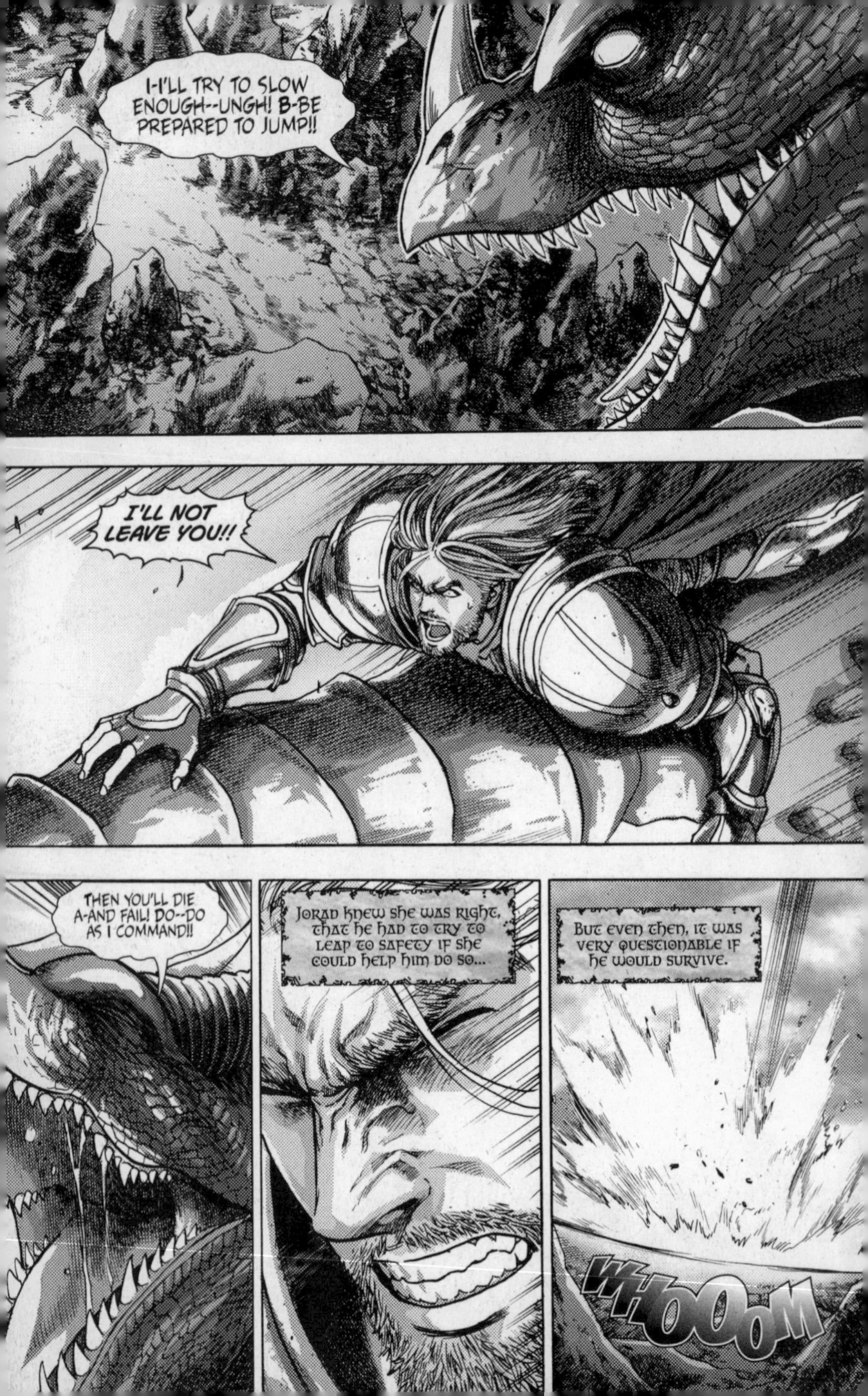
I-I'LL TRY TO SLOW ENOUGH--UNGH! B-BE PREPARED TO JUMP!!
I'LL NOT LEAVE YOU!!
THEN YOU'LL DIE A-AND FAIL! DO--DO AS I COMMAND!!
Jorad knew she was right, that he had to try to leap to safety if she could help him do so...
But even then, it was very questionable if he would survive.
WHOOOM

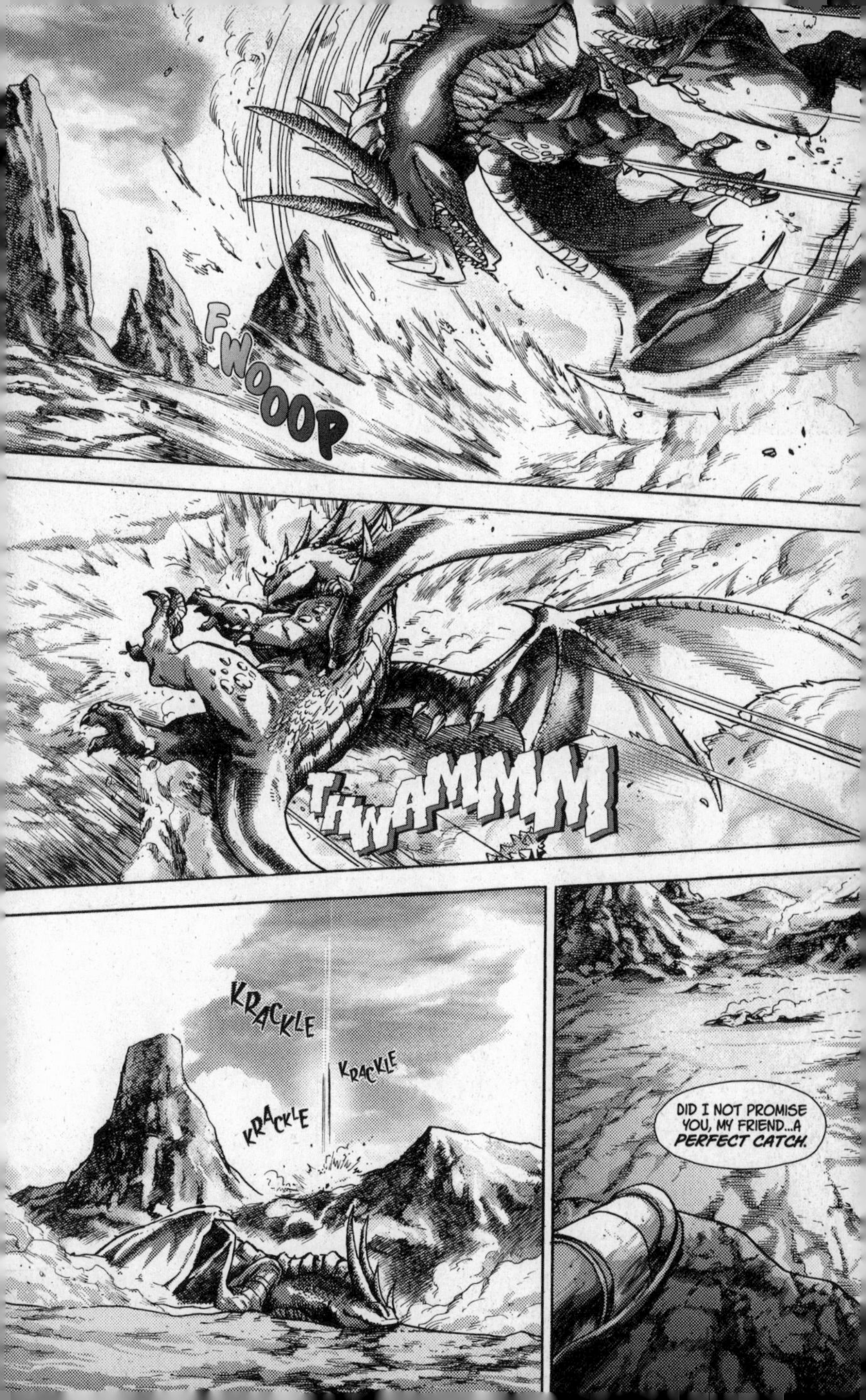
FWOOOOP
THWAMMMM
KRACKLE
KRACKLE
KRACKLE
DID I NOT PROMISE YOU, MY FRIEND...A *PERFECT CATCH.*

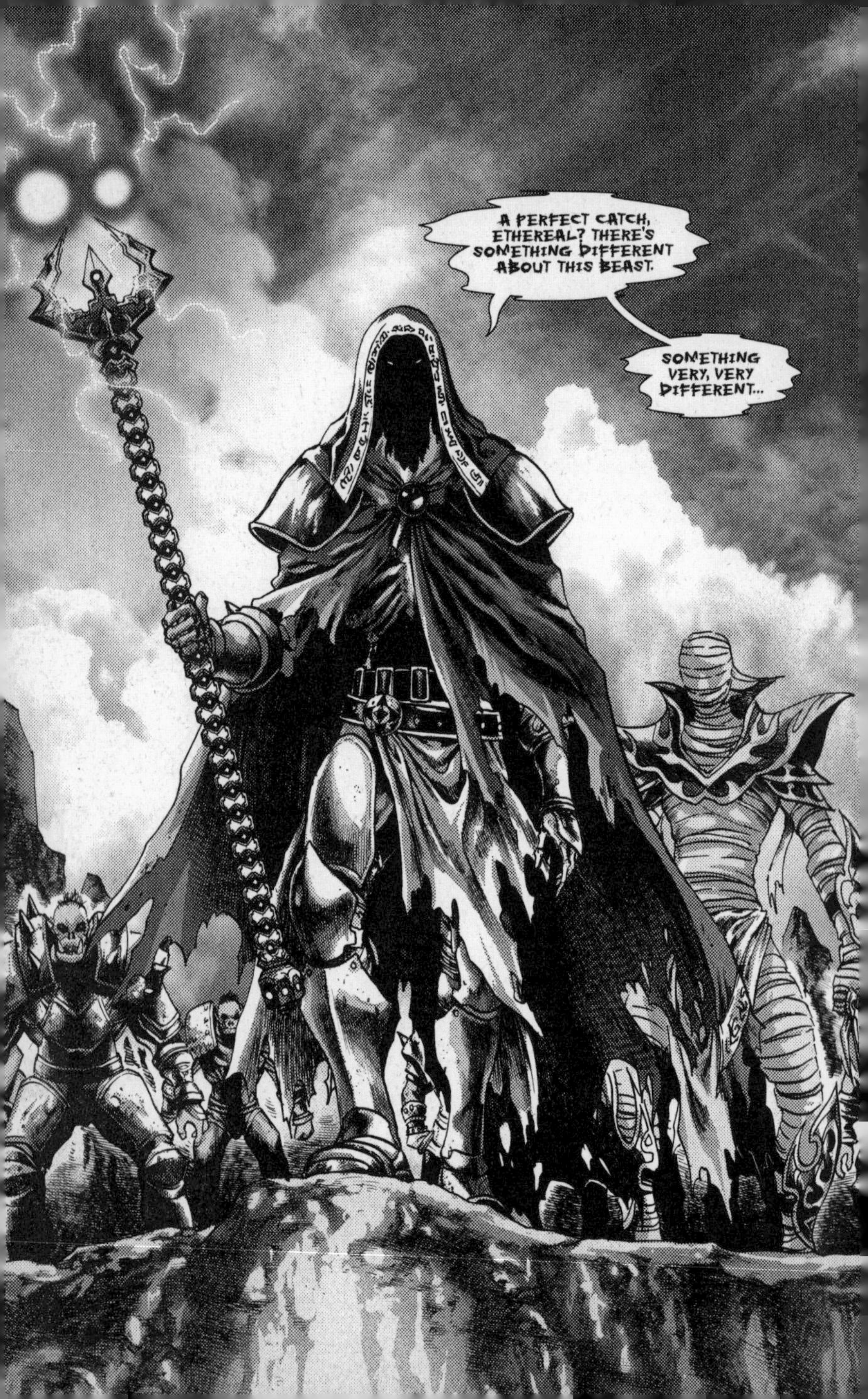
A PERFECT CATCH, ETHEREAL? THERE'S SOMETHING DIFFERENT ABOUT THIS BEAST.
SOMETHING VERY, VERY DIFFERENT...

OUTLAND'S CHILDREN

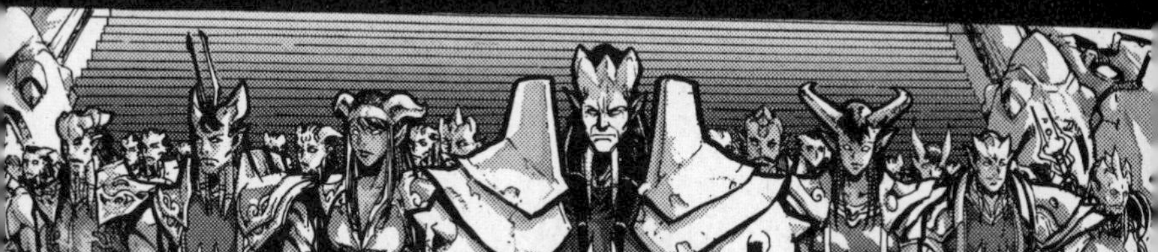
HAIL TO YOU, ENEMIES OF THE DEMONS...

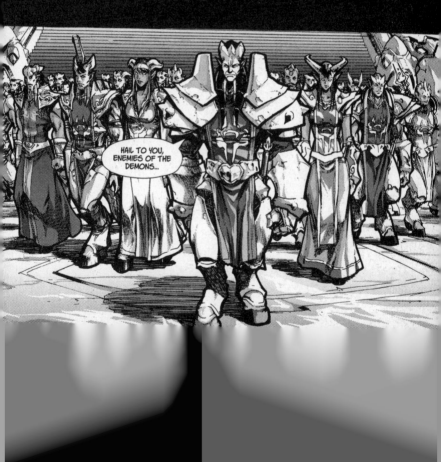

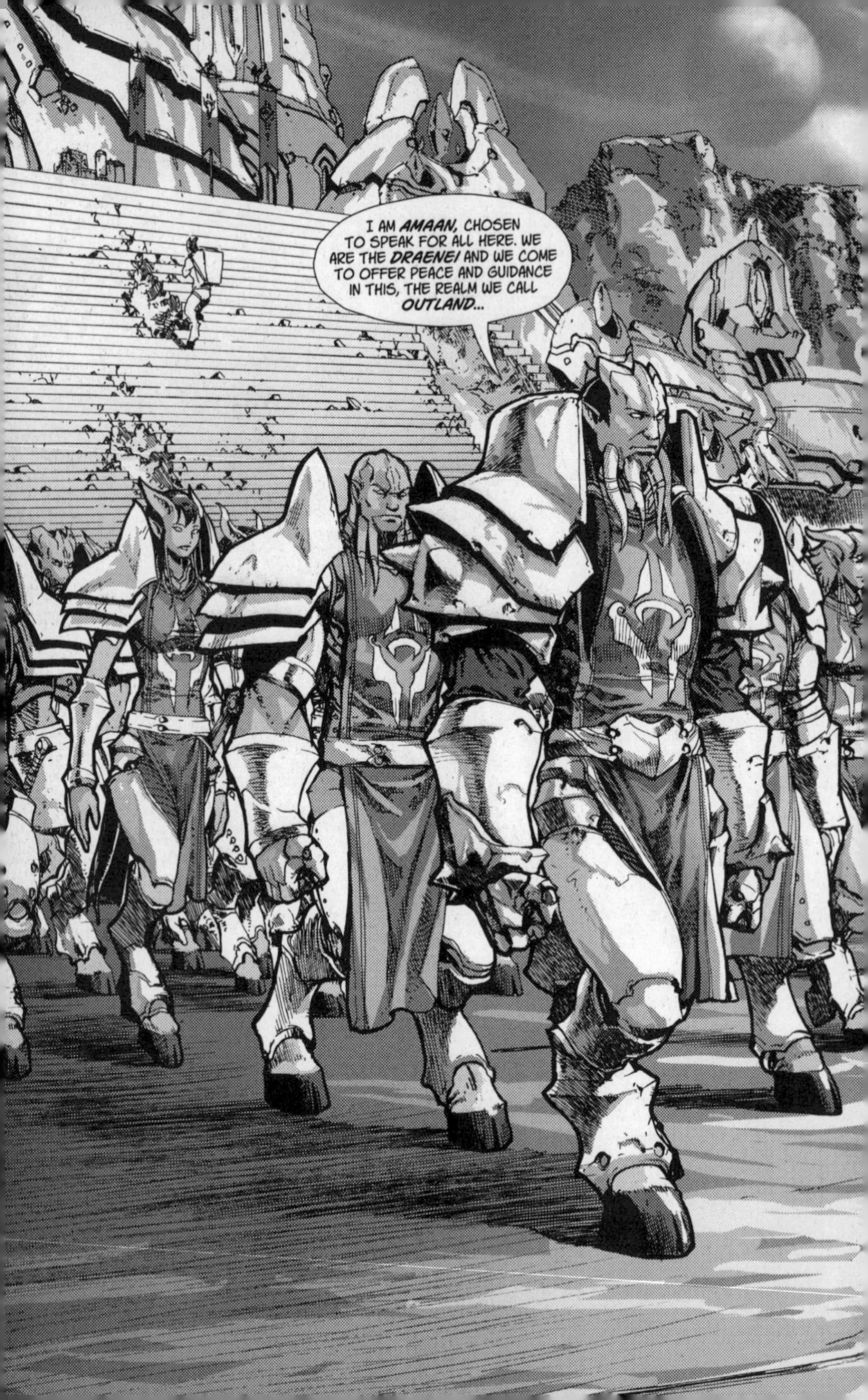
I AM *AMAAN,* CHOSEN TO SPEAK FOR ALL HERE. WE ARE THE *DRAENEI* AND WE COME TO OFFER PEACE AND GUIDANCE IN THIS, THE REALM WE CALL *OUTLAND...*

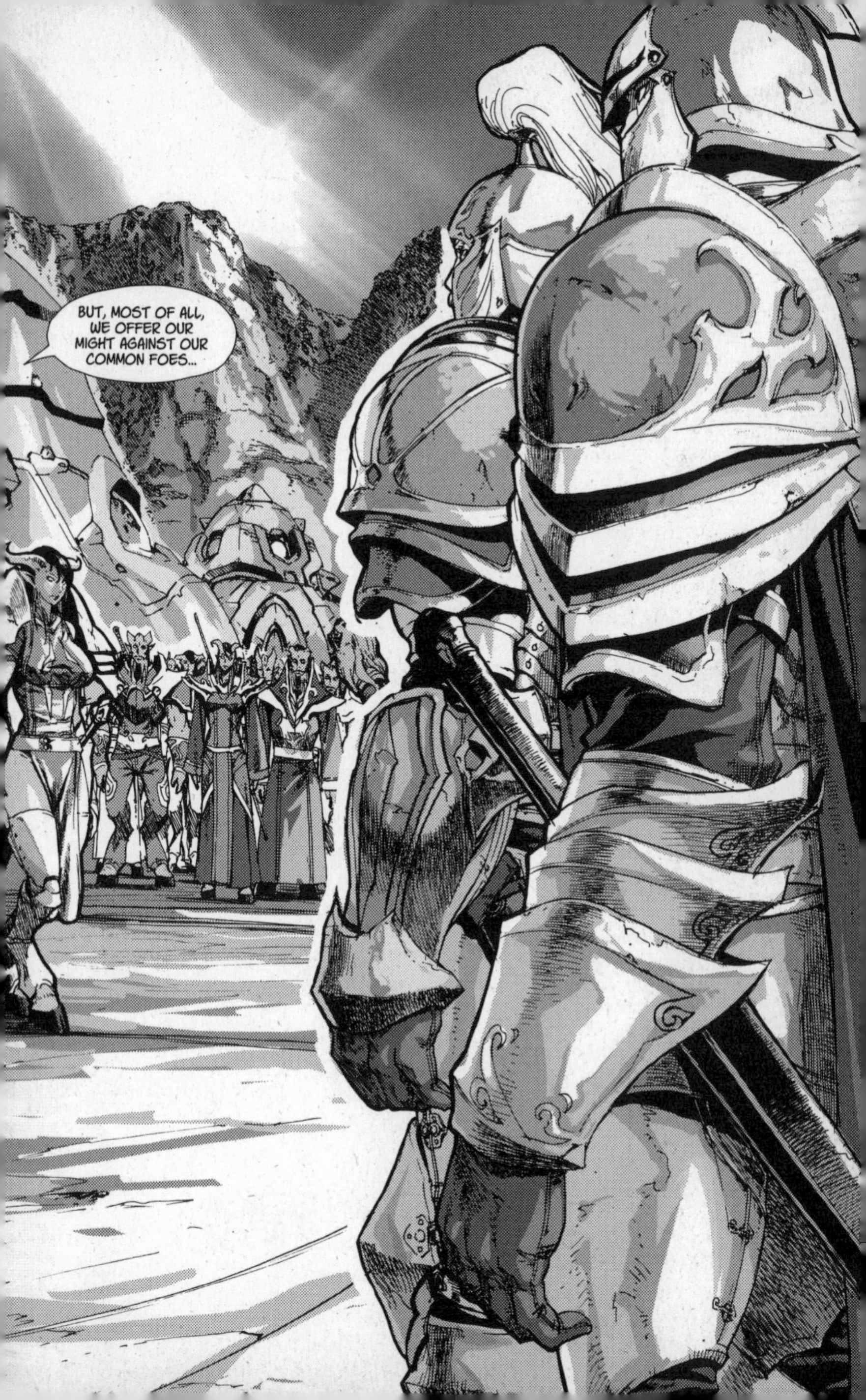
BUT, MOST OF ALL, WE OFFER OUR MIGHT AGAINST OUR COMMON FOES...

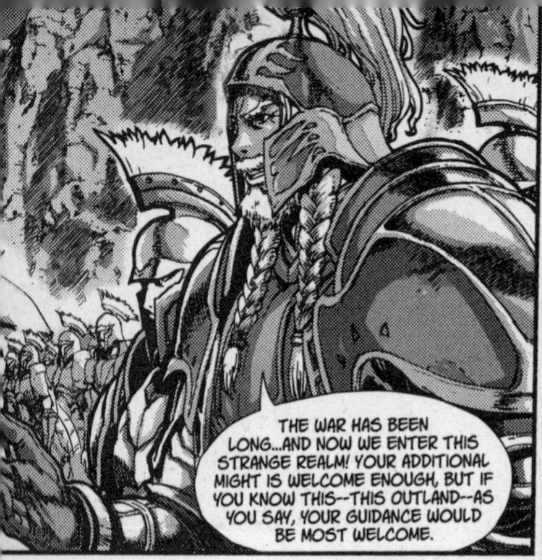
THE WAR HAS BEEN LONG...AND NOW WE ENTER THIS STRANGE REALM! YOUR ADDITIONAL MIGHT IS WELCOME ENOUGH, BUT IF YOU KNOW THIS--THIS OUTLAND--AS YOU SAY, YOUR GUIDANCE WOULD BE MOST WELCOME.
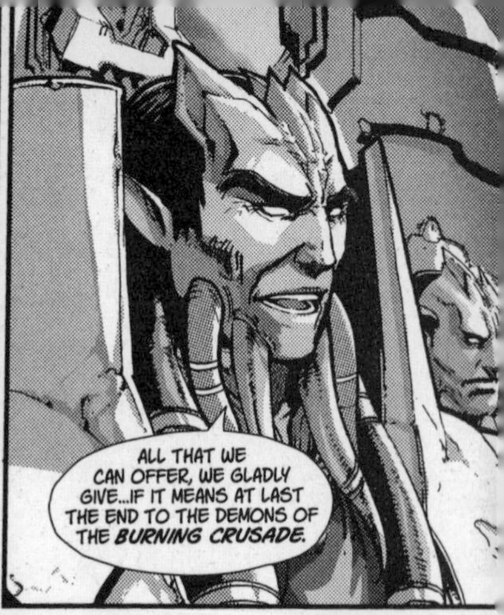
ALL THAT WE CAN OFFER, WE GLADLY GIVE...IF IT MEANS AT LAST THE END TO THE DEMONS OF THE ***BURNING CRUSADE***.
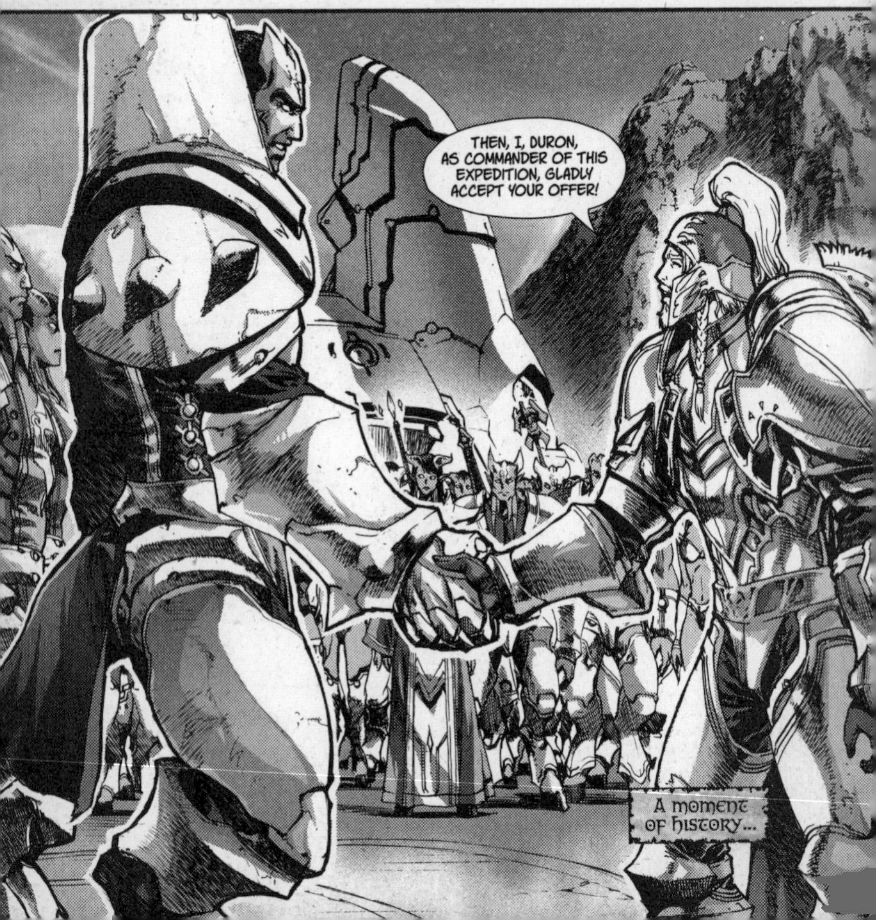
THEN, I, DURON, AS COMMANDER OF THIS EXPEDITION, GLADLY ACCEPT YOUR OFFER!
A moment of history...

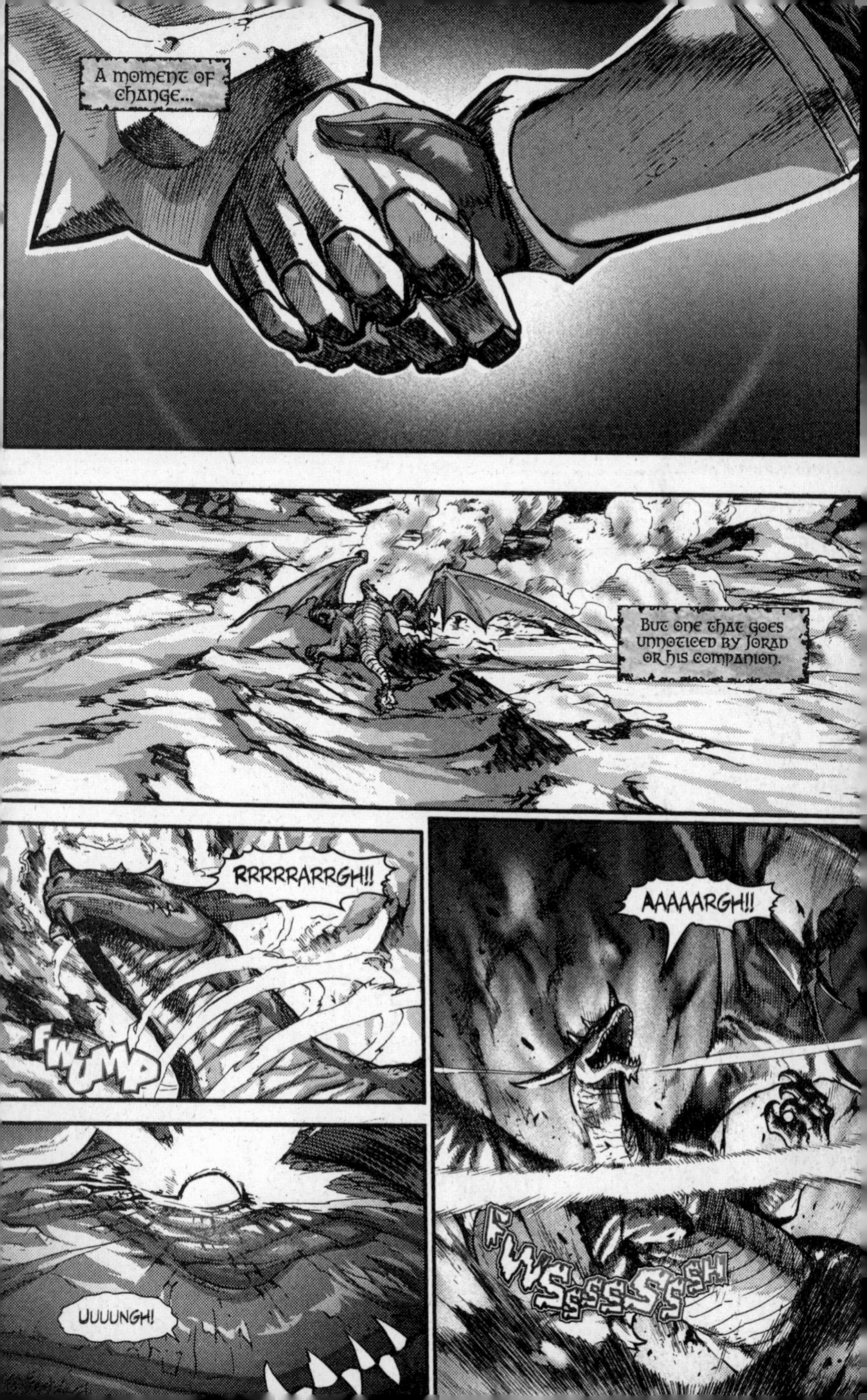
A moment of change...
But one that goes unnoticed by Jorad or his companion.
RRRRARRGH!!
FWUMP
UUUUNGH!
AAAAARGH!!
FWSSSSSSSH

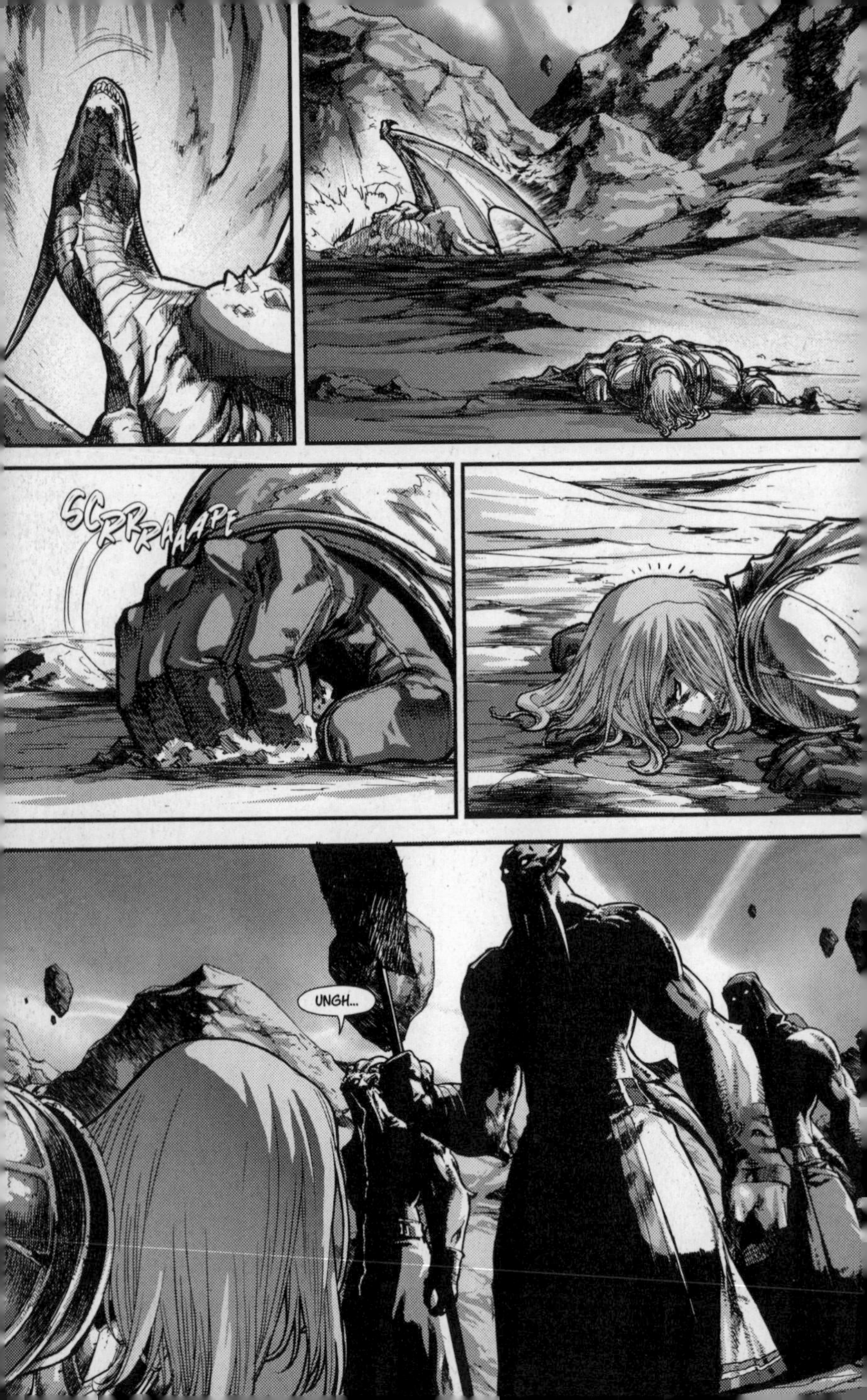
SCRRRAAAPE
UNGH...

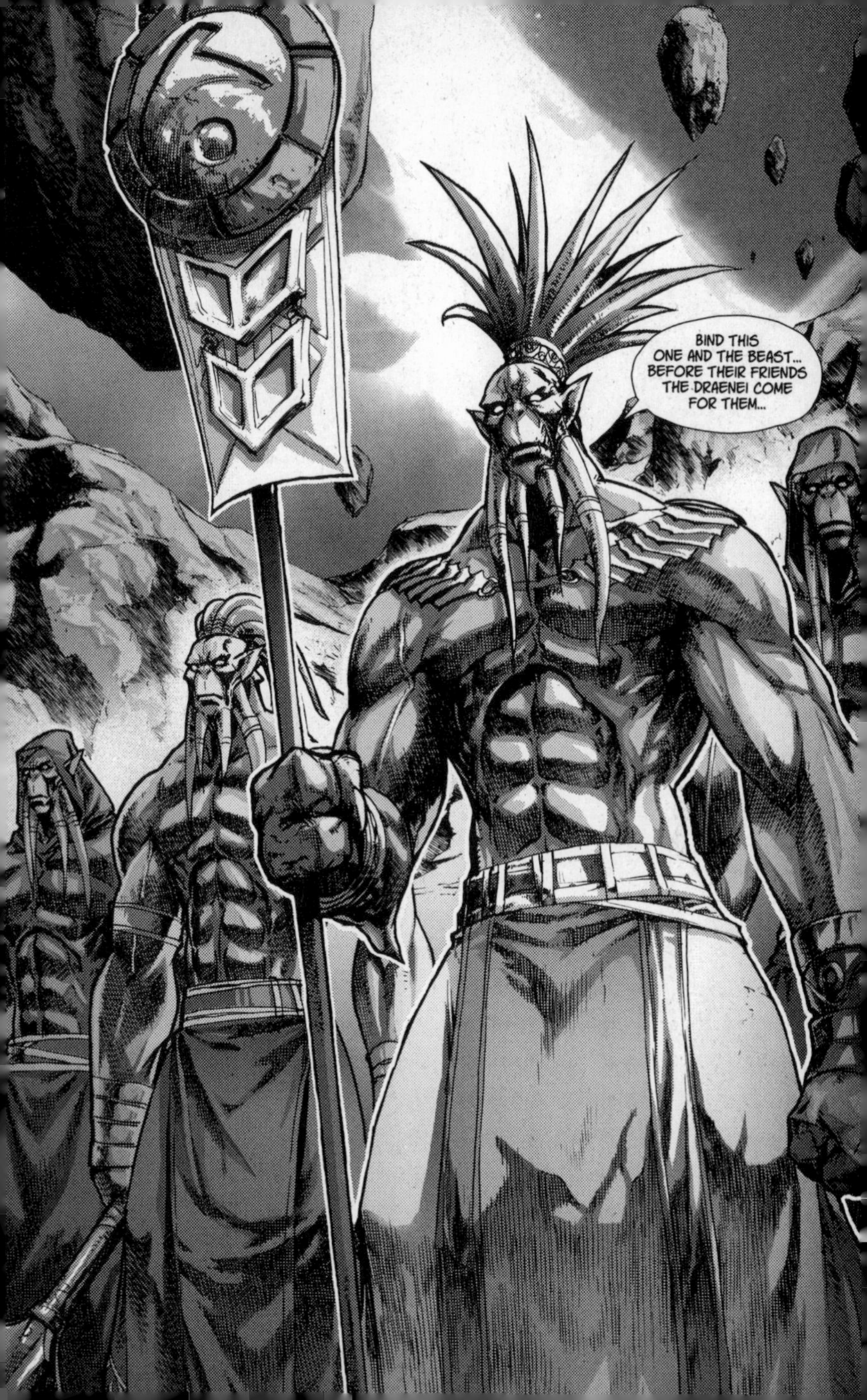
BIND THIS ONE AND THE BEAST... BEFORE THEIR FRIENDS THE DRAENEI COME FOR THEM...

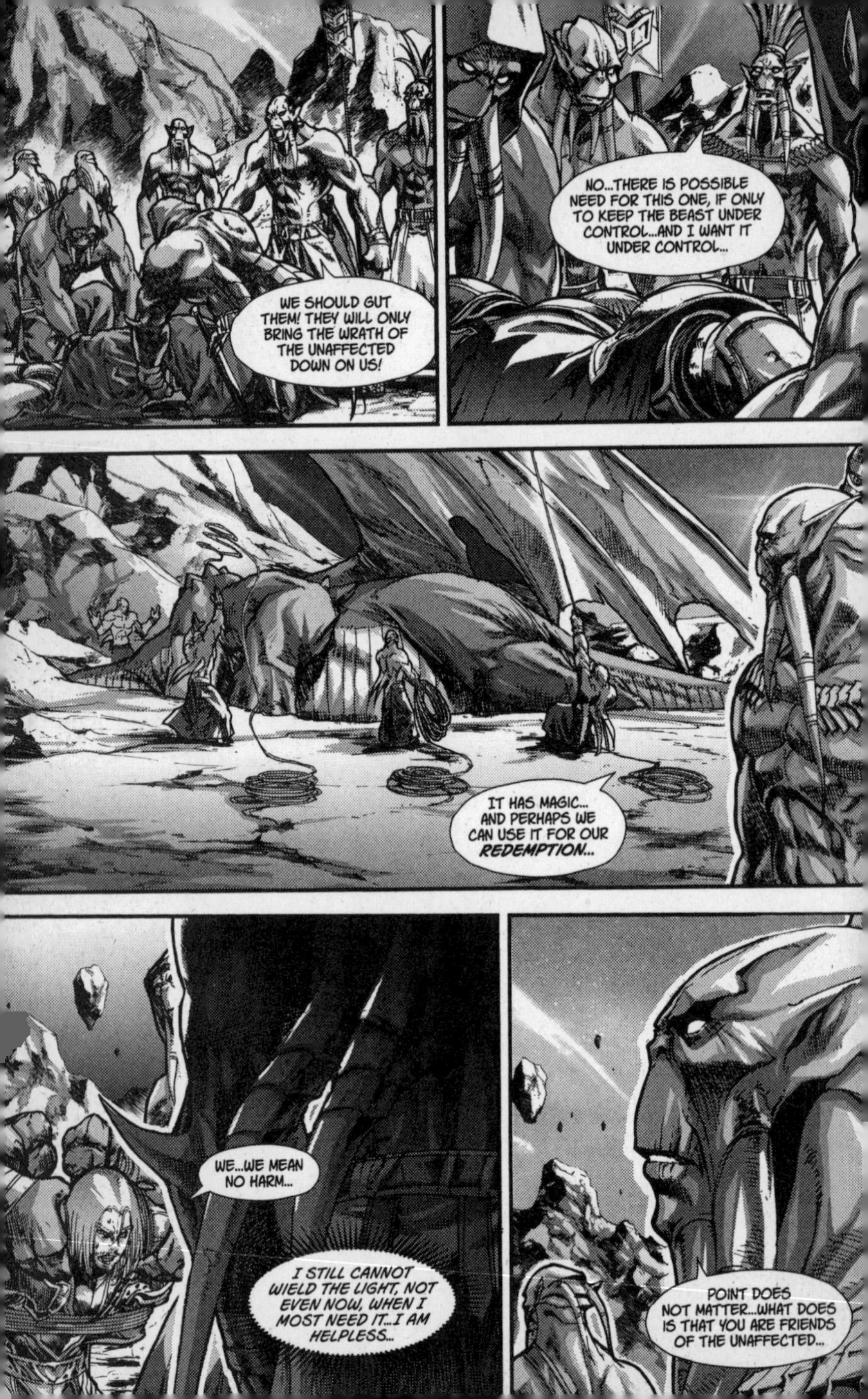
WE SHOULD GUT THEM! THEY WILL ONLY BRING THE WRATH OF THE UNAFFECTED DOWN ON US!
NO...THERE IS POSSIBLE NEED FOR THIS ONE, IF ONLY TO KEEP THE BEAST UNDER CONTROL...AND I WANT IT UNDER CONTROL...
IT HAS MAGIC... AND PERHAPS WE CAN USE IT FOR OUR ***REDEMPTION...***
WE...WE MEAN NO HARM...
I STILL CANNOT WIELD THE LIGHT, NOT EVEN NOW, WHEN I MOST NEED IT...I AM HELPLESS...
POINT DOES NOT MATTER...WHAT DOES IS THAT YOU ARE FRIENDS OF THE UNAFFECTED...

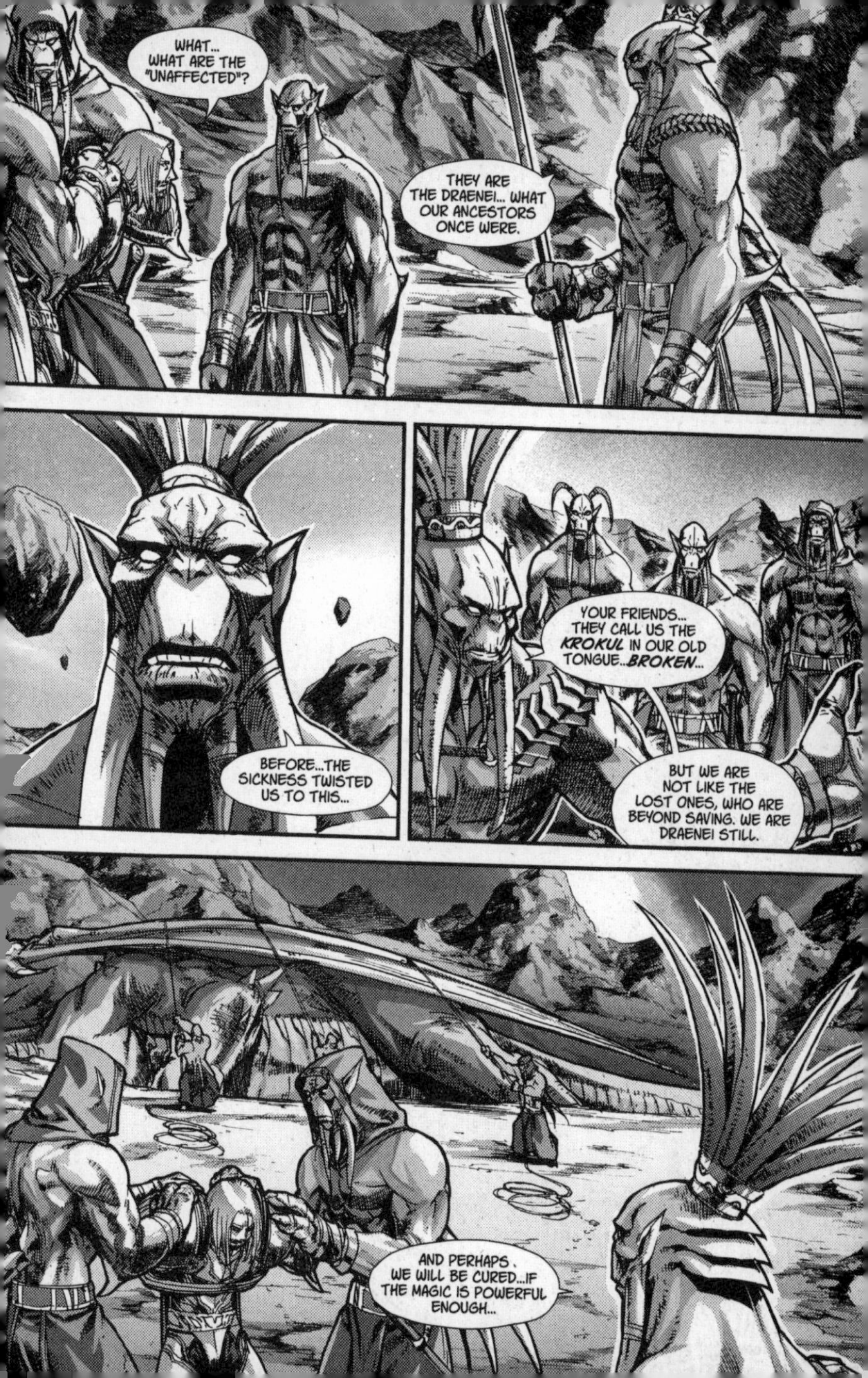
WHAT... WHAT ARE THE "UNAFFECTED"?
THEY ARE THE DRAENEI... WHAT OUR ANCESTORS ONCE WERE.
BEFORE...THE SICKNESS TWISTED US TO THIS...
YOUR FRIENDS... THEY CALL US THE KROKUL IN OUR OLD TONGUE...BROKEN...
BUT WE ARE NOT LIKE THE LOST ONES, WHO ARE BEYOND SAVING. WE ARE DRAENEI STILL.
AND PERHAPS . WE WILL BE CURED...IF THE MAGIC IS POWERFUL ENOUGH...

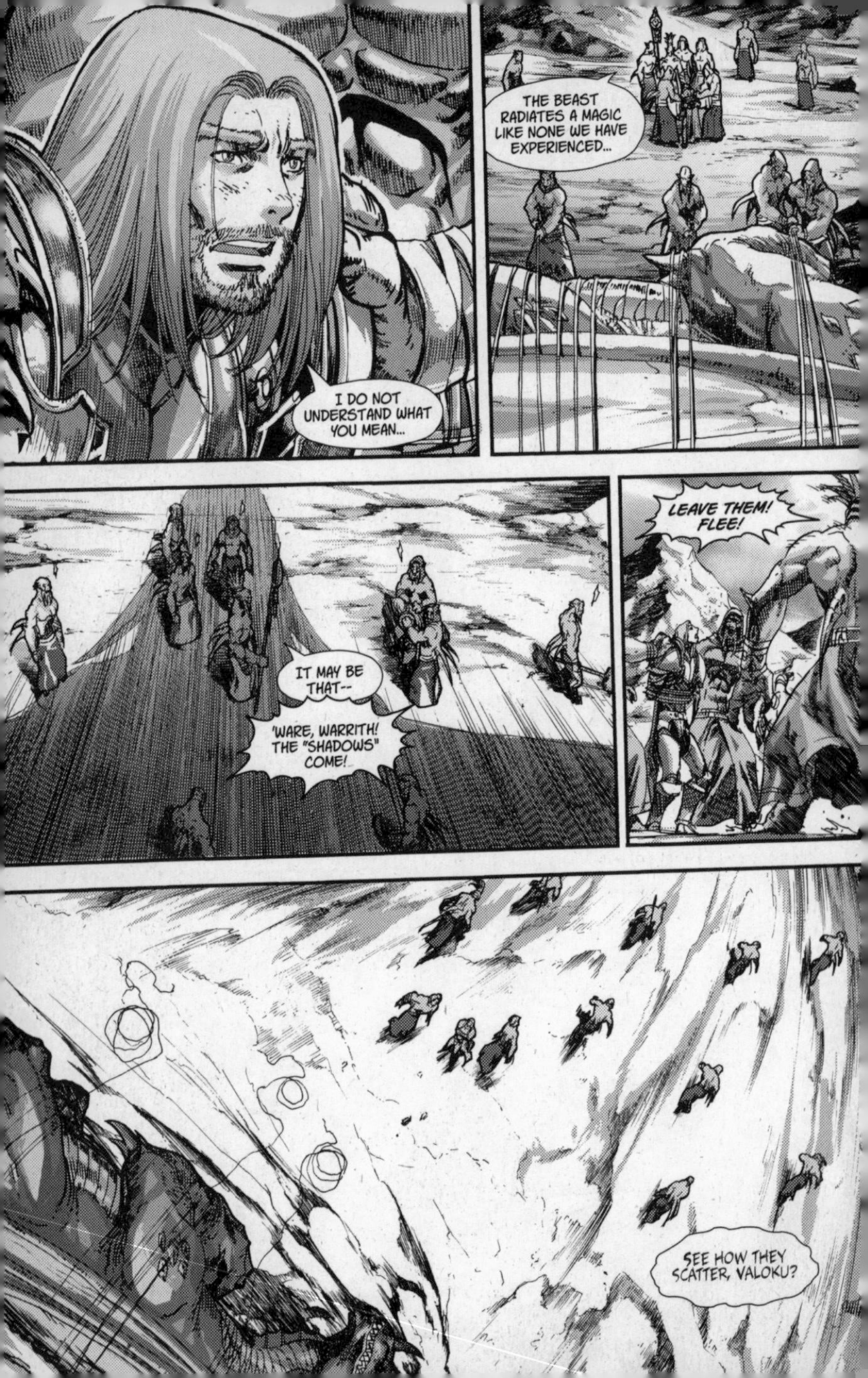
I DO NOT UNDERSTAND WHAT YOU MEAN...
THE BEAST RADIATES A MAGIC LIKE NONE WE HAVE EXPERIENCED...
IT MAY BE THAT--
'WARE, WARRITH! THE "SHADOWS" COME!
LEAVE THEM! FLEE!
SEE HOW THEY SCATTER, VALOKU?

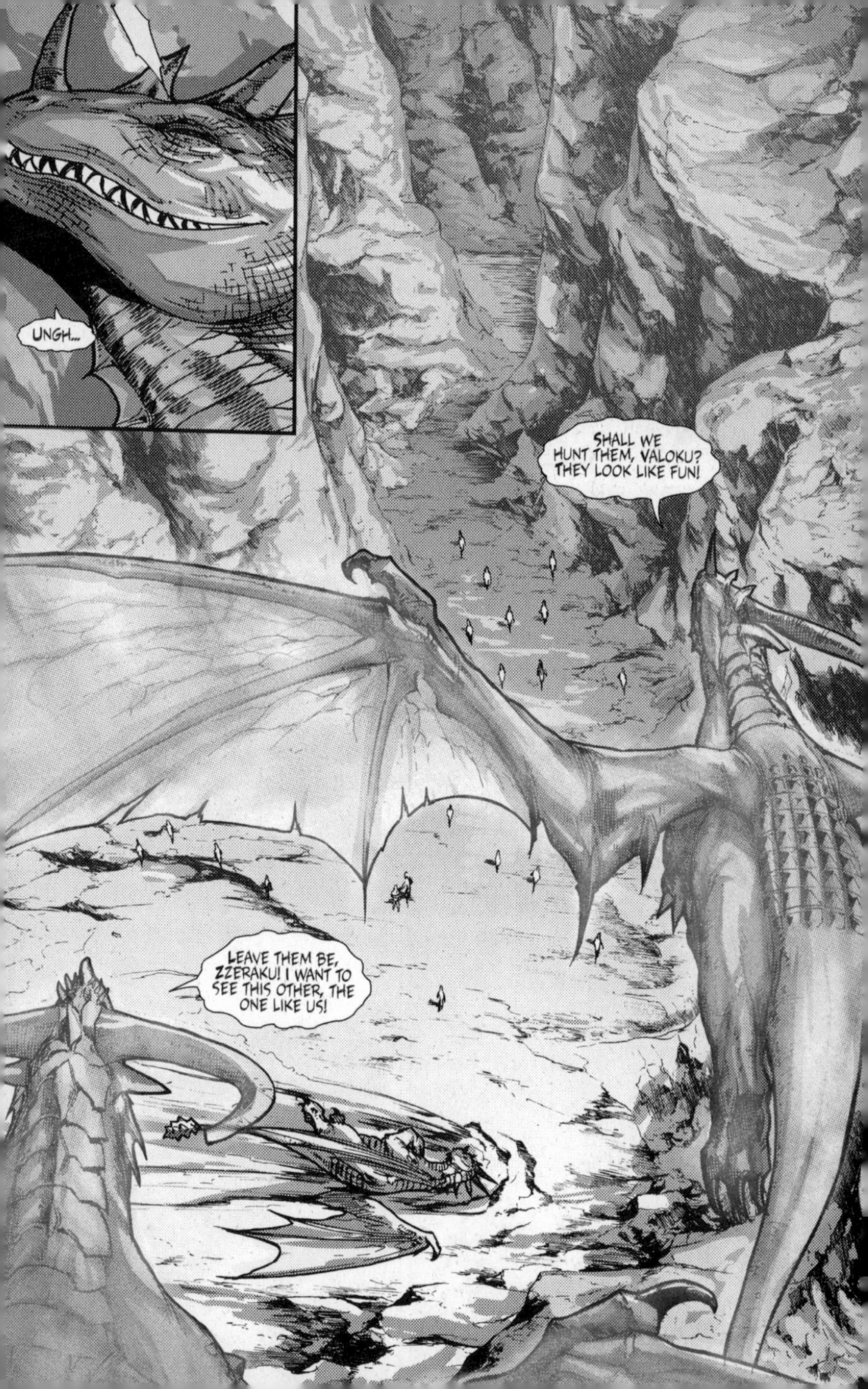
UNGH...
SHALL WE HUNT THEM, VALOKU? THEY LOOK LIKE FUN!
LEAVE THEM BE, ZZERAKU! I WANT TO SEE THIS OTHER, THE ONE LIKE US!

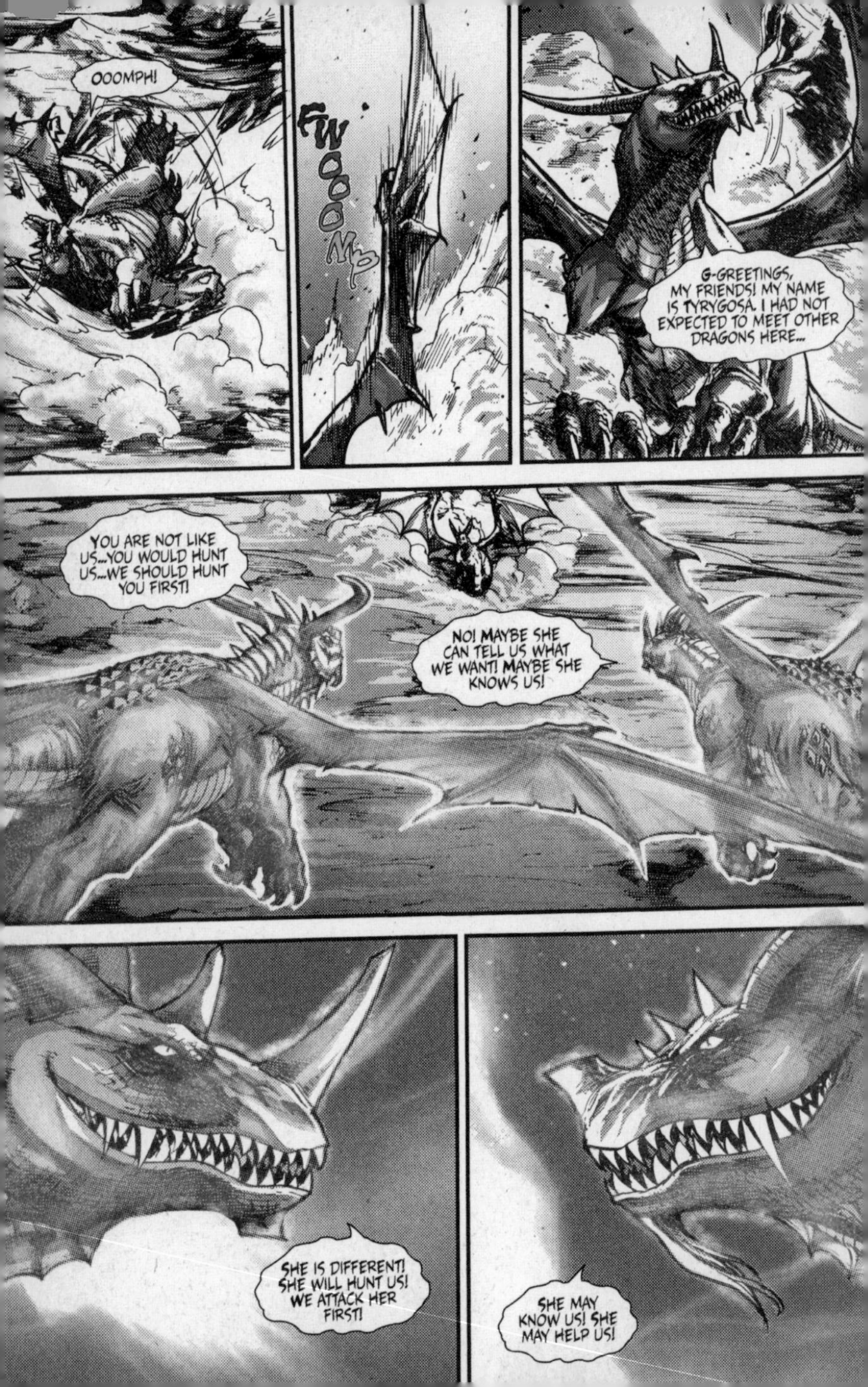
OOOMPH!
FWOOOOMP
G-GREETINGS, MY FRIENDS! MY NAME IS TYRYGOSA. I HAD NOT EXPECTED TO MEET OTHER DRAGONS HERE...
YOU ARE NOT LIKE US...YOU WOULD HUNT US...WE SHOULD HUNT YOU FIRST!
NO! MAYBE SHE CAN TELL US WHAT WE WANT! MAYBE SHE KNOWS US!
SHE IS DIFFERENT! SHE WILL HUNT US! WE ATTACK HER FIRST!
SHE MAY KNOW US! SHE MAY HELP US!

FWWWOOOSSHHHH

HUNT HER!

HELP HER!

HHHISSSS!!

RRRROOOARRRR!!

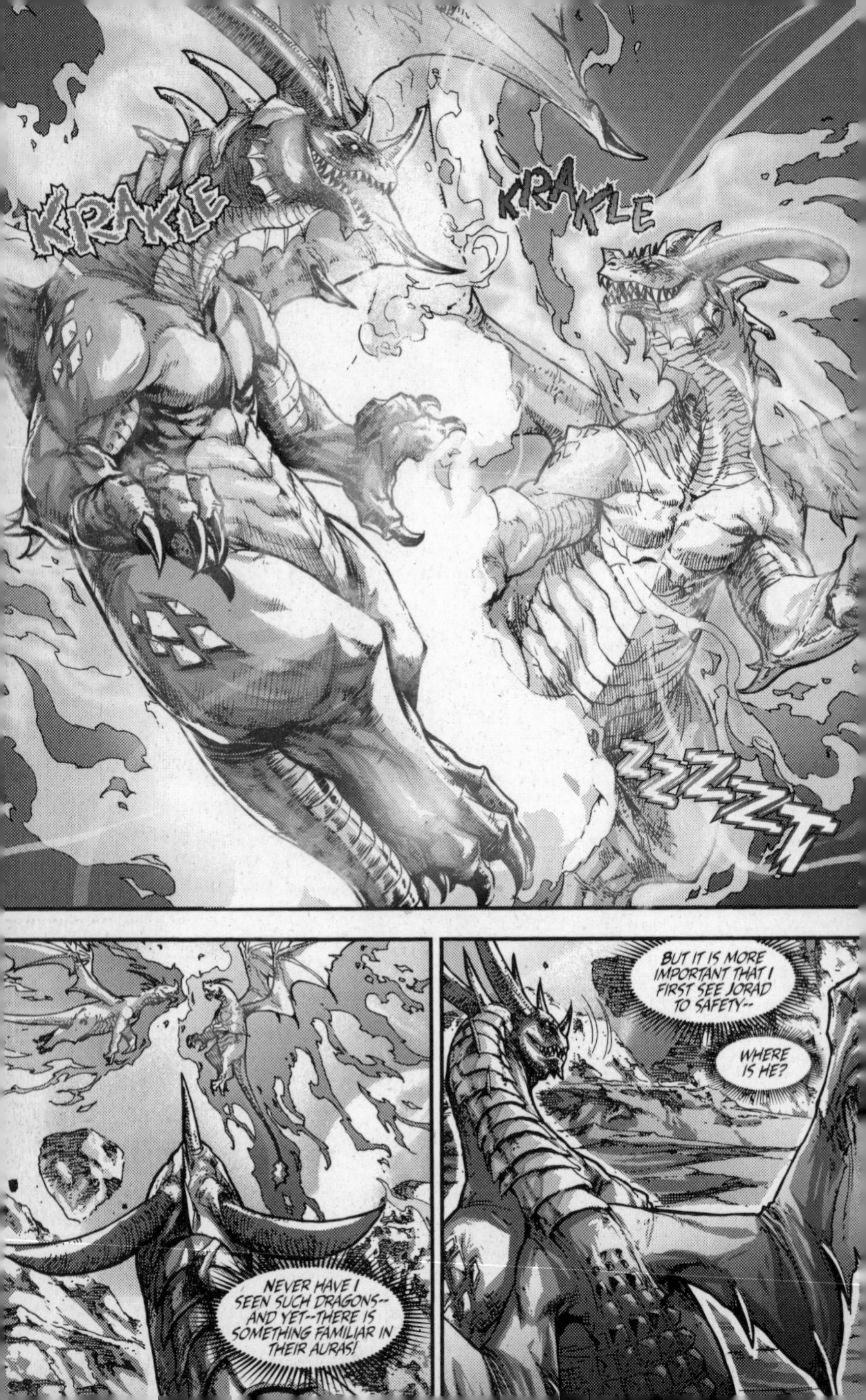
KRAKLE
KRAKLE
ZZZZZT
NEVER HAVE I SEEN SUCH DRAGONS--AND YET--THERE IS SOMETHING FAMILIAR IN THEIR AURAS!
BUT IT IS MORE IMPORTANT THAT I FIRST SEE JORAD TO SAFETY--
WHERE IS HE?

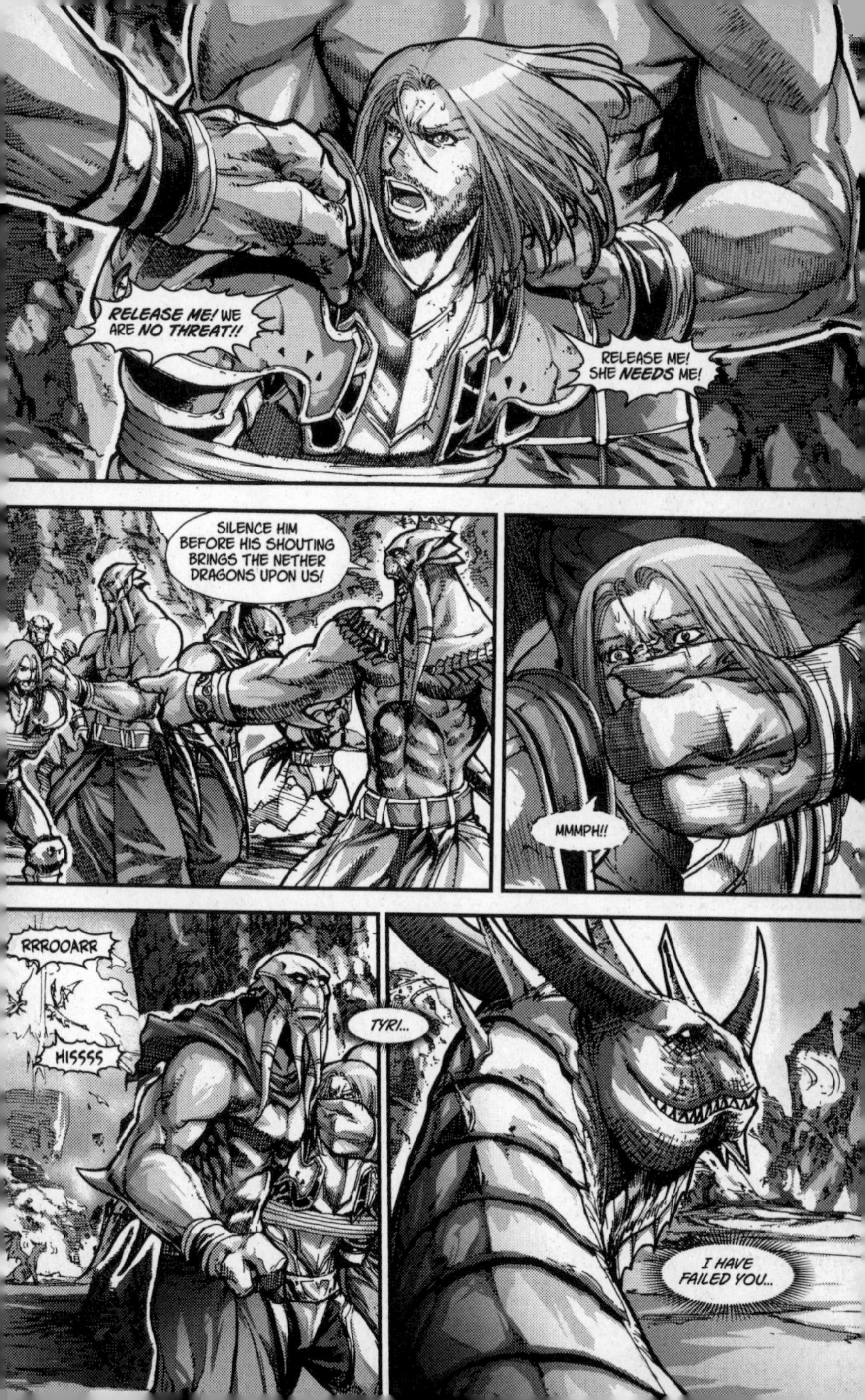
RELEASE ME! WE ARE NO THREAT!!
RELEASE ME! SHE NEEDS ME!
SILENCE HIM BEFORE HIS SHOUTING BRINGS THE NETHER DRAGONS UPON US!
MMMPH!!
RRROOARR
HISSSS
TYRI...
I HAVE FAILED YOU...

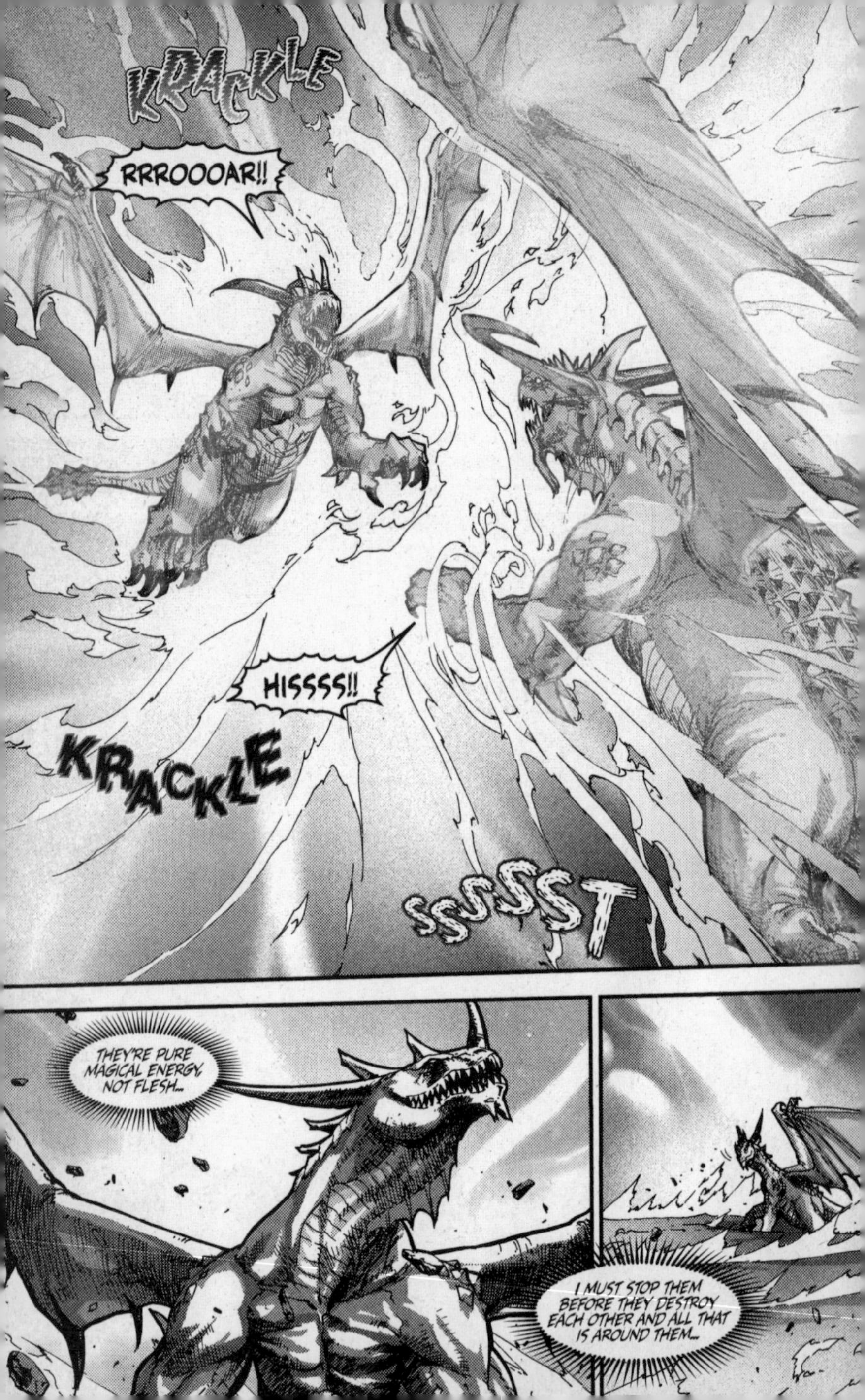
KRACKLE
RRROOOAR!!
HISSSS!!
KRACKLE
SSSSST
THEY'RE PURE MAGICAL ENERGY, NOT FLESH...
I MUST STOP THEM BEFORE THEY DESTROY EACH OTHER AND ALL THAT IS AROUND THEM...

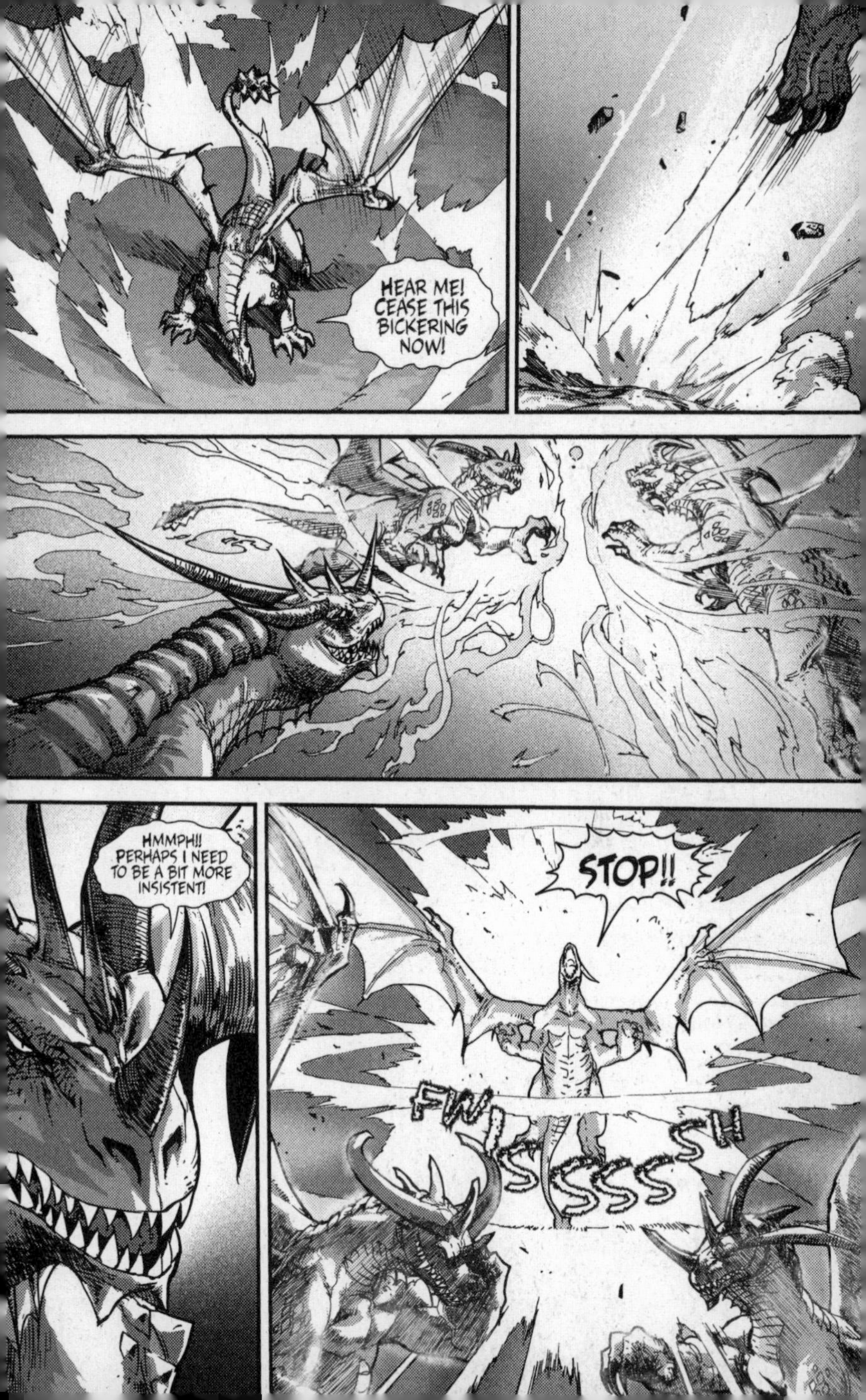
HEAR ME! CEASE THIS BICKERING NOW!
HMMPH!! PERHAPS I NEED TO BE A BIT MORE INSISTENT!
STOP!!
FWISSSSSSH

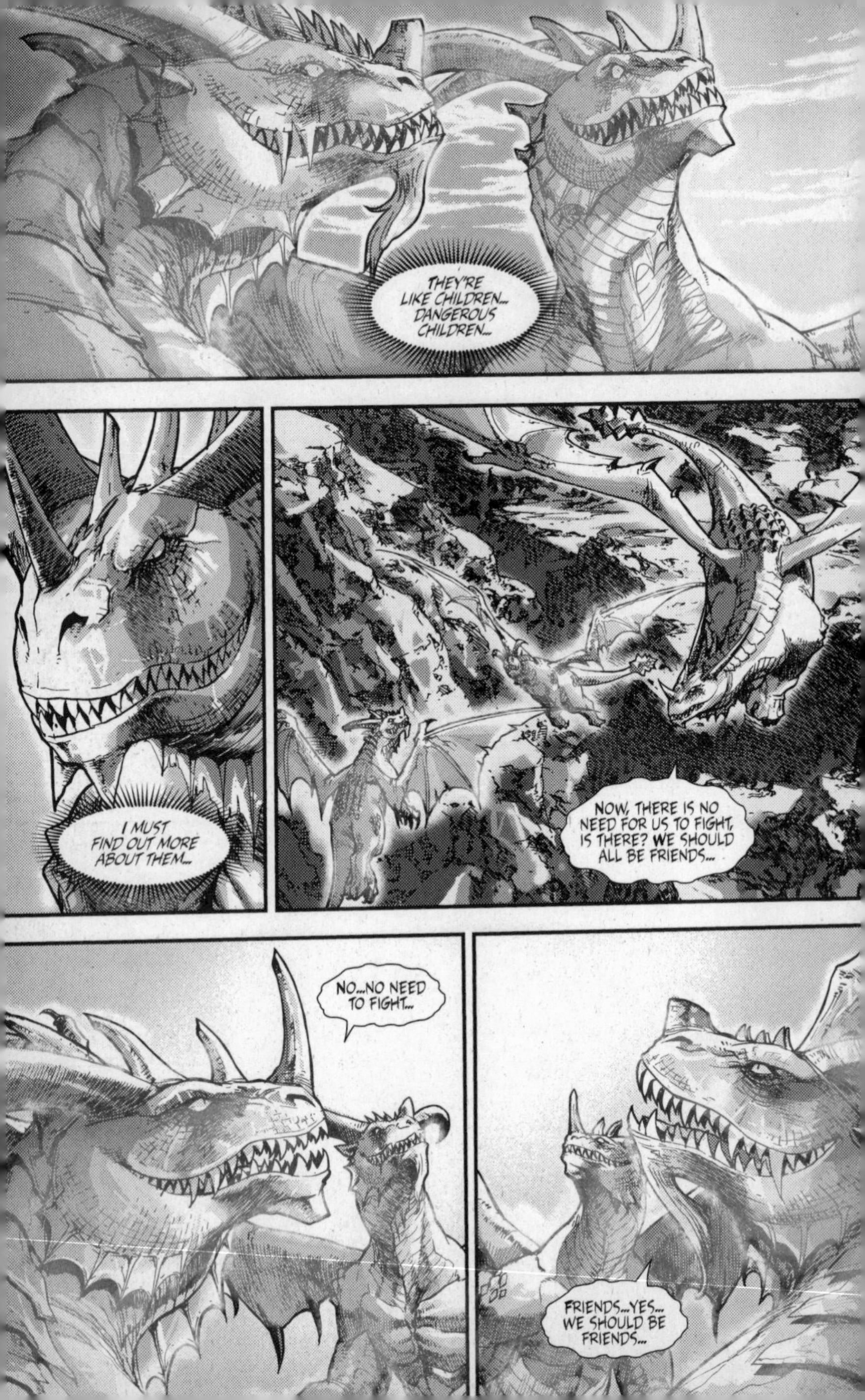
THEY'RE LIKE CHILDREN... DANGEROUS CHILDREN...
I MUST FIND OUT MORE ABOUT THEM...
NOW, THERE IS NO NEED FOR US TO FIGHT, IS THERE? WE SHOULD ALL BE FRIENDS...
NO...NO NEED TO FIGHT...
FRIENDS...YES... WE SHOULD BE FRIENDS...

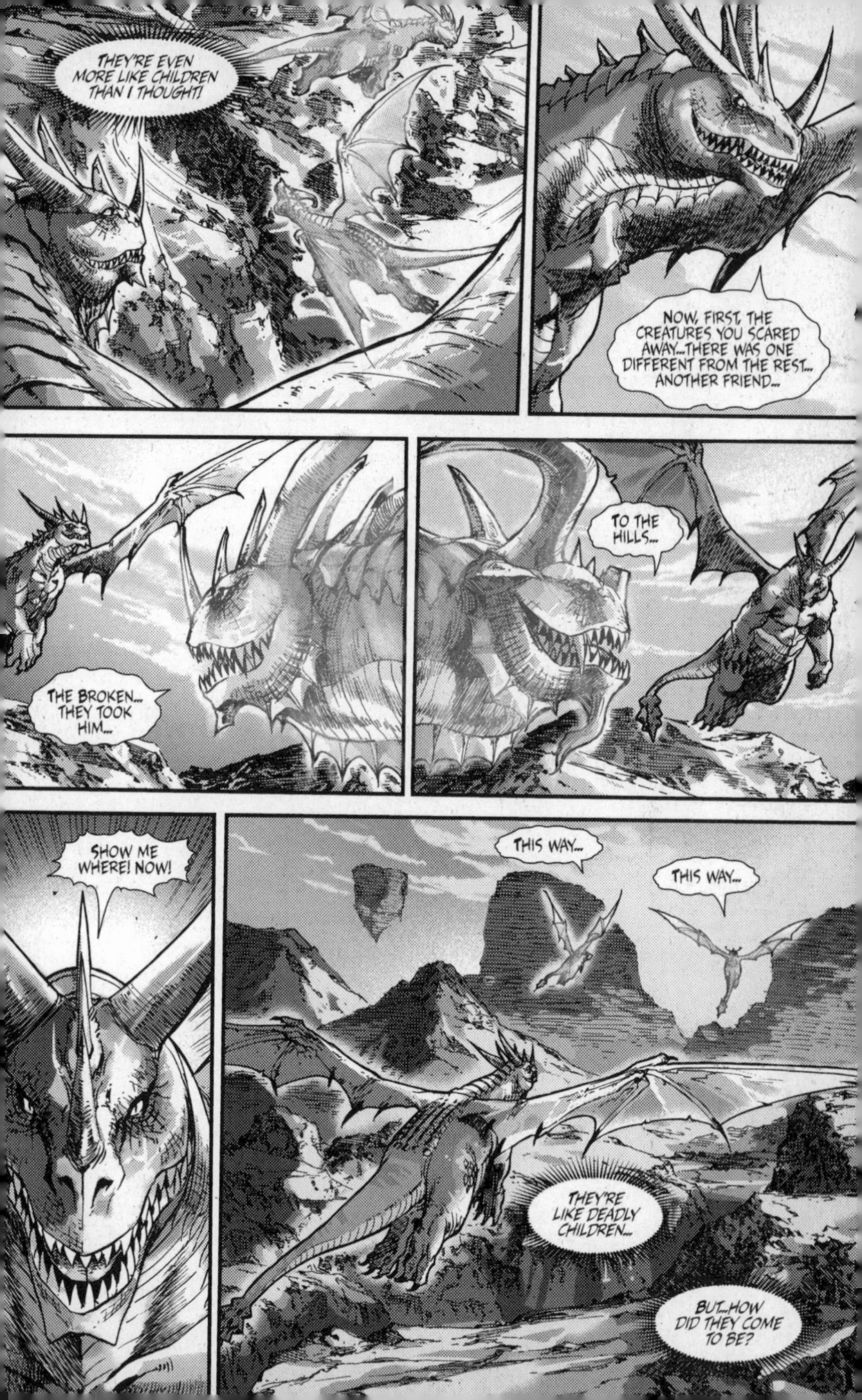
THEY'RE EVEN MORE LIKE CHILDREN THAN I THOUGHT!
NOW, FIRST, THE CREATURES YOU SCARED AWAY...THERE WAS ONE DIFFERENT FROM THE REST... ANOTHER FRIEND...
THE BROKEN... THEY TOOK HIM...
TO THE HILLS...
SHOW ME WHERE! NOW!
THIS WAY...
THIS WAY...
THEY'RE LIKE DEADLY CHILDREN...
BUT...HOW DID THEY COME TO BE?

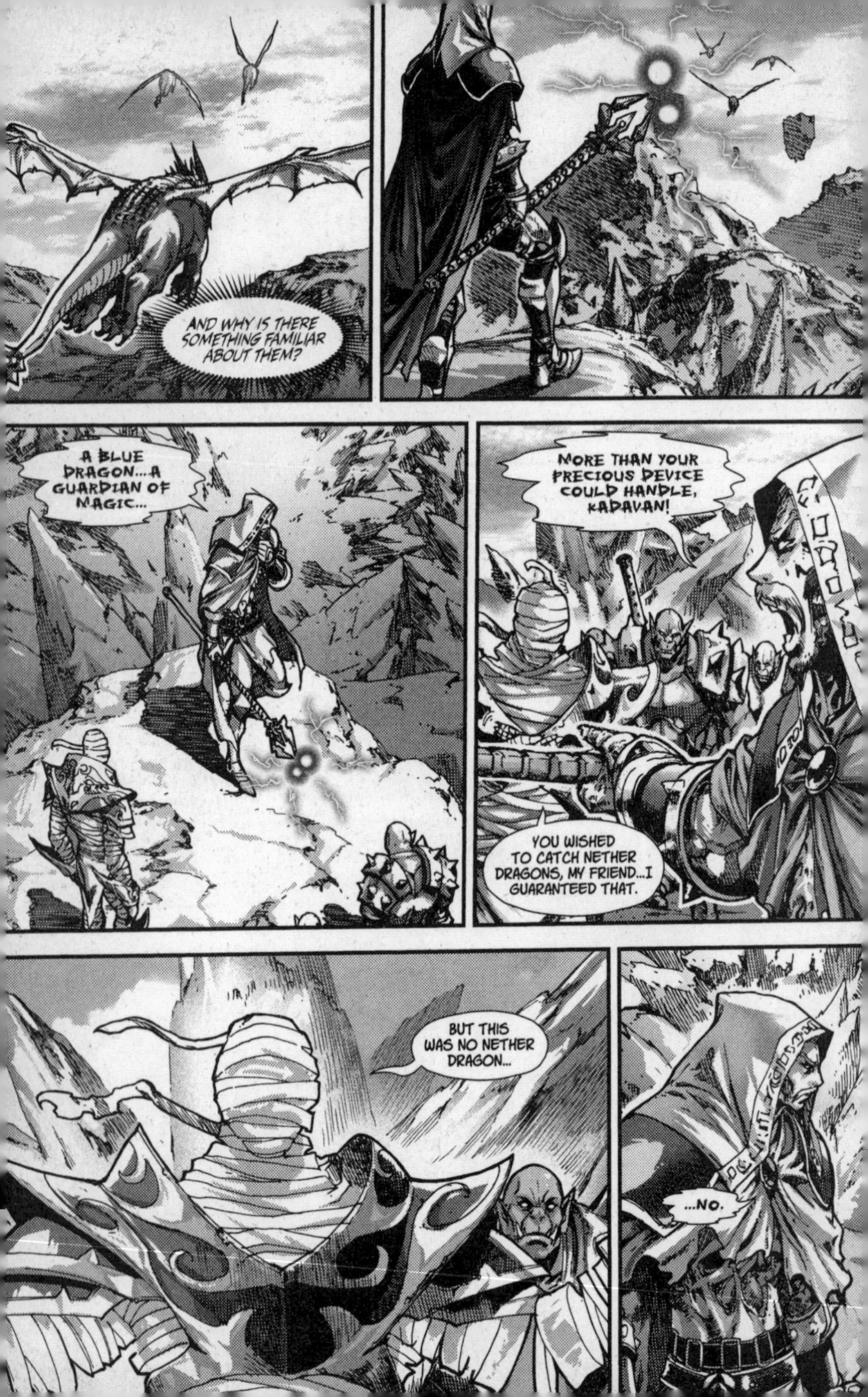
AND WHY IS THERE SOMETHING FAMILIAR ABOUT THEM?
A BLUE DRAGON...A GUARDIAN OF MAGIC...
MORE THAN YOUR PRECIOUS DEVICE COULD HANDLE, KADAVAN!
YOU WISHED TO CATCH NETHER DRAGONS, MY FRIEND...I GUARANTEED THAT.
BUT THIS WAS NO NETHER DRAGON...
...NO.

IN SOME WAYS, THIS WAS EVEN MORE...

BLUE DRAGONS ARE THE KEEPERS OF MAGIC... THEY WIELD IT LIKE NO OTHER...

WITH THE POWER OF A BLUE DRAGON AT MY BECK AND CALL...

IT COULD BE DONE...

FOR A PRICE... AS USUAL?

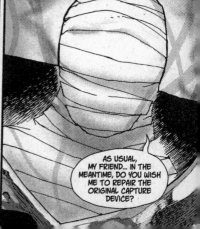

AS USUAL, MY FRIEND... IN THE MEANTIME, DO YOU WISH ME TO REPAIR THE ORIGINAL CAPTURE DEVICE?

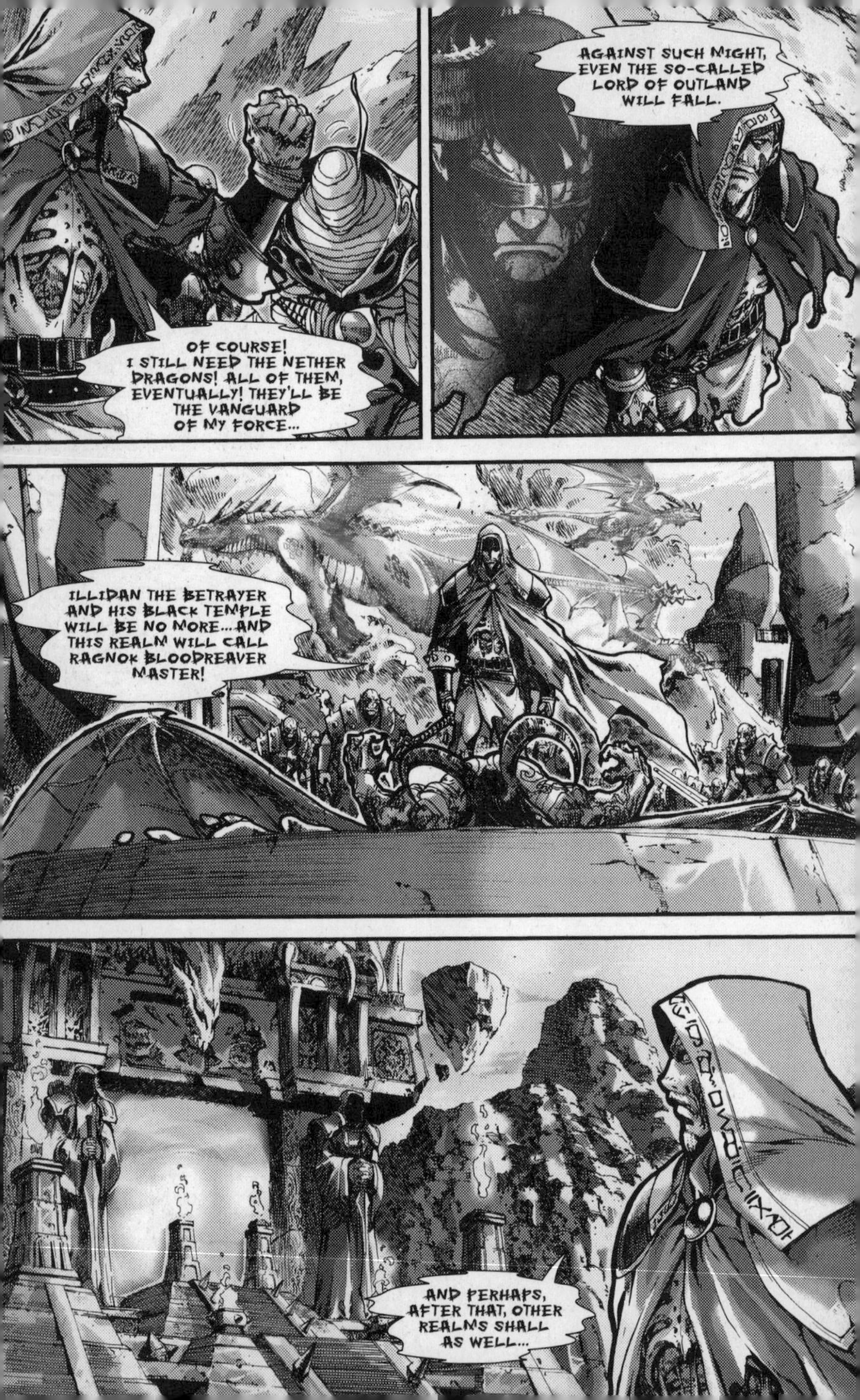
OF COURSE! I STILL NEED THE NETHER DRAGONS! ALL OF THEM, EVENTUALLY! THEY'LL BE THE VANGUARD OF MY FORCE...
AGAINST SUCH MIGHT, EVEN THE SO-CALLED LORD OF OUTLAND WILL FALL.
ILLIDAN THE BETRAYER AND HIS BLACK TEMPLE WILL BE NO MORE...AND THIS REALM WILL CALL RAGNOK BLOODREAVER MASTER!
AND PERHAPS, AFTER THAT, OTHER REALMS SHALL AS WELL...

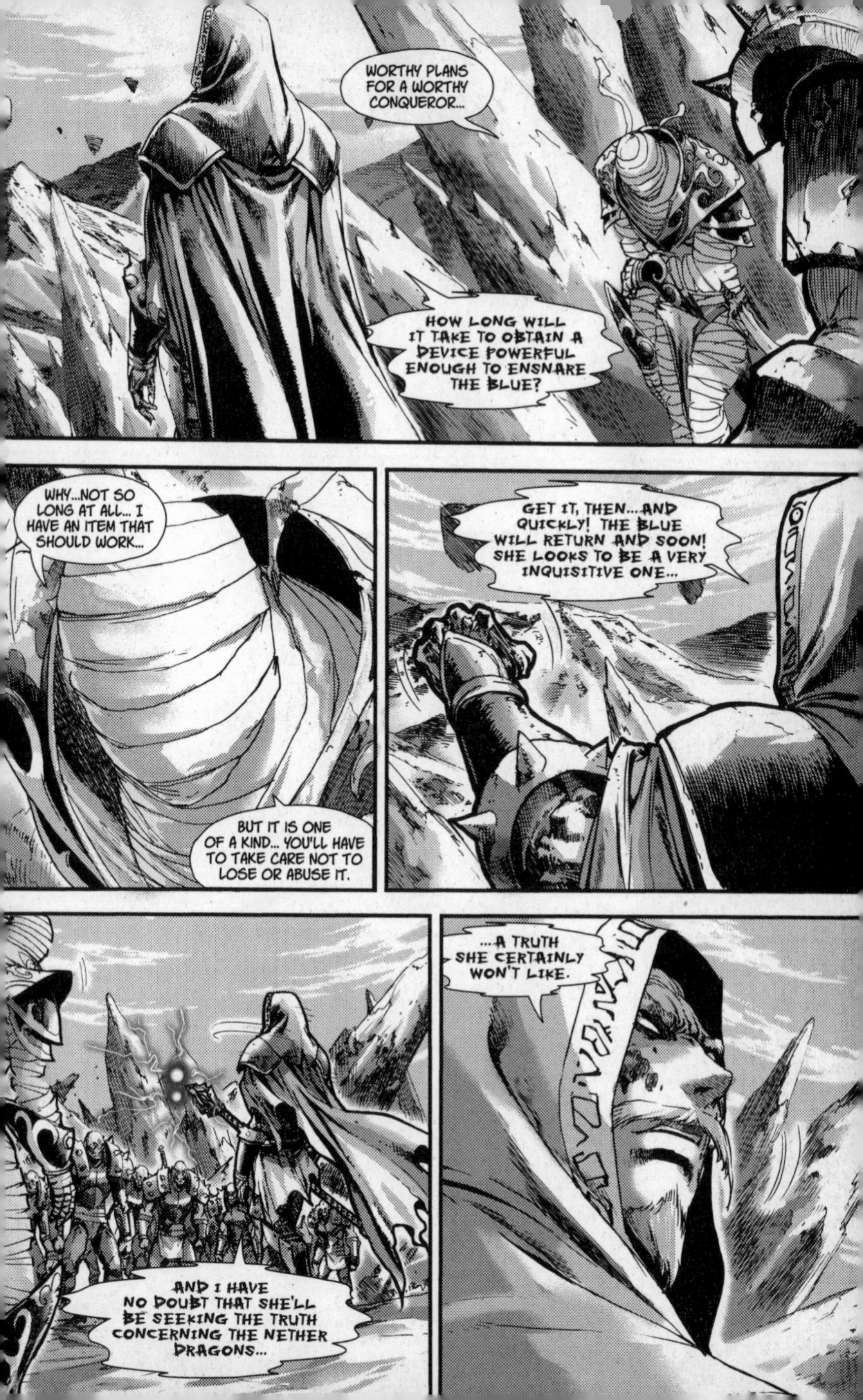
WORTHY PLANS FOR A WORTHY CONQUEROR...
HOW LONG WILL IT TAKE TO OBTAIN A DEVICE POWERFUL ENOUGH TO ENSNARE THE BLUE?
WHY...NOT SO LONG AT ALL... I HAVE AN ITEM THAT SHOULD WORK...
BUT IT IS ONE OF A KIND... YOU'LL HAVE TO TAKE CARE NOT TO LOSE OR ABUSE IT.
GET IT, THEN... AND QUICKLY! THE BLUE WILL RETURN AND SOON! SHE LOOKS TO BE A VERY INQUISITIVE ONE...
AND I HAVE NO DOUBT THAT SHE'LL BE SEEKING THE TRUTH CONCERNING THE NETHER DRAGONS...
...A TRUTH SHE CERTAINLY WON'T LIKE.

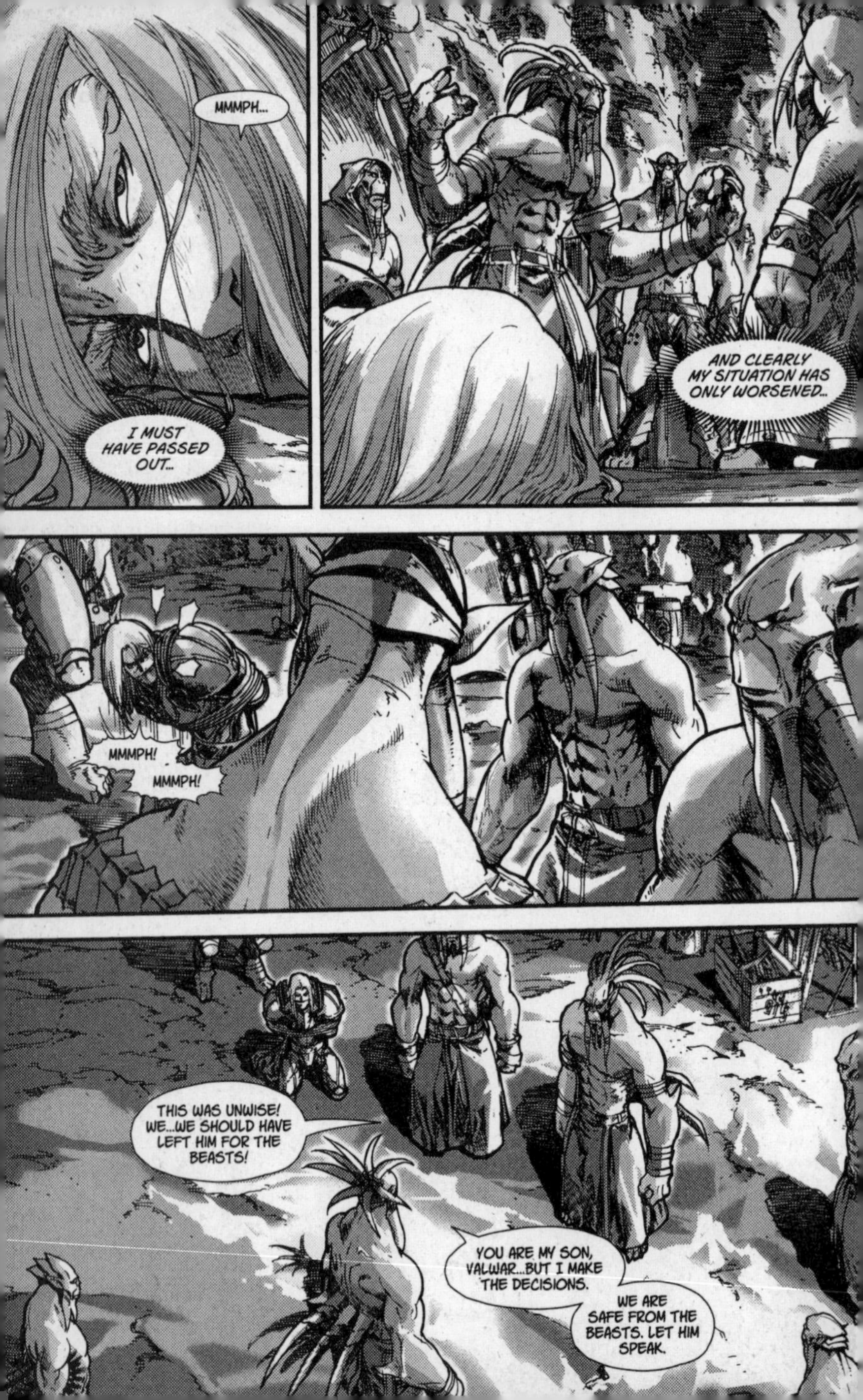
MMMPH...
I MUST HAVE PASSED OUT...
AND CLEARLY MY SITUATION HAS ONLY WORSENED...
MMMPH!
MMMPH!
THIS WAS UNWISE! WE...WE SHOULD HAVE LEFT HIM FOR THE BEASTS!
YOU ARE MY SON, VALWAR...BUT I MAKE THE DECISIONS.
WE ARE SAFE FROM THE BEASTS. LET HIM SPEAK.

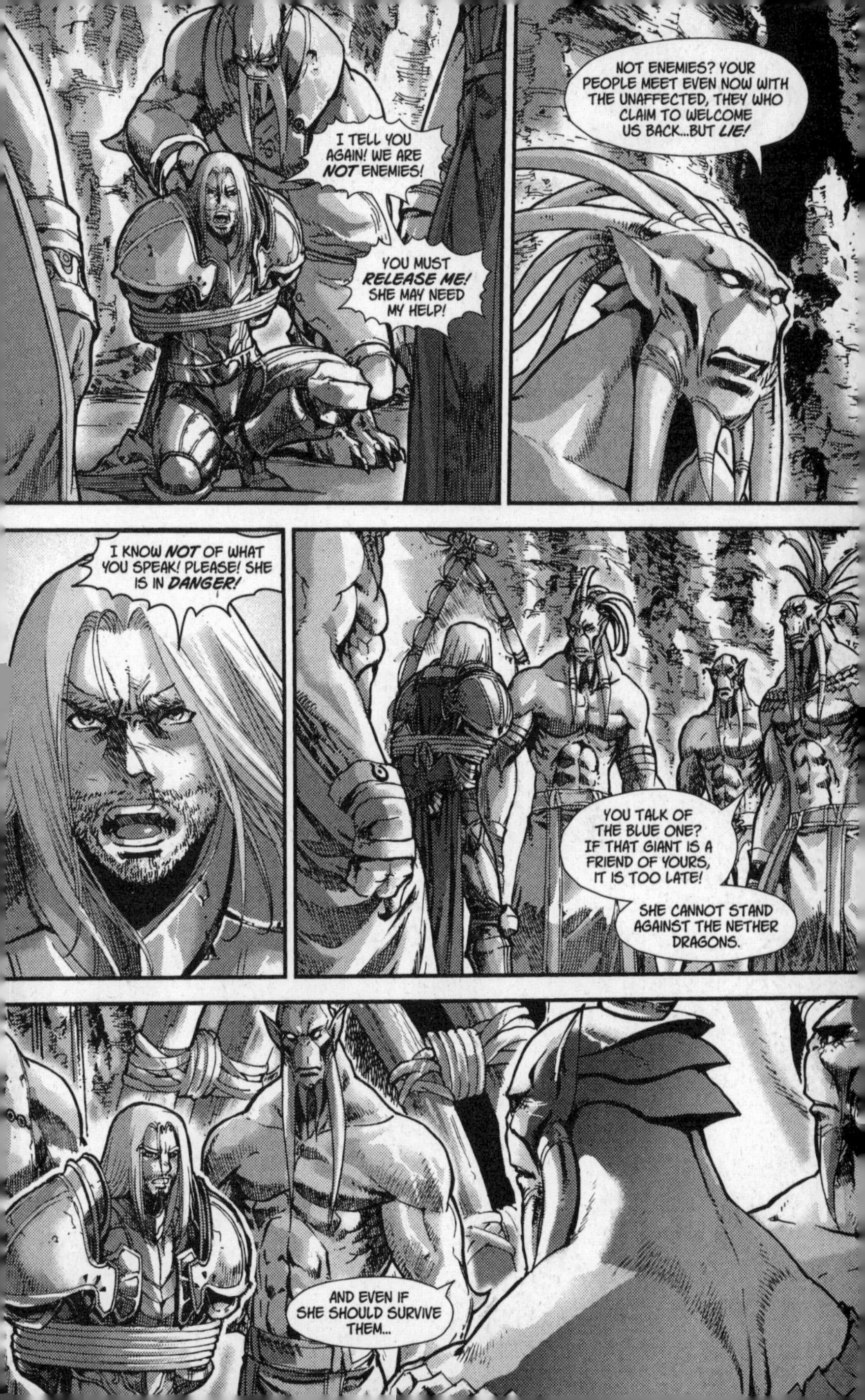
I TELL YOU AGAIN! WE ARE *NOT* ENEMIES!
YOU MUST *RELEASE ME!* SHE MAY NEED MY HELP!
NOT ENEMIES? YOUR PEOPLE MEET EVEN NOW WITH THE UNAFFECTED, THEY WHO CLAIM TO WELCOME US BACK...BUT *LIE!*
I KNOW *NOT* OF WHAT YOU SPEAK! PLEASE! SHE IS IN *DANGER!*
YOU TALK OF THE BLUE ONE? IF THAT GIANT IS A FRIEND OF YOURS, IT IS TOO LATE!
SHE CANNOT STAND AGAINST THE NETHER DRAGONS.
AND EVEN IF SHE SHOULD SURVIVE THEM...

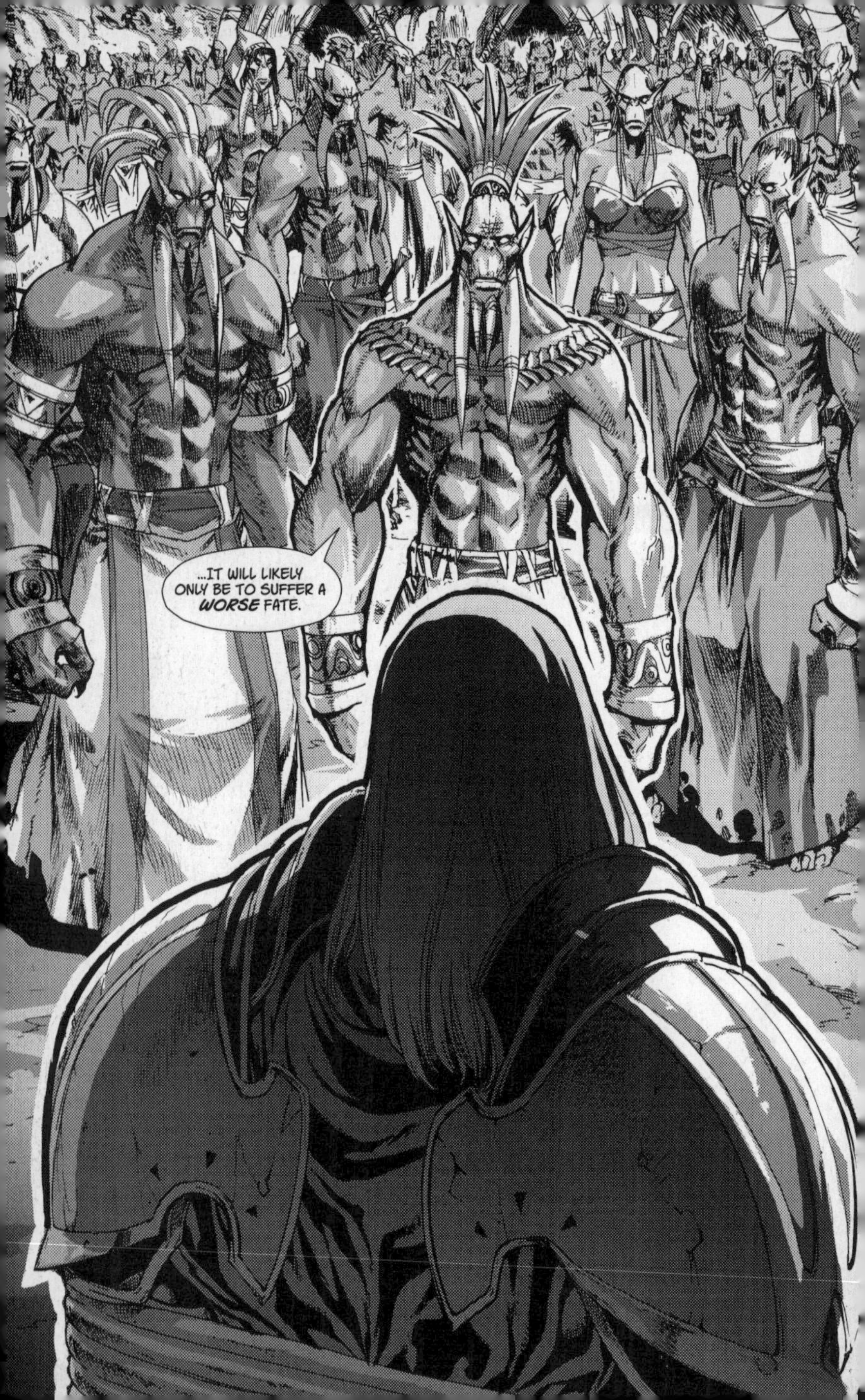
...IT WILL LIKELY ONLY BE TO SUFFER A WORSE FATE.

CHAPTER THREE
TREACHERY

SO ASTOUNDING...
SO FANTASTIC...

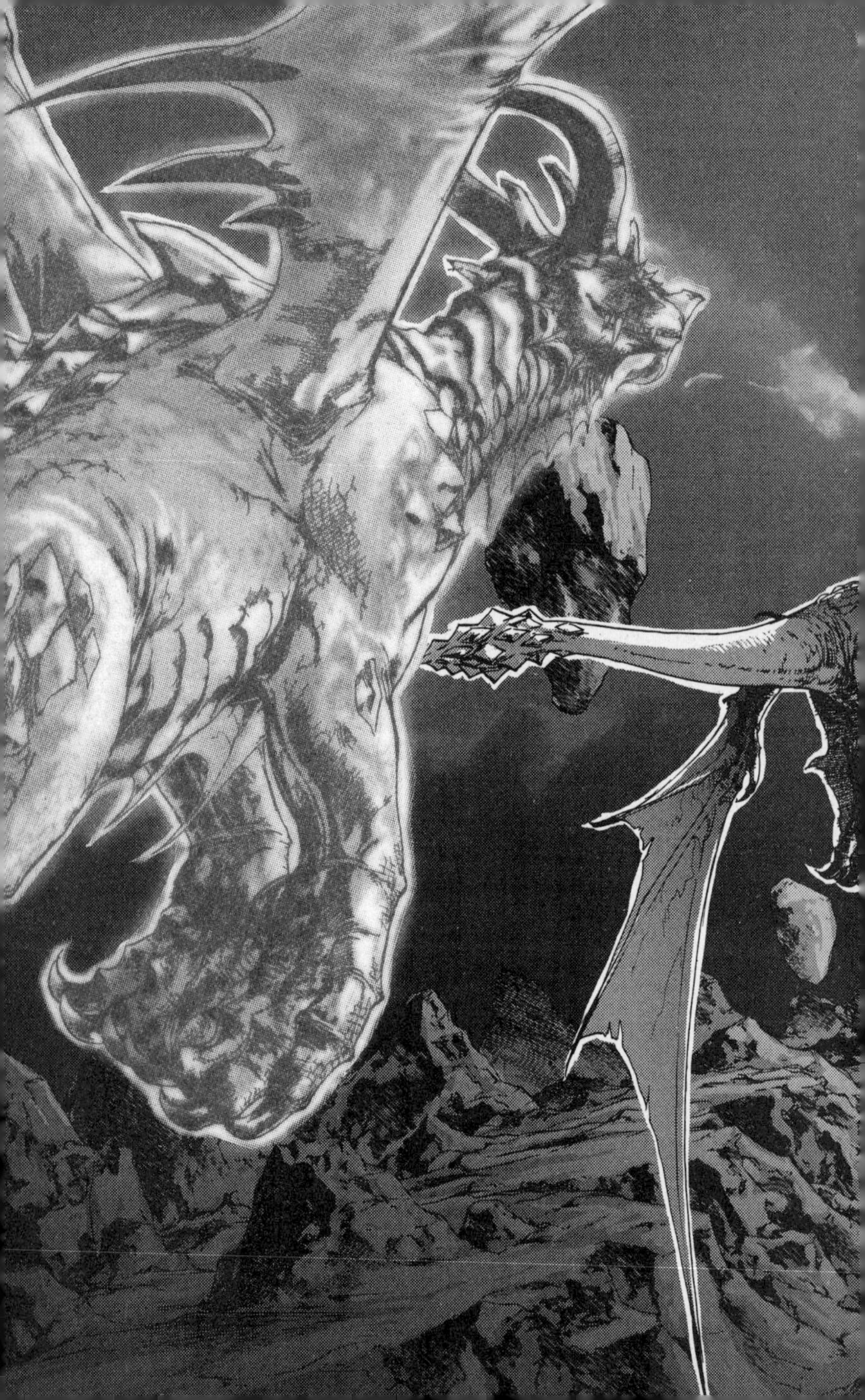

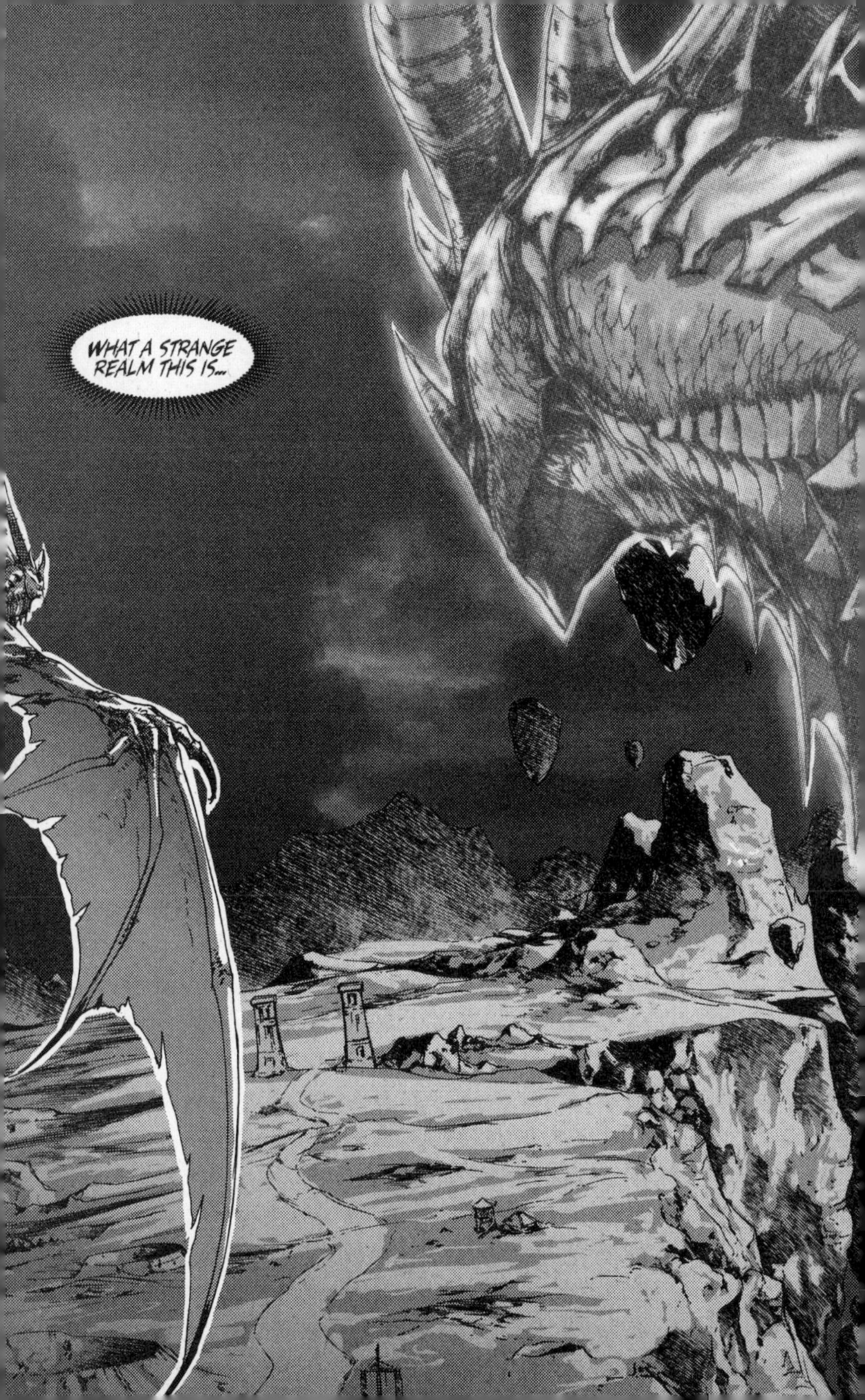
WHAT A STRANGE REALM THIS IS...

A TRAGIC, SHATTERED WORLD STILL FILLED WITH LIFE...

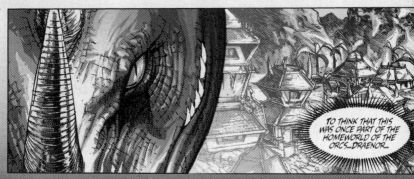

TO THINK THAT THIS WAS ONCE PART OF THE HOMEWORLD OF THE ORCS...DRAENOR...

A WILD, BRUTAL PLACE WHERE CORRUPTION BY DEMONS FIRST ALTERED THE BROWN-SKINNED ORCS INTO A FETID GREEN, MONSTROUS EVIL...

A WORLD TIED TO OURS ONLY BY THE DARK PORTAL.

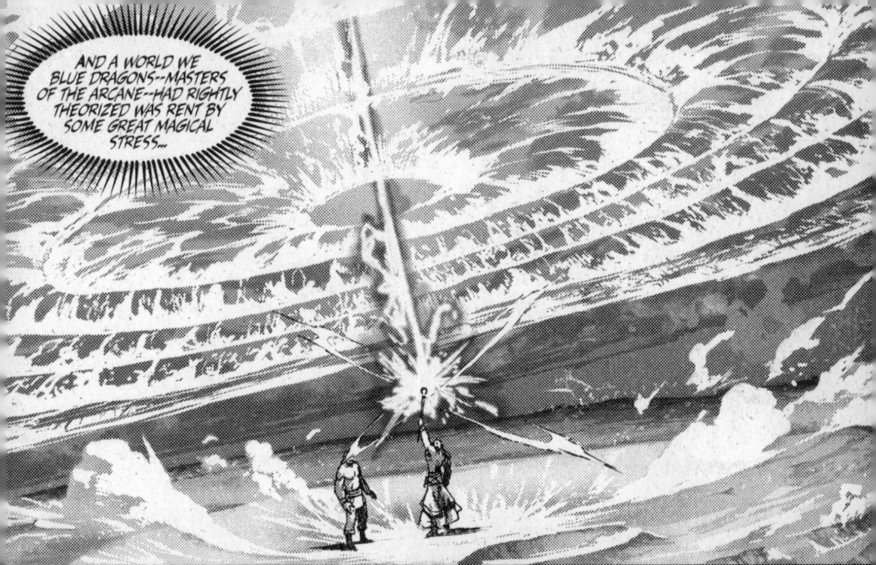
AND A WORLD WE BLUE DRAGONS--MASTERS OF THE ARCANE--HAD RIGHTLY THEORIZED WAS RENT BY SOME GREAT MAGICAL STRESS...

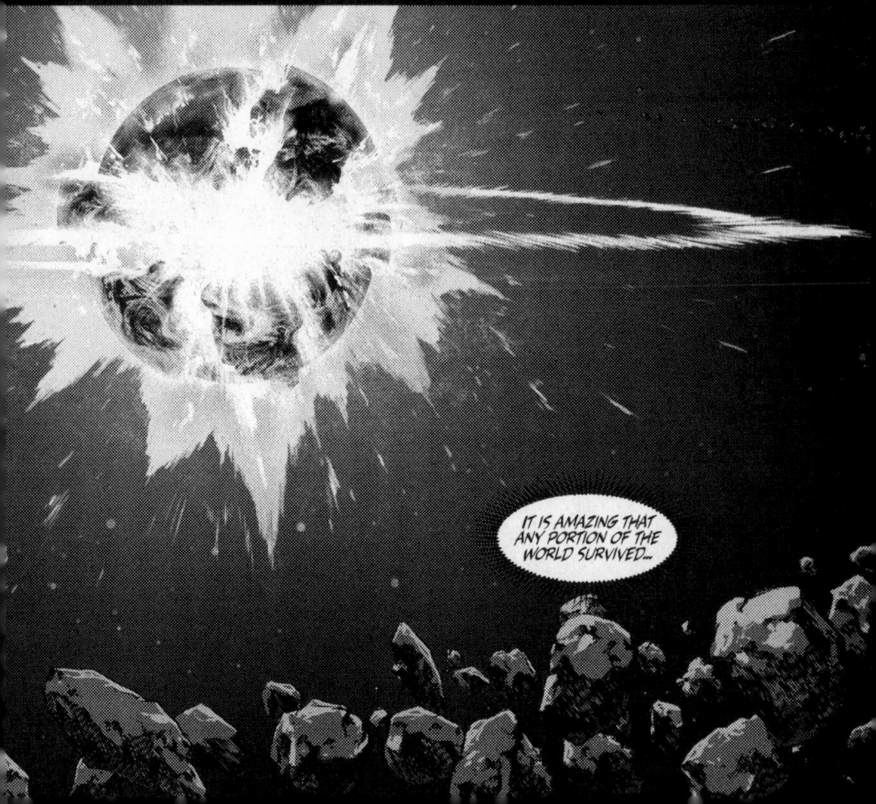
IT IS AMAZING THAT ANY PORTION OF THE WORLD SURVIVED...

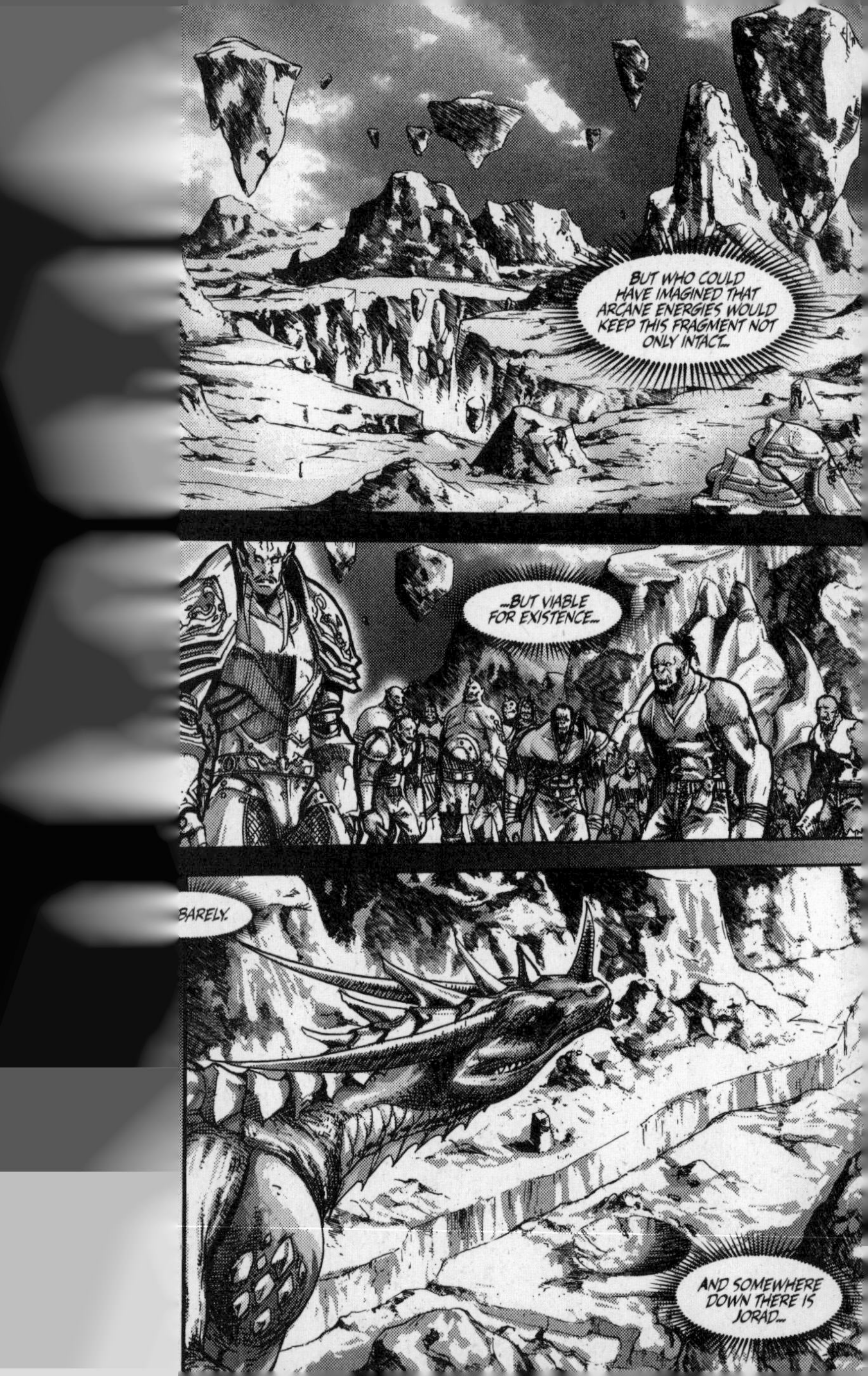
BUT WHO COULD HAVE IMAGINED THAT ARCANE ENERGIES WOULD KEEP THIS FRAGMENT NOT ONLY INTACT...
...BUT VIABLE FOR EXISTENCE...
BARELY.
AND SOMEWHERE DOWN THERE IS JORAD...

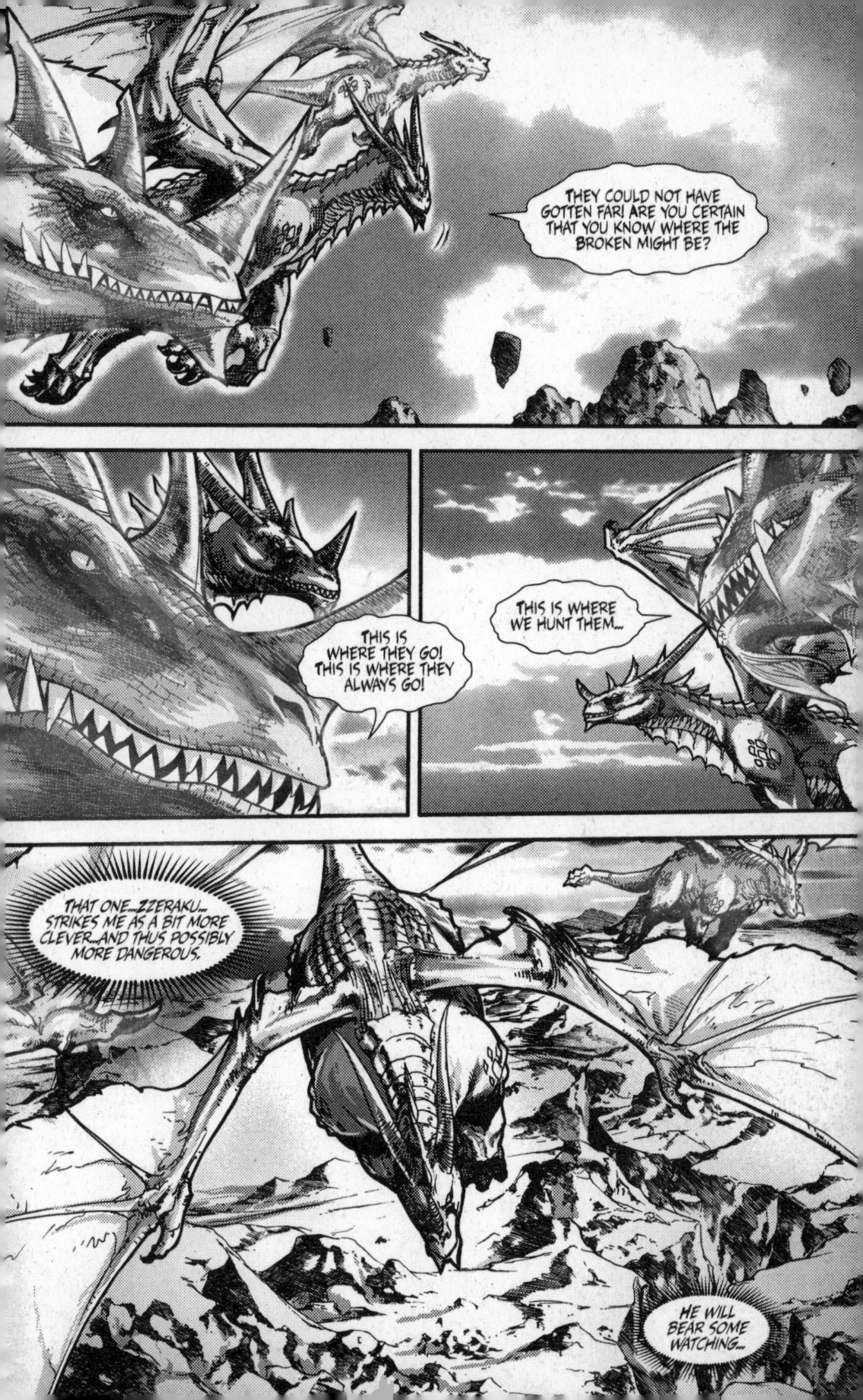
THEY COULD NOT HAVE GOTTEN FAR! ARE YOU CERTAIN THAT YOU KNOW WHERE THE BROKEN MIGHT BE?
THIS IS WHERE THEY GO! THIS IS WHERE THEY ALWAYS GO!
THIS IS WHERE WE HUNT THEM...
THAT ONE...ZZERAKU... STRIKES ME AS A BIT MORE CLEVER...AND THUS POSSIBLY MORE DANGEROUS.
HE WILL BEAR SOME WATCHING...

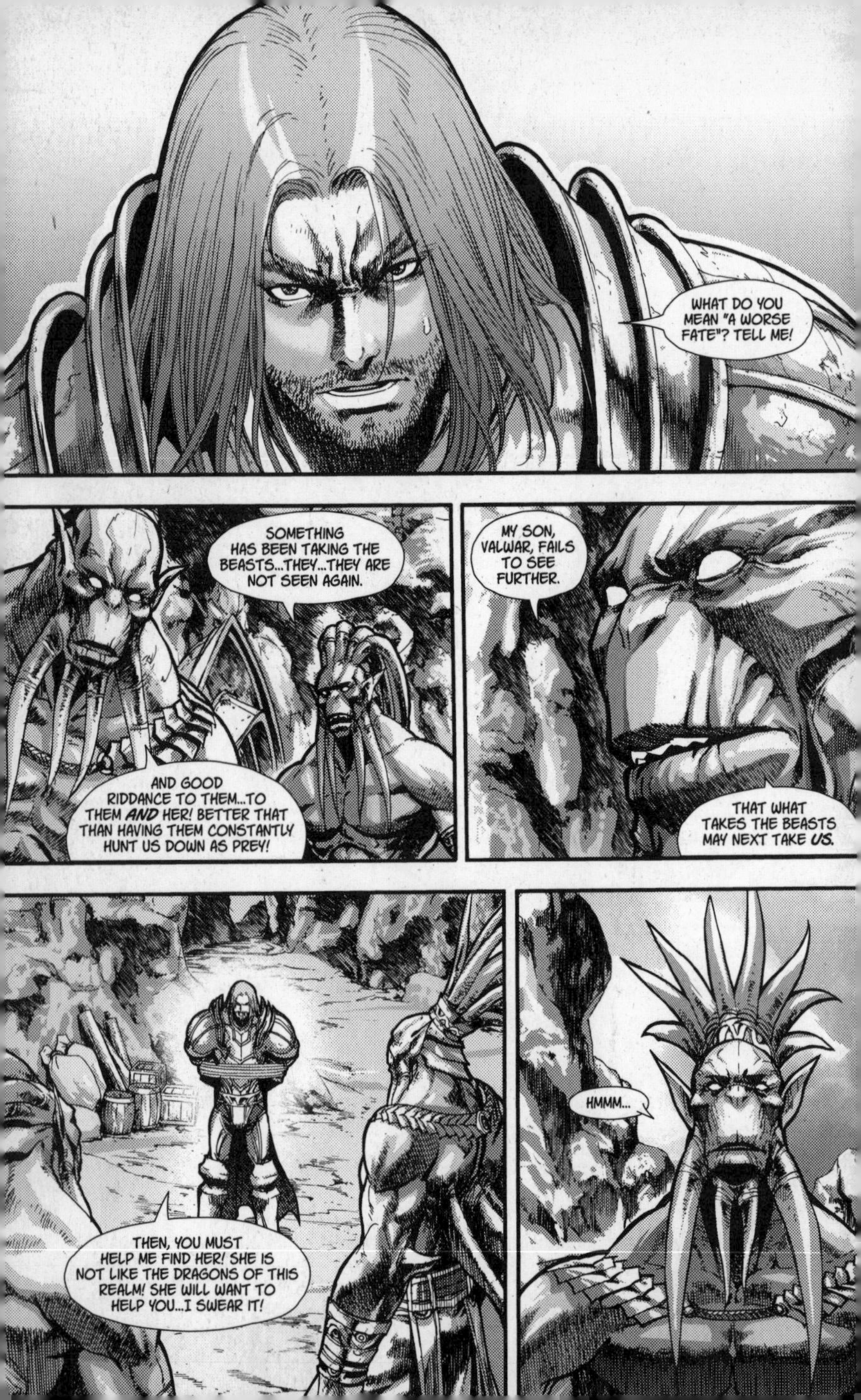
WHAT DO YOU MEAN "A WORSE FATE"? TELL ME!
SOMETHING HAS BEEN TAKING THE BEASTS...THEY...THEY ARE NOT SEEN AGAIN.
AND GOOD RIDDANCE TO THEM...TO THEM AND HER! BETTER THAT THAN HAVING THEM CONSTANTLY HUNT US DOWN AS PREY!
MY SON, VALWAR, FAILS TO SEE FURTHER.
THAT WHAT TAKES THE BEASTS MAY NEXT TAKE US.
THEN, YOU MUST HELP ME FIND HER! SHE IS NOT LIKE THE DRAGONS OF THIS REALM! SHE WILL WANT TO HELP YOU...I SWEAR IT!
HMMM...

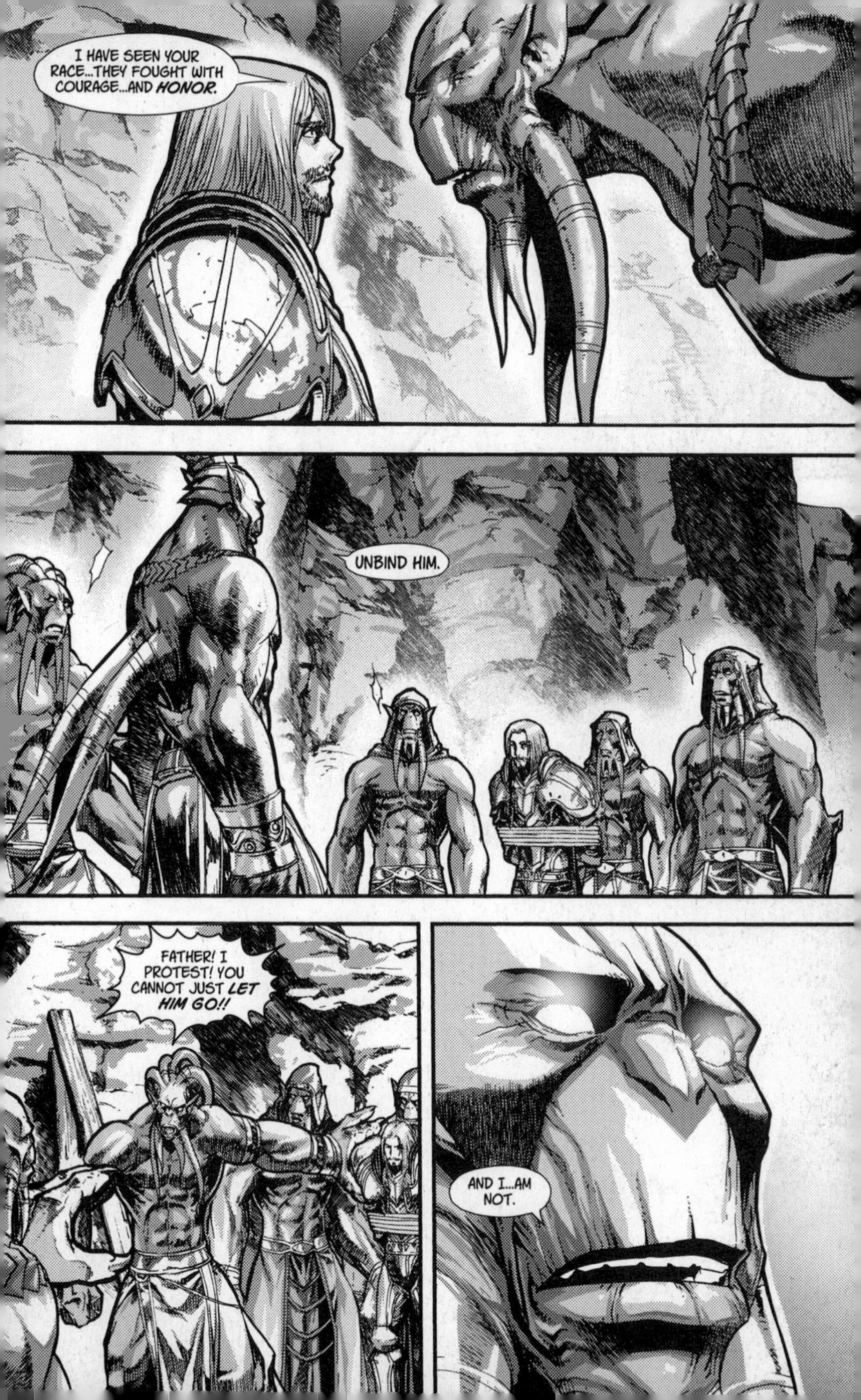
I HAVE SEEN YOUR RACE...THEY FOUGHT WITH COURAGE...AND HONOR.
UNBIND HIM.
FATHER! I PROTEST! YOU CANNOT JUST LET HIM GO!!
AND I...AM NOT.

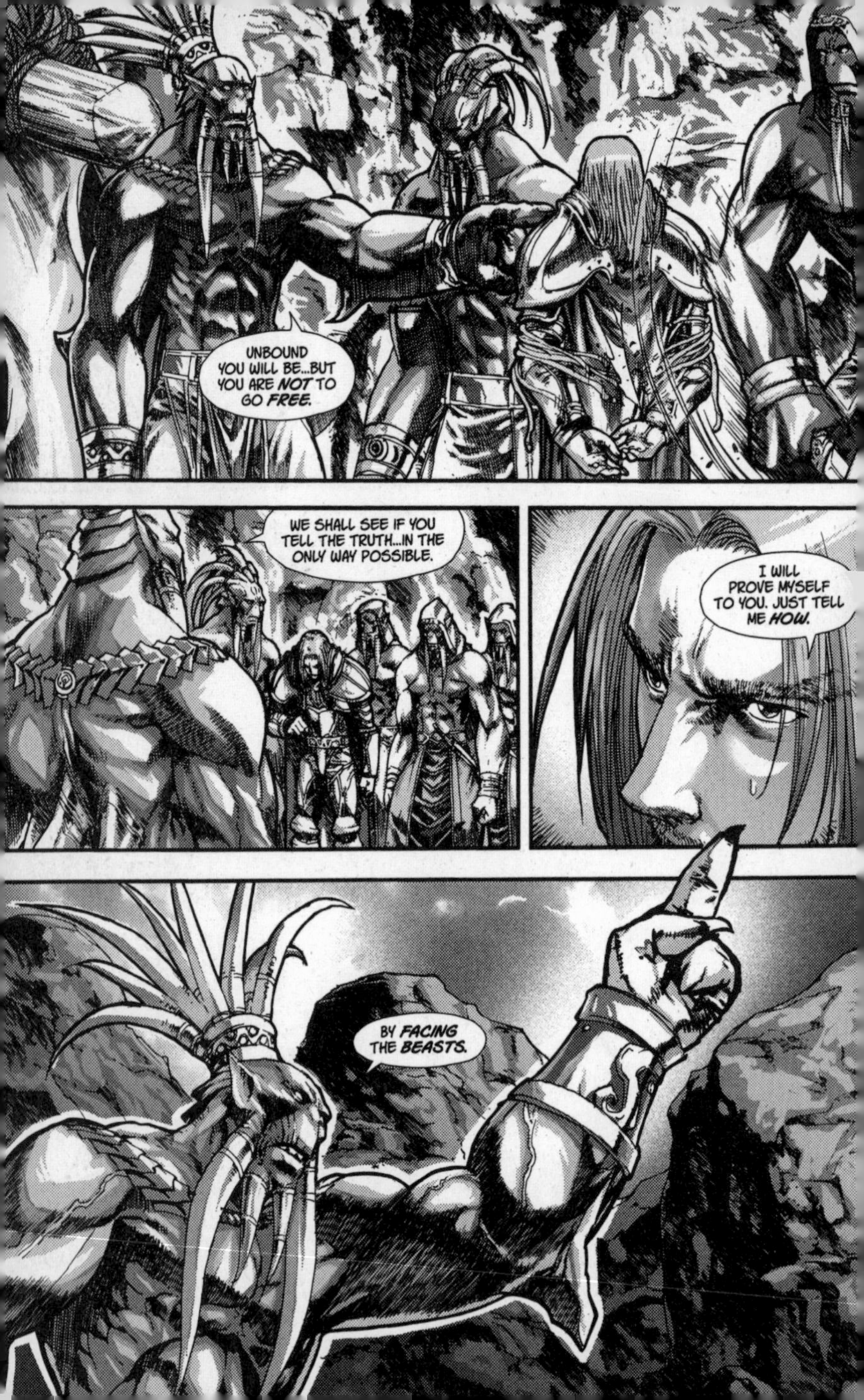
UNBOUND YOU WILL BE...BUT YOU ARE NOT TO GO FREE.
WE SHALL SEE IF YOU TELL THE TRUTH...IN THE ONLY WAY POSSIBLE.
I WILL PROVE MYSELF TO YOU. JUST TELL ME HOW.
BY FACING THE BEASTS.

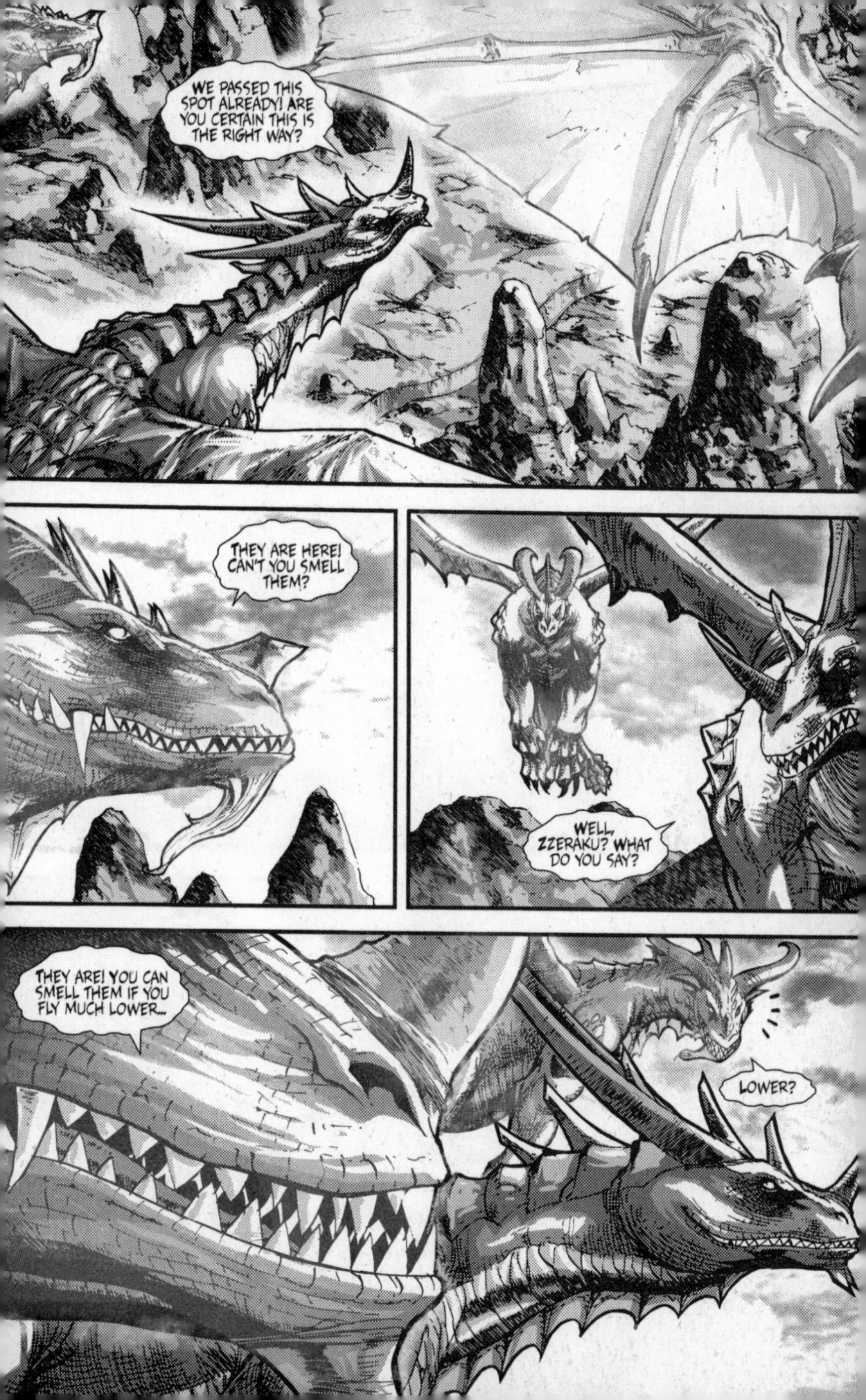
WE PASSED THIS SPOT ALREADY! ARE YOU CERTAIN THIS IS THE RIGHT WAY?
THEY ARE HERE! CAN'T YOU SMELL THEM?
WELL, ZZERAKU? WHAT DO YOU SAY?
THEY ARE! YOU CAN SMELL THEM IF YOU FLY MUCH LOWER...
LOWER?

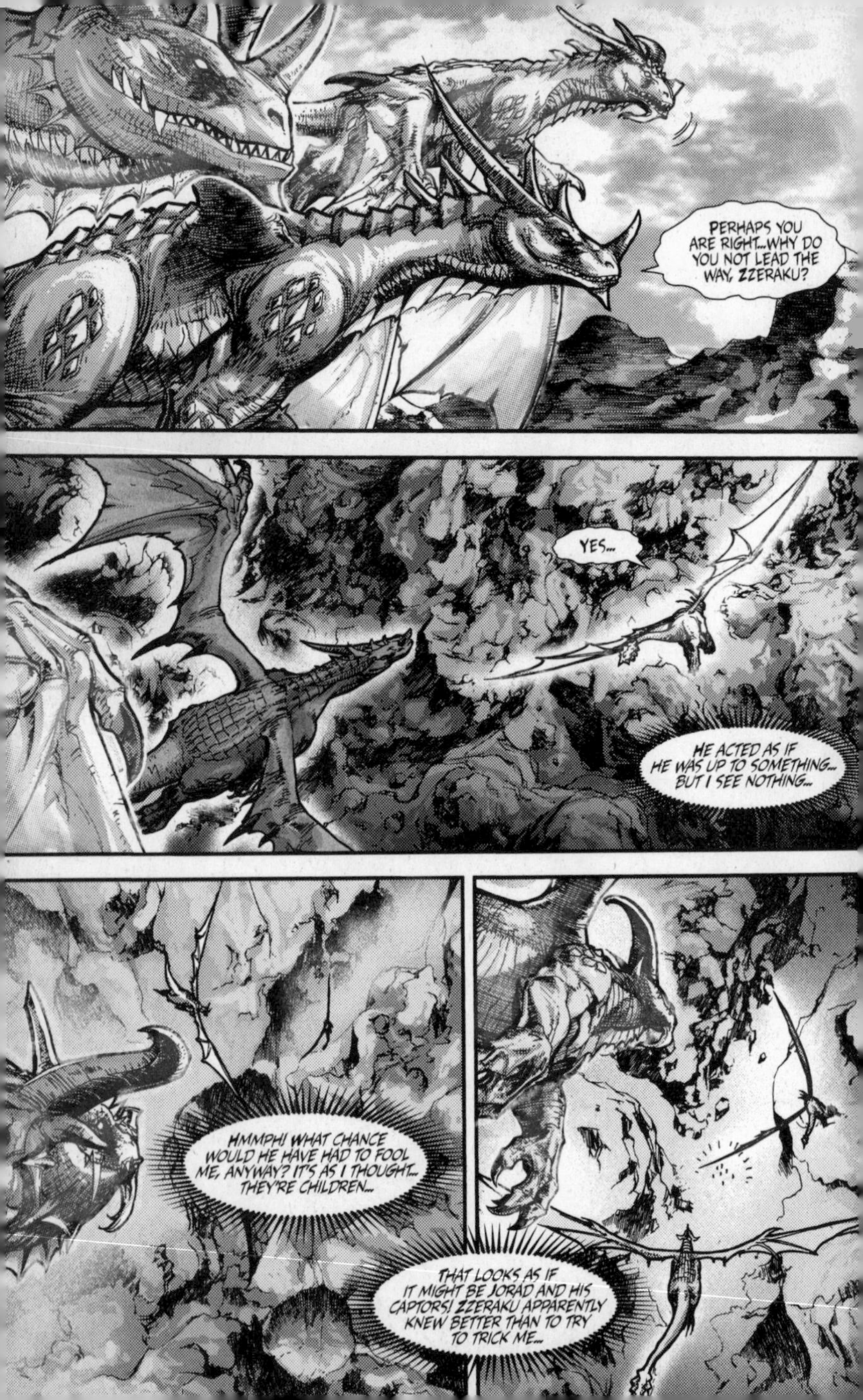
PERHAPS YOU ARE RIGHT...WHY DO YOU NOT LEAD THE WAY, ZZERAKU?
YES...
HE ACTED AS IF HE WAS UP TO SOMETHING... BUT I SEE NOTHING...
HMMPH! WHAT CHANCE WOULD HE HAVE HAD TO FOOL ME, ANYWAY? IT'S AS I THOUGHT... THEY'RE CHILDREN...
THAT LOOKS AS IF IT MIGHT BE JORAD AND HIS CAPTORS! ZZERAKU APPARENTLY KNEW BETTER THAN TO TRY TO TRICK ME...

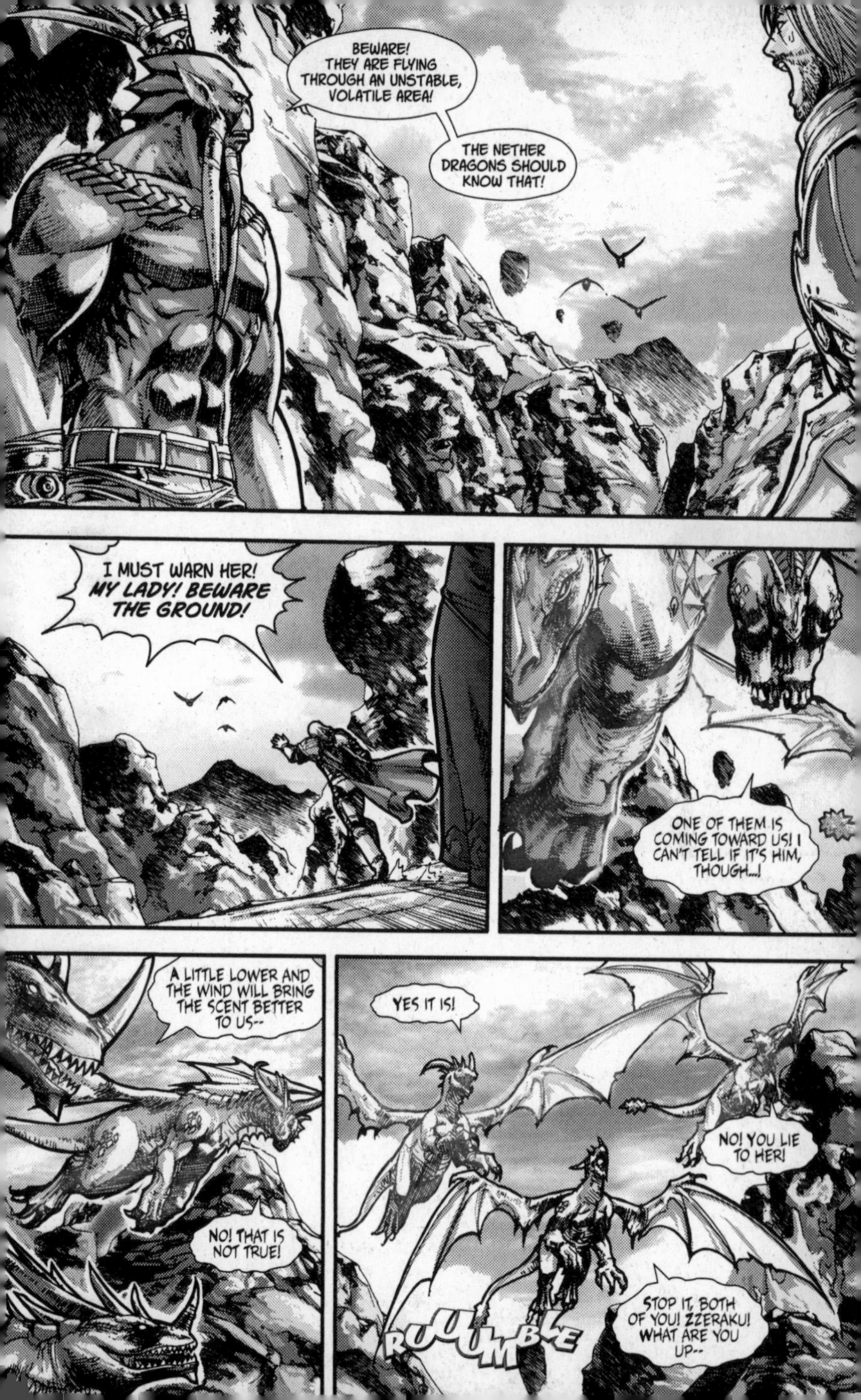
BEWARE! THEY ARE FLYING THROUGH AN UNSTABLE, VOLATILE AREA!
THE NETHER DRAGONS SHOULD KNOW THAT!
I MUST WARN HER! MY LADY! BEWARE THE GROUND!
ONE OF THEM IS COMING TOWARD US! I CAN'T TELL IF IT'S HIM, THOUGH...!
A LITTLE LOWER AND THE WIND WILL BRING THE SCENT BETTER TO US--
NO! THAT IS NOT TRUE!
YES IT IS!
NO! YOU LIE TO HER!
ROOUUMBLE
STOP IT, BOTH OF YOU! ZZERAKU! WHAT ARE YOU UP--

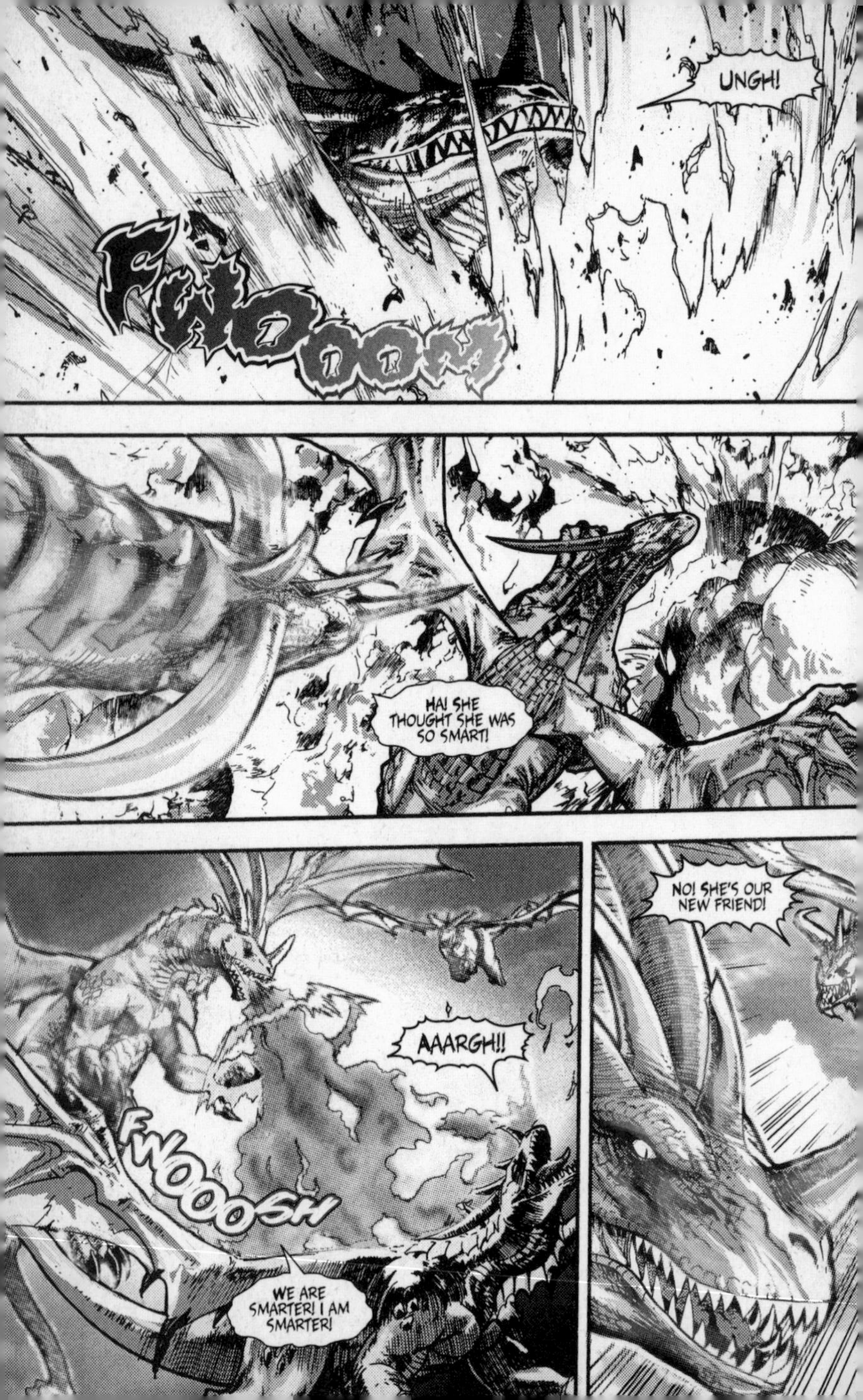
UNGH!
FWOOOM
HA! SHE THOUGHT SHE WAS SO SMART!
NO! SHE'S OUR NEW FRIEND!
AAARGH!!
FWOOOSH
WE ARE SMARTER! I AM SMARTER!

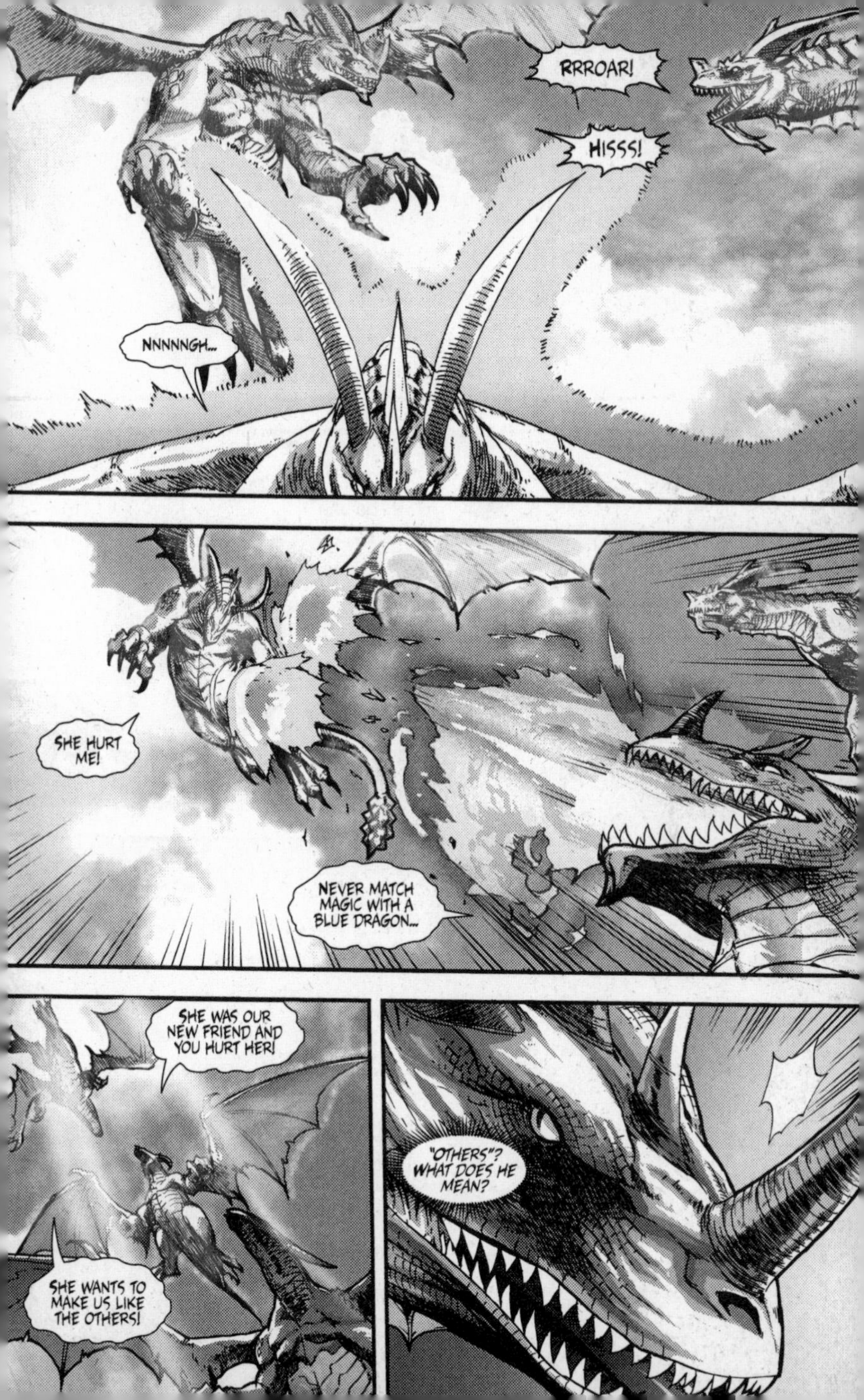
RRROAR!
HISSS!
NNNNNGH...
SHE HURT ME!
NEVER MATCH MAGIC WITH A BLUE DRAGON...
SHE WAS OUR NEW FRIEND AND YOU HURT HER!
SHE WANTS TO MAKE US LIKE THE OTHERS!
"OTHERS"? WHAT DOES HE MEAN?

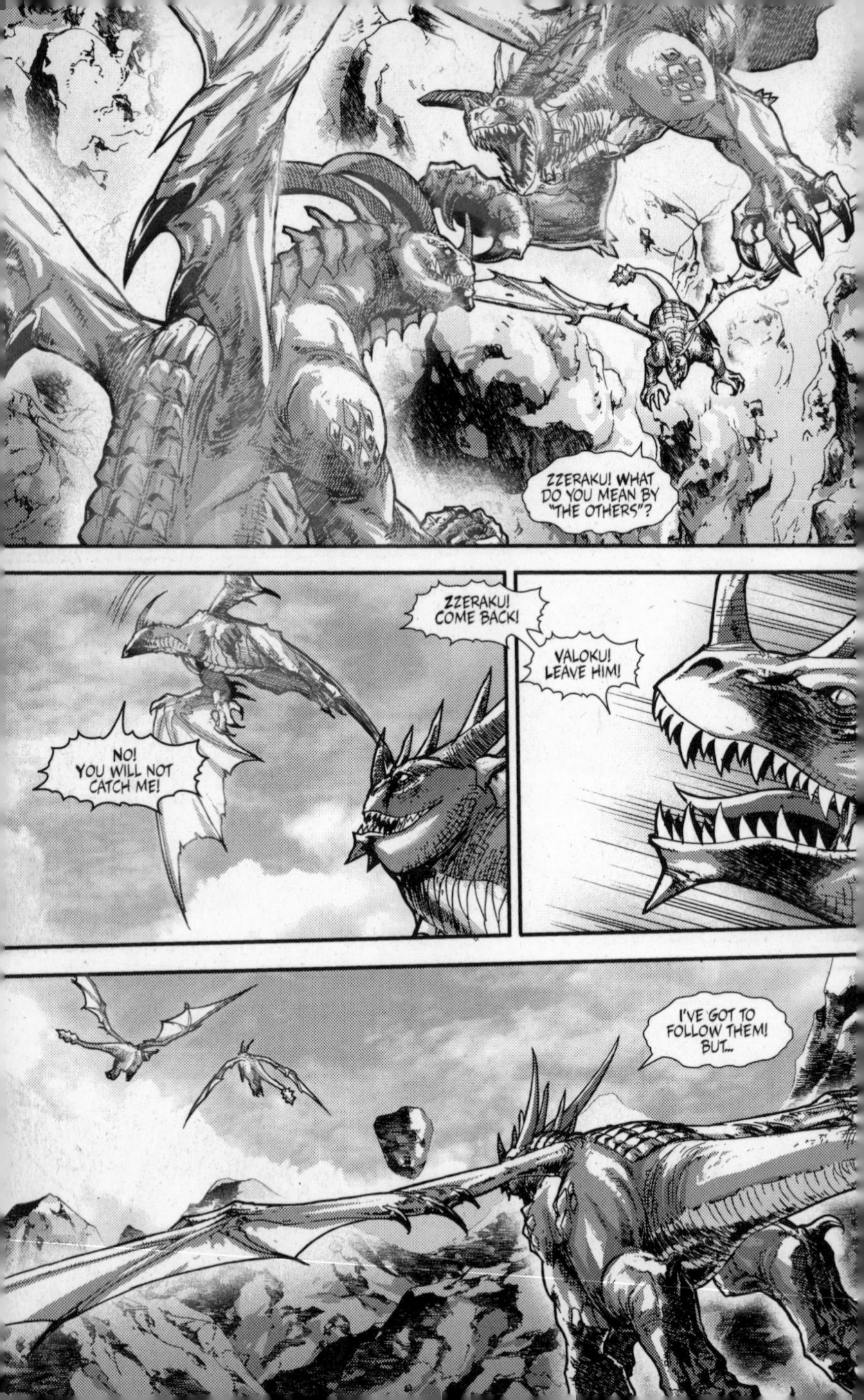
ZZERAKU! WHAT DO YOU MEAN BY "THE OTHERS"?
NO! YOU WILL NOT CATCH ME!
ZZERAKU! COME BACK!
VALOKU! LEAVE HIM!
I'VE GOT TO FOLLOW THEM! BUT...

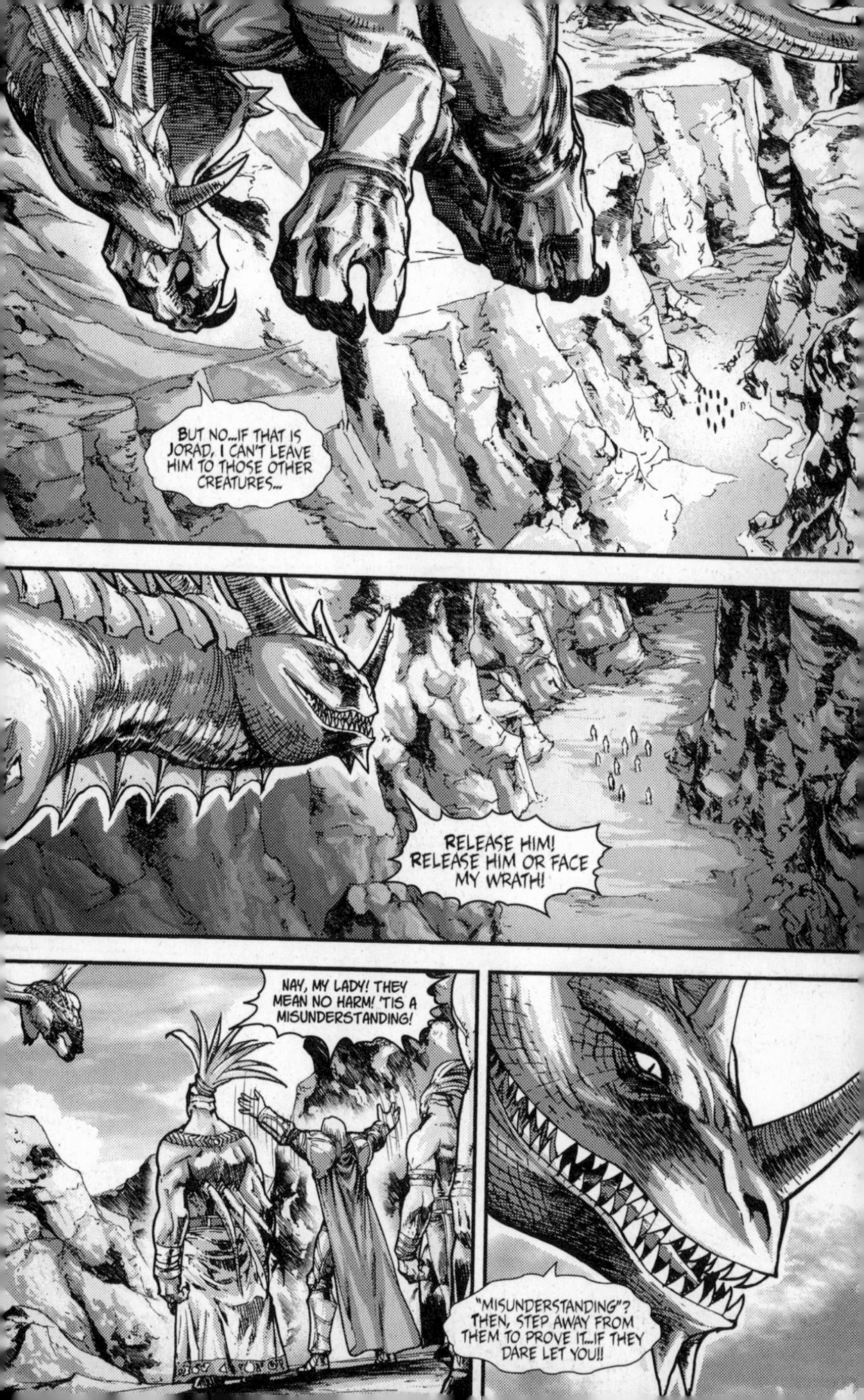
BUT NO...IF THAT IS JORAD, I CAN'T LEAVE HIM TO THOSE OTHER CREATURES...
RELEASE HIM! RELEASE HIM OR FACE MY WRATH!
NAY, MY LADY! THEY MEAN NO HARM! 'TIS A MISUNDERSTANDING!
"MISUNDERSTANDING"? THEN, STEP AWAY FROM THEM TO PROVE IT...IF THEY DARE LET YOU!!

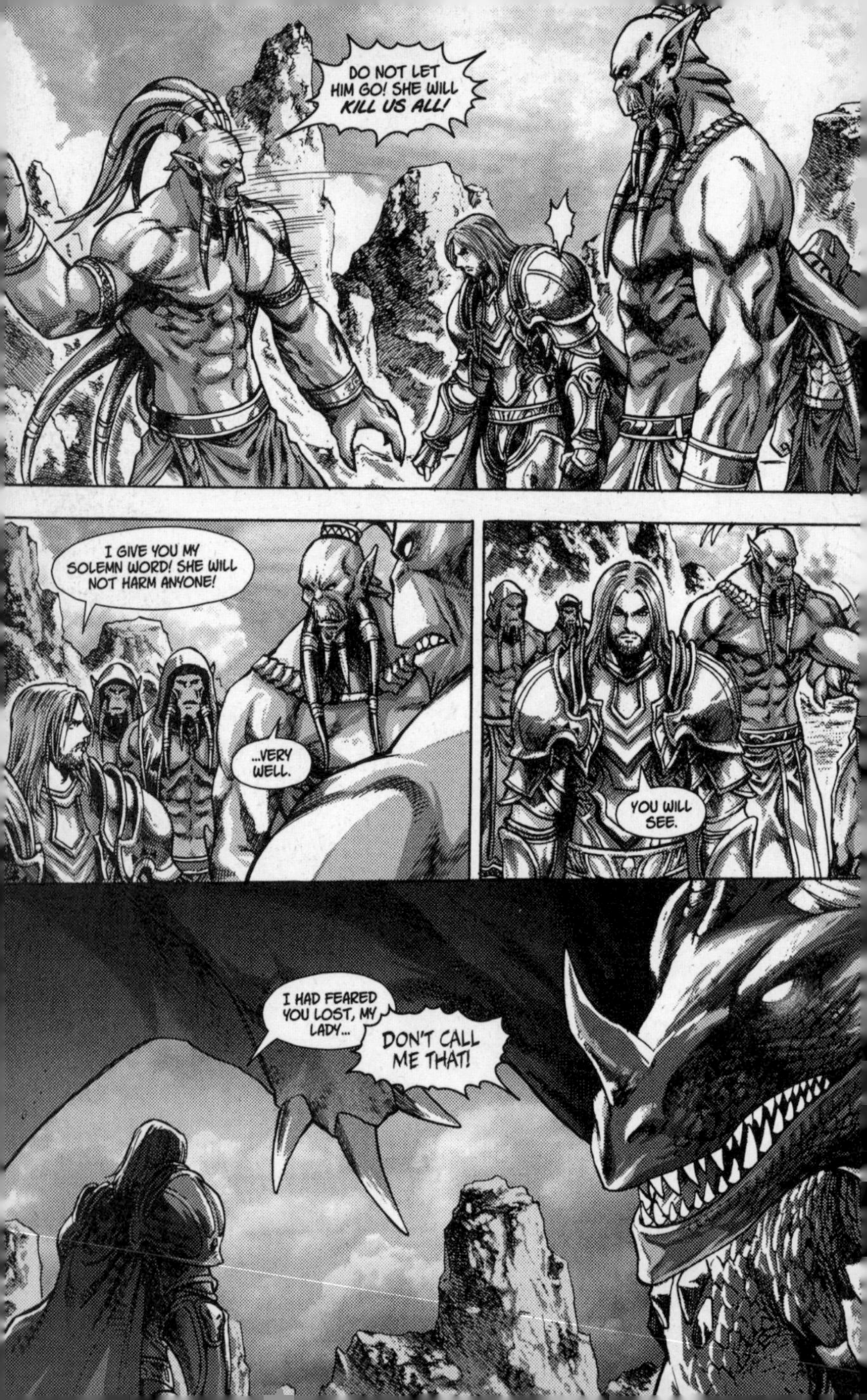
DO NOT LET HIM GO! SHE WILL KILL US ALL!
I GIVE YOU MY SOLEMN WORD! SHE WILL NOT HARM ANYONE!
...VERY WELL.
YOU WILL SEE.
I HAD FEARED YOU LOST, MY LADY...
DON'T CALL ME THAT!

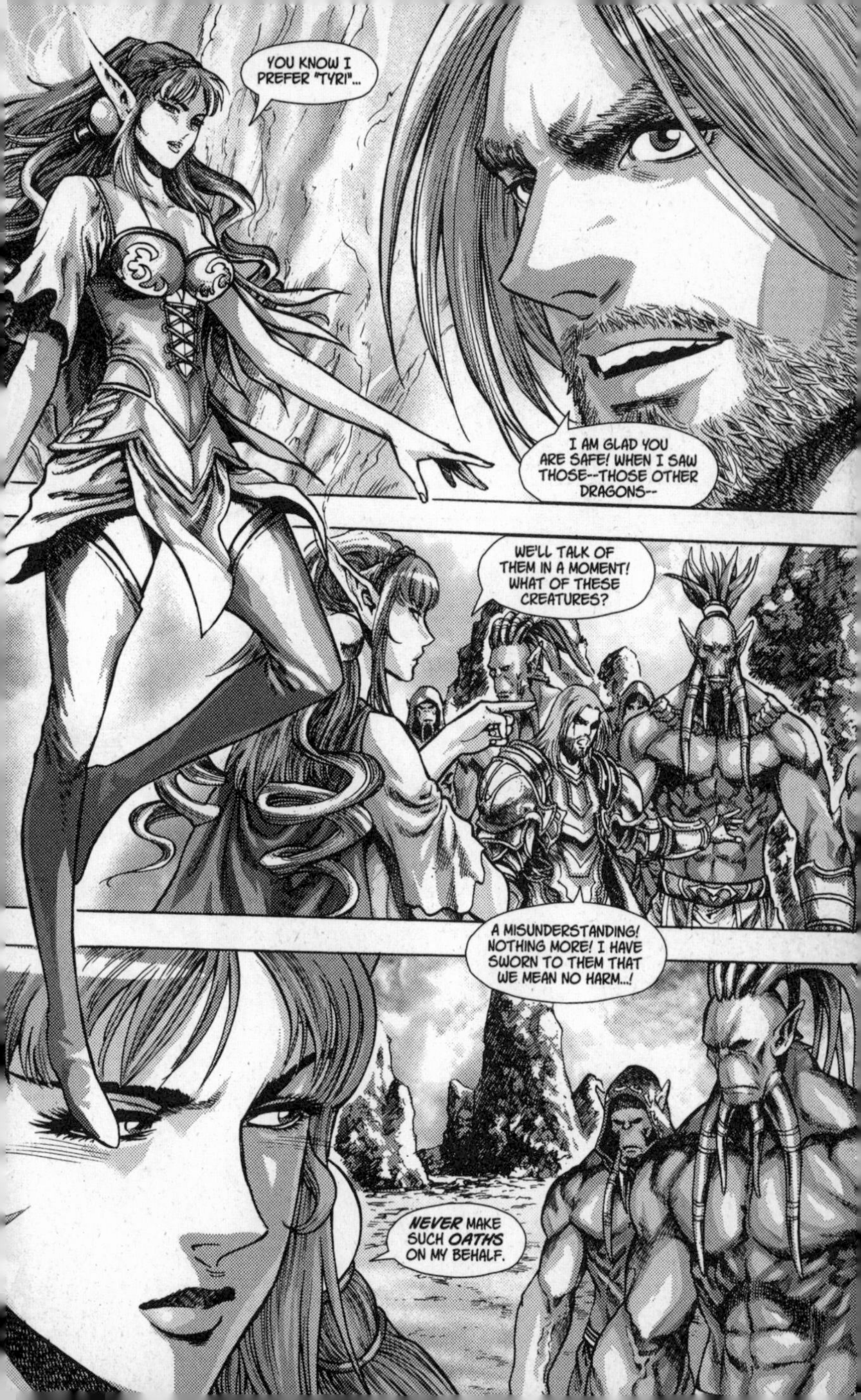
YOU KNOW I PREFER "TYRI"...
I AM GLAD YOU ARE SAFE! WHEN I SAW THOSE--THOSE OTHER DRAGONS--
WE'LL TALK OF THEM IN A MOMENT! WHAT OF THESE CREATURES?
A MISUNDERSTANDING! NOTHING MORE! I HAVE SWORN TO THEM THAT WE MEAN NO HARM...!
NEVER MAKE SUCH ***OATHS*** ON MY BEHALF.

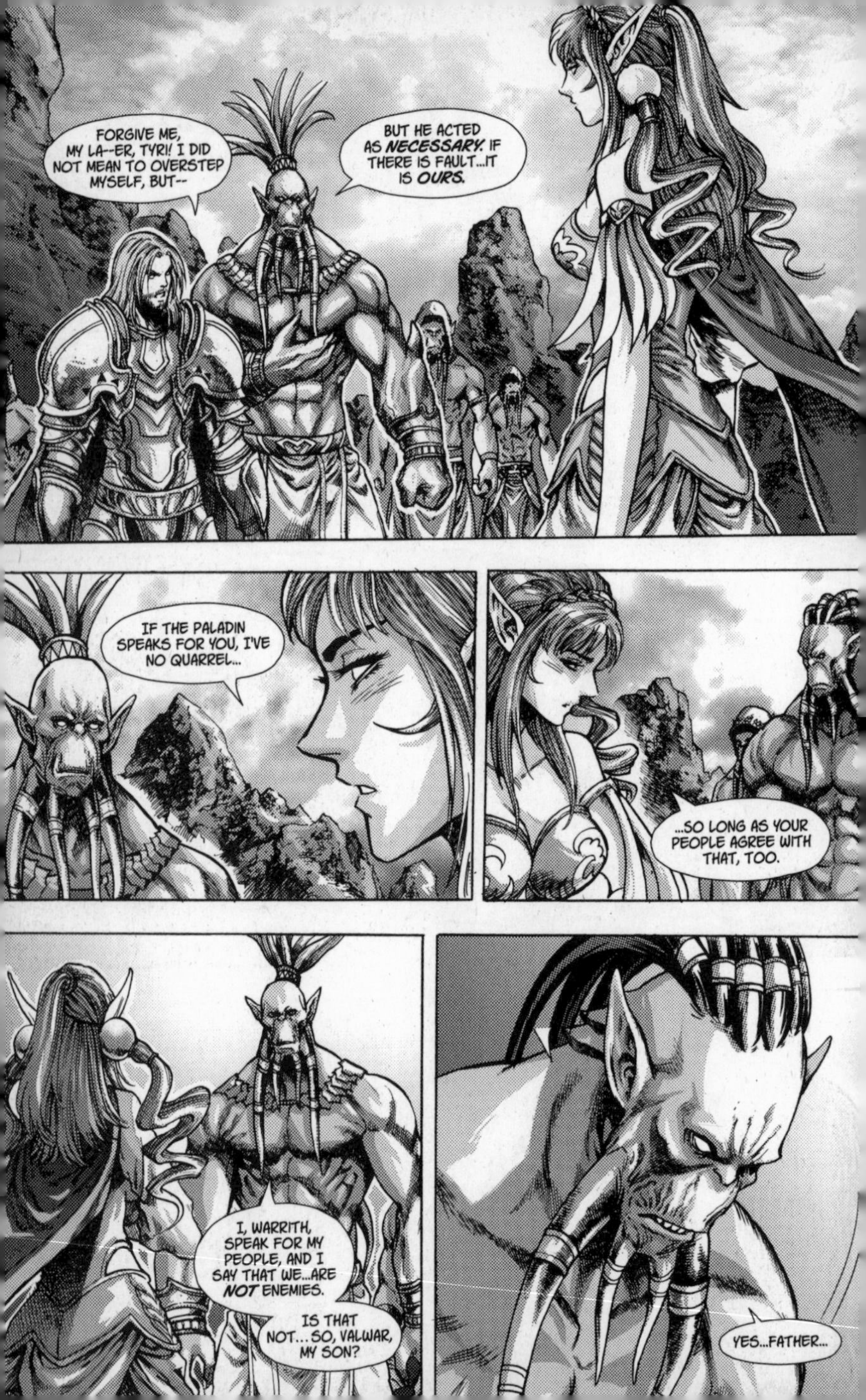
FORGIVE ME, MY LA--ER, TYRI! I DID NOT MEAN TO OVERSTEP MYSELF, BUT--
BUT HE ACTED AS *NECESSARY.* IF THERE IS FAULT...IT IS *OURS.*
IF THE PALADIN SPEAKS FOR YOU, I'VE NO QUARREL...
...SO LONG AS YOUR PEOPLE AGREE WITH THAT, TOO.
I, WARRITH, SPEAK FOR MY PEOPLE, AND I SAY THAT WE...ARE *NOT* ENEMIES.
IS THAT NOT... SO, VALWAR, MY SON?
YES...FATHER...

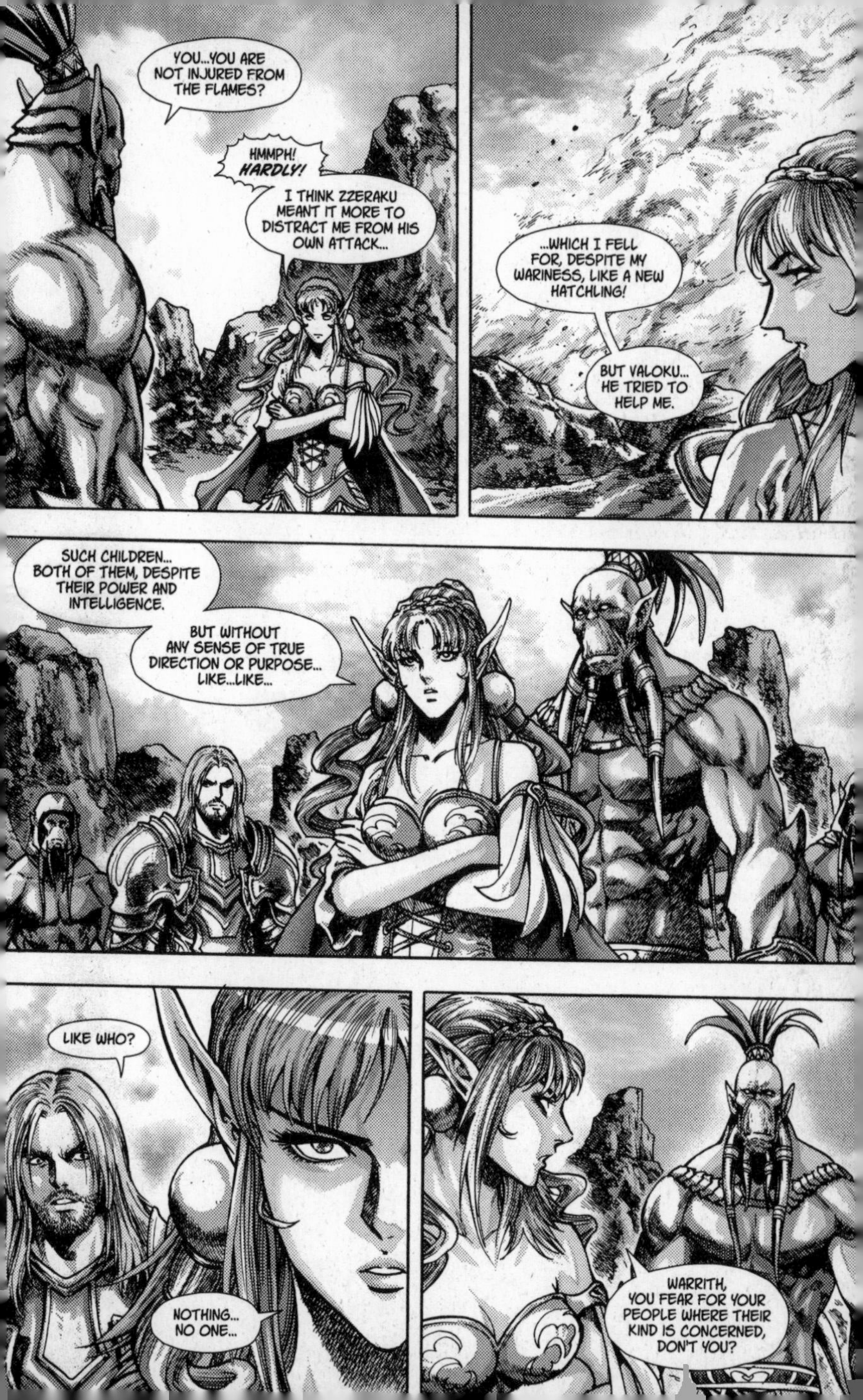
YOU...YOU ARE NOT INJURED FROM THE FLAMES?
HMMPH! **HARDLY!**
I THINK ZZERAKU MEANT IT MORE TO DISTRACT ME FROM HIS OWN ATTACK...
...WHICH I FELL FOR, DESPITE MY WARINESS, LIKE A NEW HATCHLING!
BUT VALOKU... HE TRIED TO HELP ME.
SUCH CHILDREN... BOTH OF THEM, DESPITE THEIR POWER AND INTELLIGENCE.
BUT WITHOUT ANY SENSE OF TRUE DIRECTION OR PURPOSE... LIKE...LIKE...
LIKE WHO?
NOTHING... NO ONE...
WARRITH, YOU FEAR FOR YOUR PEOPLE WHERE THEIR KIND IS CONCERNED, DON'T YOU?

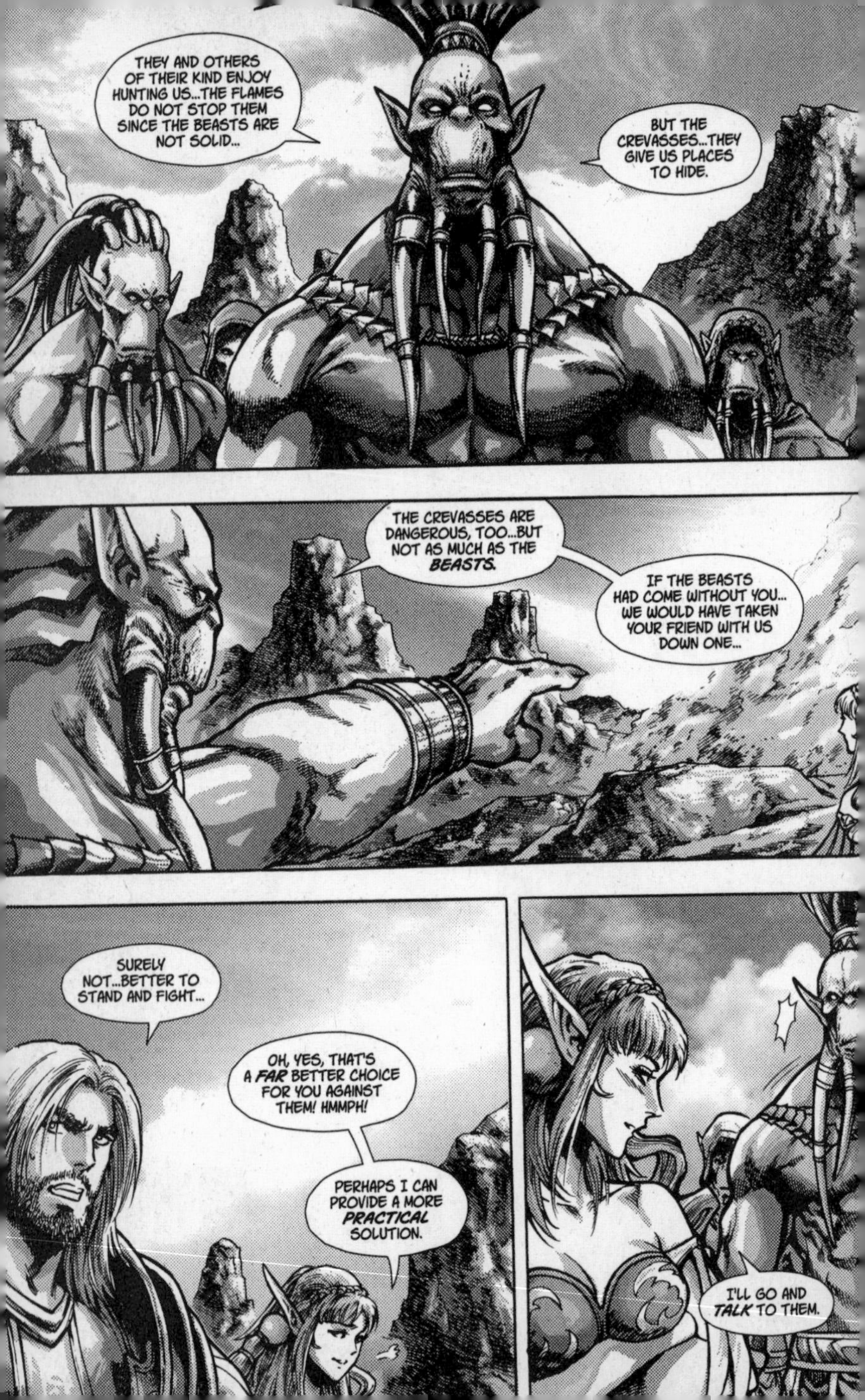
THEY AND OTHERS OF THEIR KIND ENJOY HUNTING US...THE FLAMES DO NOT STOP THEM SINCE THE BEASTS ARE NOT SOLID...
BUT THE CREVASSES...THEY GIVE US PLACES TO HIDE.
THE CREVASSES ARE DANGEROUS, TOO...BUT NOT AS MUCH AS THE BEASTS.
IF THE BEASTS HAD COME WITHOUT YOU... WE WOULD HAVE TAKEN YOUR FRIEND WITH US DOWN ONE...
SURELY NOT...BETTER TO STAND AND FIGHT...
OH, YES, THAT'S A FAR BETTER CHOICE FOR YOU AGAINST THEM! HMMPH!
PERHAPS I CAN PROVIDE A MORE PRACTICAL SOLUTION.
I'LL GO AND TALK TO THEM.

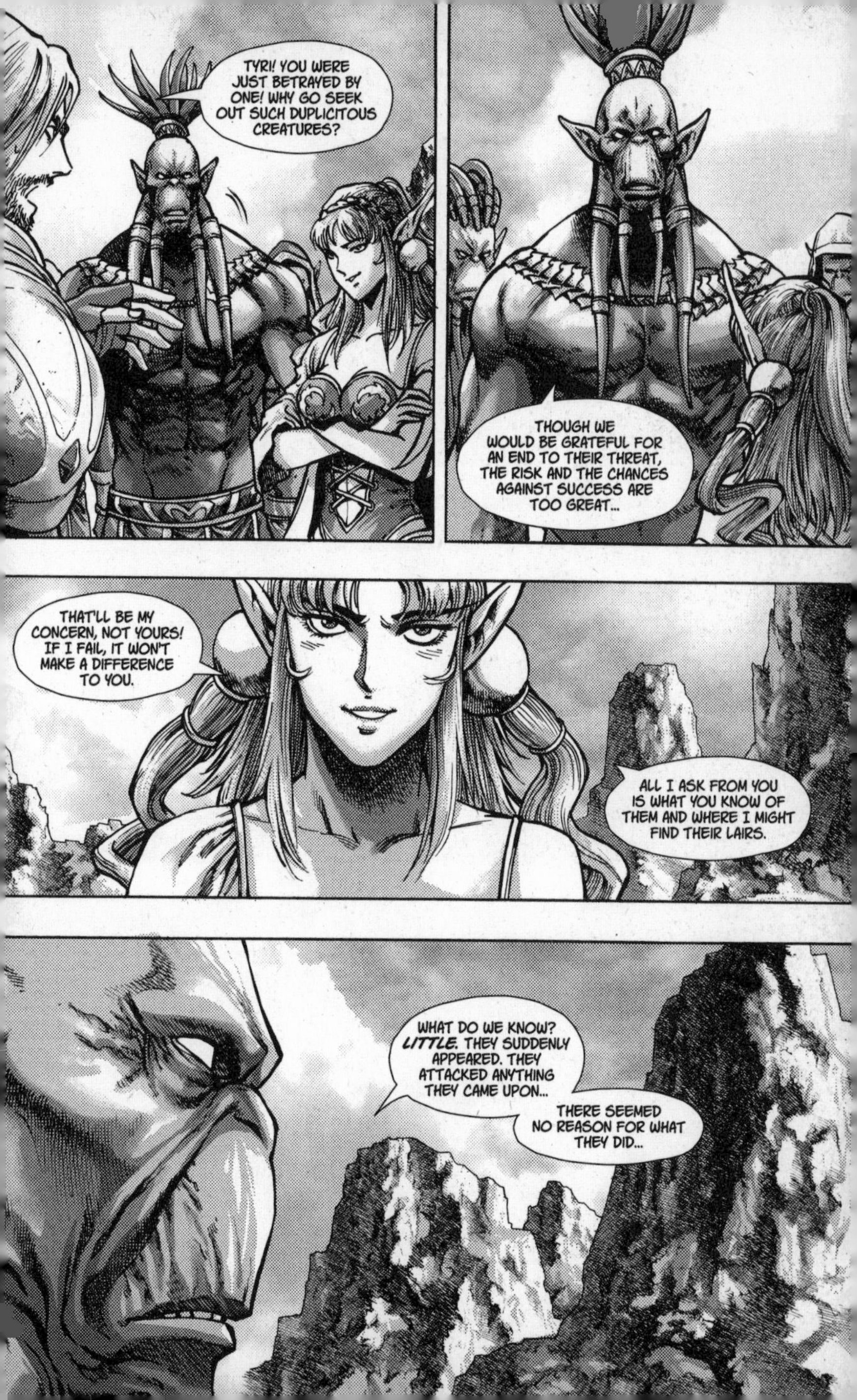
TYRI! YOU WERE JUST BETRAYED BY ONE! WHY GO SEEK OUT SUCH DUPLICITOUS CREATURES?
THOUGH WE WOULD BE GRATEFUL FOR AN END TO THEIR THREAT, THE RISK AND THE CHANCES AGAINST SUCCESS ARE TOO GREAT...
THAT'LL BE MY CONCERN, NOT YOURS! IF I FAIL, IT WON'T MAKE A DIFFERENCE TO YOU.
ALL I ASK FROM YOU IS WHAT YOU KNOW OF THEM AND WHERE I MIGHT FIND THEIR LAIRS.
WHAT DO WE KNOW? *LITTLE*. THEY SUDDENLY APPEARED. THEY ATTACKED ANYTHING THEY CAME UPON...
THERE SEEMED NO REASON FOR WHAT THEY DID...

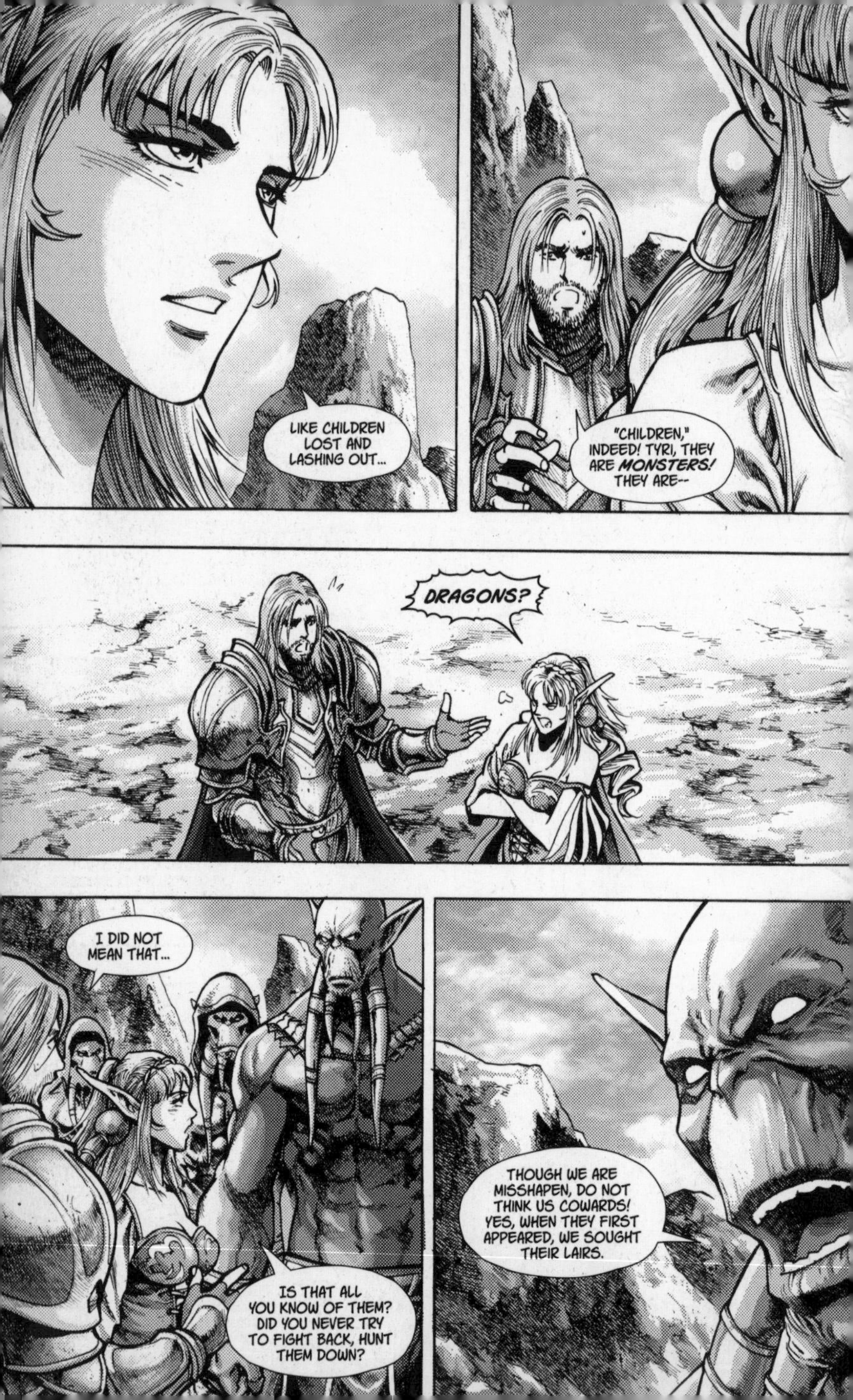
LIKE CHILDREN LOST AND LASHING OUT...
"CHILDREN," INDEED! TYRI, THEY ARE *MONSTERS!* THEY ARE--
DRAGONS?
I DID NOT MEAN THAT...
IS THAT ALL YOU KNOW OF THEM? DID YOU NEVER TRY TO FIGHT BACK, HUNT THEM DOWN?
THOUGH WE ARE MISSHAPEN, DO NOT THINK US COWARDS! YES, WHEN THEY FIRST APPEARED, WE SOUGHT THEIR LAIRS.

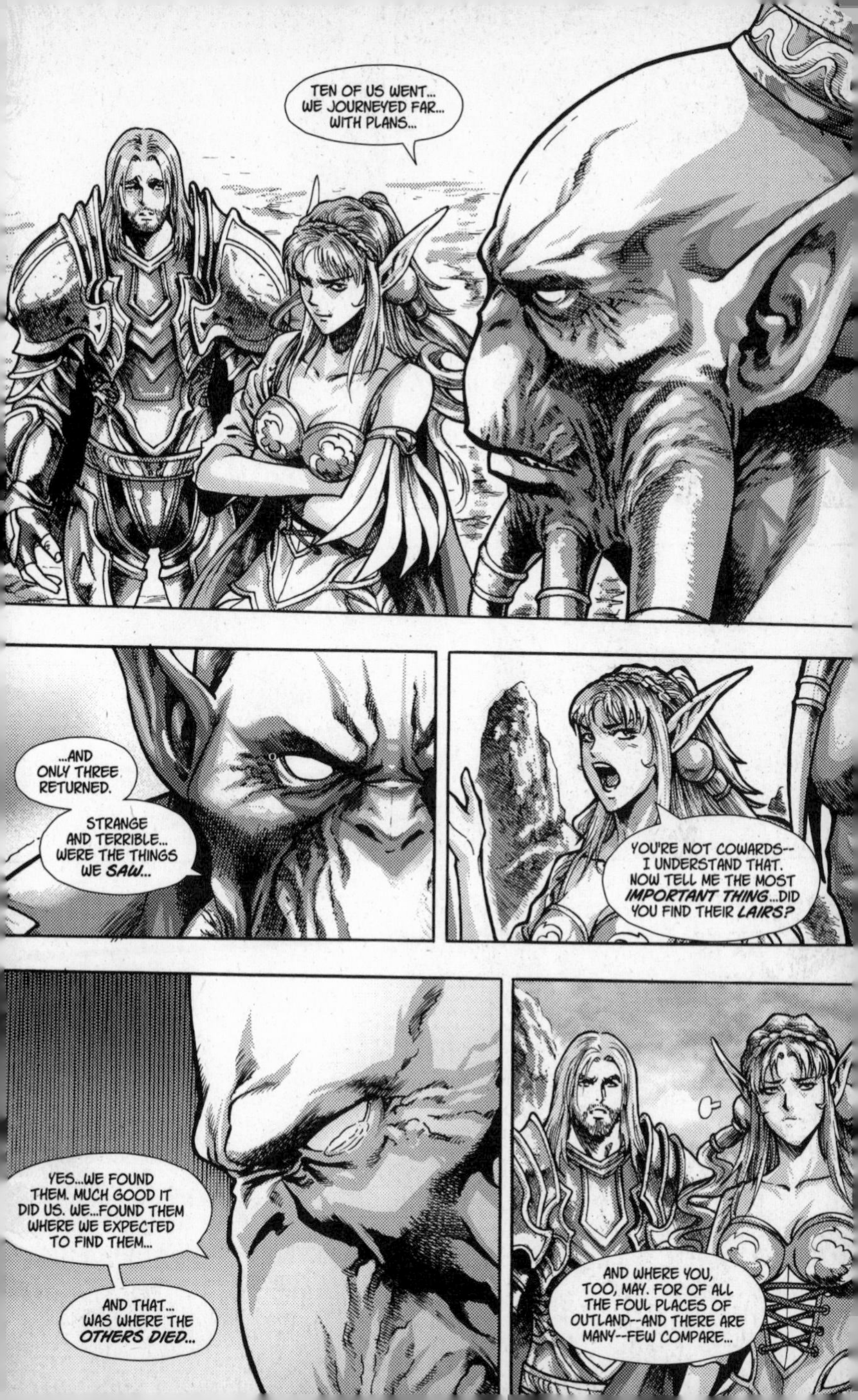
TEN OF US WENT... WE JOURNEYED FAR... WITH PLANS...
...AND ONLY THREE RETURNED.
STRANGE AND TERRIBLE... WERE THE THINGS WE *SAW...*
YOU'RE NOT COWARDS-- I UNDERSTAND THAT. NOW TELL ME THE MOST *IMPORTANT THING*...DID YOU FIND THEIR *LAIRS?*
YES...WE FOUND THEM. MUCH GOOD IT DID US. WE...FOUND THEM WHERE WE EXPECTED TO FIND THEM...
AND THAT... WAS WHERE THE *OTHERS DIED...*
AND WHERE YOU, TOO, MAY. FOR OF ALL THE FOUL PLACES OF OUTLAND--AND THERE ARE MANY--FEW COMPARE...

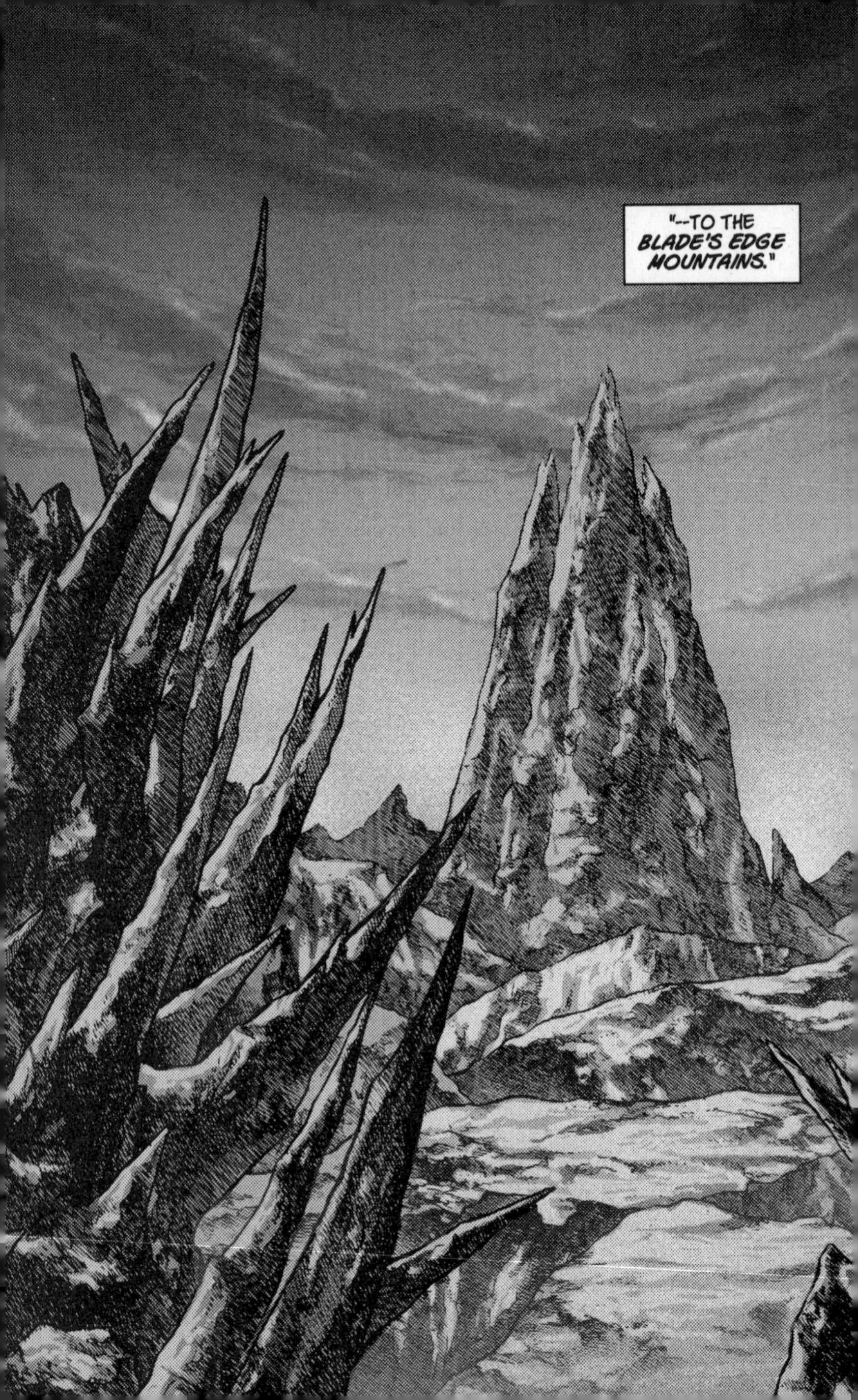
"--TO THE BLADE'S EDGE MOUNTAINS."

CHAPTER FOUR
BLADE'S EDGE

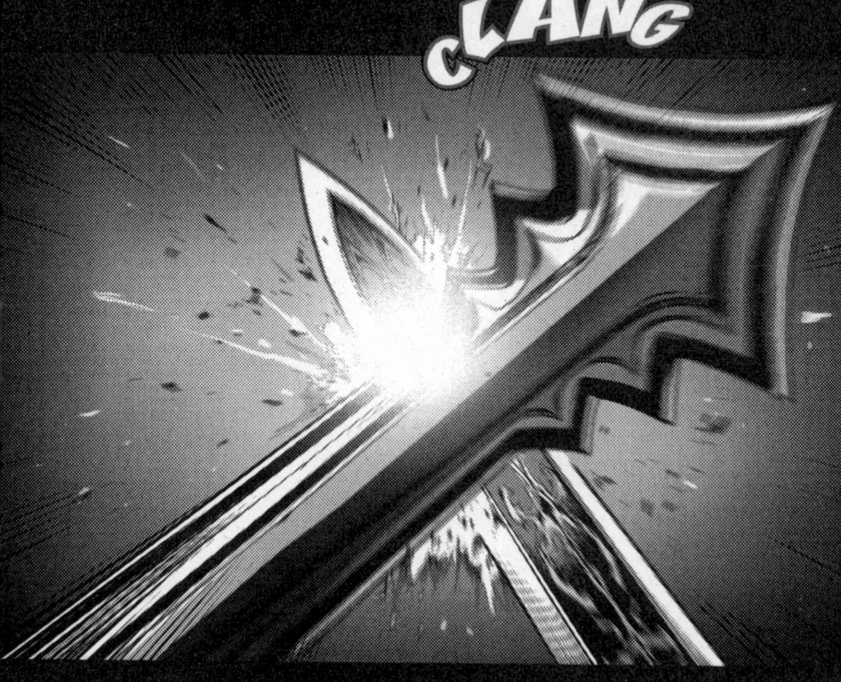
CLANG

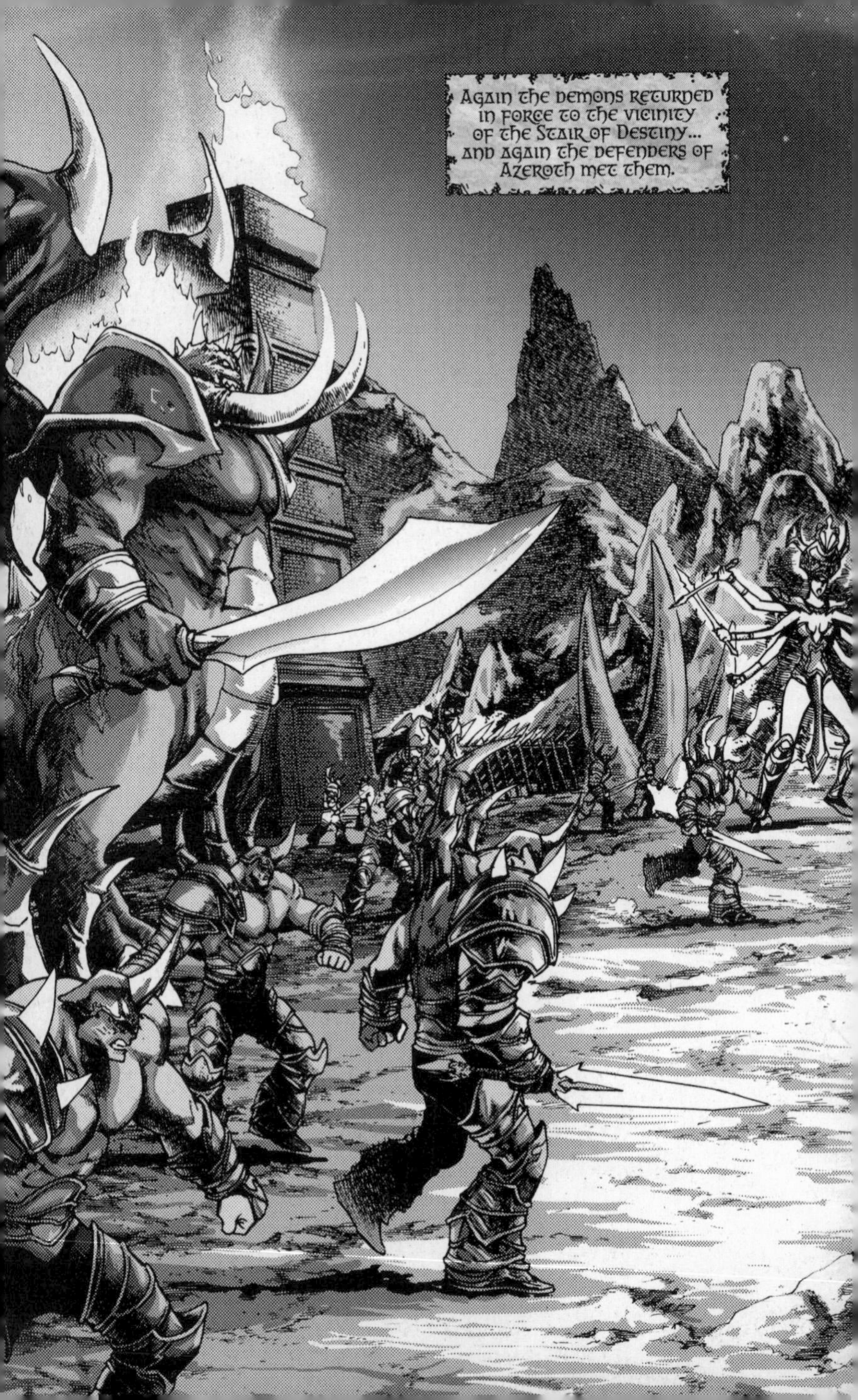
Again the demons returned in force to the vicinity of the Stair of Destiny... and again the defenders of Azeroth met them.

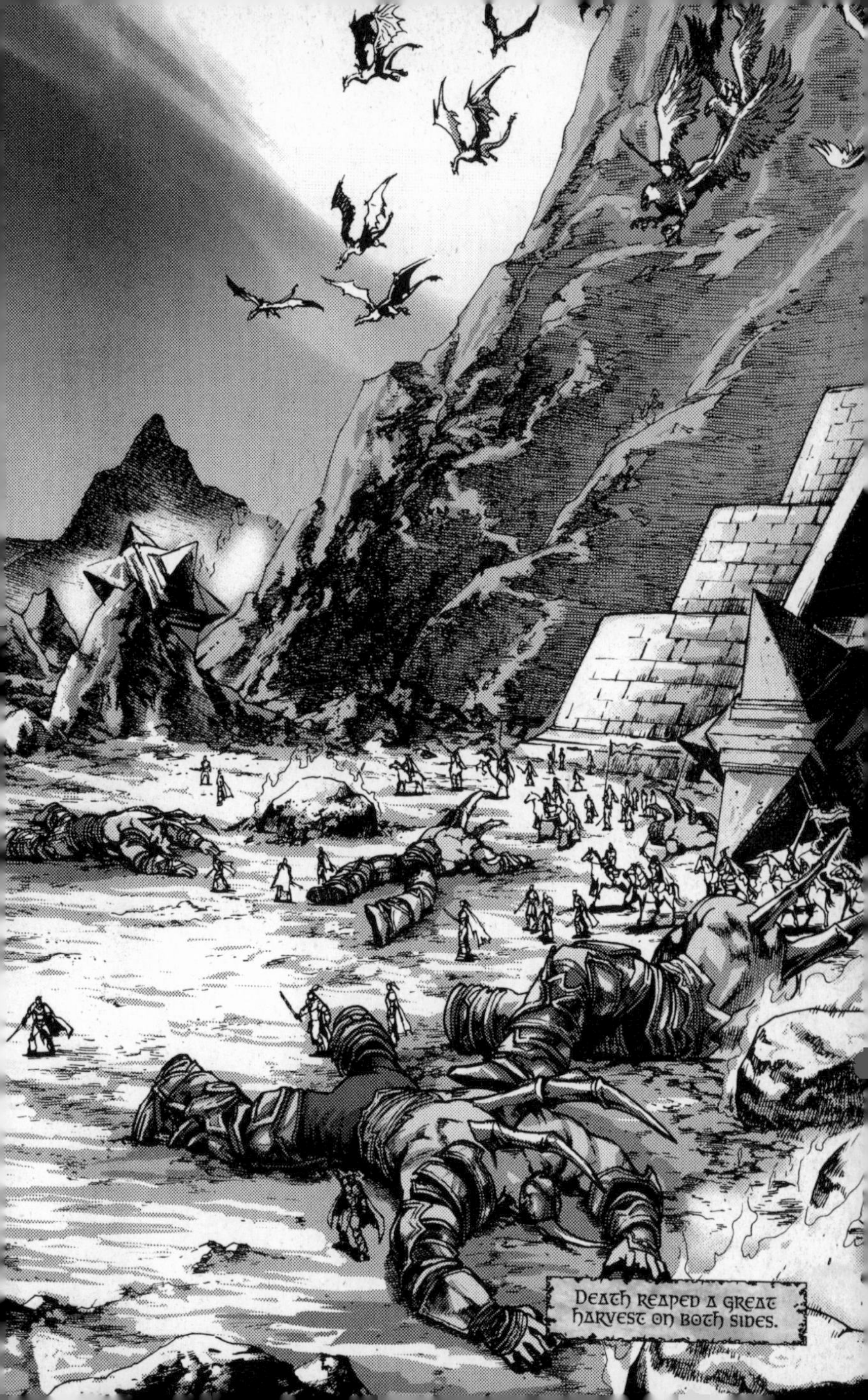
Death reaped a great harvest on both sides.

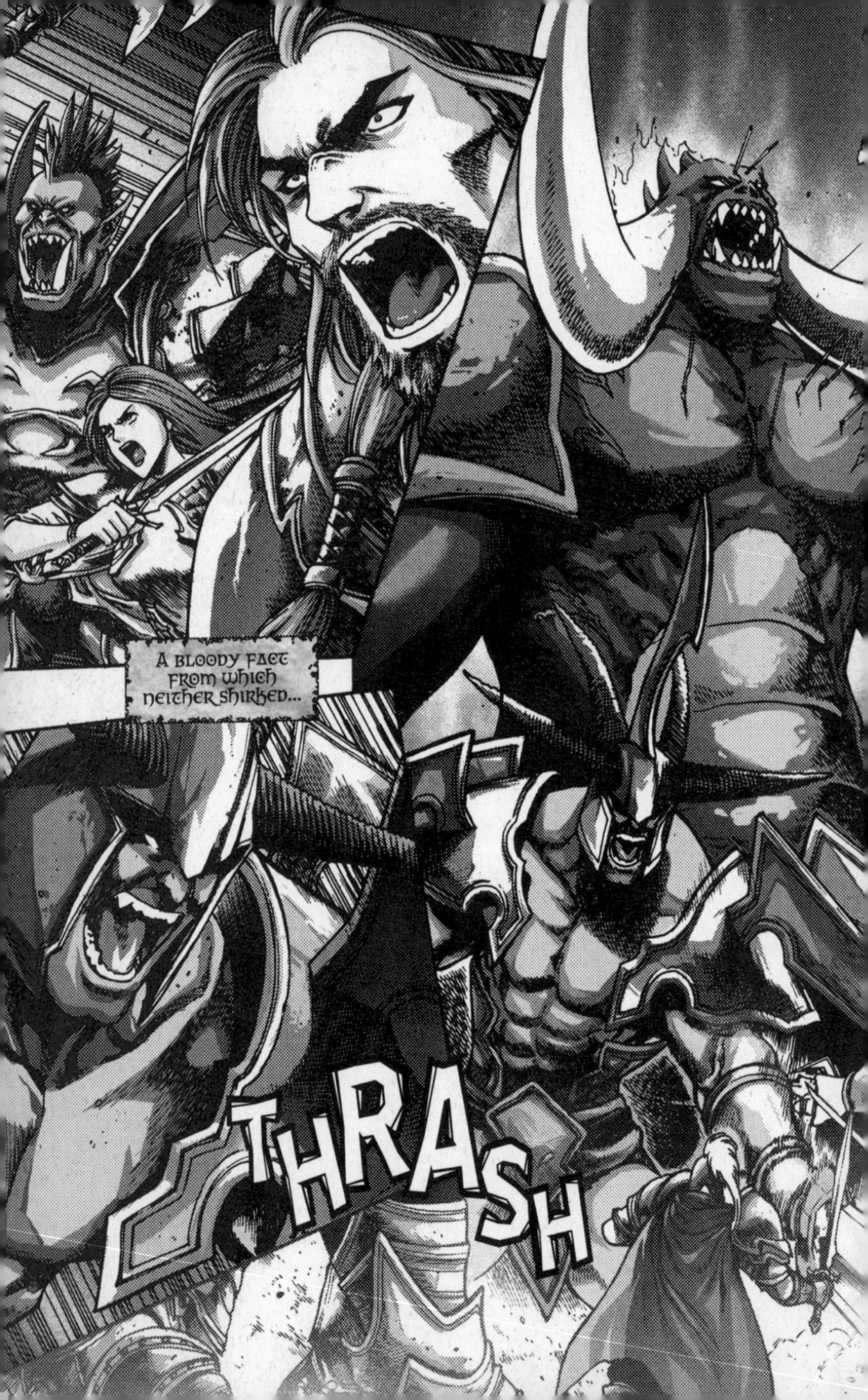
A BLOODY FACT FROM WHICH NEITHER SHIRKED...
THRASH

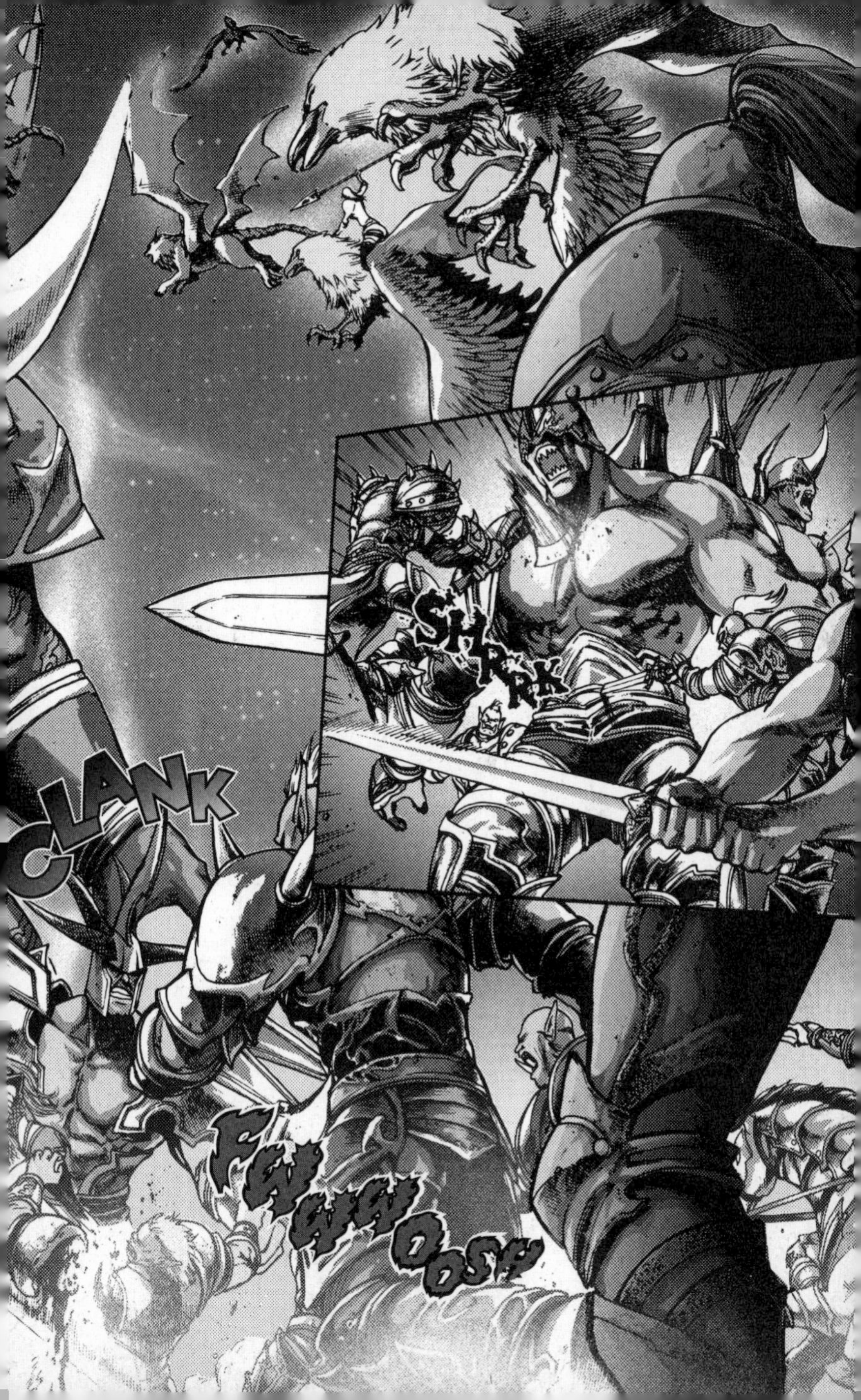
SHRRK
CLANK
FWWOOSH

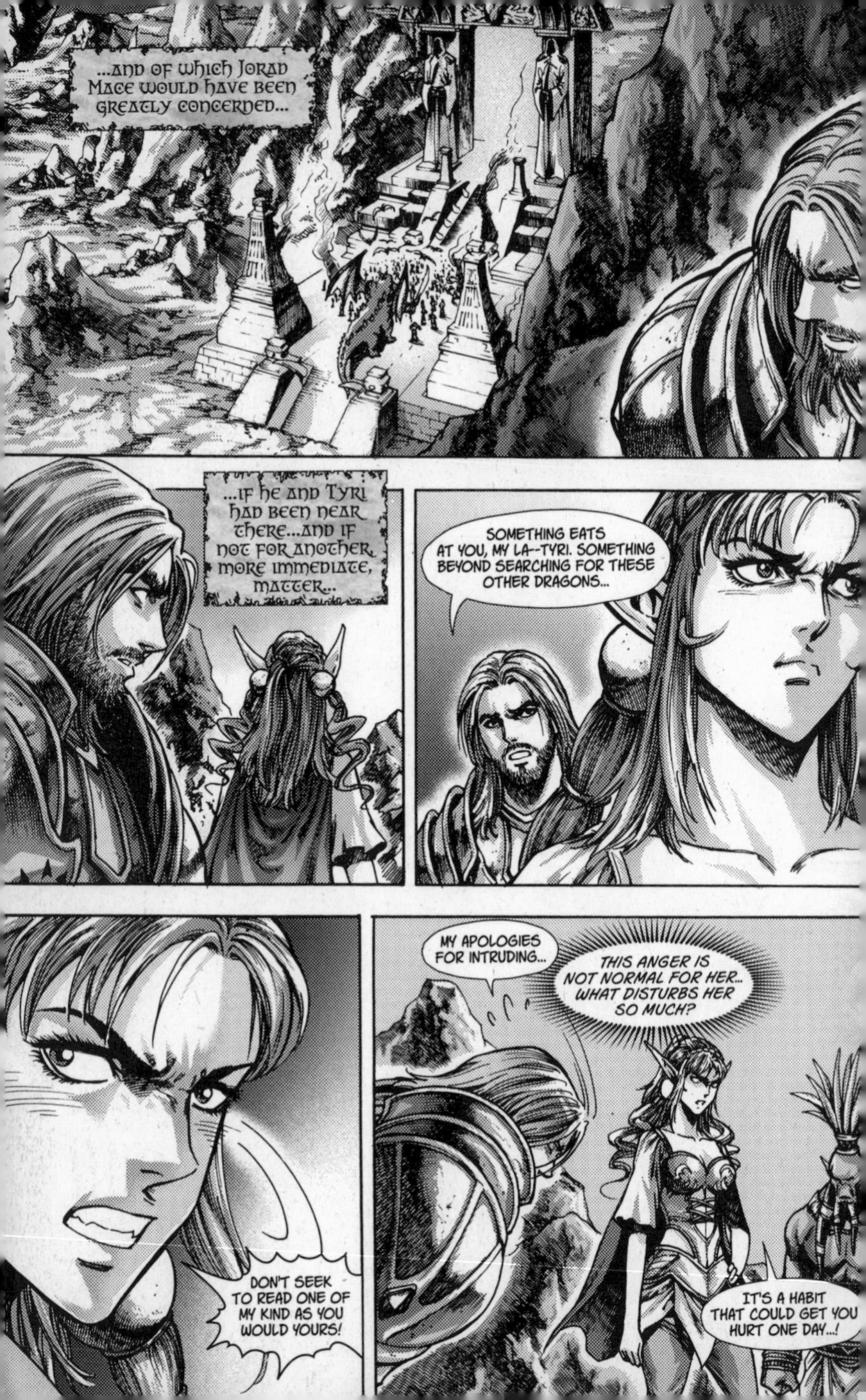
...AND OF WHICH JORAD MACE WOULD HAVE BEEN GREATLY CONCERNED...
...IF HE AND TYRI HAD BEEN NEAR THERE...AND IF NOT FOR ANOTHER, MORE IMMEDIATE, MATTER...
SOMETHING EATS AT YOU, MY LA--TYRI. SOMETHING BEYOND SEARCHING FOR THESE OTHER DRAGONS...
DON'T SEEK TO READ ONE OF MY KIND AS YOU WOULD YOURS!
MY APOLOGIES FOR INTRUDING...
THIS ANGER IS NOT NORMAL FOR HER... WHAT DISTURBS HER SO MUCH?
IT'S A HABIT THAT COULD GET YOU HURT ONE DAY...!

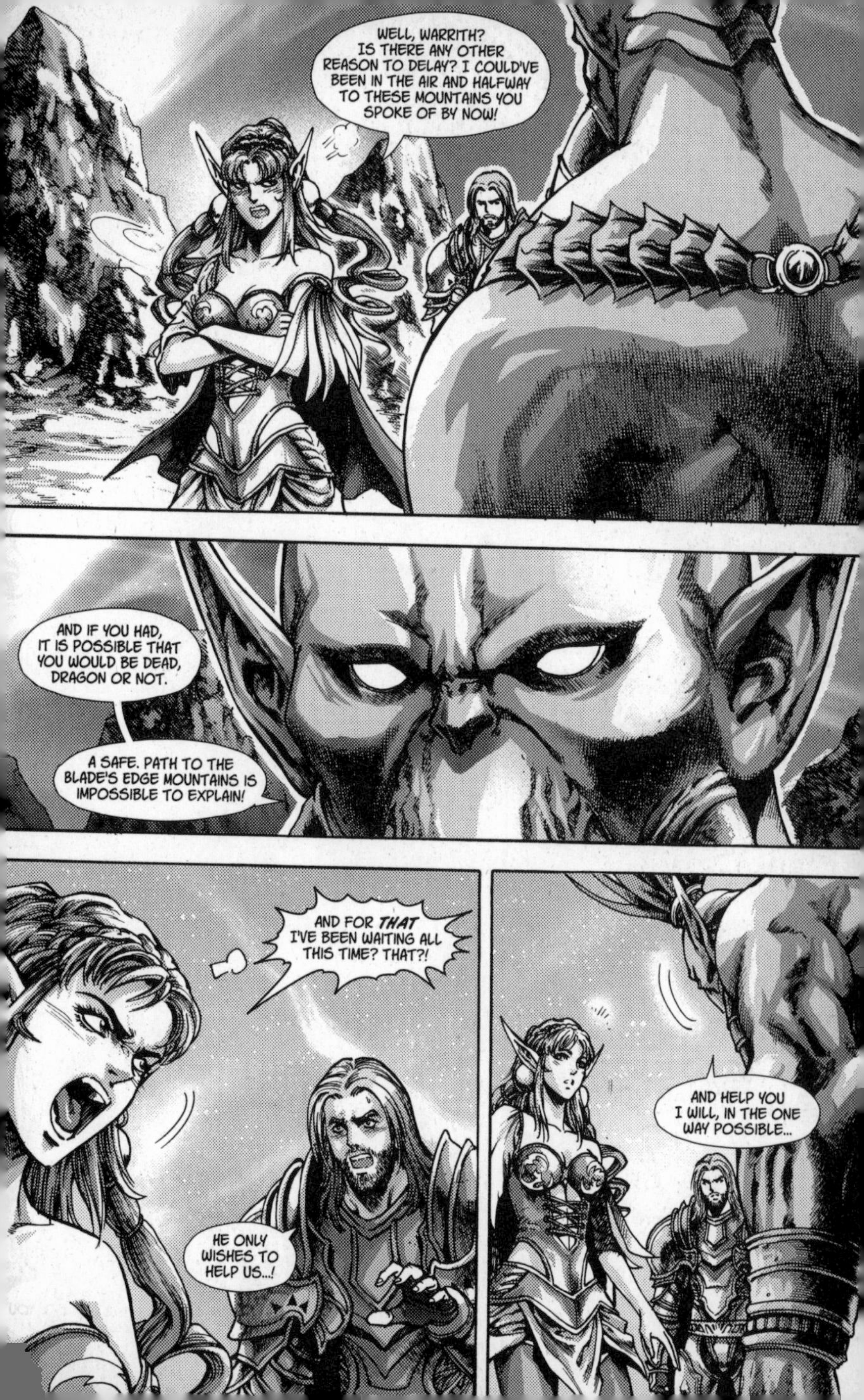
WELL, WARRITH? IS THERE ANY OTHER REASON TO DELAY? I COULD'VE BEEN IN THE AIR AND HALFWAY TO THESE MOUNTAINS YOU SPOKE OF BY NOW!
AND IF YOU HAD, IT IS POSSIBLE THAT YOU WOULD BE DEAD, DRAGON OR NOT.
A SAFE. PATH TO THE BLADE'S EDGE MOUNTAINS IS IMPOSSIBLE TO EXPLAIN!
AND FOR *THAT* I'VE BEEN WAITING ALL THIS TIME? THAT?!
HE ONLY WISHES TO HELP US...!
AND HELP YOU I WILL, IN THE ONE WAY POSSIBLE...

I WILL BE YOUR *GUIDE.*

THERE'S NO NEED FOR YOU TO ACCOMPANY US...

I STILL *PROTEST* THIS DECISION, FATHER!

THERE IS EVERY NEED! THERE IS NO ARGUMENT. IF YOU WISH TO SAFELY REACH THE NETHER DRAKES...THEN I AM YOUR BEST HOPE.

I MUST MAKE AMENDS FOR MY SUSPICIONS ABOUT THE TWO OF YOU...

...AND FOR MY FAILURE TO MY COMRADES THE LAST TIME.

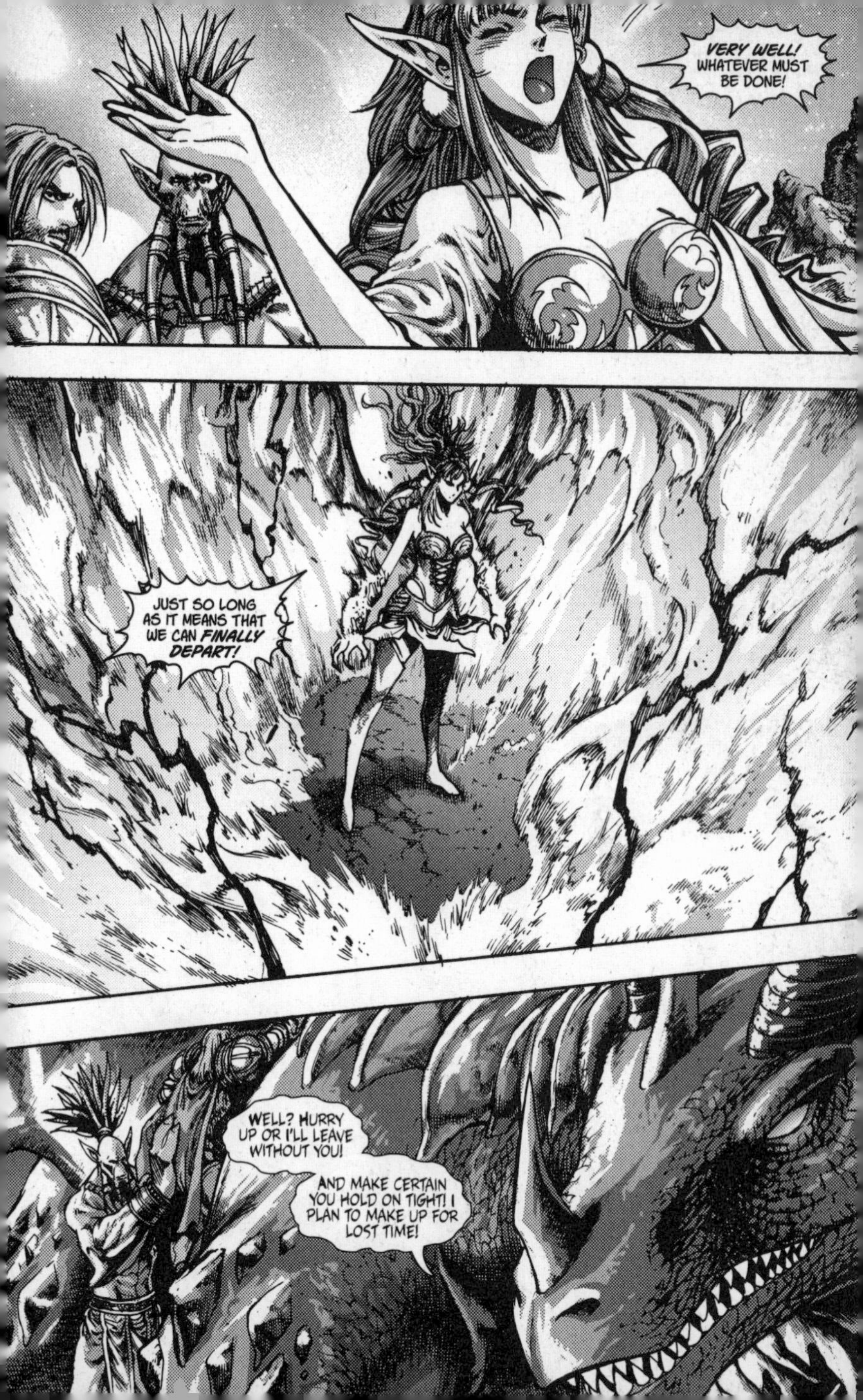
VERY WELL! WHATEVER MUST BE DONE!
JUST SO LONG AS IT MEANS THAT WE CAN ***FINALLY DEPART!***
WELL? HURRY UP OR I'LL LEAVE WITHOUT YOU!
AND MAKE CERTAIN YOU HOLD ON TIGHT! I PLAN TO MAKE UP FOR LOST TIME!

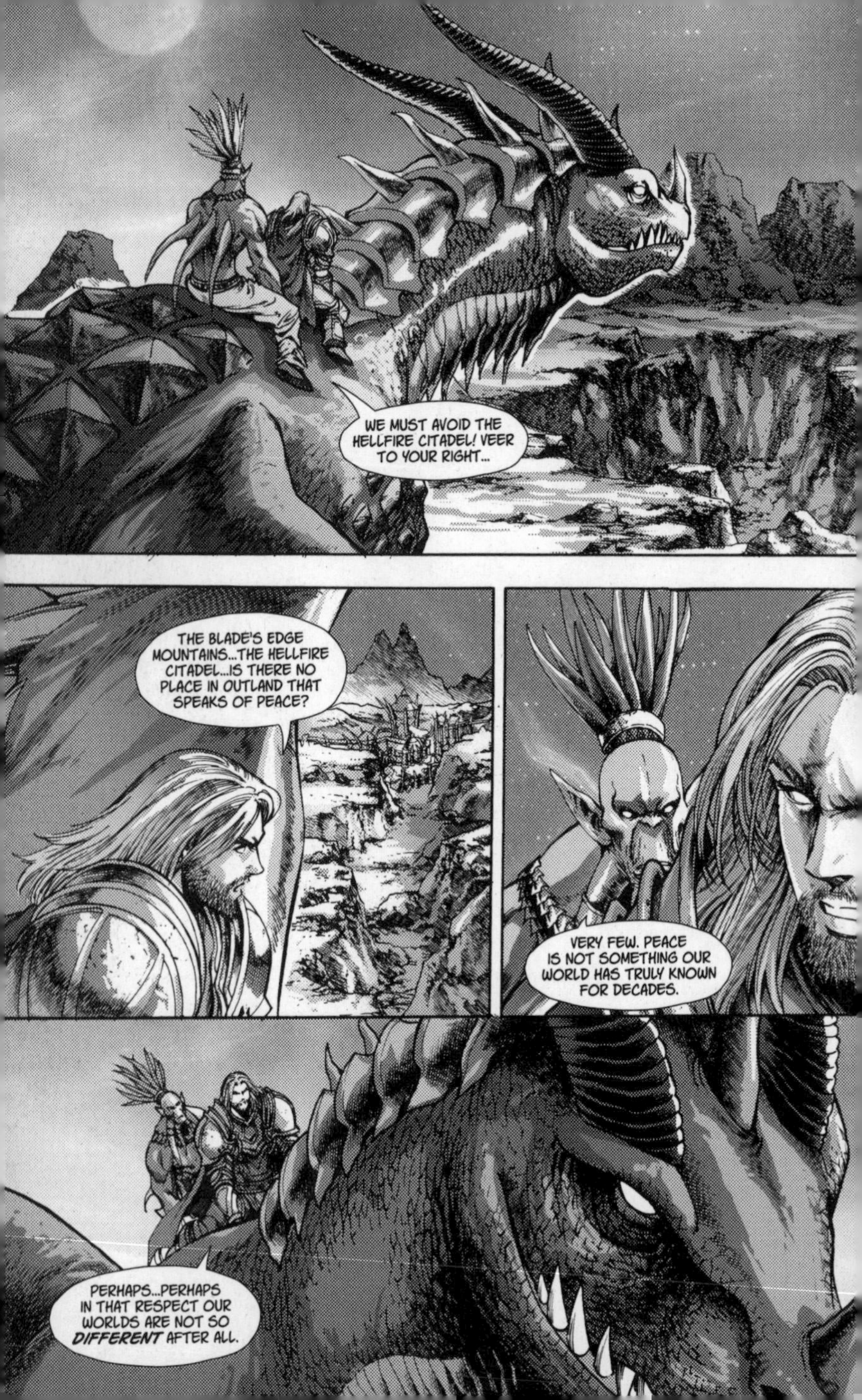
WE MUST AVOID THE HELLFIRE CITADEL! VEER TO YOUR RIGHT...
THE BLADE'S EDGE MOUNTAINS...THE HELLFIRE CITADEL...IS THERE NO PLACE IN OUTLAND THAT SPEAKS OF PEACE?
VERY FEW. PEACE IS NOT SOMETHING OUR WORLD HAS TRULY KNOWN FOR DECADES.
PERHAPS...PERHAPS IN THAT RESPECT OUR WORLDS ARE NOT SO *DIFFERENT* AFTER ALL.

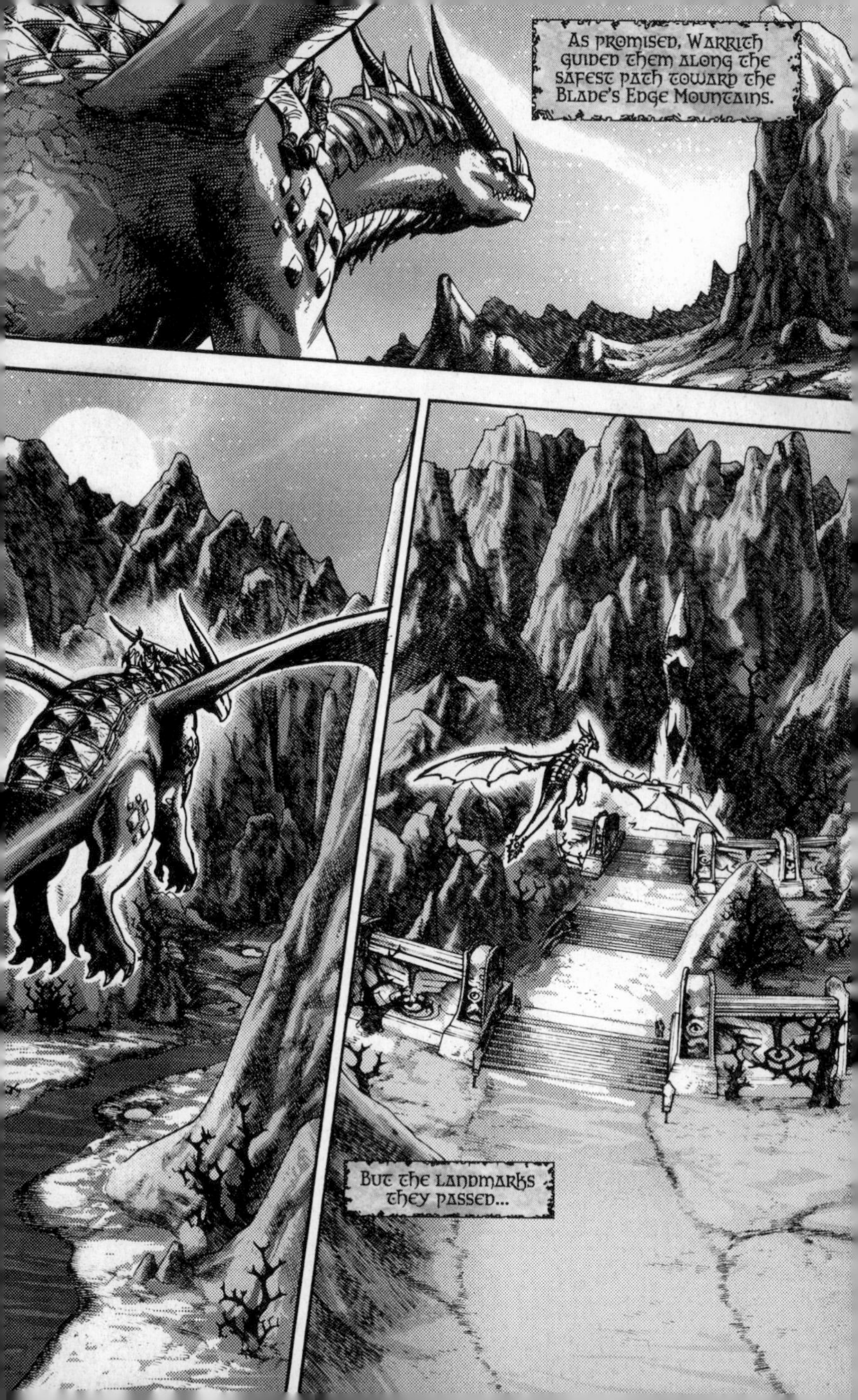
As promised, Warrith guided them along the safest path toward the Blade's Edge Mountains.
But the landmarks they passed...

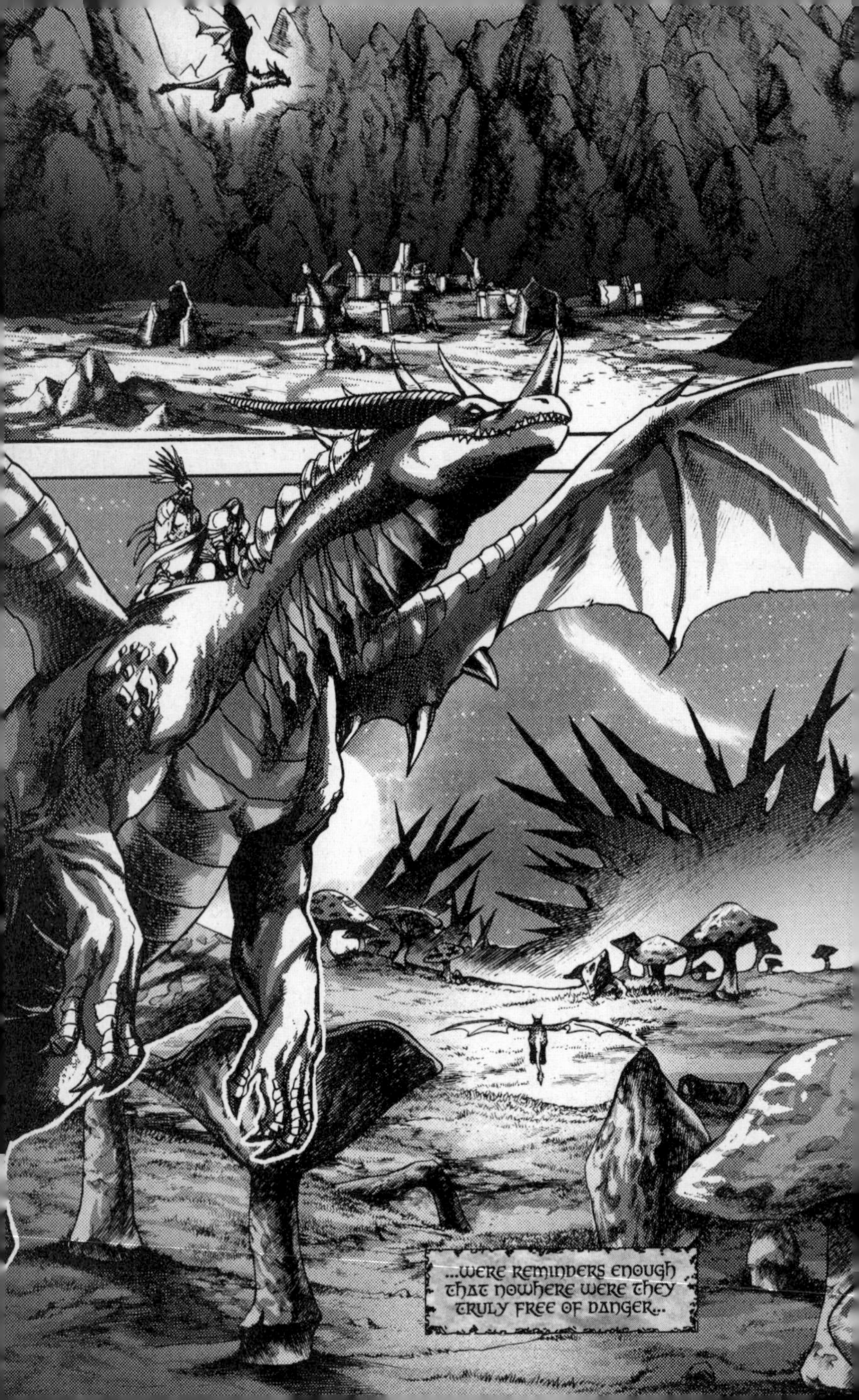
...WERE REMINDERS ENOUGH THAT NOWHERE WERE THEY TRULY FREE OF DANGER...

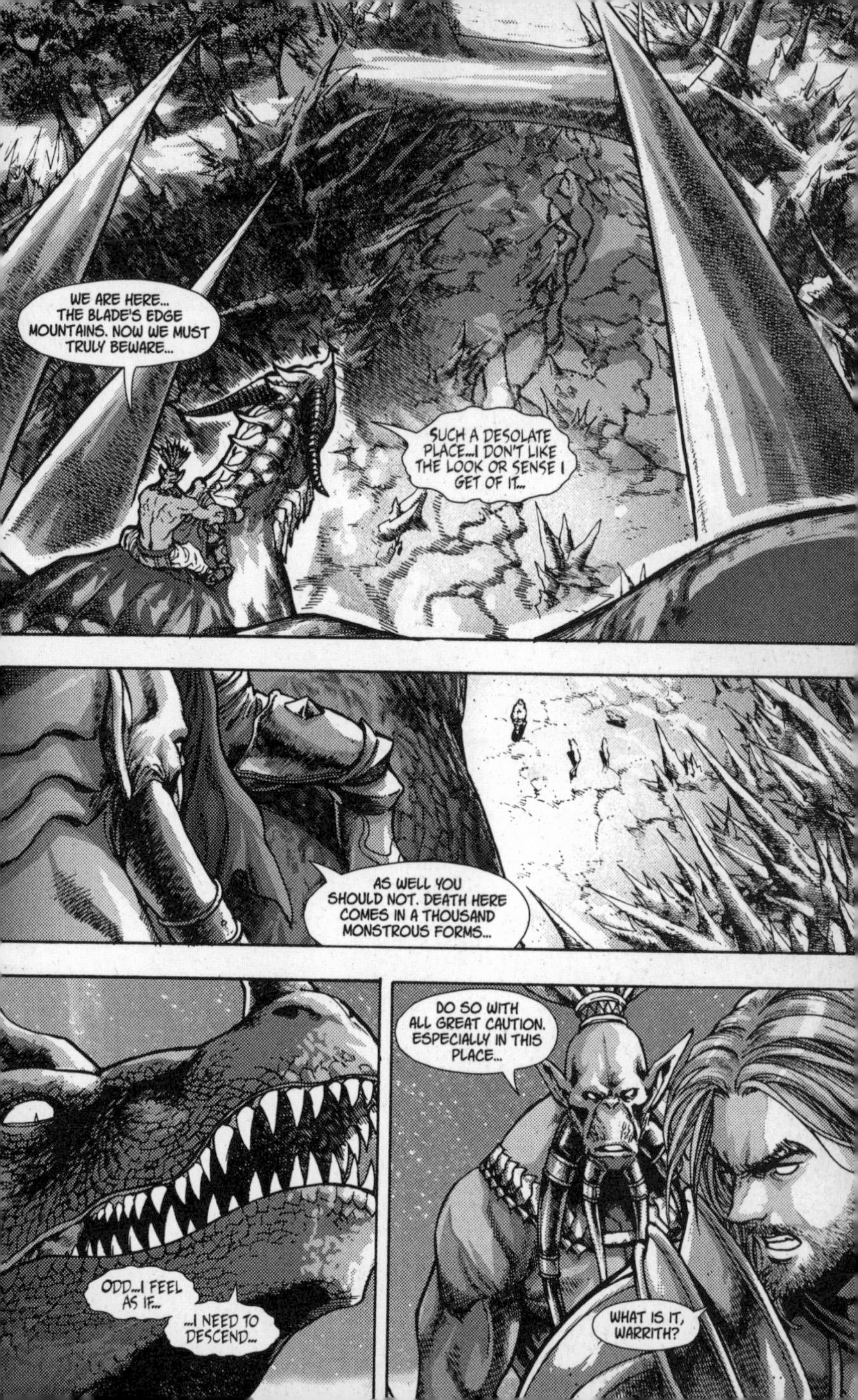
WE ARE HERE... THE BLADE'S EDGE MOUNTAINS. NOW WE MUST TRULY BEWARE...
SUCH A DESOLATE PLACE...I DON'T LIKE THE LOOK OR SENSE I GET OF IT...
AS WELL YOU SHOULD NOT. DEATH HERE COMES IN A THOUSAND MONSTROUS FORMS...
ODD...I FEEL AS IF...
...I NEED TO DESCEND...
DO SO WITH ALL GREAT CAUTION. ESPECIALLY IN THIS PLACE...
WHAT IS IT, WARRITH?

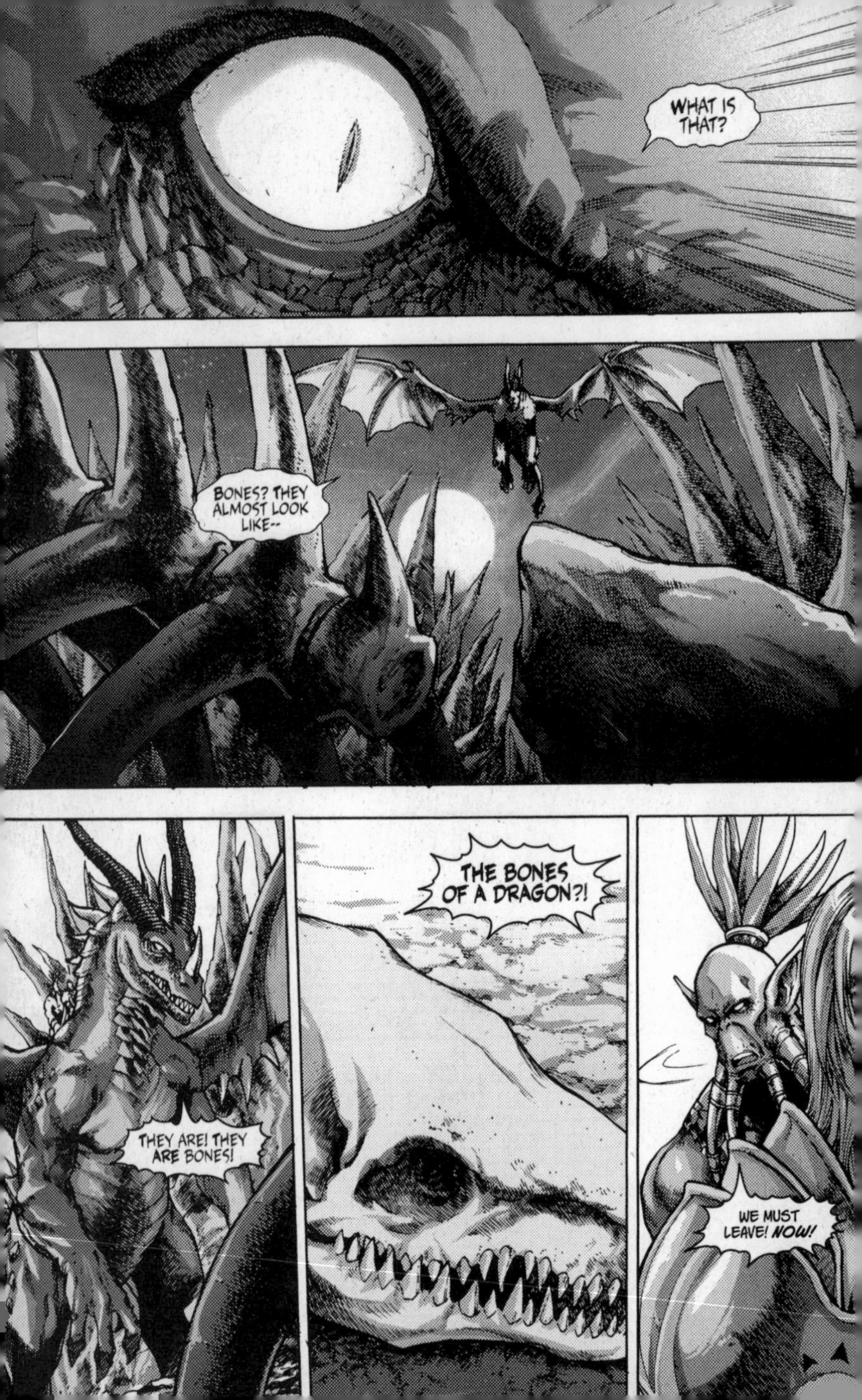
WHAT IS THAT?
BONES? THEY ALMOST LOOK LIKE--
THEY ARE! THEY ARE BONES!
THE BONES OF A DRAGON?!
WE MUST LEAVE! NOW!

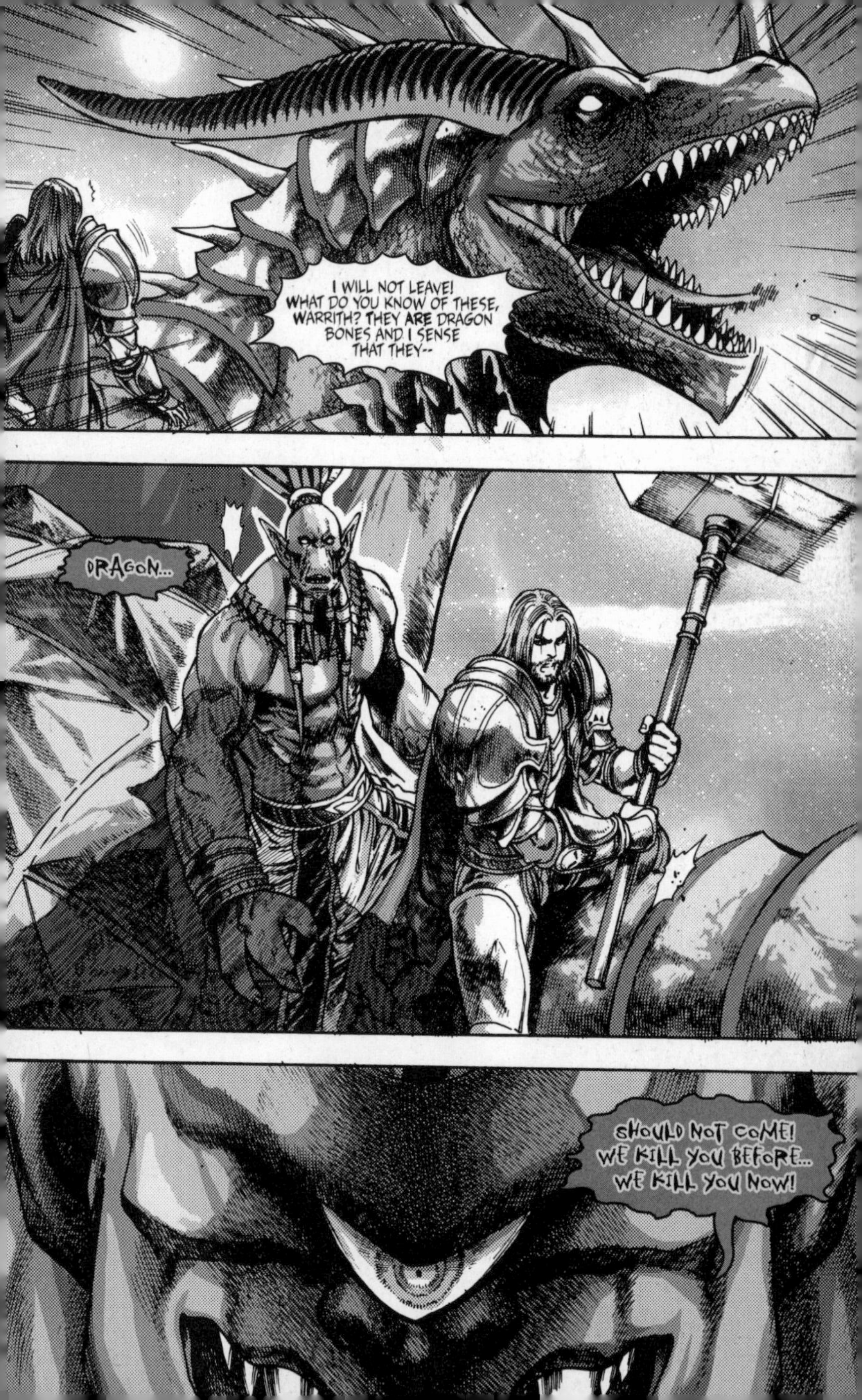
I WILL NOT LEAVE! WHAT DO YOU KNOW OF THESE, WARRITH? THEY ARE DRAGON BONES AND I SENSE THAT THEY--
DRAGON...
SHOULD NOT COME! WE KILL YOU BEFORE... WE KILL YOU NOW!

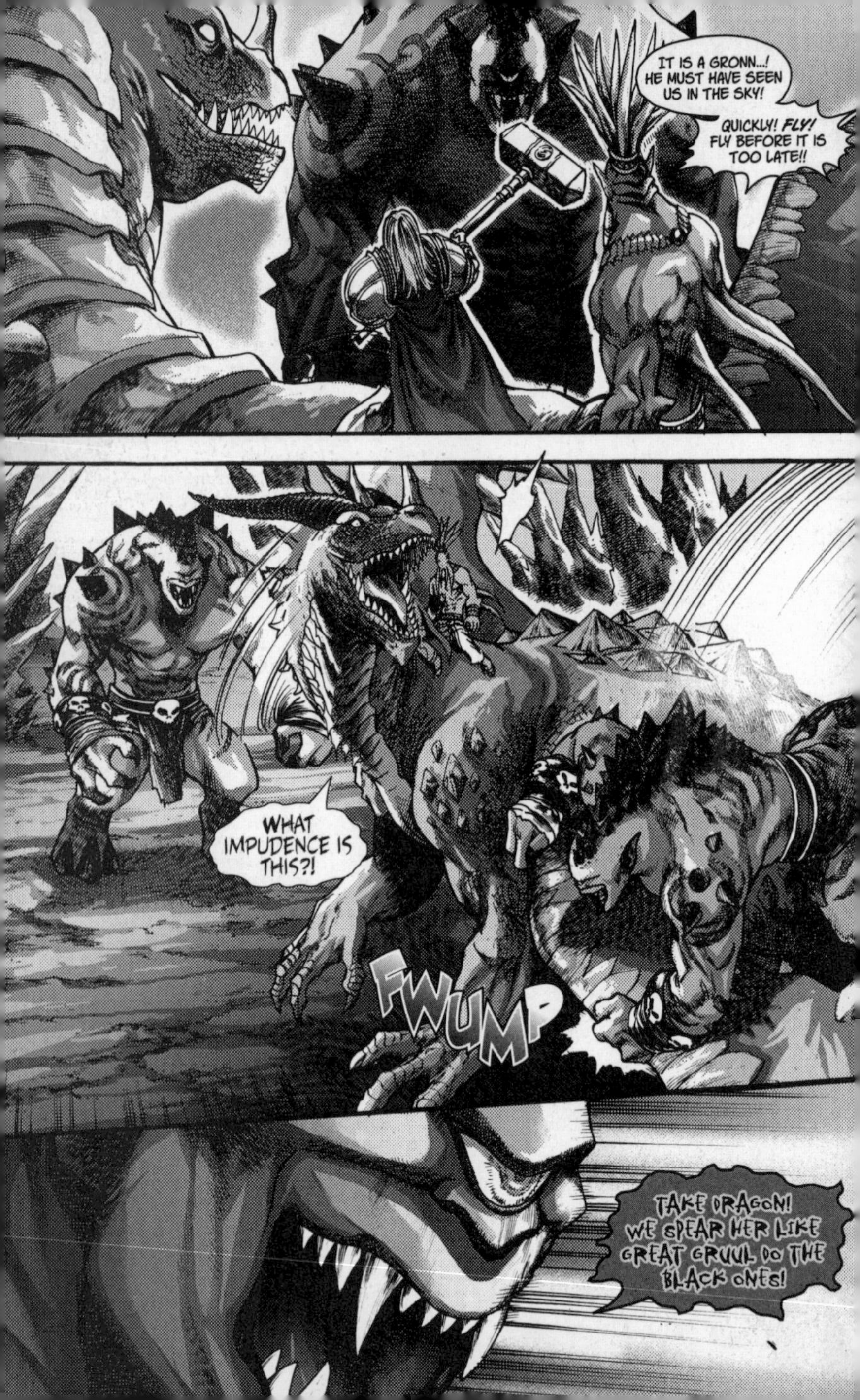
IT IS A GRONN...! HE MUST HAVE SEEN US IN THE SKY!
QUICKLY! *FLY!* FLY BEFORE IT IS TOO LATE!!
WHAT IMPUDENCE IS THIS?!
FWUMP
TAKE DRAGON! WE SPEAR HER LIKE GREAT GRUUL DO THE BLACK ONES!

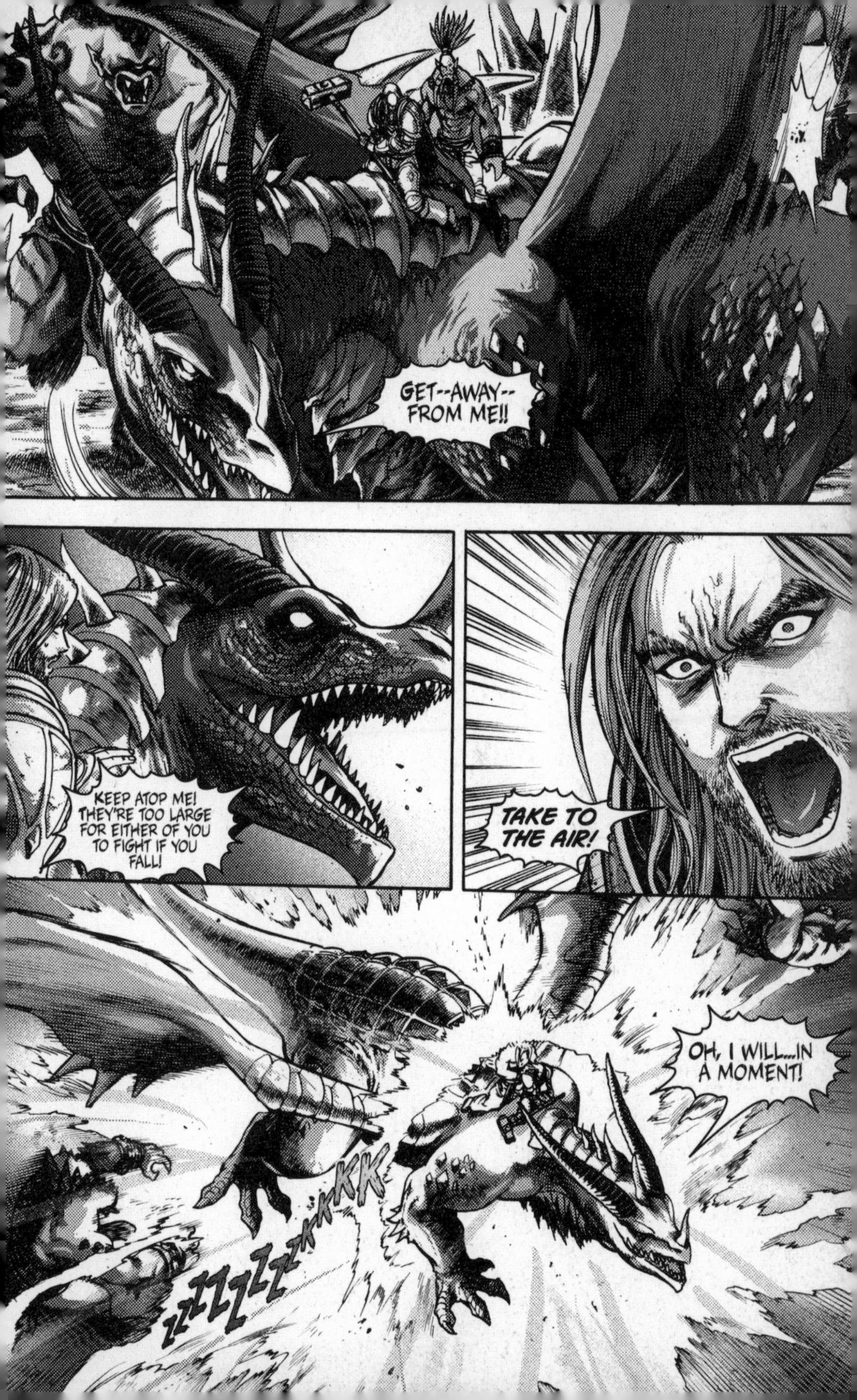
GET--AWAY--
FROM ME!!
KEEP ATOP ME! THEY'RE TOO LARGE FOR EITHER OF YOU TO FIGHT IF YOU FALL!
TAKE TO THE AIR!
OH, I WILL...IN A MOMENT!
ZZZZZZZZZKKKKK

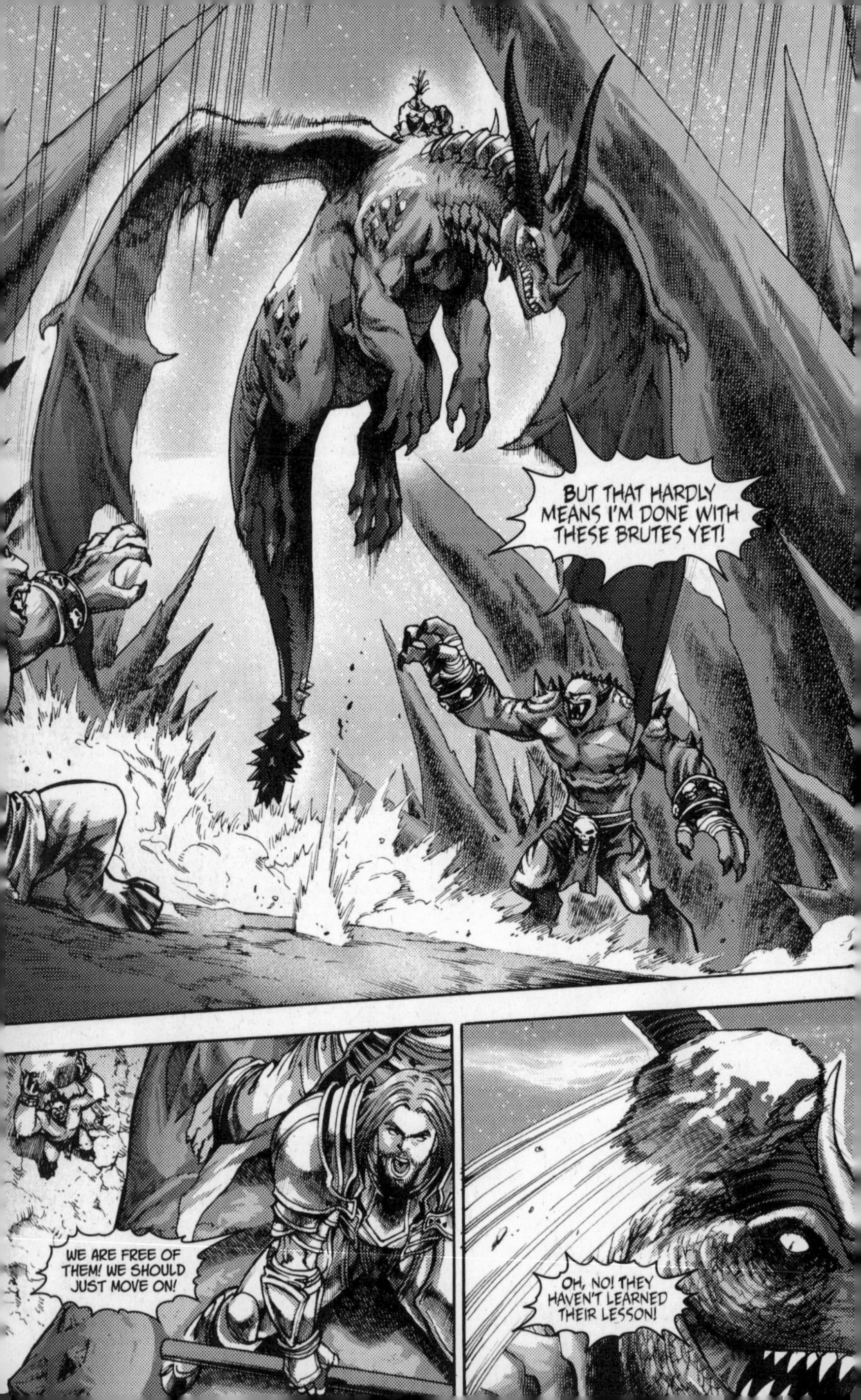
BUT THAT HARDLY MEANS I'M DONE WITH THESE BRUTES YET!
WE ARE FREE OF THEM! WE SHOULD JUST MOVE ON!
OH, NO! THEY HAVEN'T LEARNED THEIR LESSON!

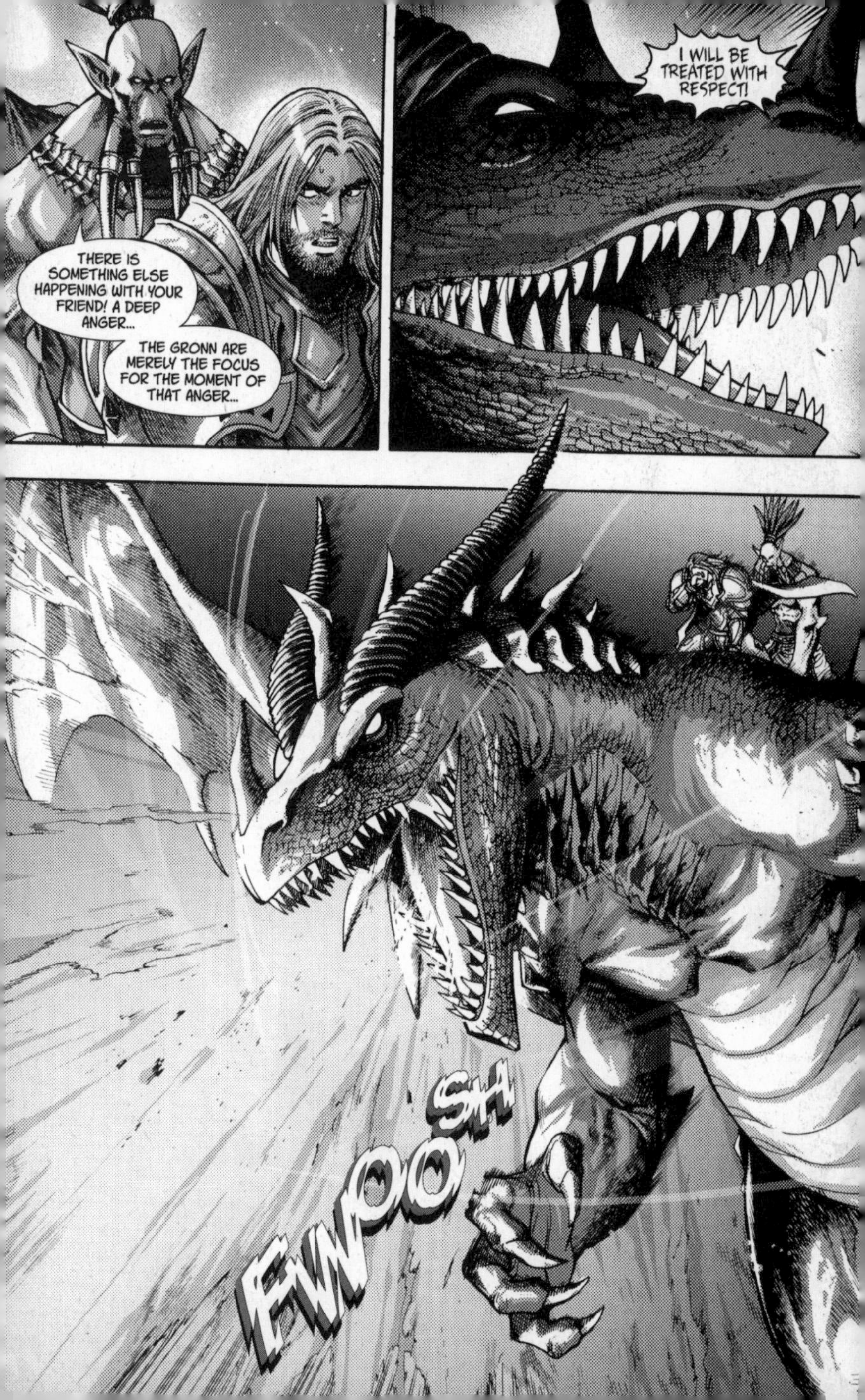
THERE IS SOMETHING ELSE HAPPENING WITH YOUR FRIEND! A DEEP ANGER...
THE GRONN ARE MERELY THE FOCUS FOR THE MOMENT OF THAT ANGER...
I WILL BE TREATED WITH RESPECT!
FWOOSH

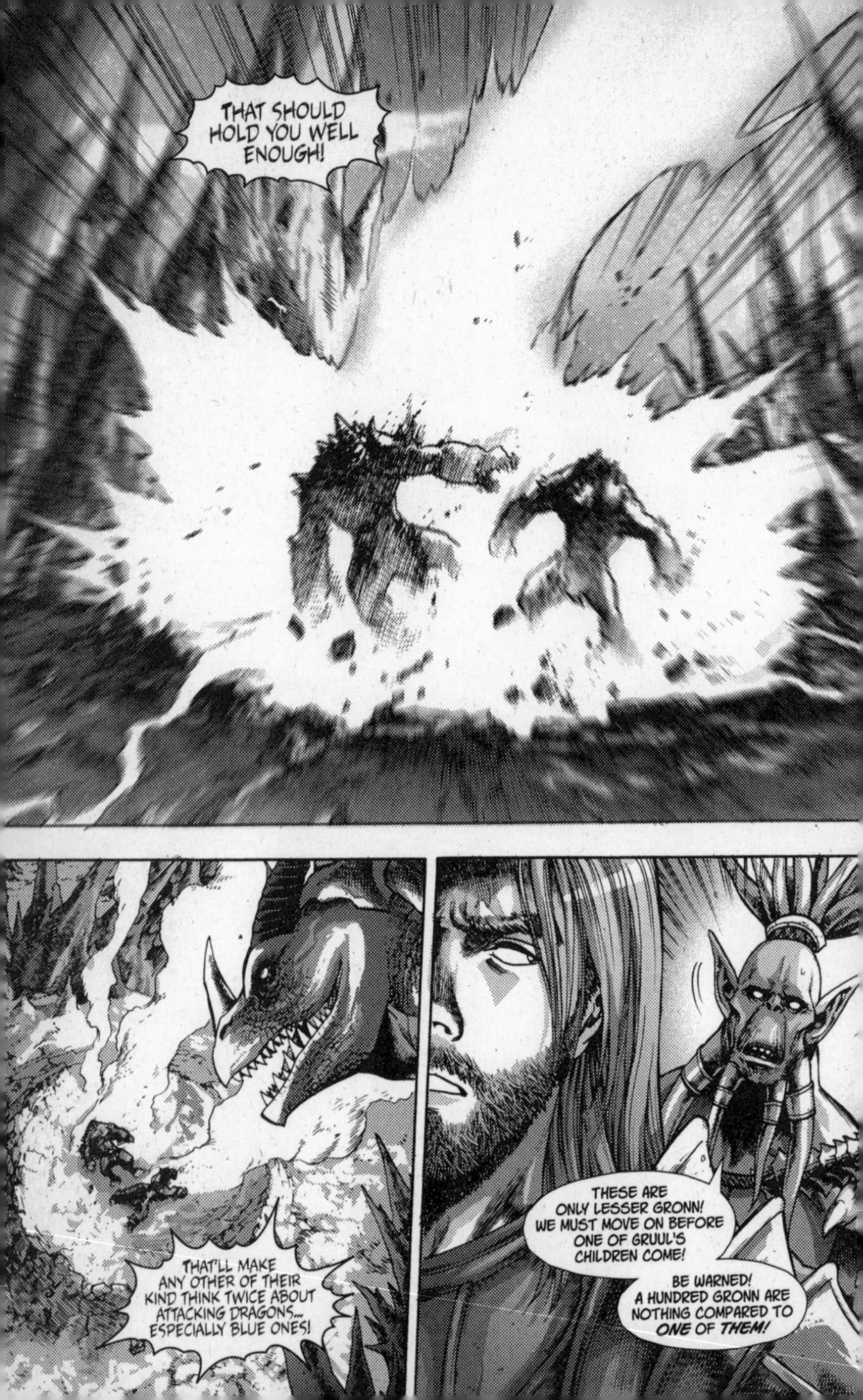
THAT SHOULD HOLD YOU WELL ENOUGH!
THAT'LL MAKE ANY OTHER OF THEIR KIND THINK TWICE ABOUT ATTACKING DRAGONS... ESPECIALLY BLUE ONES!
THESE ARE ONLY LESSER GRONN! WE MUST MOVE ON BEFORE ONE OF GRUUL'S CHILDREN COME!
BE WARNED! A HUNDRED GRONN ARE NOTHING COMPARED TO *ONE* OF *THEM!*

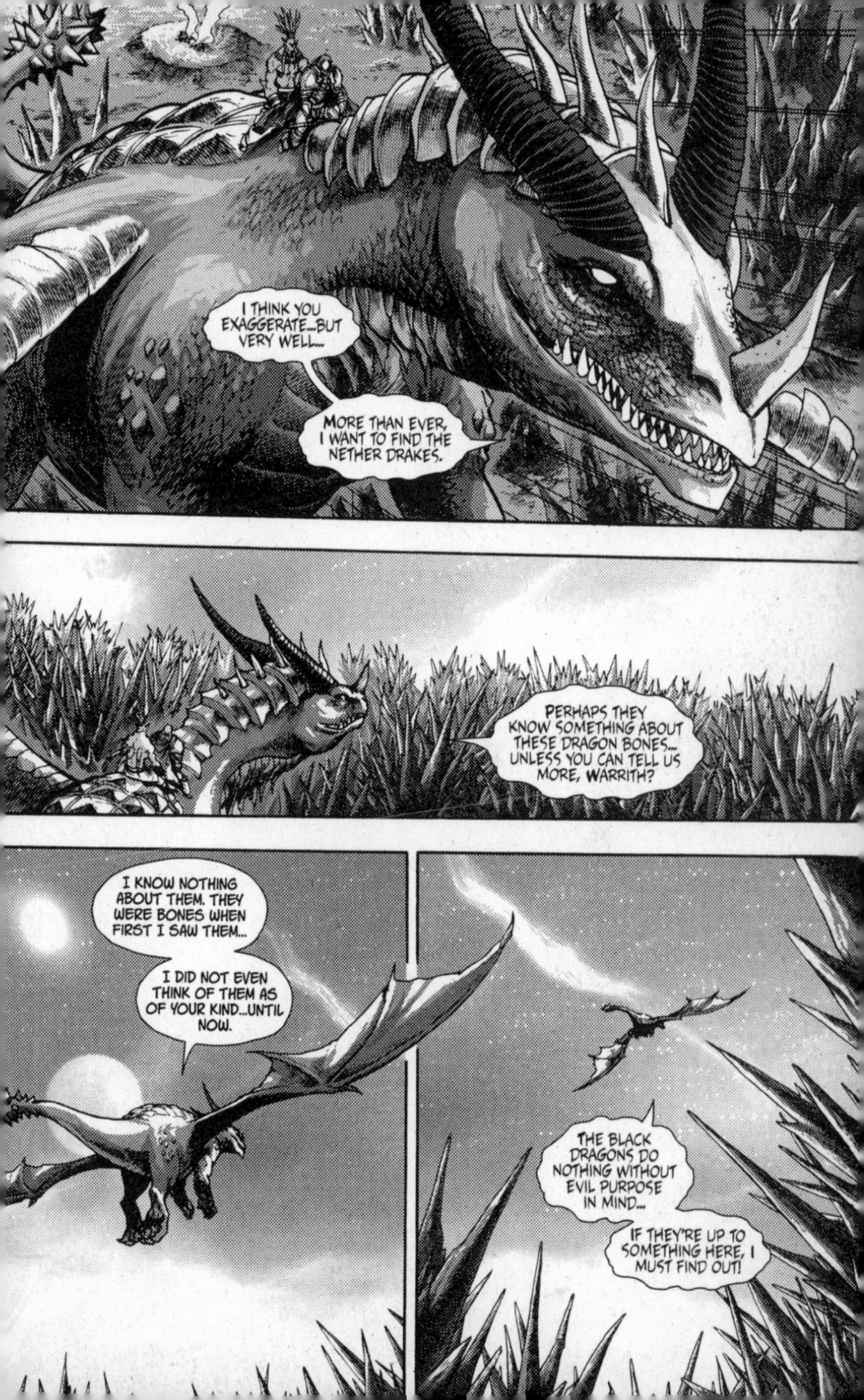
I THINK YOU EXAGGERATE...BUT VERY WELL...
MORE THAN EVER, I WANT TO FIND THE NETHER DRAKES.
PERHAPS THEY KNOW SOMETHING ABOUT THESE DRAGON BONES... UNLESS YOU CAN TELL US MORE, WARRITH?
I KNOW NOTHING ABOUT THEM. THEY WERE BONES WHEN FIRST I SAW THEM...
I DID NOT EVEN THINK OF THEM AS OF YOUR KIND...UNTIL NOW.
THE BLACK DRAGONS DO NOTHING WITHOUT EVIL PURPOSE IN MIND...
IF THEY'RE UP TO SOMETHING HERE, I MUST FIND OUT!

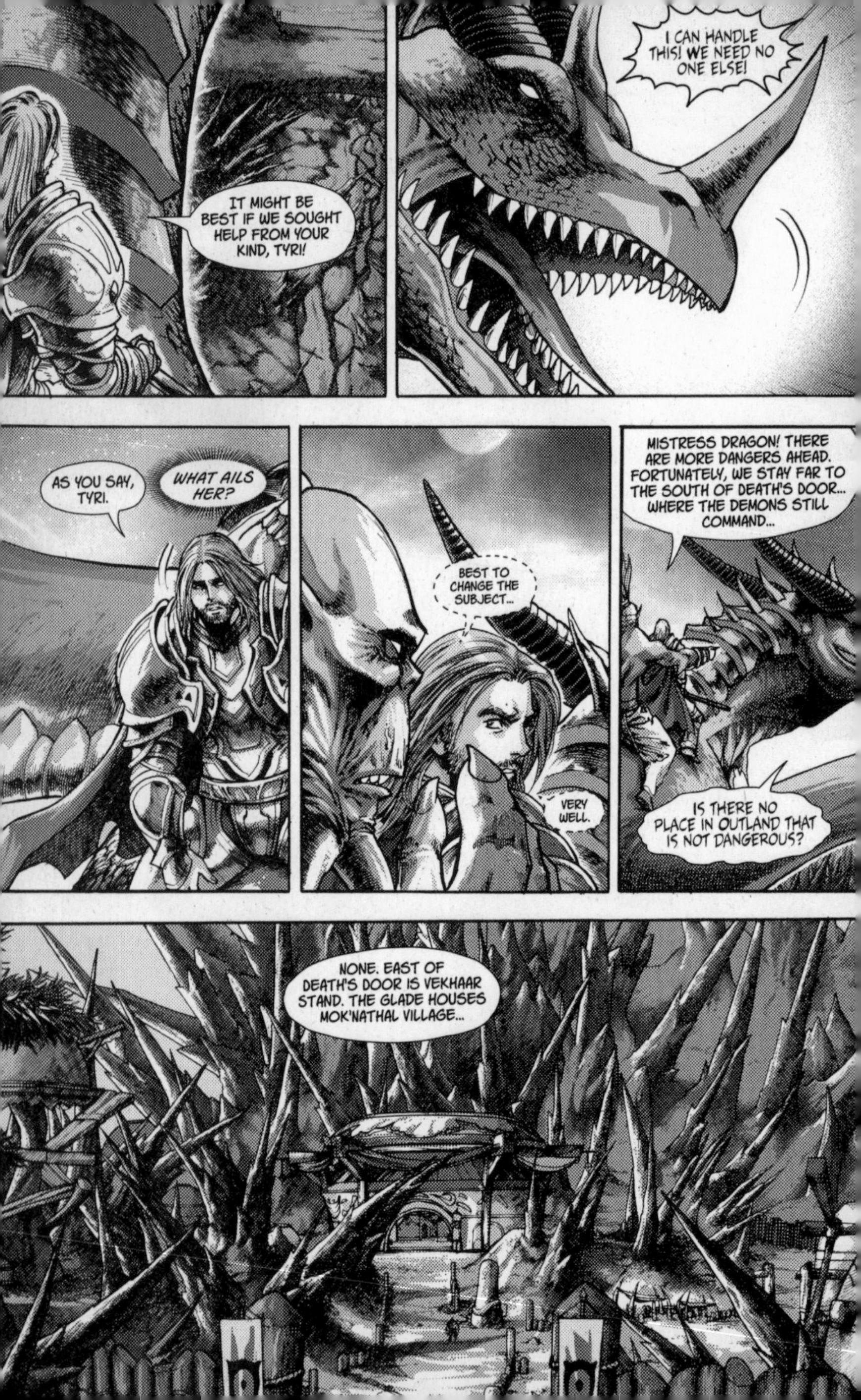
IT MIGHT BE BEST IF WE SOUGHT HELP FROM YOUR KIND, TYRI!
I CAN HANDLE THIS! WE NEED NO ONE ELSE!
AS YOU SAY, TYRI.
WHAT AILS HER?
BEST TO CHANGE THE SUBJECT...
VERY WELL.
MISTRESS DRAGON! THERE ARE MORE DANGERS AHEAD. FORTUNATELY, WE STAY FAR TO THE SOUTH OF DEATH'S DOOR... WHERE THE DEMONS STILL COMMAND...
IS THERE NO PLACE IN OUTLAND THAT IS NOT DANGEROUS?
NONE. EAST OF DEATH'S DOOR IS VEKHAAR STAND. THE GLADE HOUSES MOK'NATHAL VILLAGE...

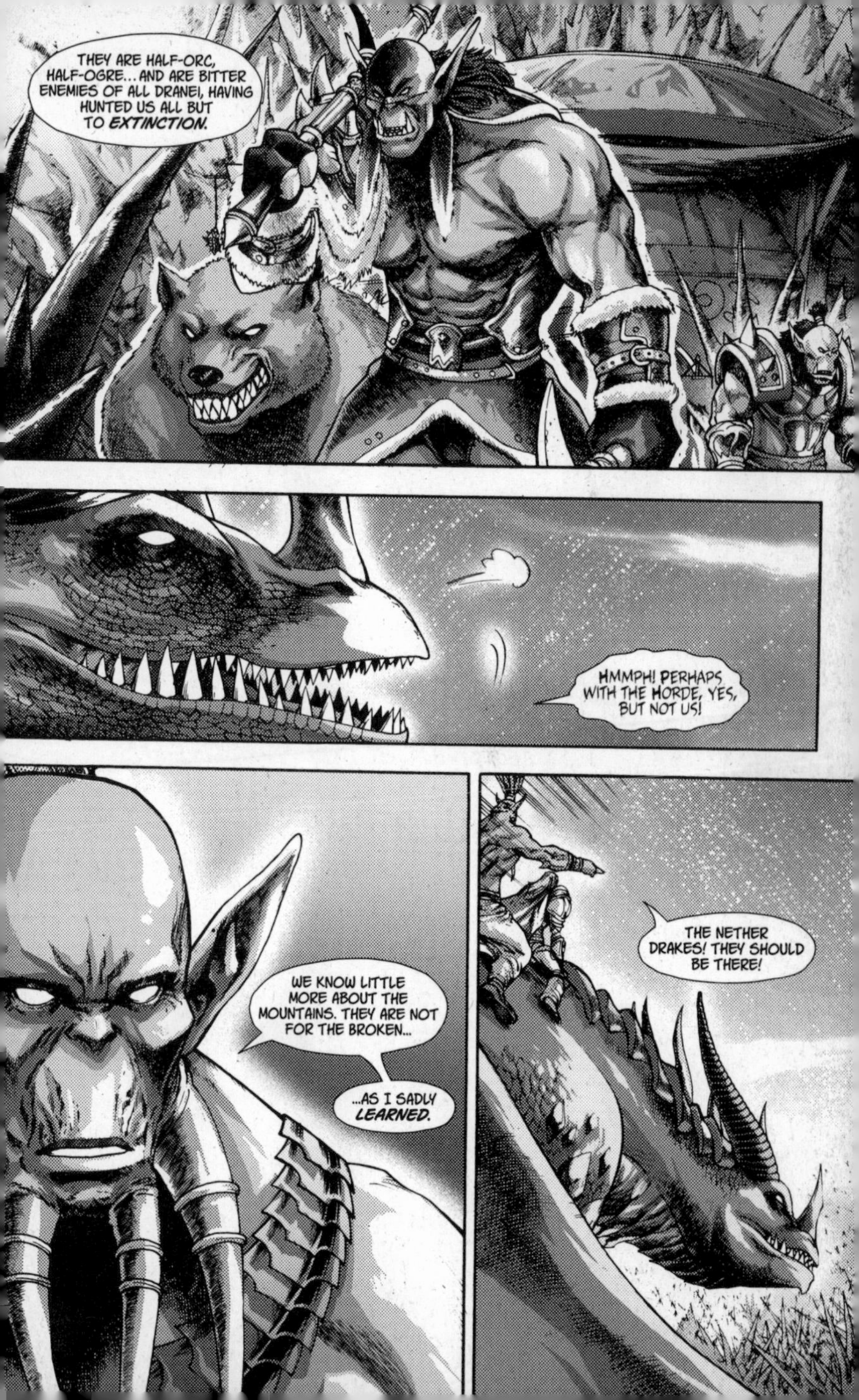
THEY ARE HALF-ORC, HALF-OGRE... AND ARE BITTER ENEMIES OF ALL DRANEI, HAVING HUNTED US ALL BUT TO EXTINCTION.
HMMPH! PERHAPS WITH THE HORDE, YES, BUT NOT US!
WE KNOW LITTLE MORE ABOUT THE MOUNTAINS. THEY ARE NOT FOR THE BROKEN...
...AS I SADLY LEARNED.
THE NETHER DRAKES! THEY SHOULD BE THERE!

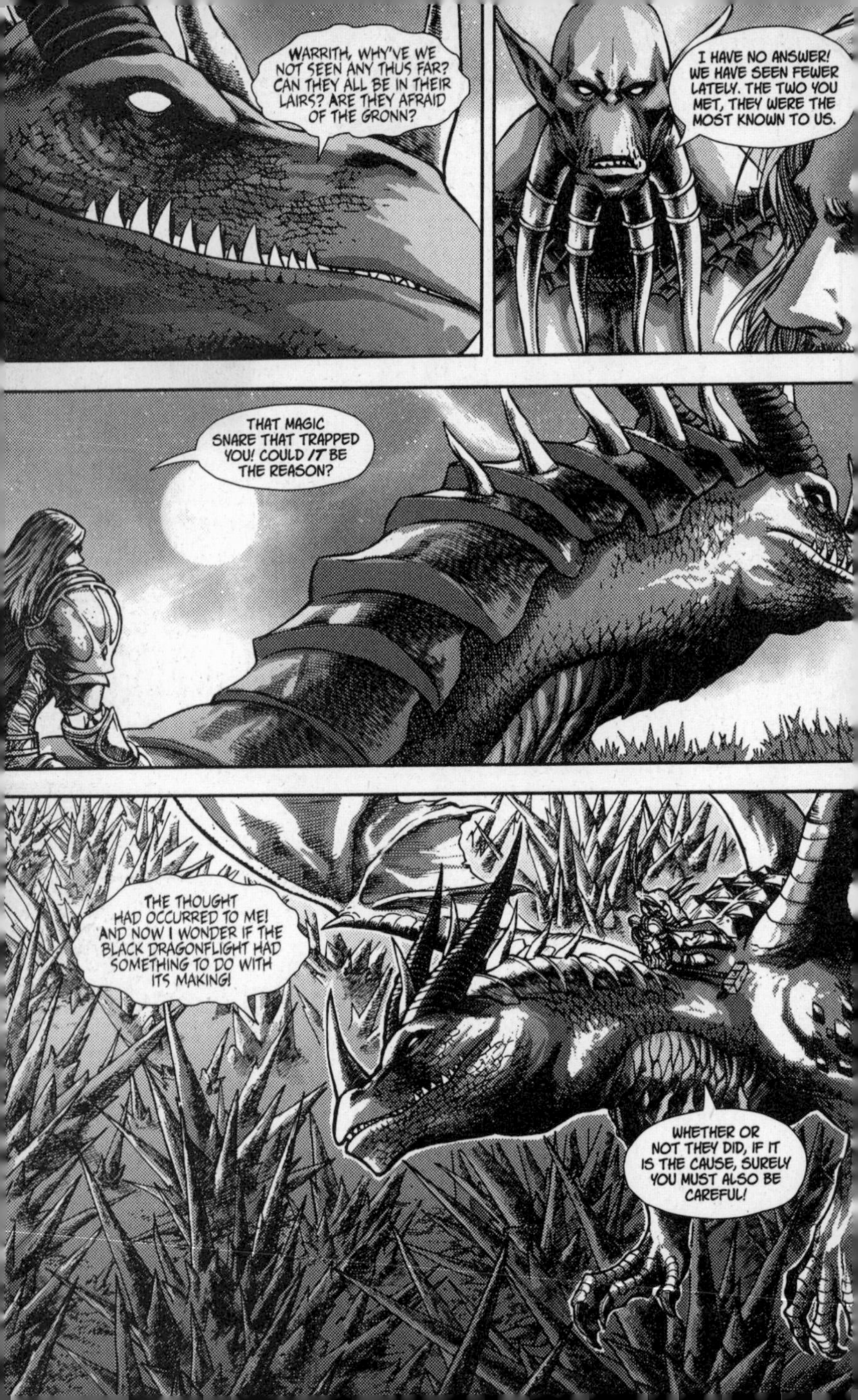
WARRITH, WHY'VE WE NOT SEEN ANY THUS FAR? CAN THEY ALL BE IN THEIR LAIRS? ARE THEY AFRAID OF THE GRONN?
I HAVE NO ANSWER! WE HAVE SEEN FEWER LATELY. THE TWO YOU MET, THEY WERE THE MOST KNOWN TO US.
THAT MAGIC SNARE THAT TRAPPED YOU! COULD *IT* BE THE REASON?
THE THOUGHT HAD OCCURRED TO ME! AND NOW I WONDER IF THE BLACK DRAGONFLIGHT HAD SOMETHING TO DO WITH ITS MAKING!
WHETHER OR NOT THEY DID, IF IT IS THE CAUSE, SURELY YOU MUST ALSO BE CAREFUL!

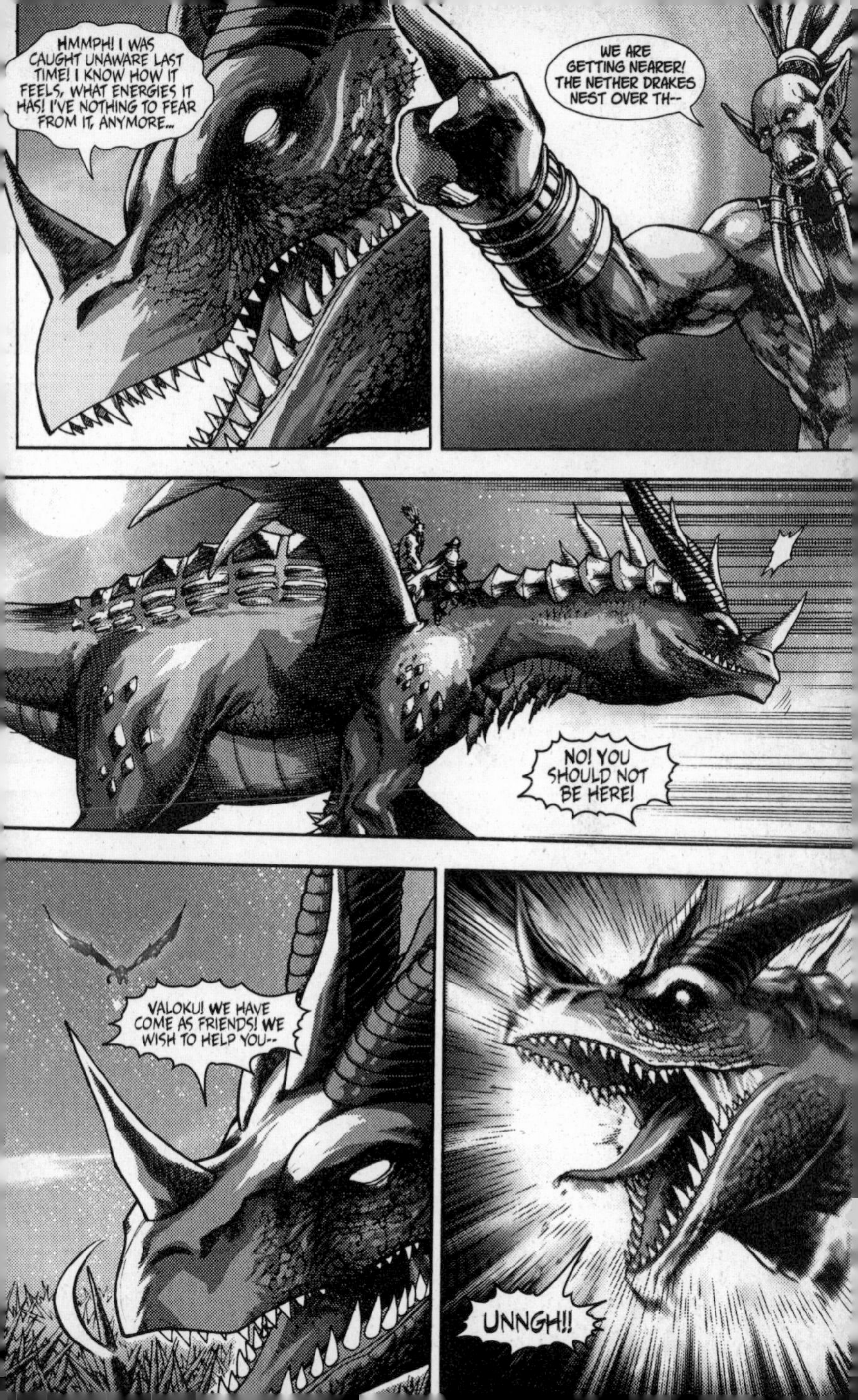
HMMPH! I WAS CAUGHT UNAWARE LAST TIME! I KNOW HOW IT FEELS, WHAT ENERGIES IT HAS! I'VE NOTHING TO FEAR FROM IT, ANYMORE...
WE ARE GETTING NEARER! THE NETHER DRAKES NEST OVER TH--
NO! YOU SHOULD NOT BE HERE!
VALOKU! WE HAVE COME AS FRIENDS! WE WISH TO HELP YOU--
UNNGH!!

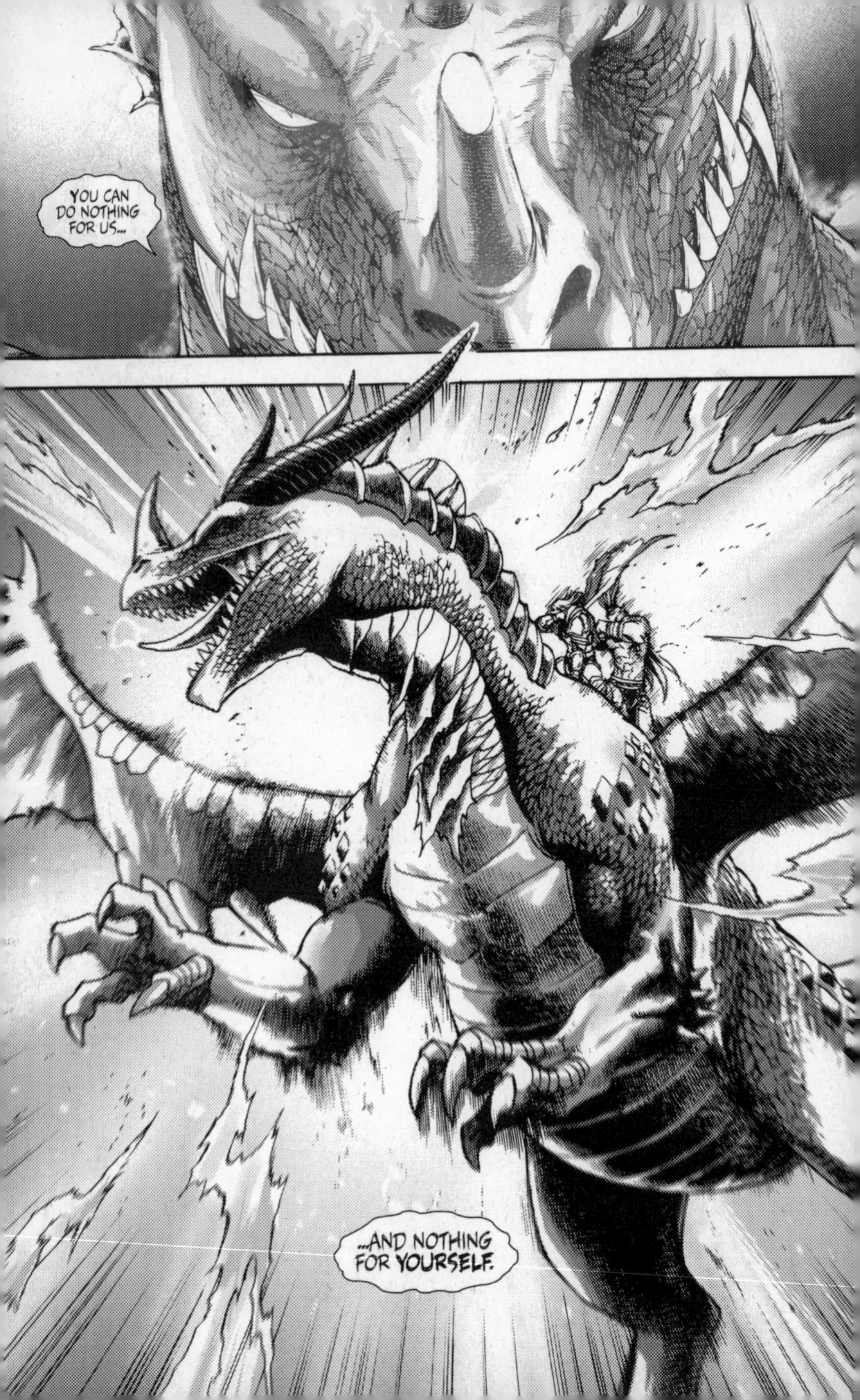
YOU CAN DO NOTHING FOR US...
...AND NOTHING FOR **YOURSELF**.

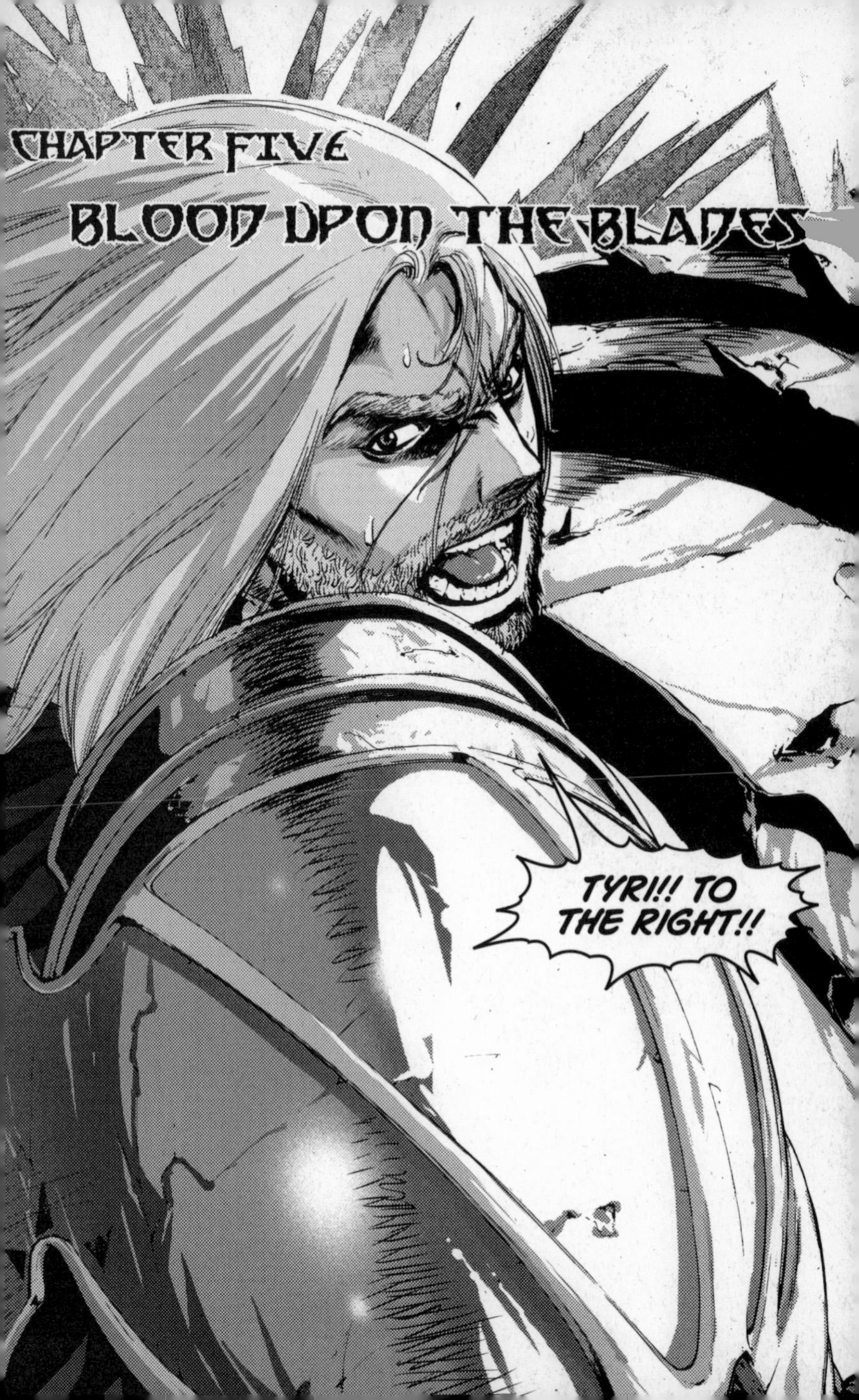
CHAPTER FIVE
BLOOD UPON THE BLADES
TYRI!! TO THE RIGHT!!

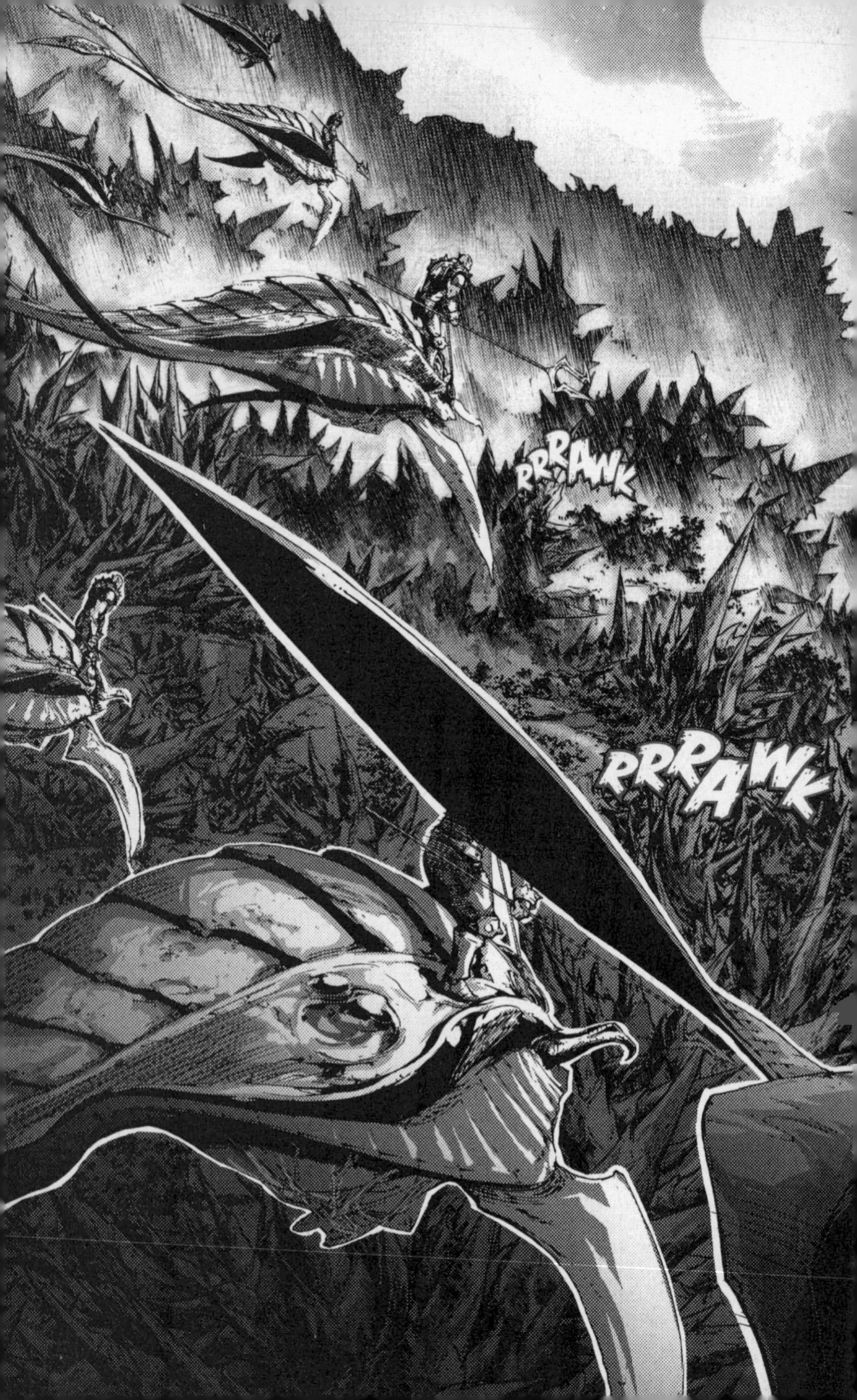
RRRAWK
RRRAWK

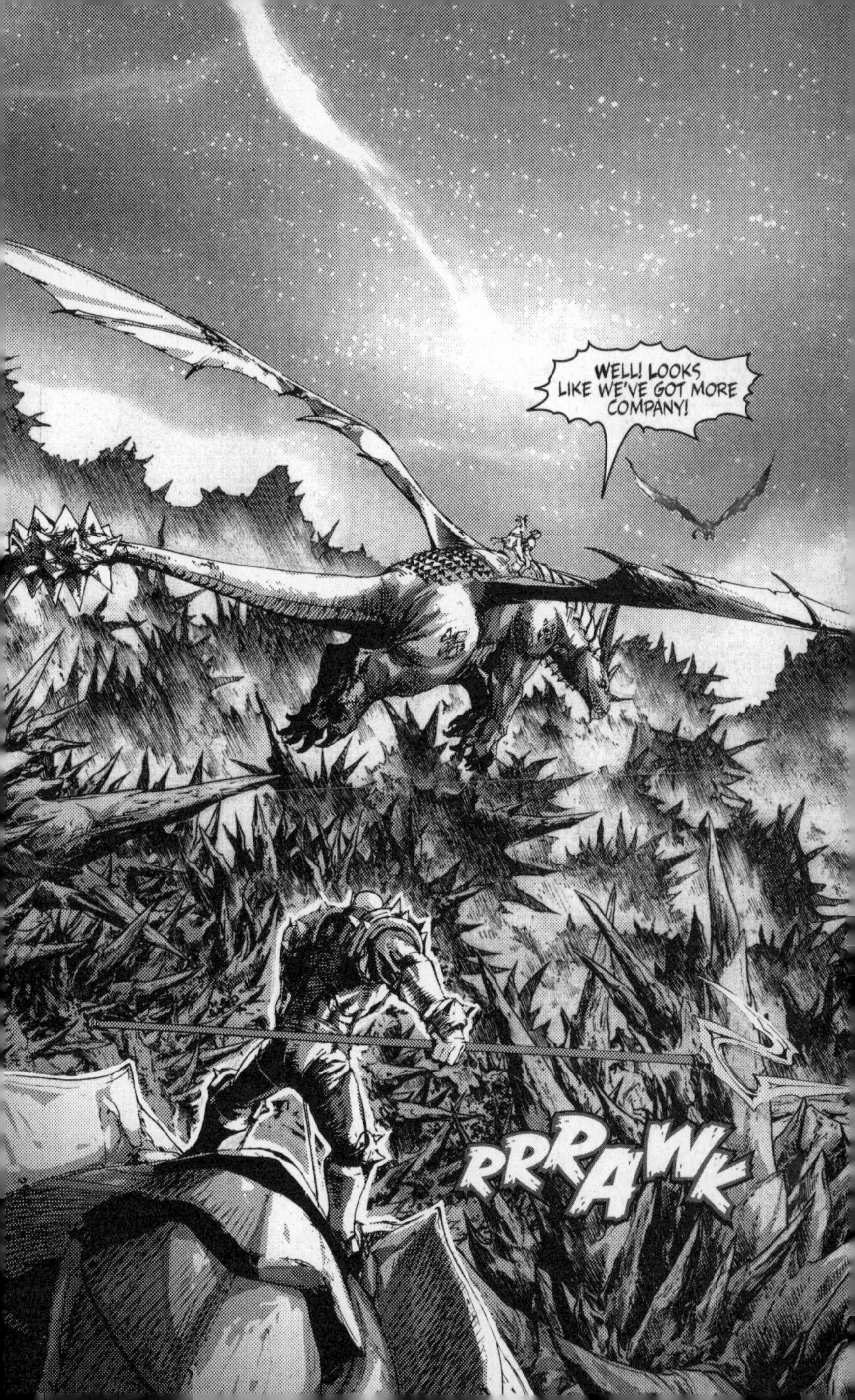
WELL! LOOKS LIKE WE'VE GOT MORE COMPANY!
RRRAWK

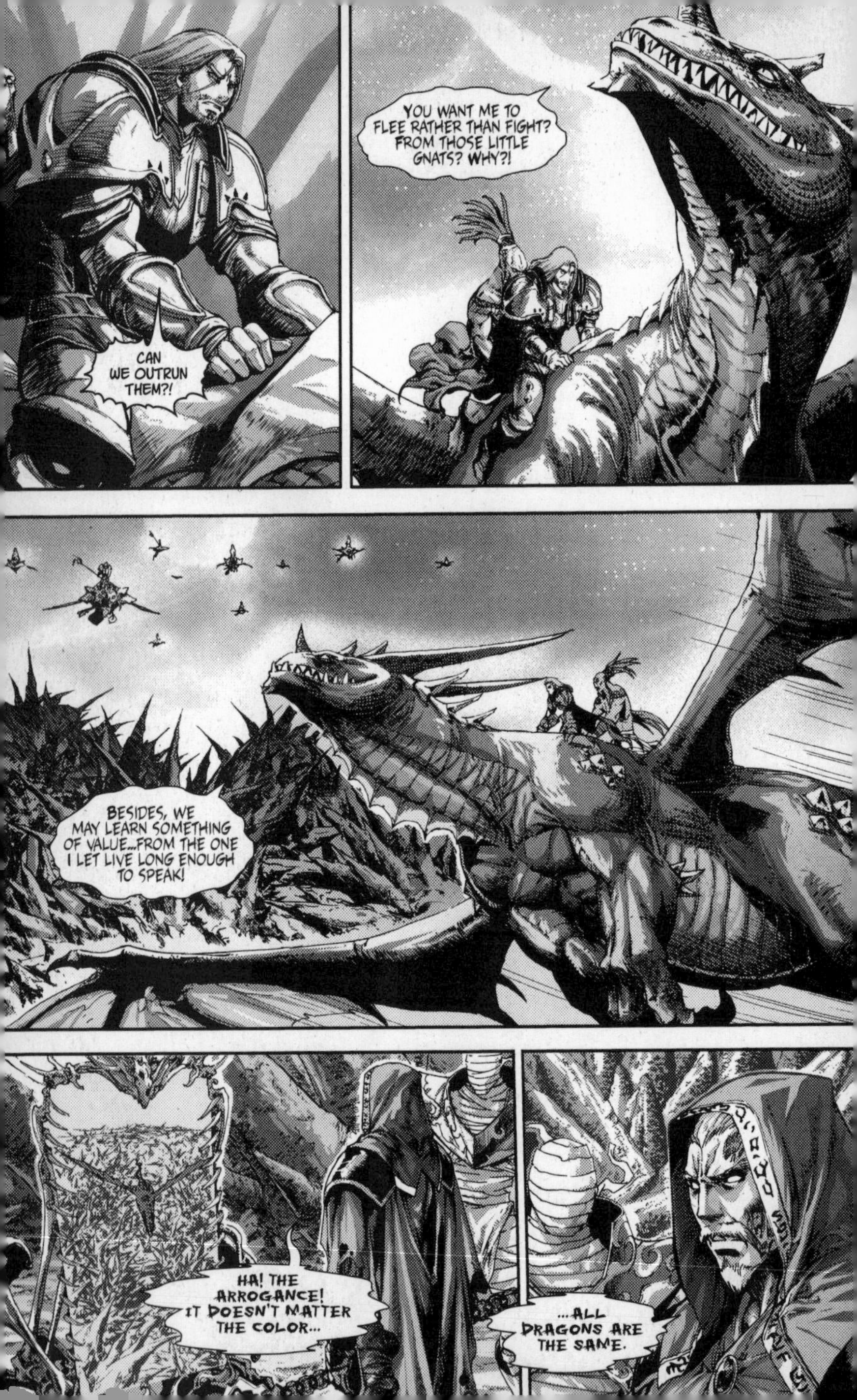
CAN WE OUTRUN THEM?!
YOU WANT ME TO FLEE RATHER THAN FIGHT? FROM THOSE LITTLE GNATS? WHY?!
BESIDES, WE MAY LEARN SOMETHING OF VALUE...FROM THE ONE I LET LIVE LONG ENOUGH TO SPEAK!
HA! THE ARROGANCE! IT DOESN'T MATTER THE COLOR...
...ALL DRAGONS ARE THE SAME.

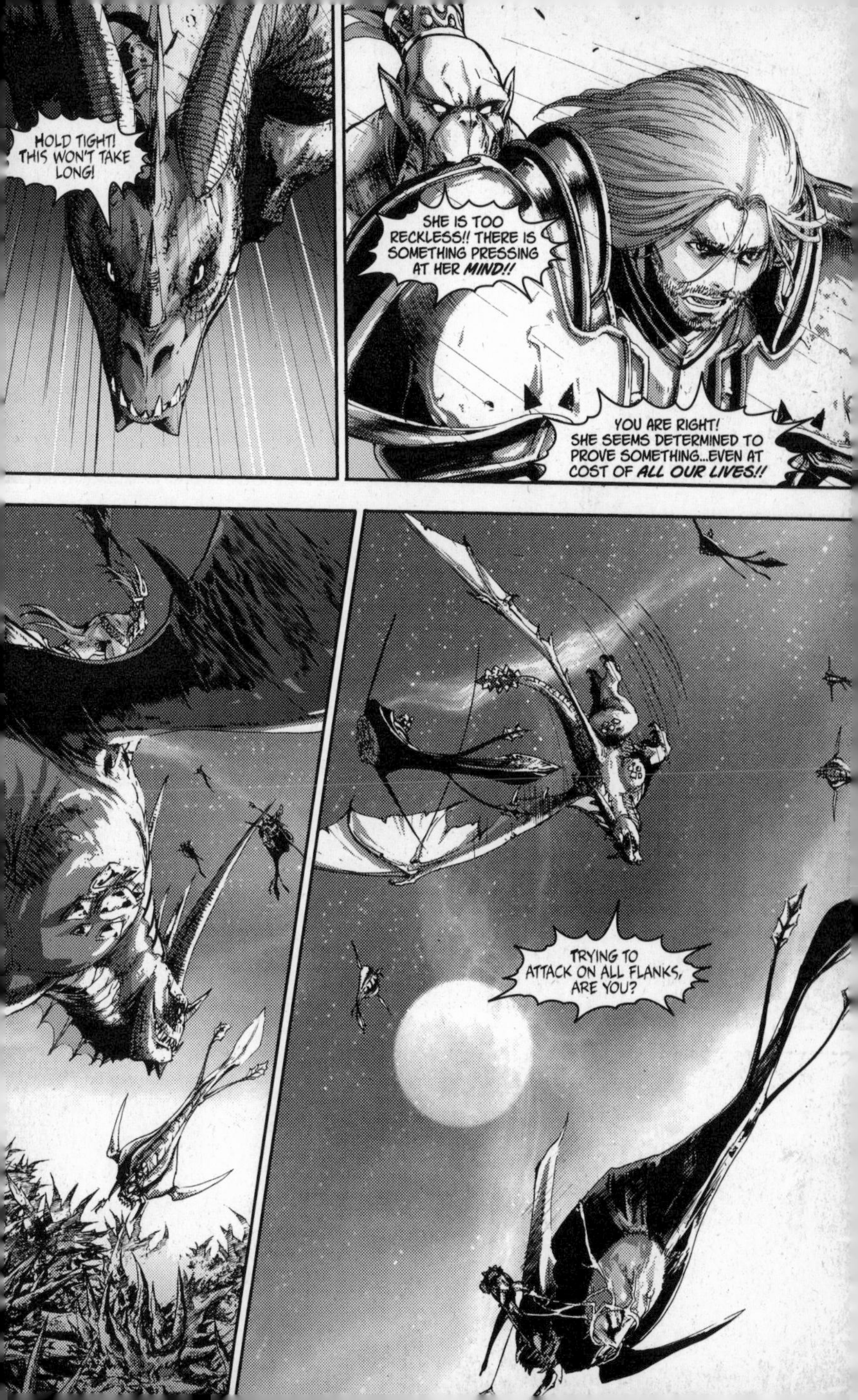
HOLD TIGHT! THIS WON'T TAKE LONG!
SHE IS TOO RECKLESS!! THERE IS SOMETHING PRESSING AT HER *MIND!!*
YOU ARE RIGHT! SHE SEEMS DETERMINED TO PROVE SOMETHING...EVEN AT COST OF ***ALL OUR LIVES!!***
TRYING TO ATTACK ON ALL FLANKS, ARE YOU?

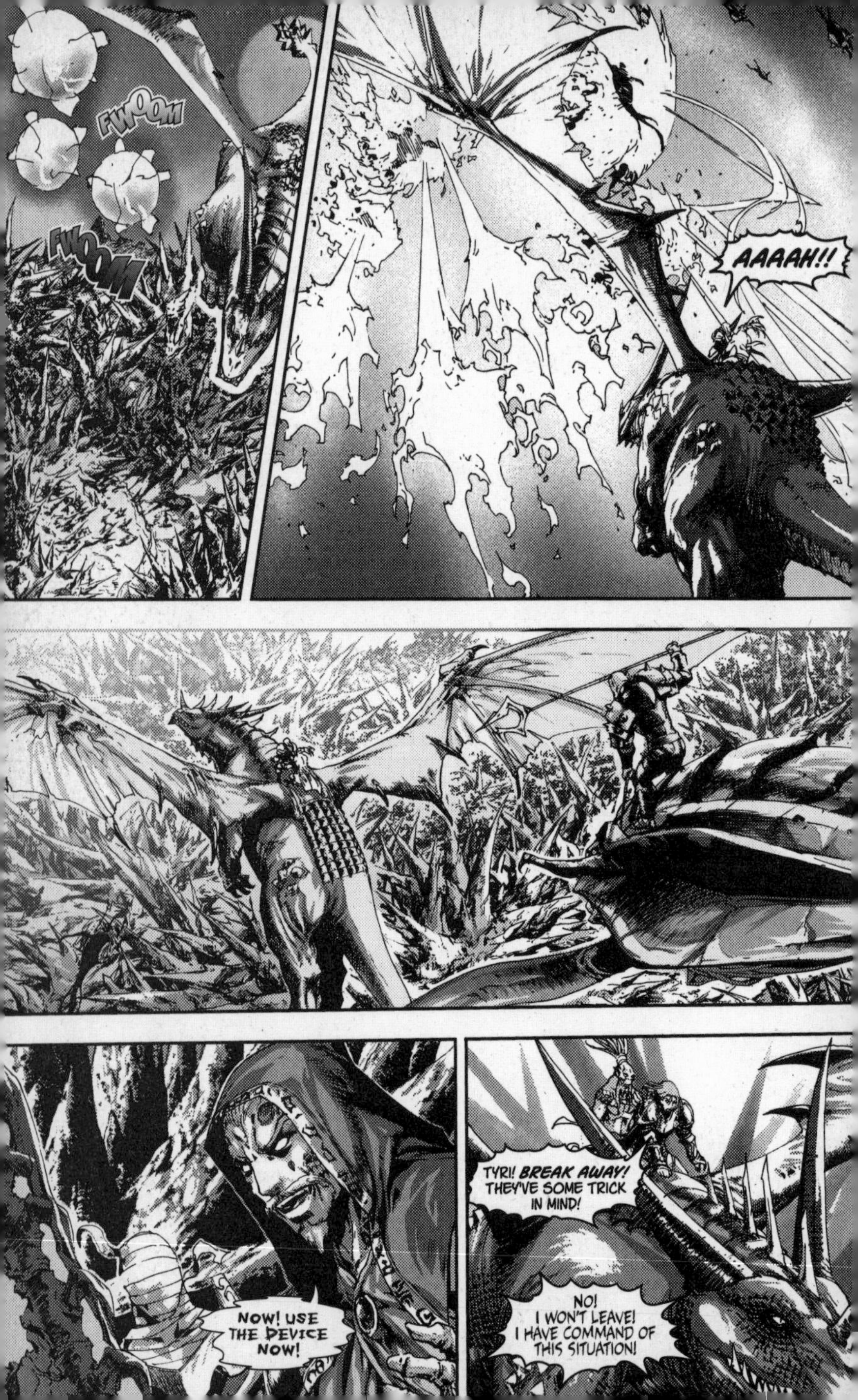
FWOOM
FWOOM
AAAAH!!
NOW! USE THE DEVICE NOW!
TYRI! BREAK AWAY! THEY'VE SOME TRICK IN MIND!
NO! I WON'T LEAVE! I HAVE COMMAND OF THIS SITUATION!

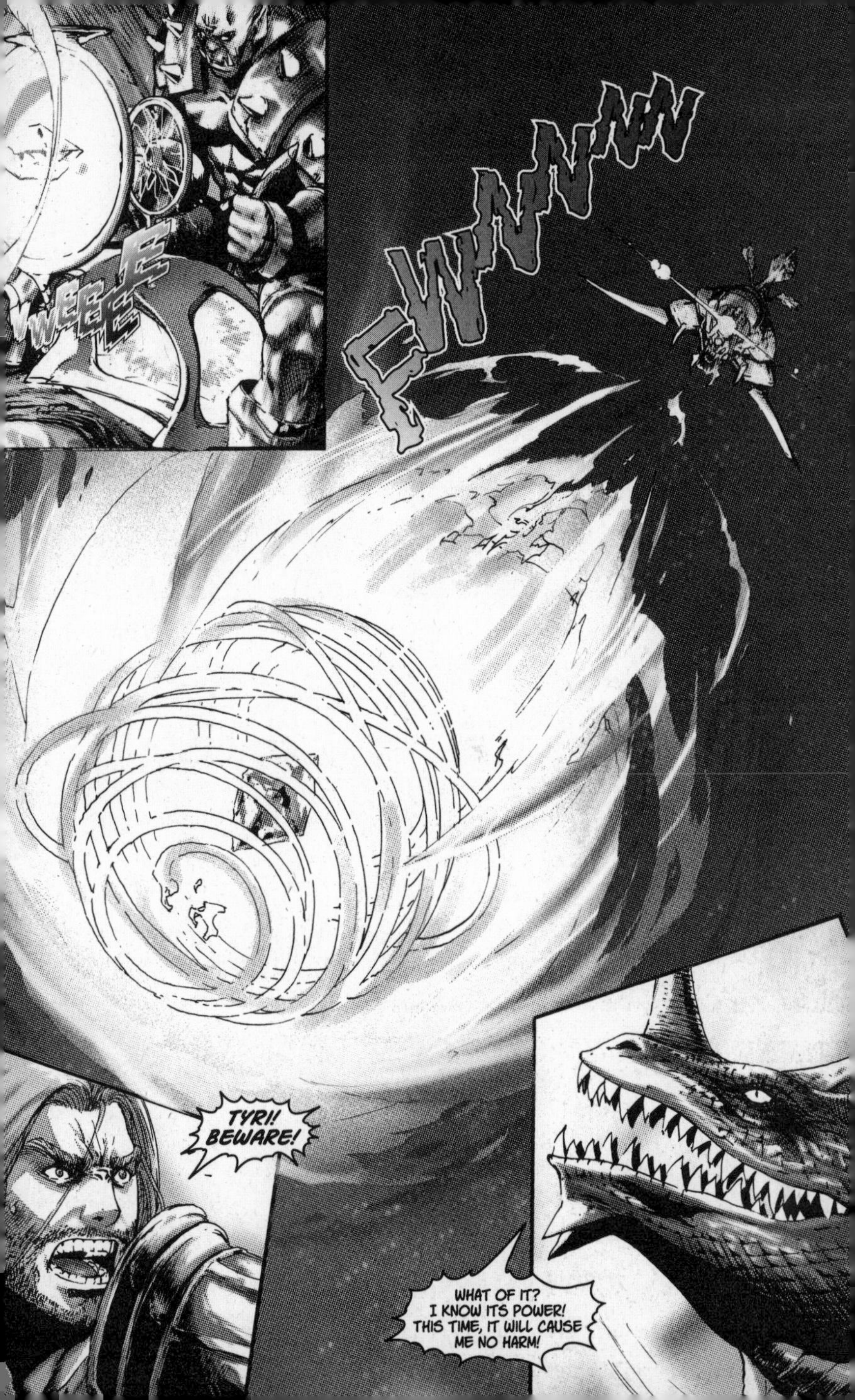
WEEEE
FWWNNNNNNN
TYRI! BEWARE!
WHAT OF IT? I KNOW ITS POWER! THIS TIME, IT WILL CAUSE ME NO HARM!

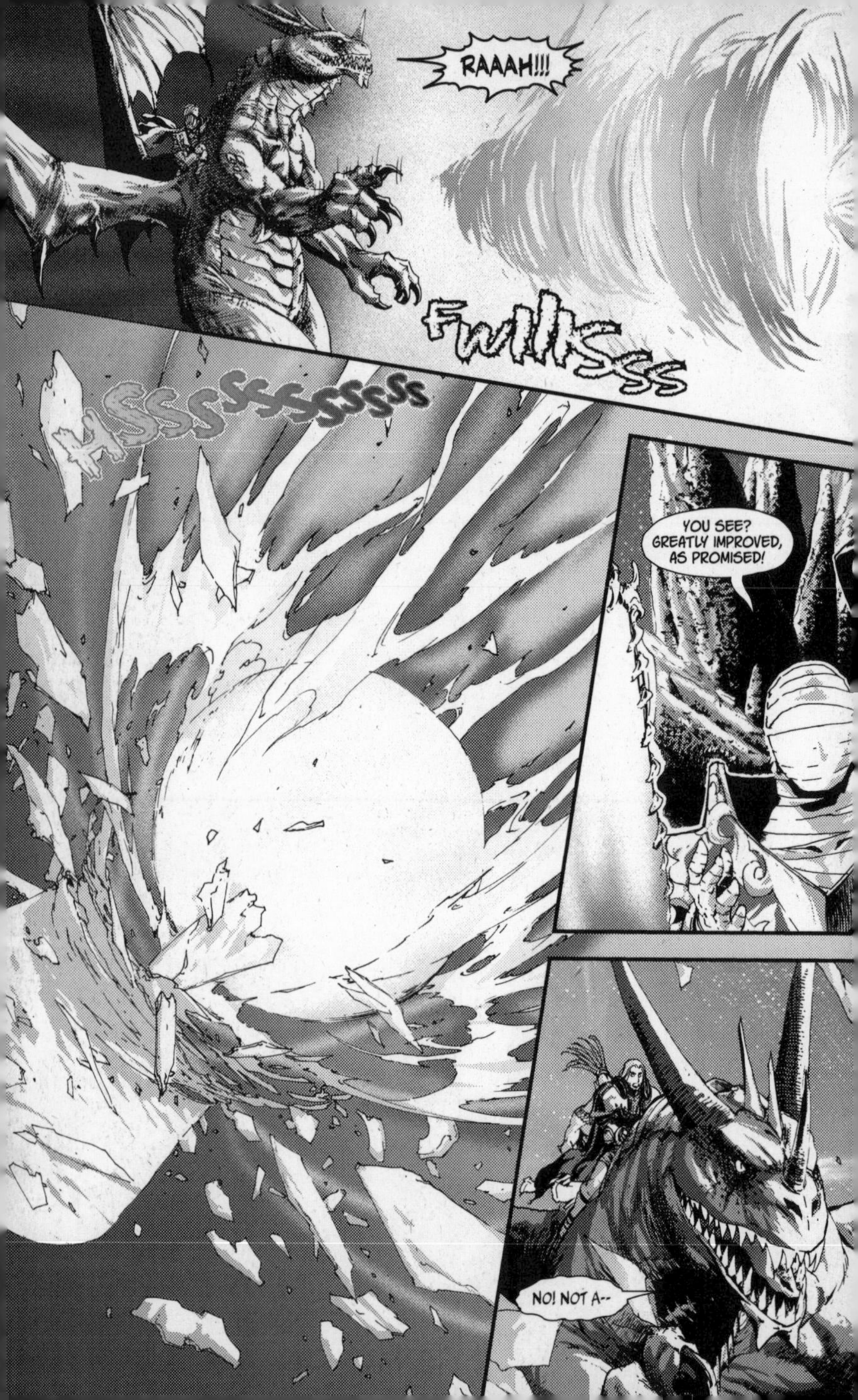
RAAAH!!!
FWllKSSS
HSSSSSSSSSS
YOU SEE? GREATLY IMPROVED, AS PROMISED!
NO! NOT A--

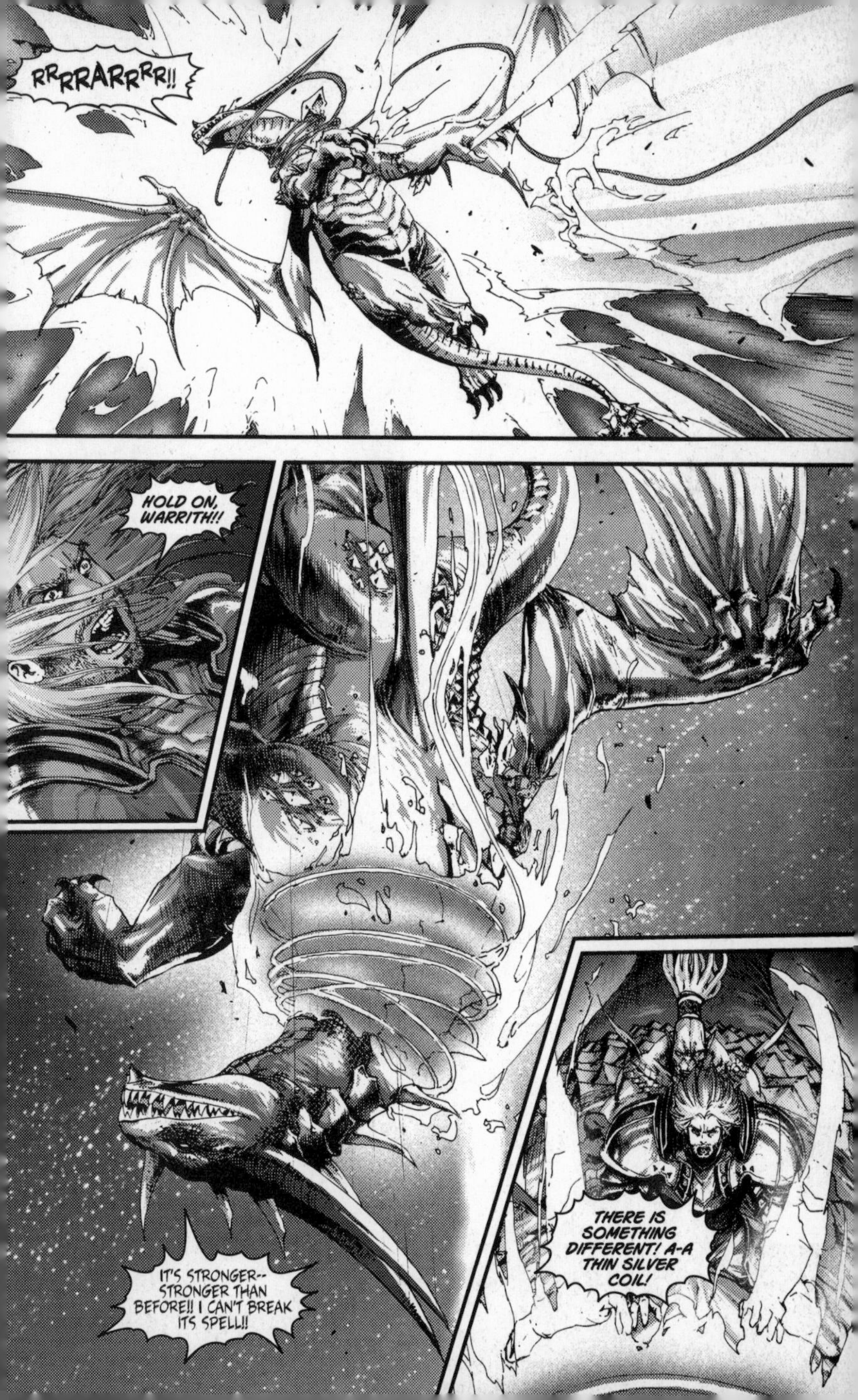
RRRRARRRRR!!
HOLD ON, WARRITH!!
IT'S STRONGER-- STRONGER THAN BEFORE!! I CAN'T BREAK ITS SPELL!!
THERE IS SOMETHING DIFFERENT! A-A THIN SILVER COIL!

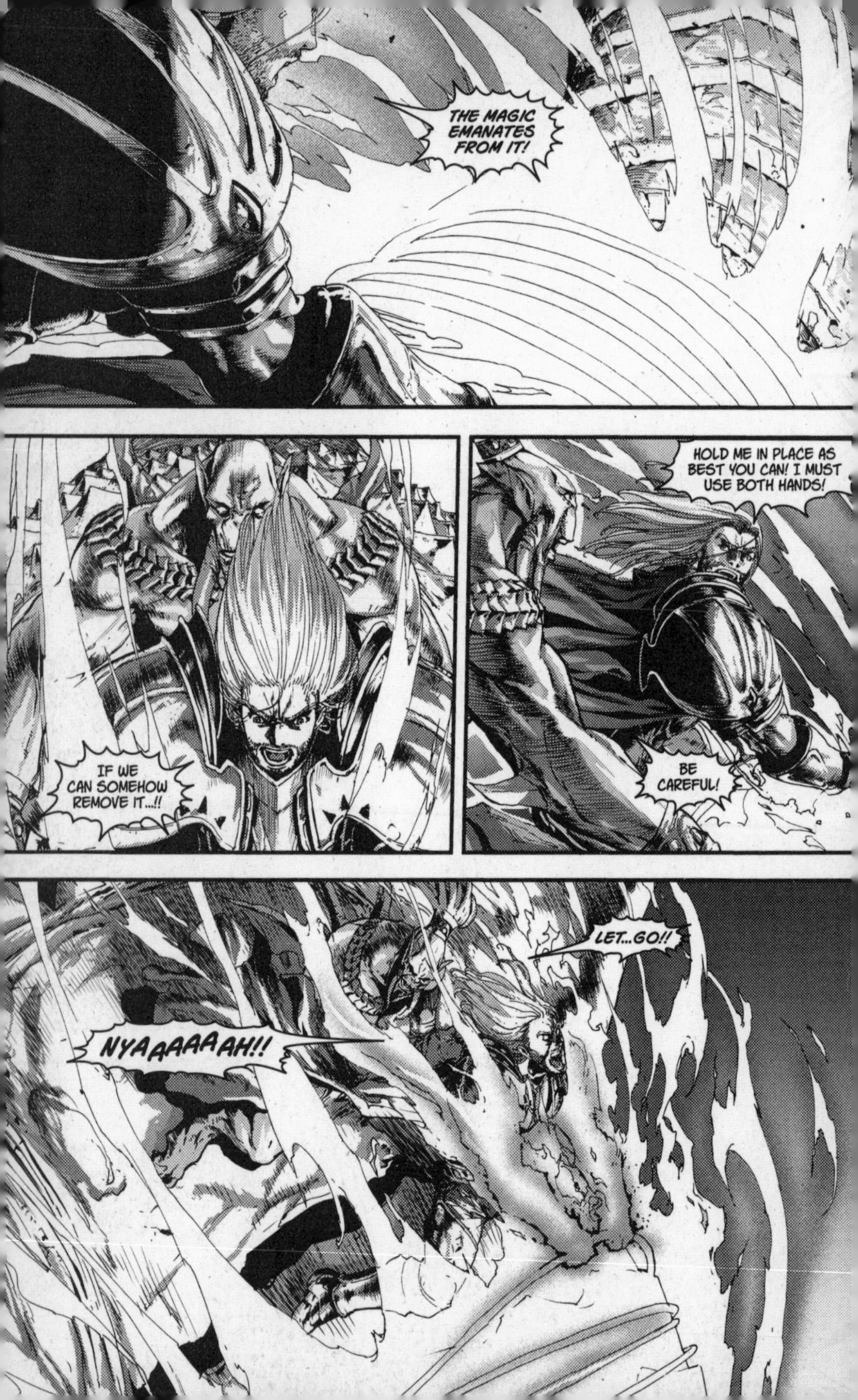
THE MAGIC EMANATES FROM IT!
IF WE CAN SOMEHOW REMOVE IT...!!
HOLD ME IN PLACE AS BEST YOU CAN! I MUST USE BOTH HANDS!
BE CAREFUL!
NYAAAAAAH!!
LET...GO!!

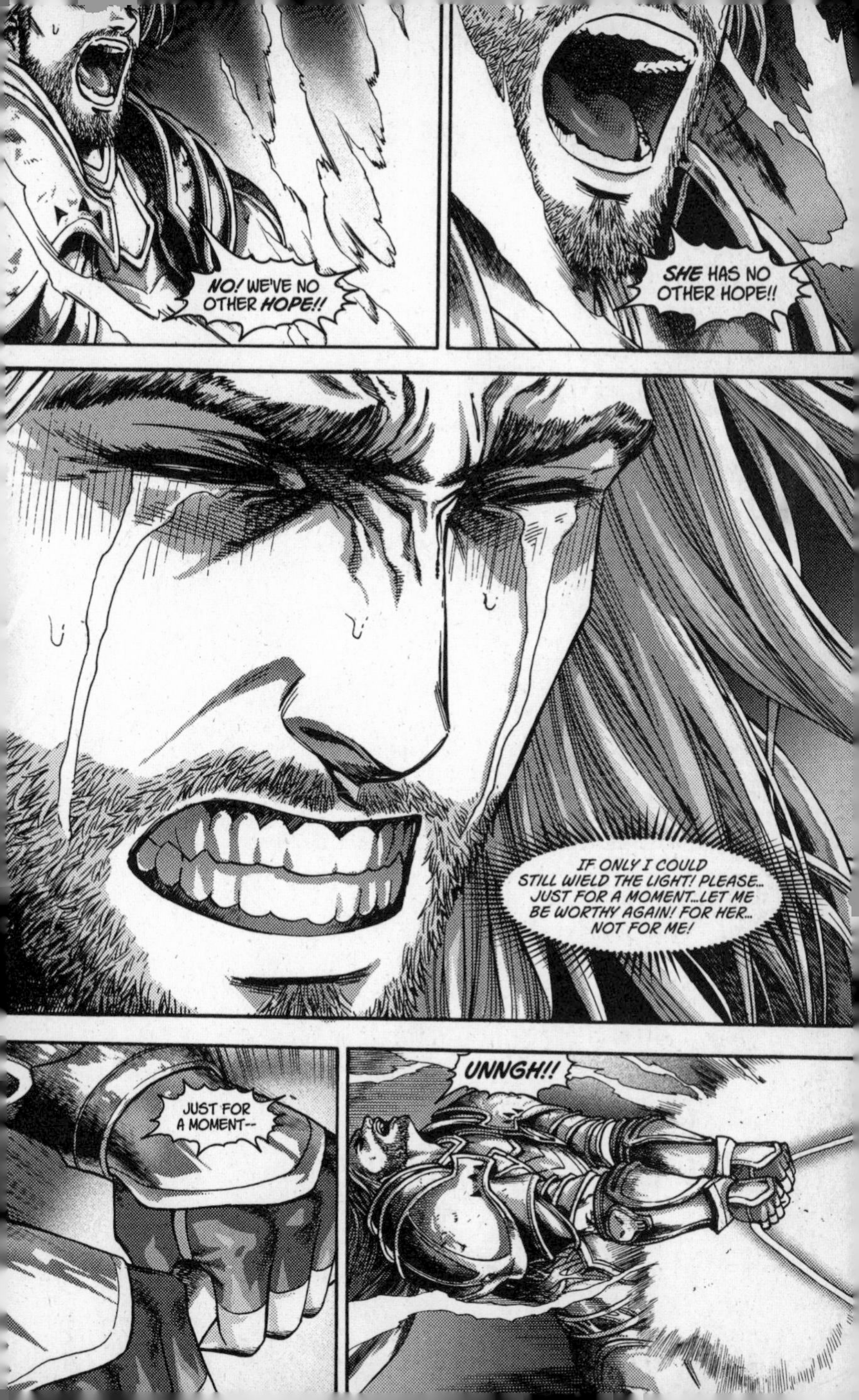
NO! WE'VE NO OTHER HOPE!!
SHE HAS NO OTHER HOPE!!
IF ONLY I COULD STILL WIELD THE LIGHT! PLEASE... JUST FOR A MOMENT...LET ME BE WORTHY AGAIN! FOR HER... NOT FOR ME!
JUST FOR A MOMENT--
UNNGH!!

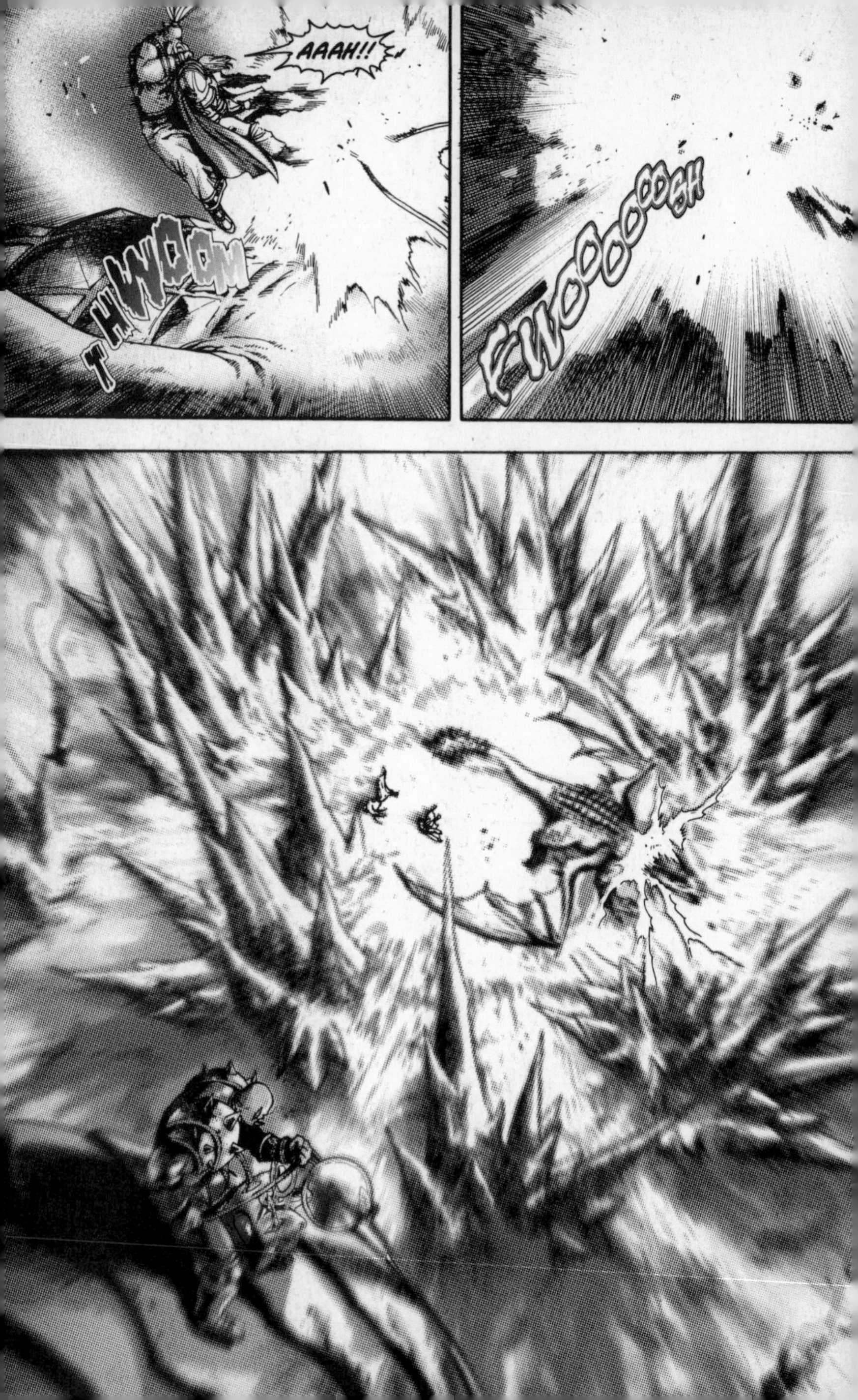
AAAH!!
THWOOM
FWOOOOOOSH

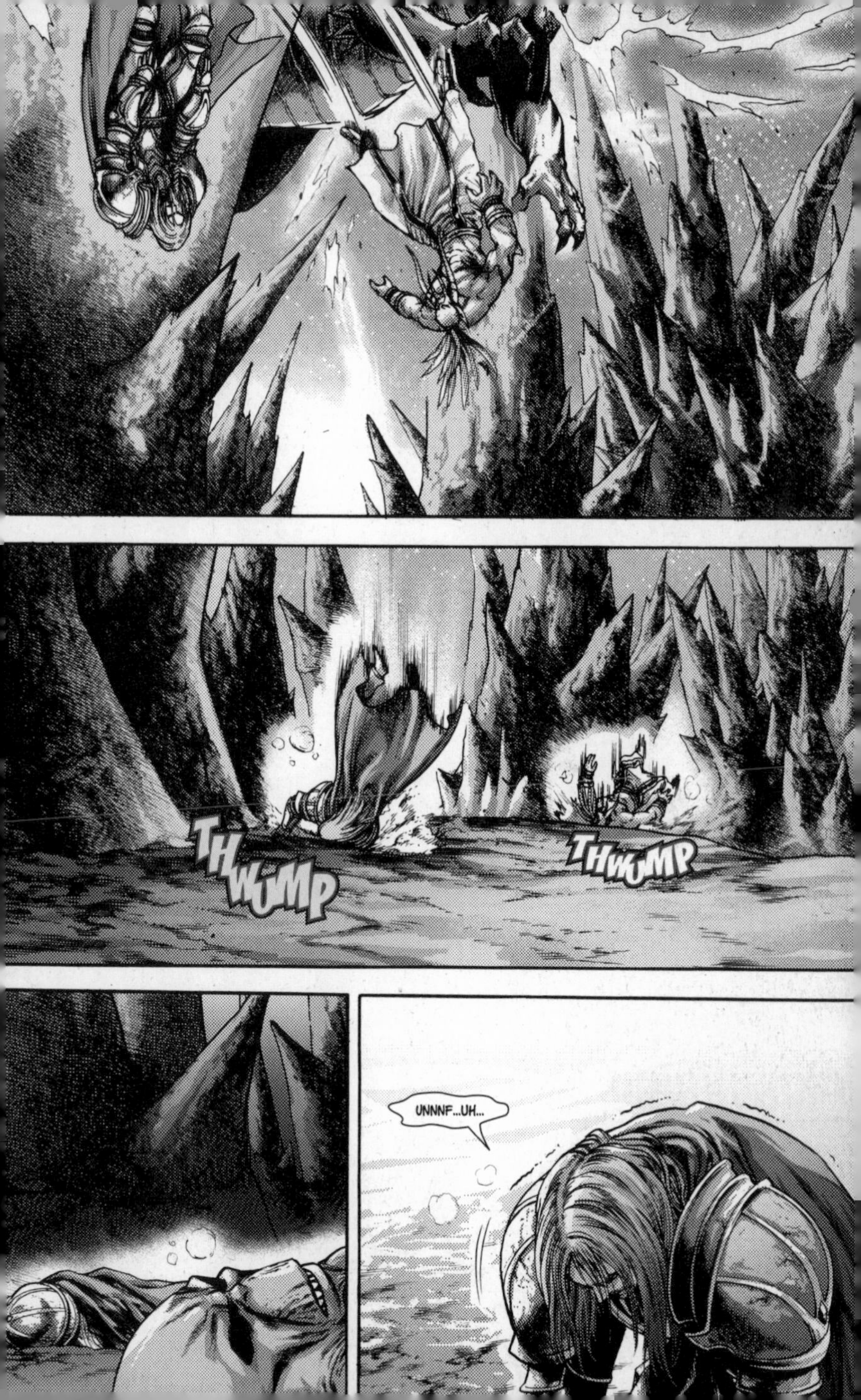
THWUMP
THWUMP
UNNNF...UH...

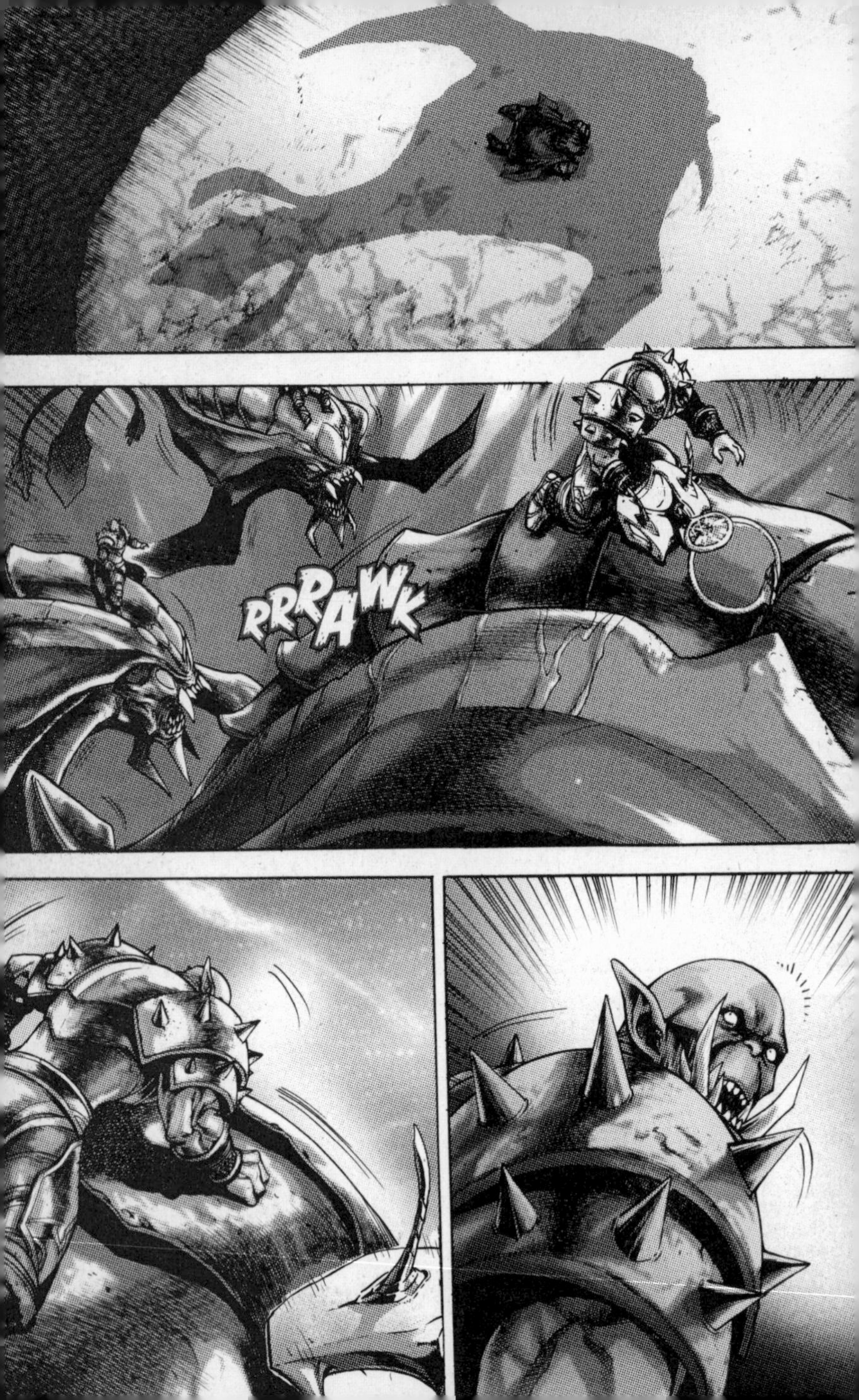
RRRAWK

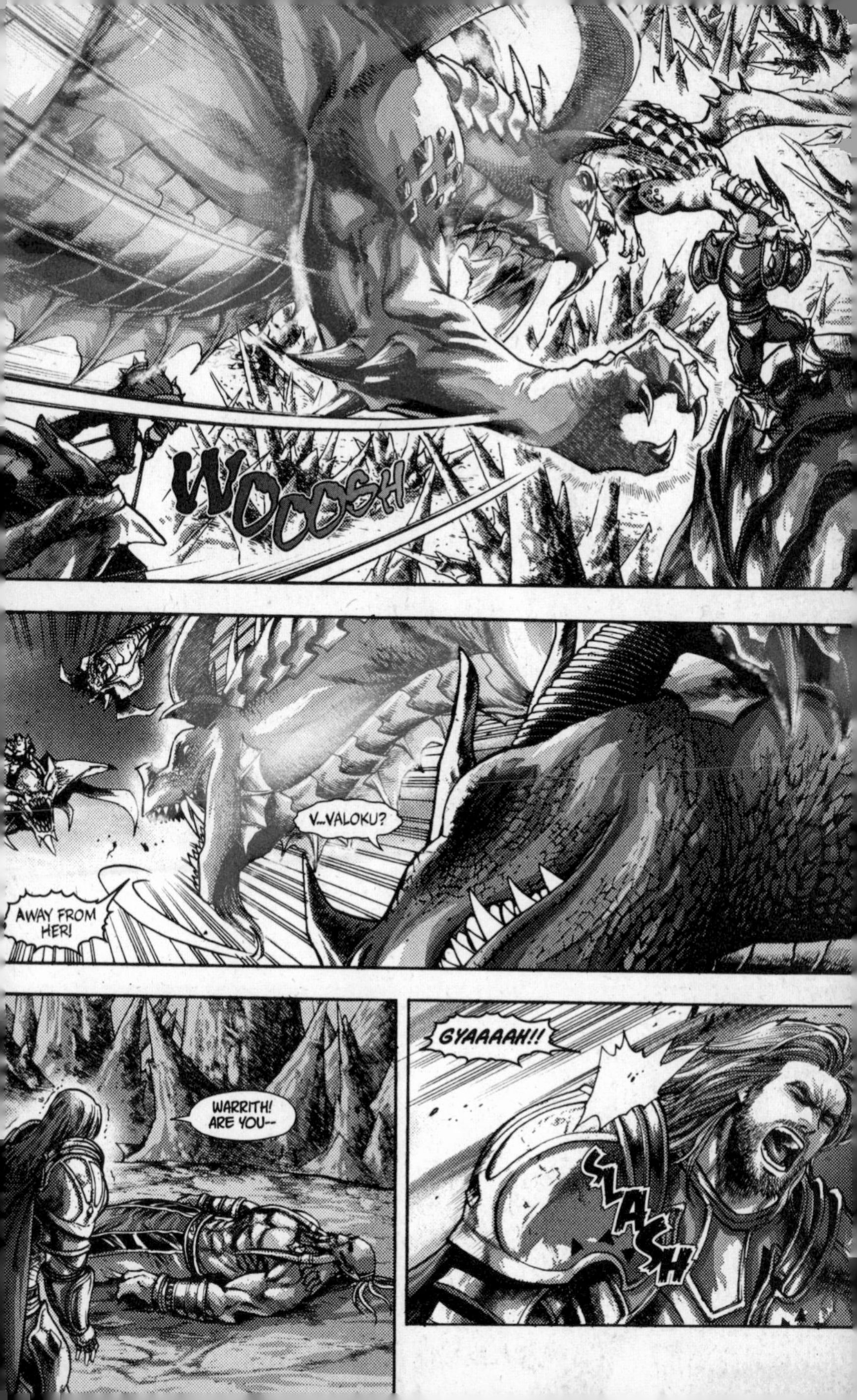
WOOOSH
V...VALOKU?
AWAY FROM HER!
WARRITH! ARE YOU--
GYAAAAH!!
SLASH

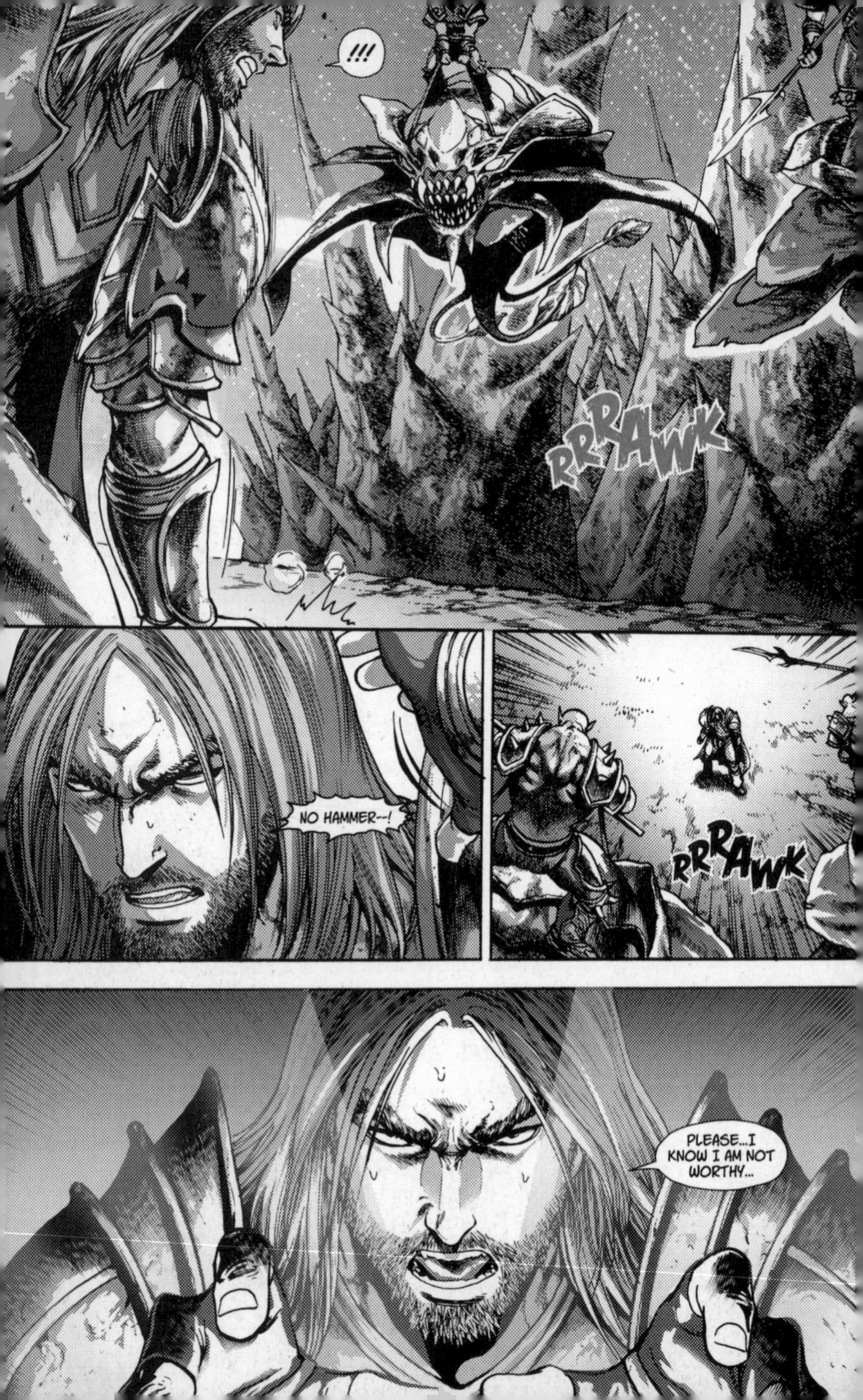
!!!
RRRAWK
NO HAMMER--!
RRRAWK
PLEASE...I KNOW I AM NOT WORTHY...

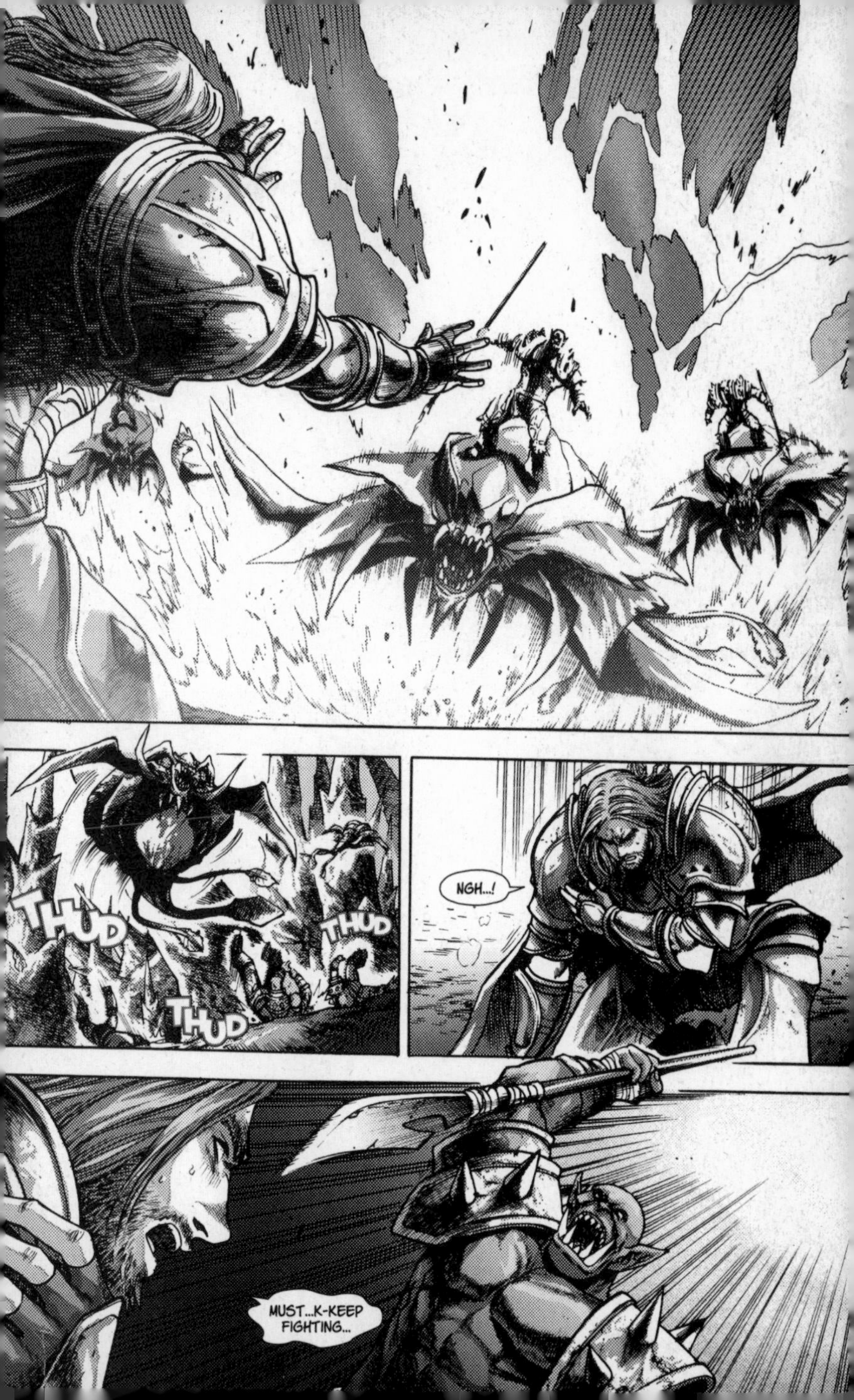
THUD
THUD
THUD
NGH...!
MUST...K-KEEP FIGHTING...

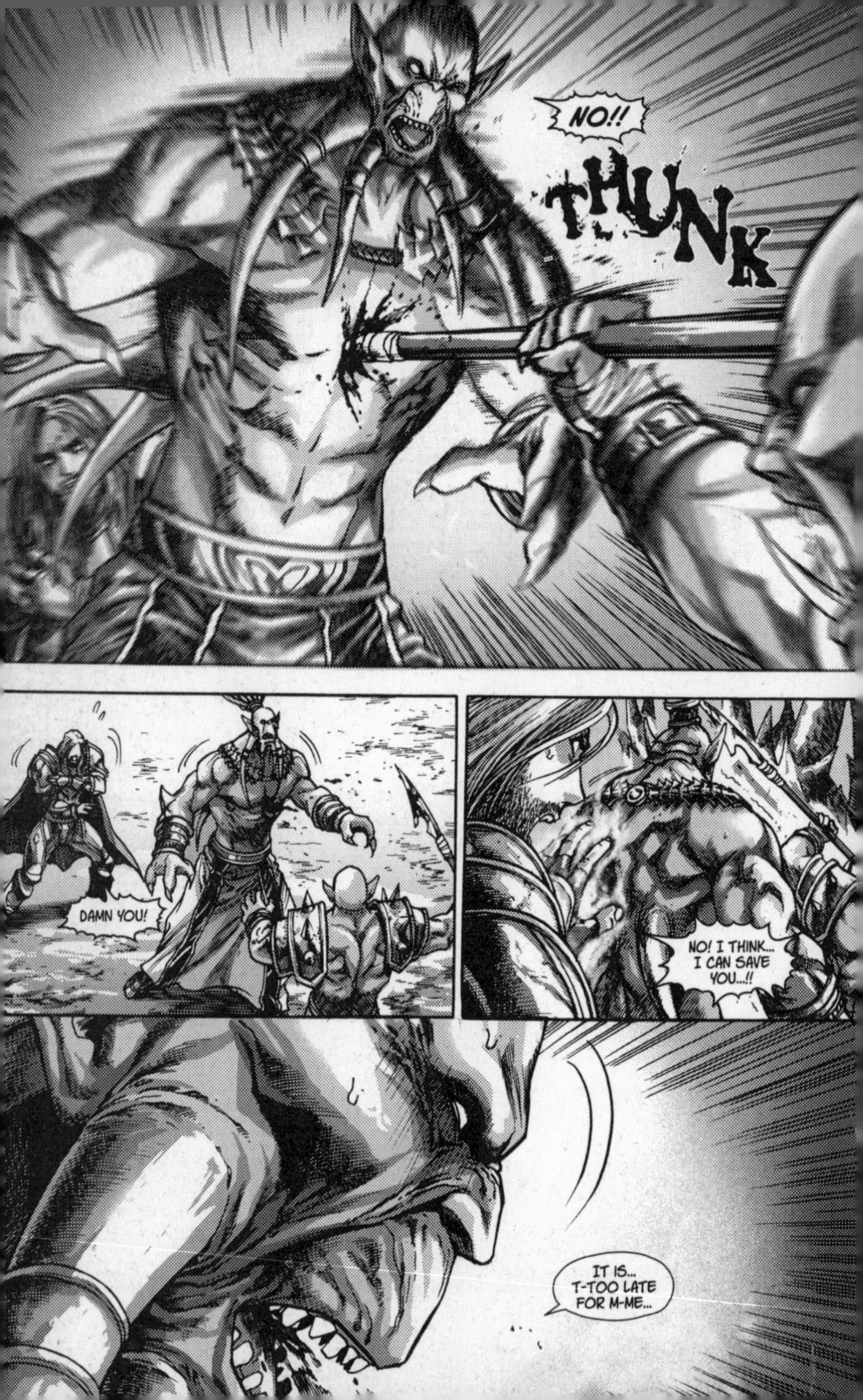
NO!!
THUNK
DAMN YOU!
NO! I THINK...
I CAN SAVE
YOU...!!
IT IS...
T-TOO LATE
FOR M-ME...

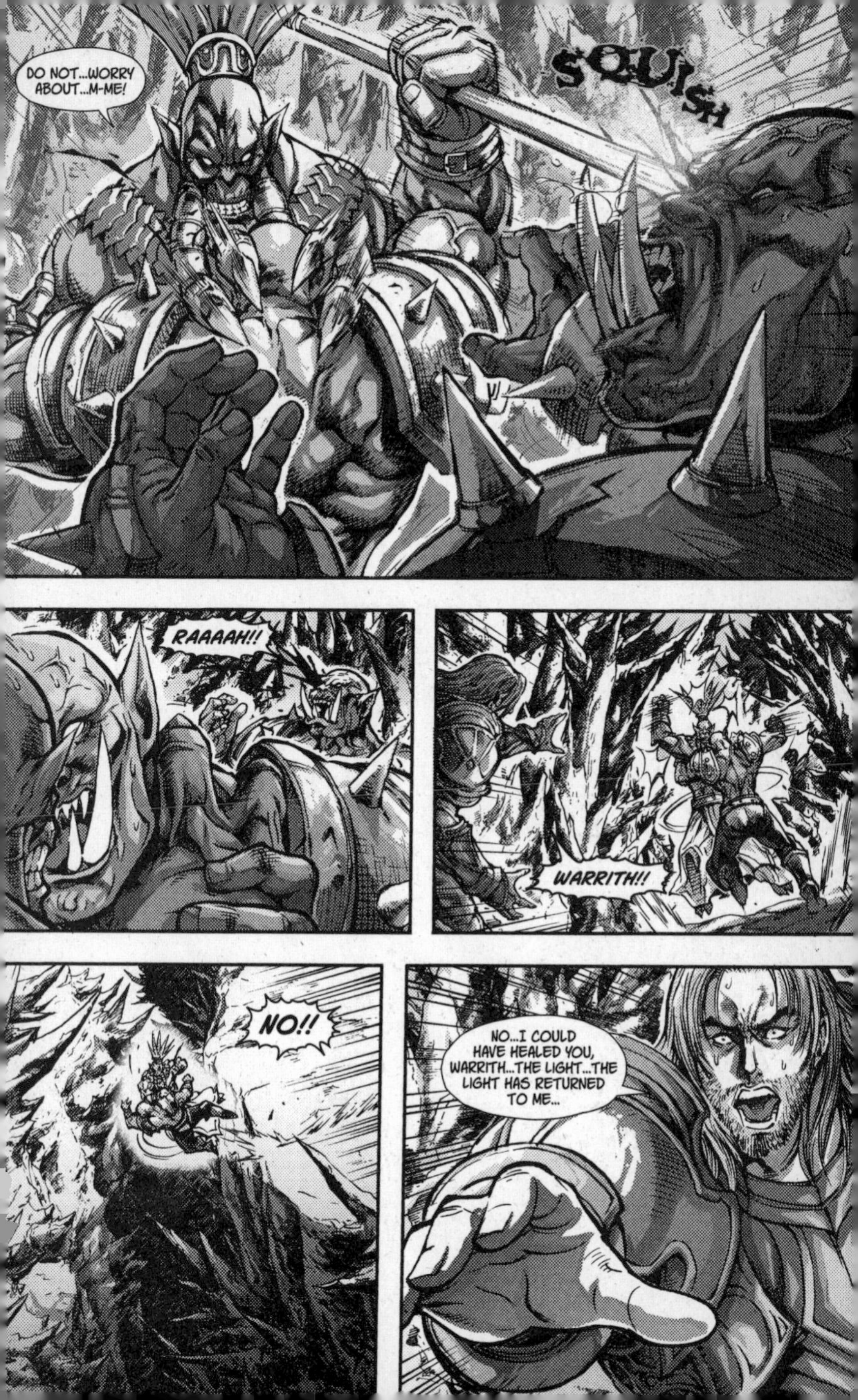
DO NOT...WORRY ABOUT...M-ME!
SQUISH
RAAAAH!!
WARRITH!!
NO!!
NO...I COULD HAVE HEALED YOU, WARRITH...THE LIGHT...THE LIGHT HAS RETURNED TO ME...

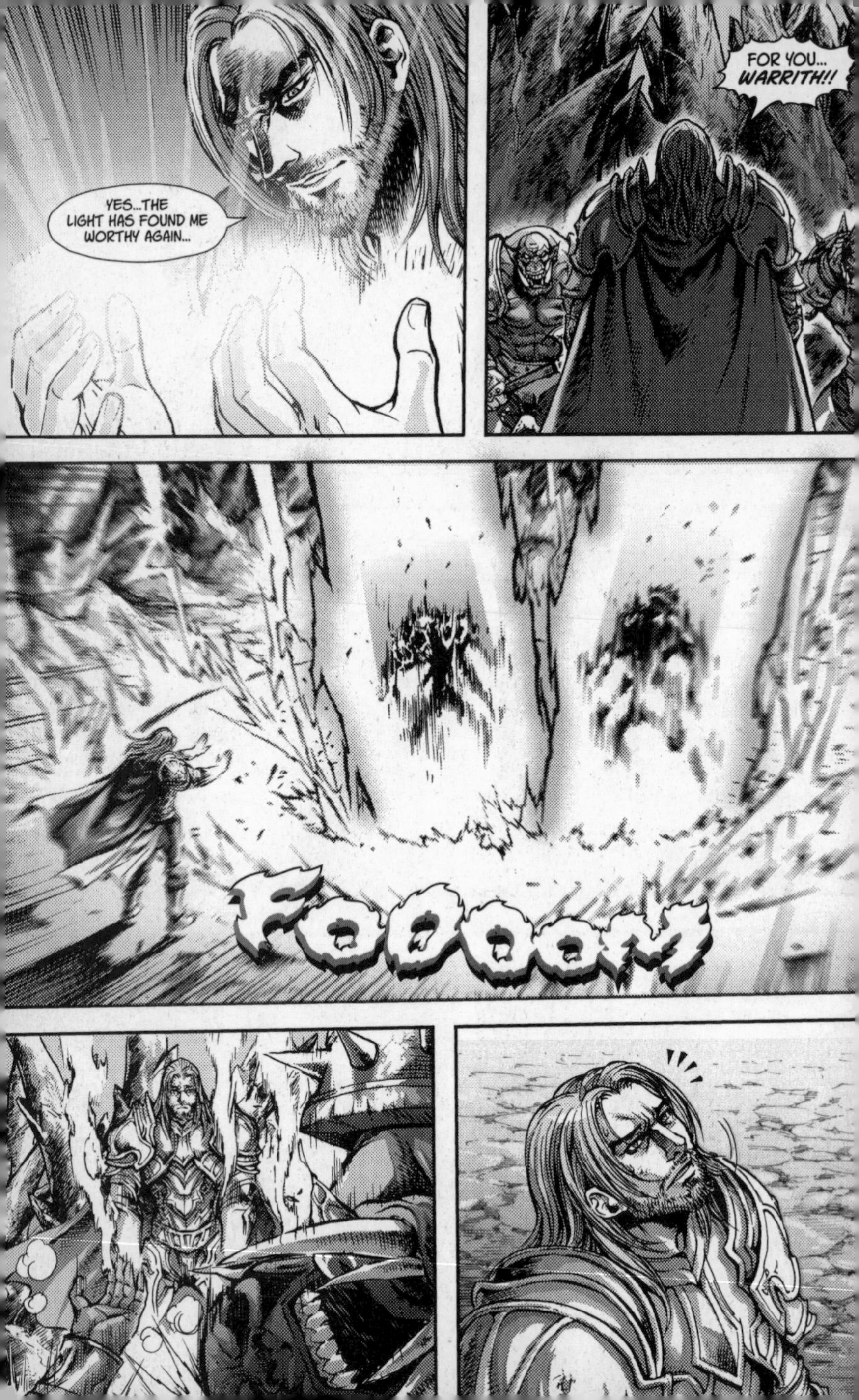
YES...THE LIGHT HAS FOUND ME WORTHY AGAIN...
FOR YOU... WARRITH!!
FOOOOM

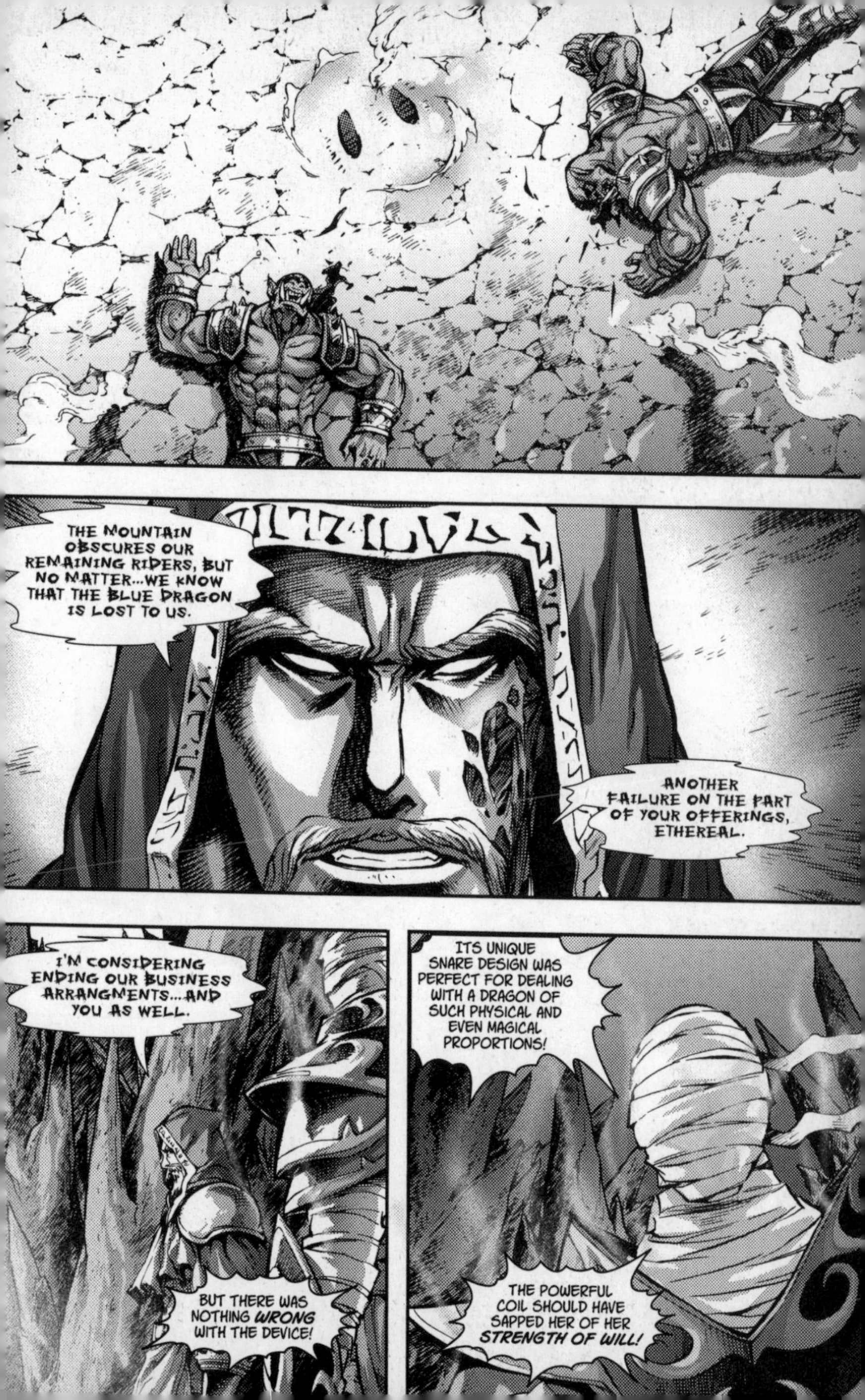
THE MOUNTAIN OBSCURES OUR REMAINING RIDERS, BUT NO MATTER...WE KNOW THAT THE BLUE DRAGON IS LOST TO US.
ANOTHER FAILURE ON THE PART OF YOUR OFFERINGS, ETHEREAL.
I'M CONSIDERING ENDING OUR BUSINESS ARRANGMENTS....AND YOU AS WELL.
BUT THERE WAS NOTHING *WRONG* WITH THE DEVICE!
ITS UNIQUE SNARE DESIGN WAS PERFECT FOR DEALING WITH A DRAGON OF SUCH PHYSICAL AND EVEN MAGICAL PROPORTIONS!
THE POWERFUL COIL SHOULD HAVE SAPPED HER OF HER ***STRENGTH OF WILL!***

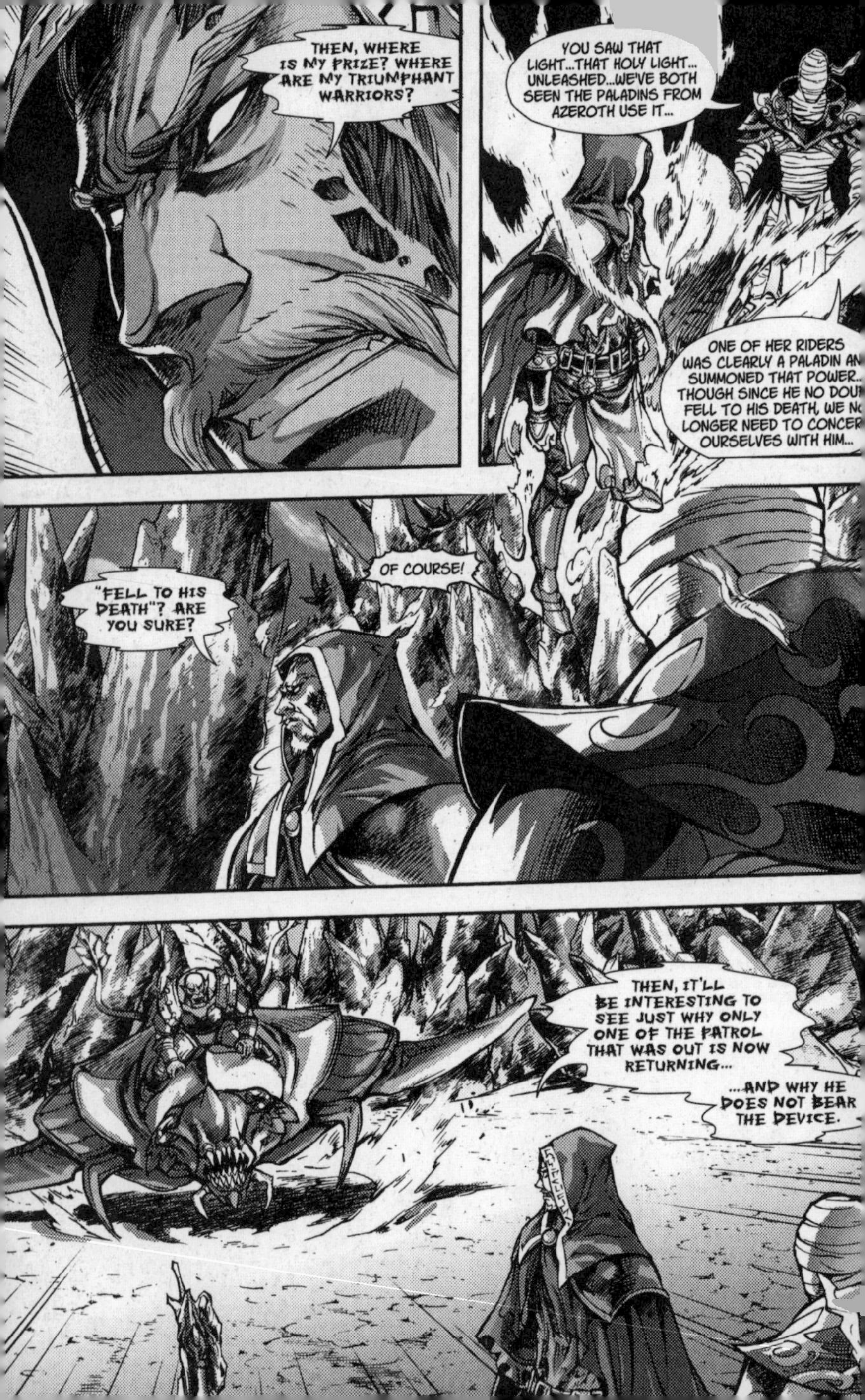
THEN, WHERE IS MY PRIZE? WHERE ARE MY TRIUMPHANT WARRIORS?
YOU SAW THAT LIGHT...THAT HOLY LIGHT... UNLEASHED...WE'VE BOTH SEEN THE PALADINS FROM AZEROTH USE IT...
ONE OF HER RIDERS WAS CLEARLY A PALADIN AN SUMMONED THAT POWER... THOUGH SINCE HE NO DOU FELL TO HIS DEATH, WE N LONGER NEED TO CONCER OURSELVES WITH HIM...
"FELL TO HIS DEATH"? ARE YOU SURE?
OF COURSE!
THEN, IT'LL BE INTERESTING TO SEE JUST WHY ONLY ONE OF THE PATROL THAT WAS OUT IS NOW RETURNING...
...AND WHY HE DOES NOT BEAR THE DEVICE.

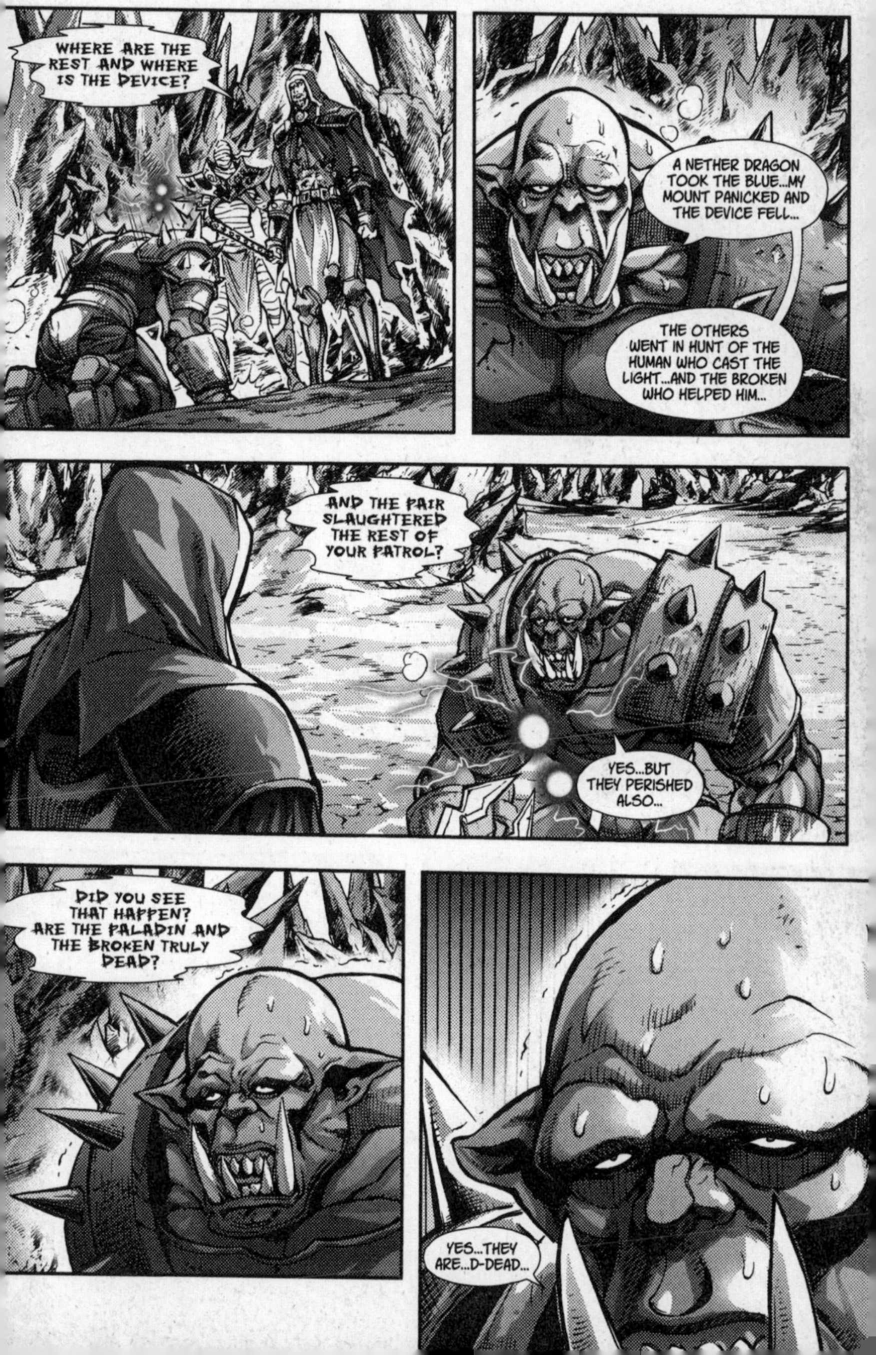
WHERE ARE THE REST AND WHERE IS THE DEVICE?
A NETHER DRAGON TOOK THE BLUE...MY MOUNT PANICKED AND THE DEVICE FELL...
THE OTHERS WENT IN HUNT OF THE HUMAN WHO CAST THE LIGHT...AND THE BROKEN WHO HELPED HIM...
AND THE PAIR SLAUGHTERED THE REST OF YOUR PATROL?
YES...BUT THEY PERISHED ALSO...
DID YOU SEE THAT HAPPEN? ARE THE PALADIN AND THE BROKEN TRULY DEAD?
YES...THEY ARE...D-DEAD...

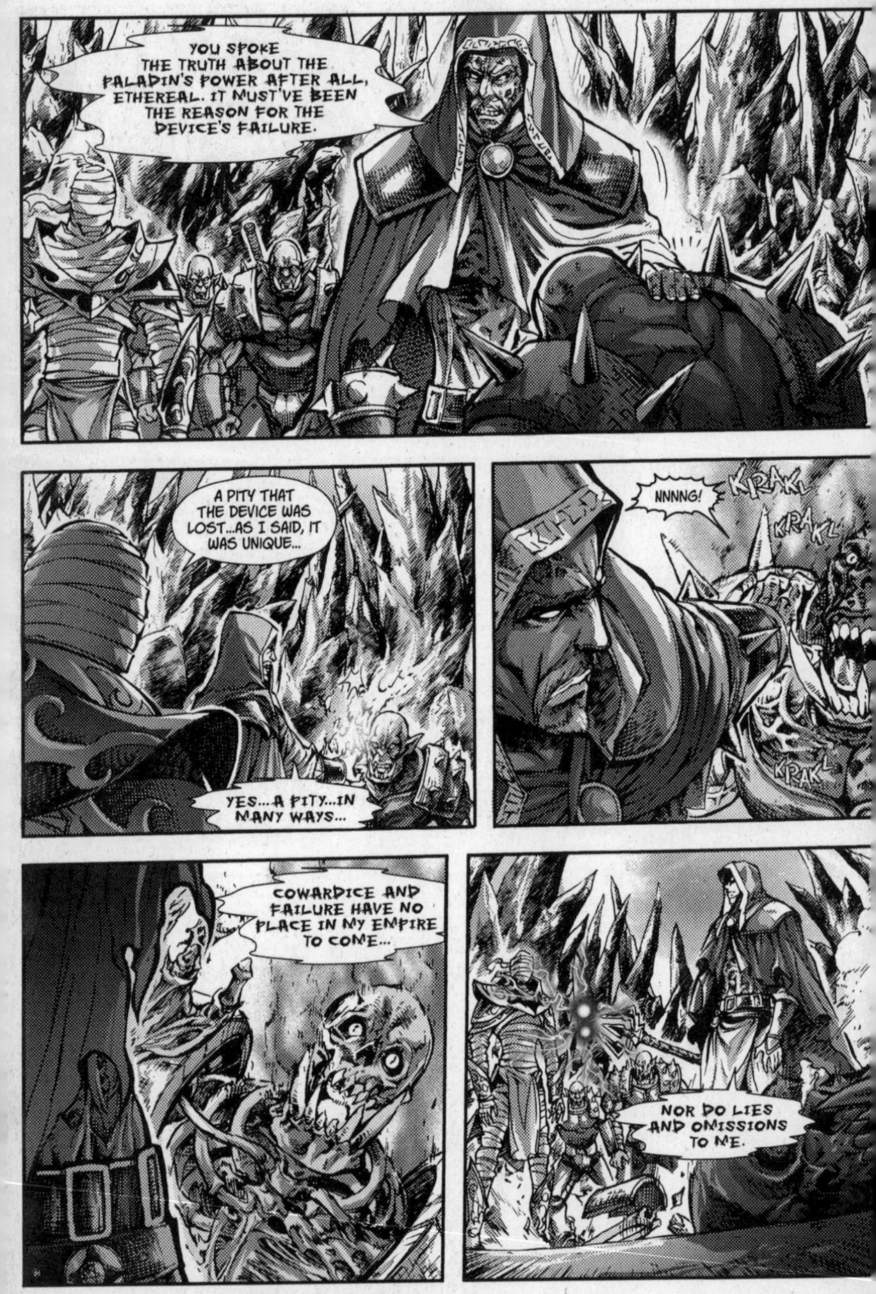
YOU SPOKE THE TRUTH ABOUT THE PALADIN'S POWER AFTER ALL, ETHEREAL. IT MUST'VE BEEN THE REASON FOR THE DEVICE'S FAILURE.
A PITY THAT THE DEVICE WAS LOST...AS I SAID, IT WAS UNIQUE...
YES...A PITY...IN MANY WAYS...
NNNNG!
KRAKL
KRAKL
KRAKL
COWARDICE AND FAILURE HAVE NO PLACE IN MY EMPIRE TO COME...
NOR DO LIES AND OMISSIONS TO ME.

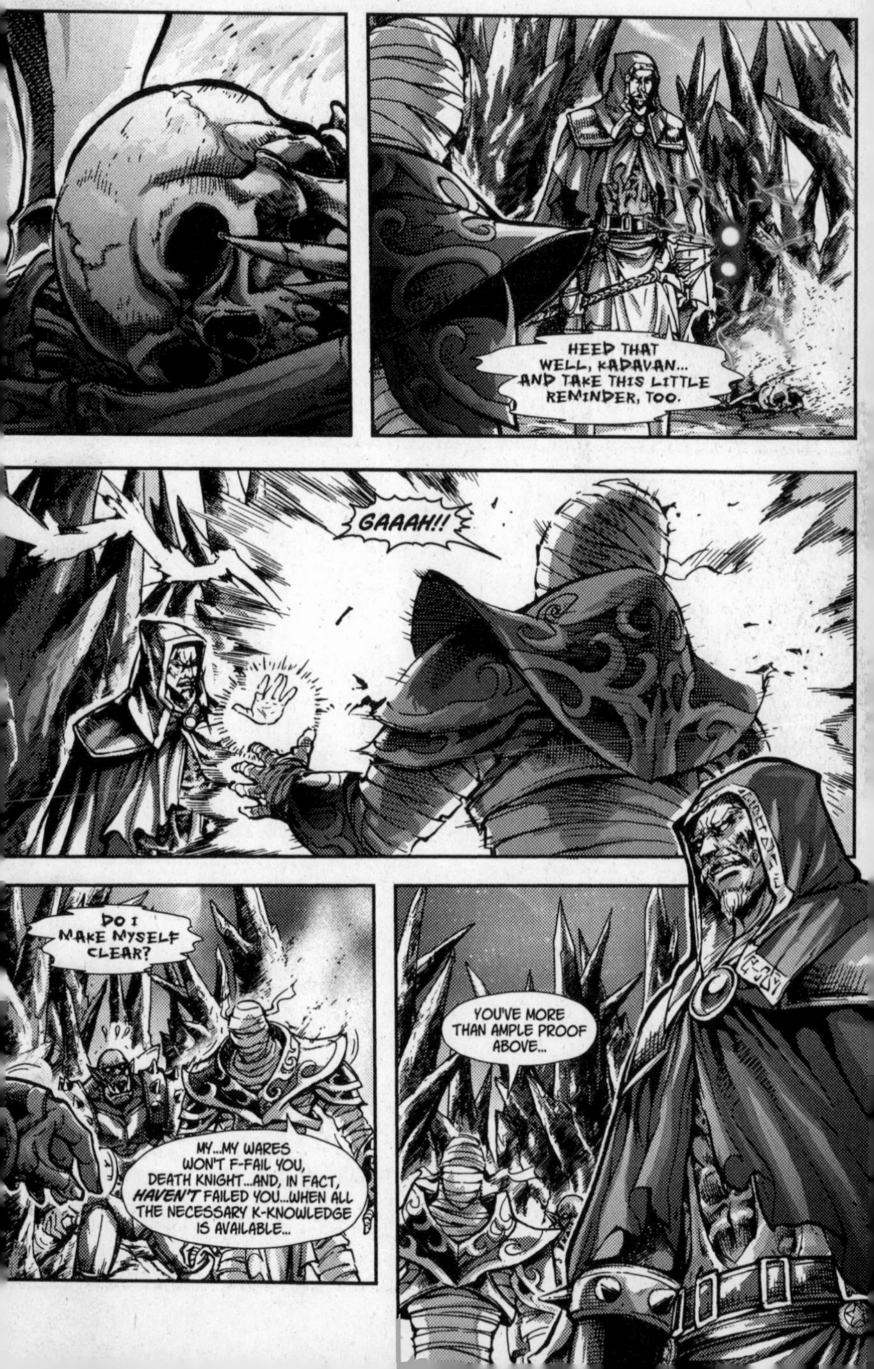
HEED THAT WELL, KADAVAN... AND TAKE THIS LITTLE REMINDER, TOO.
GAAAH!!
DO I MAKE MYSELF CLEAR?
MY...MY WARES WON'T F-FAIL YOU, DEATH KNIGHT...AND, IN FACT, *HAVEN'T* FAILED YOU...WHEN ALL THE NECESSARY K-KNOWLEDGE IS AVAILABLE...
YOU'VE MORE THAN AMPLE PROOF ABOVE...

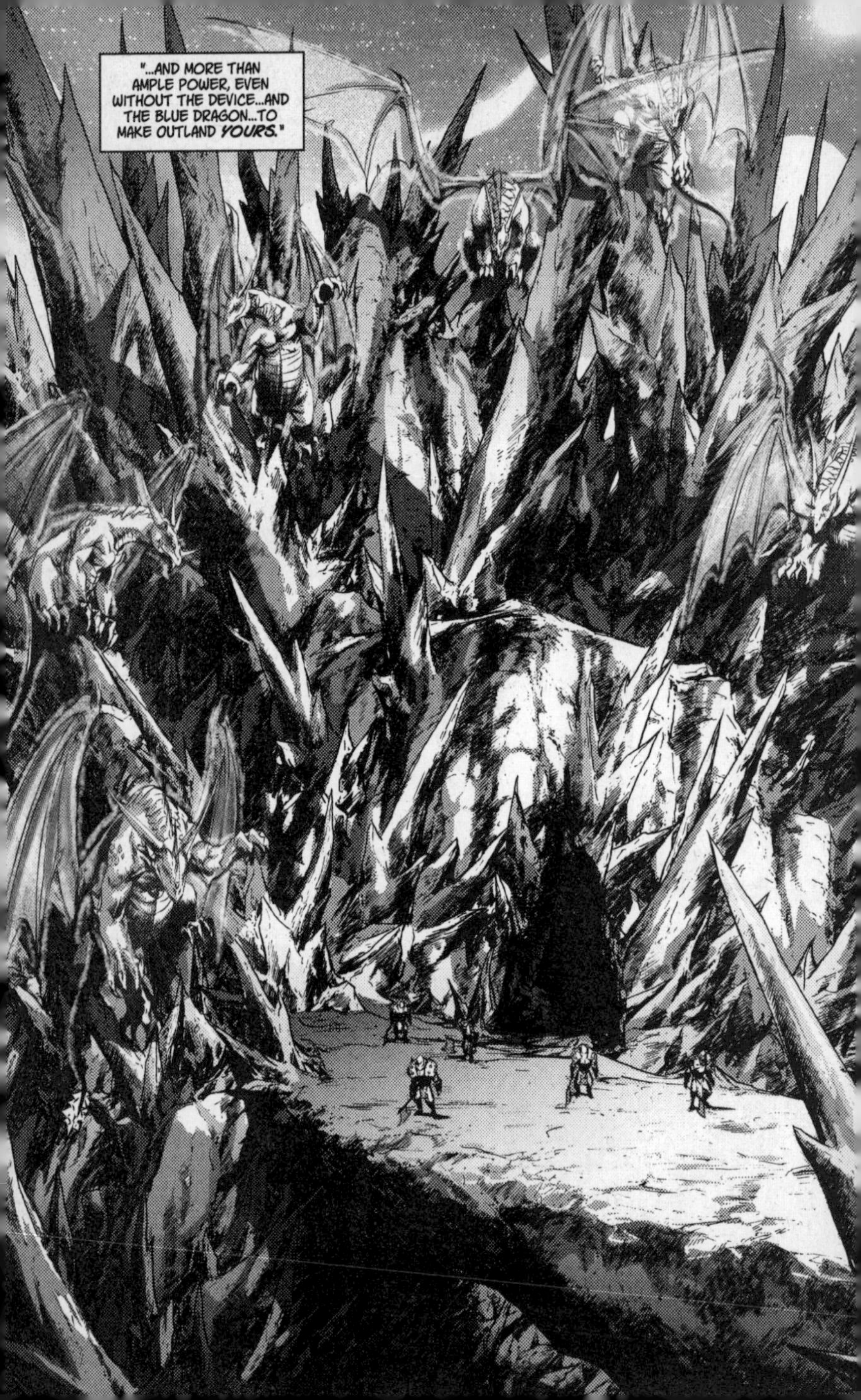
"...AND MORE THAN AMPLE POWER, EVEN WITHOUT THE DEVICE...AND THE BLUE DRAGON...TO MAKE OUTLAND *YOURS*."

CHAPTER SIX
SHADOW'S LEGACY

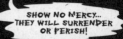

SHOW NO MERCY...
THEY WILL SURRENDER
OR PERISH!

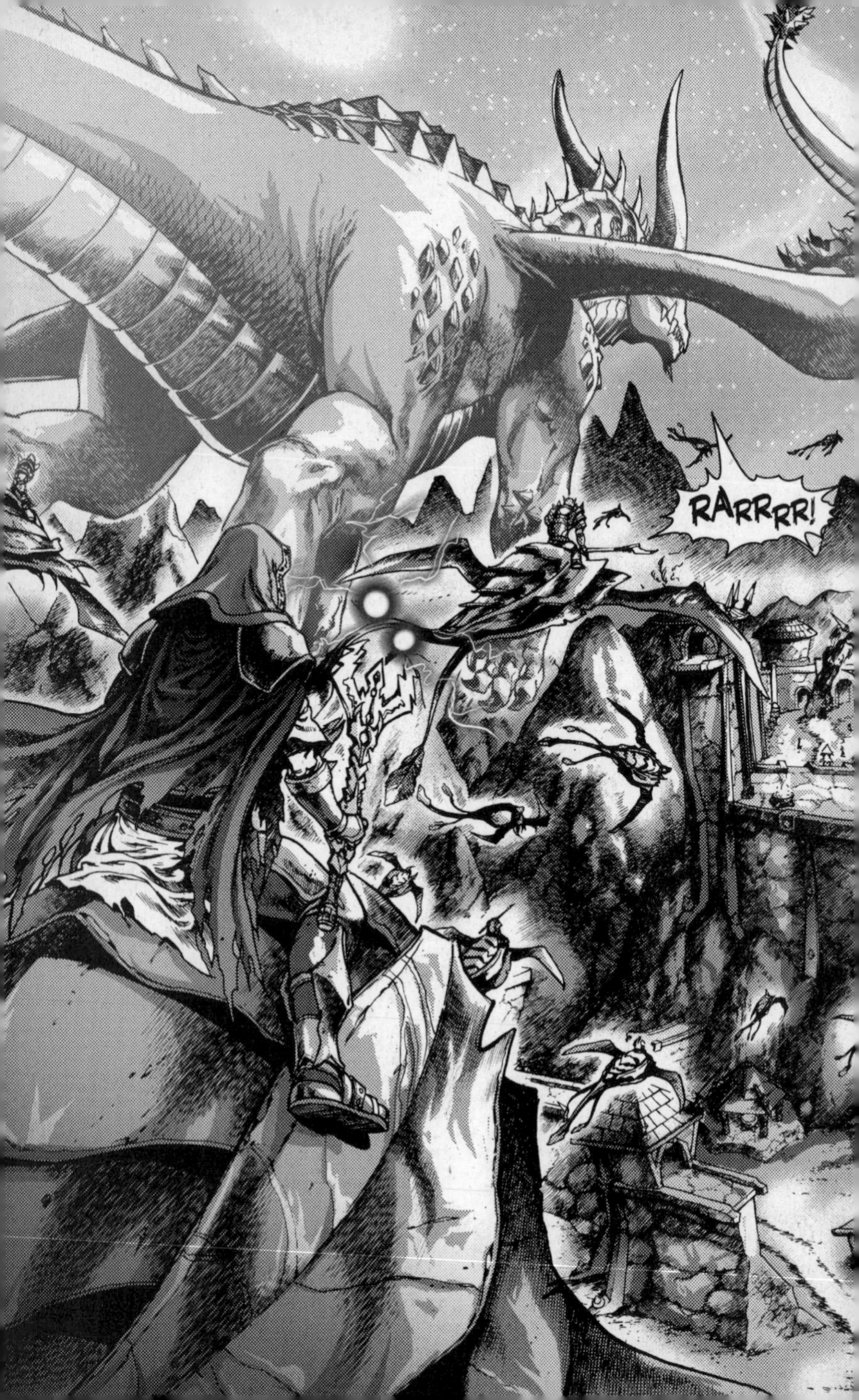
RARRRR!

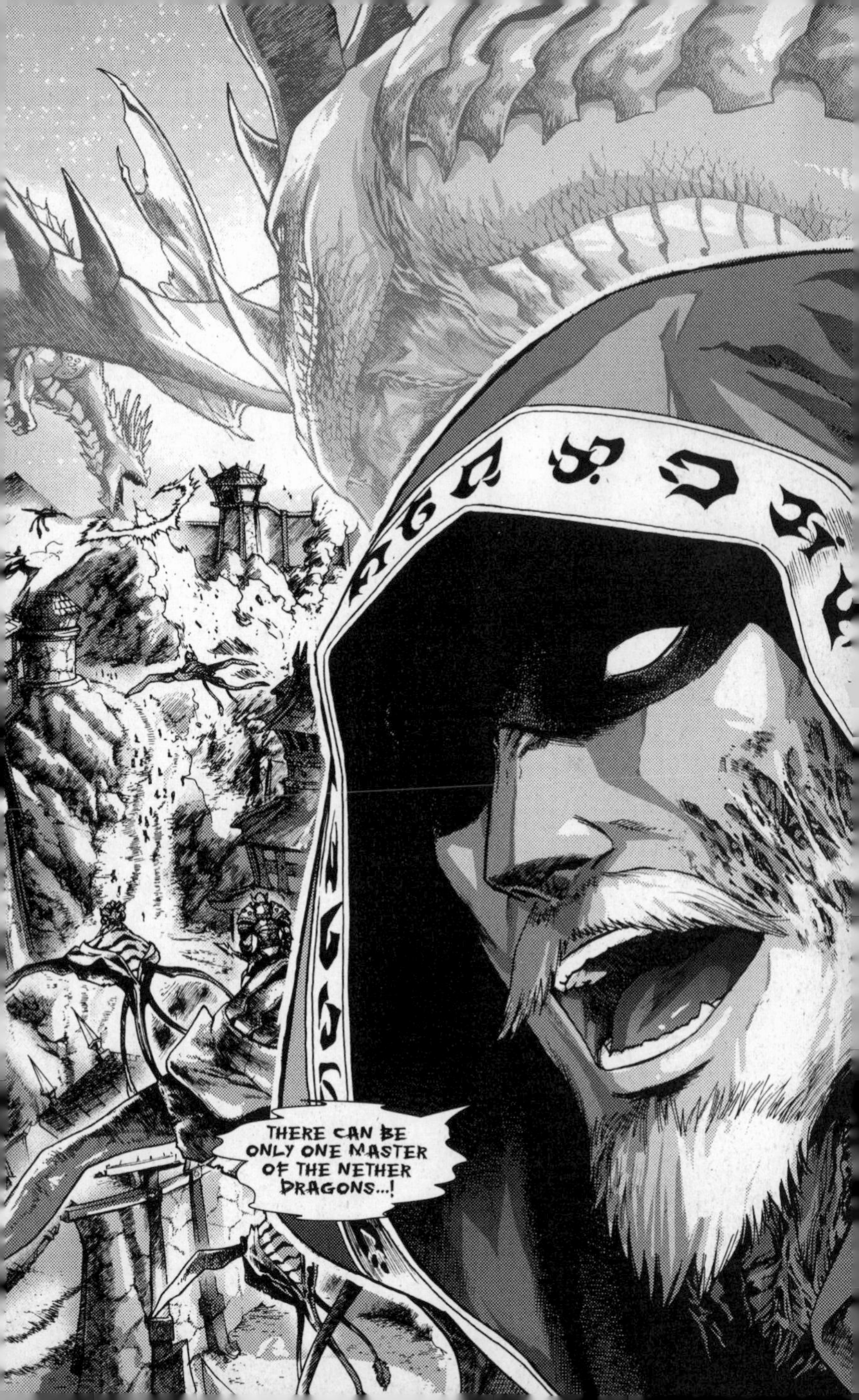
THERE CAN BE ONLY ONE MASTER OF THE NETHER DRAGONS...!

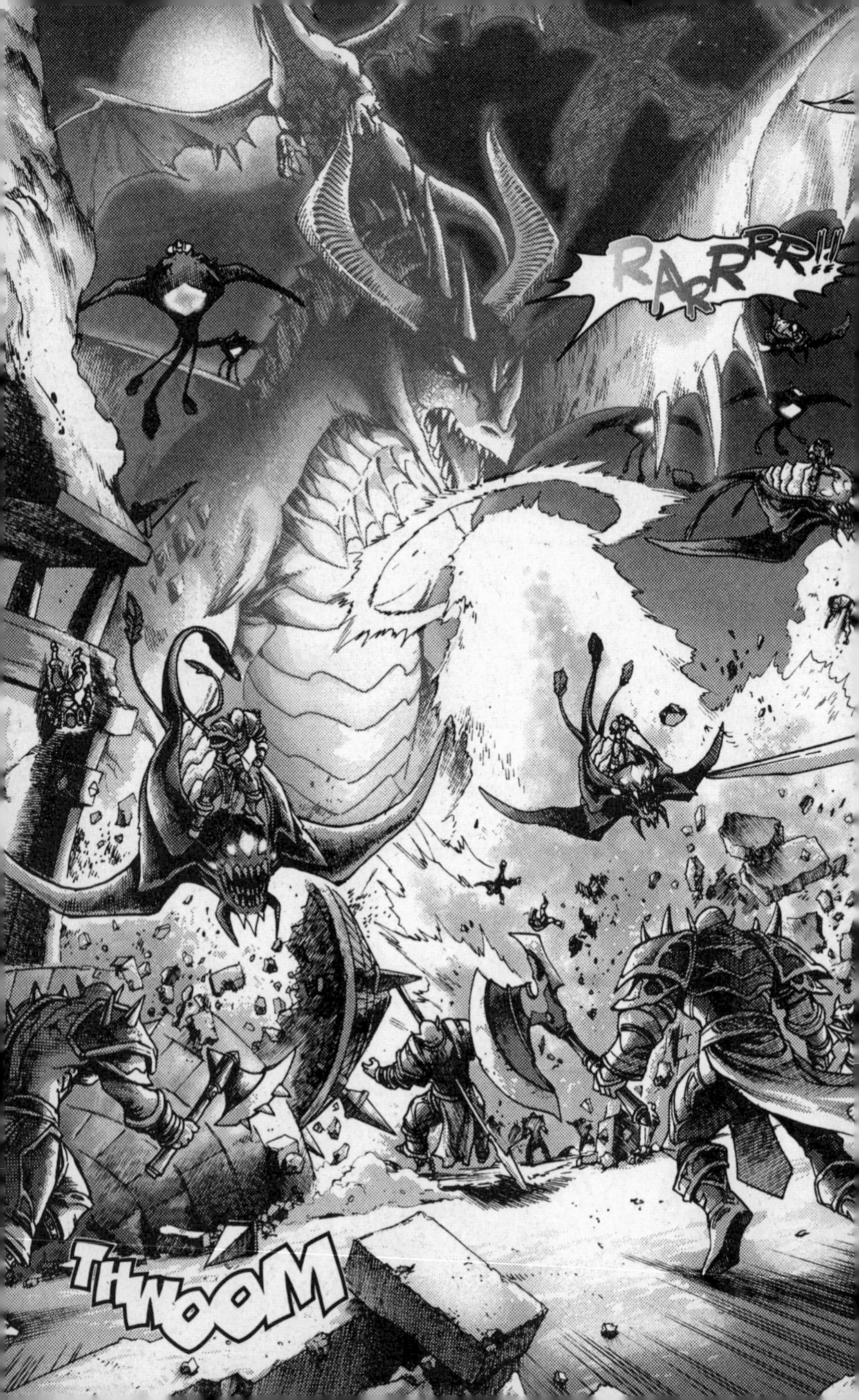
RARRRRR!!
THWOOM

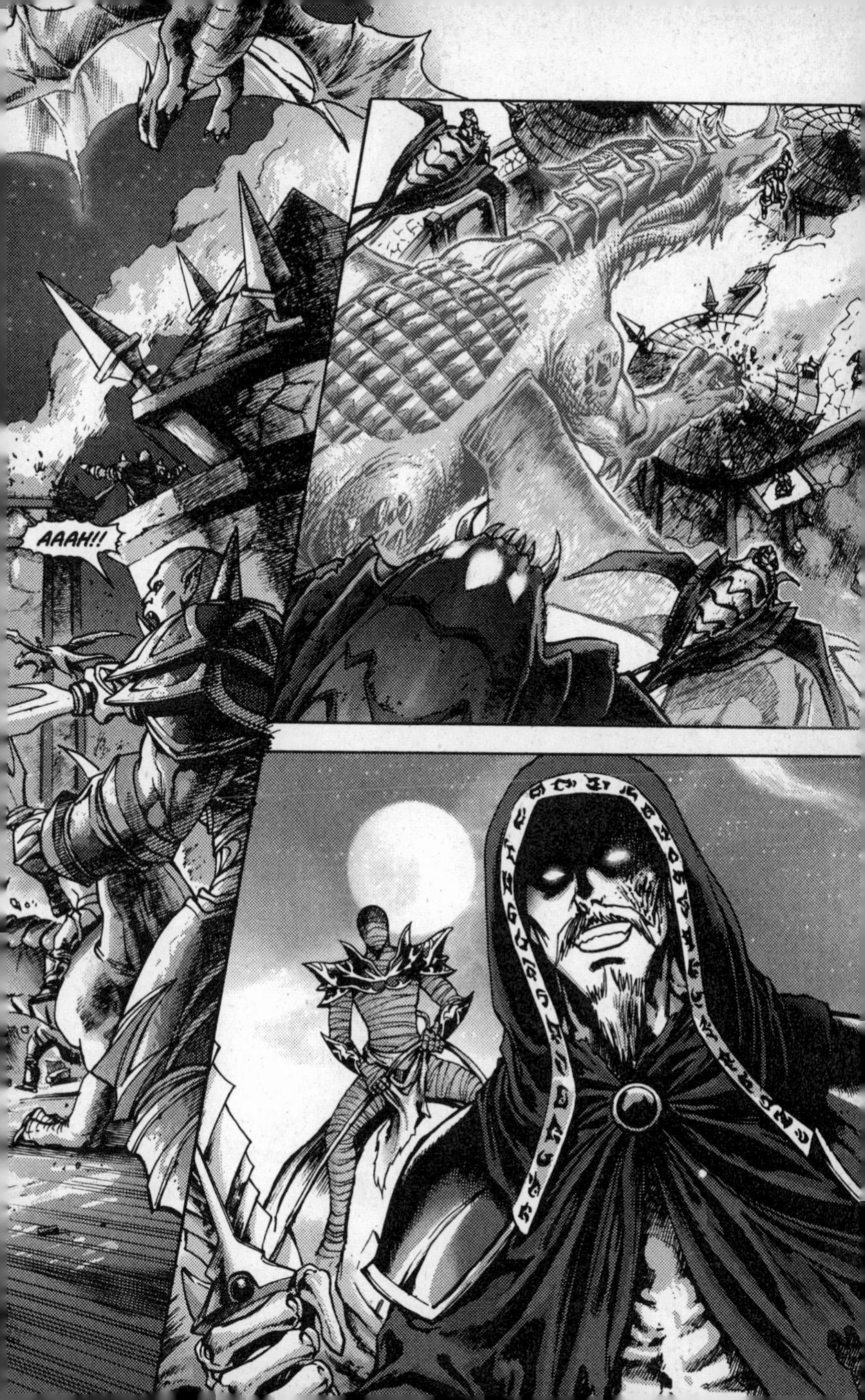
AAAH!!

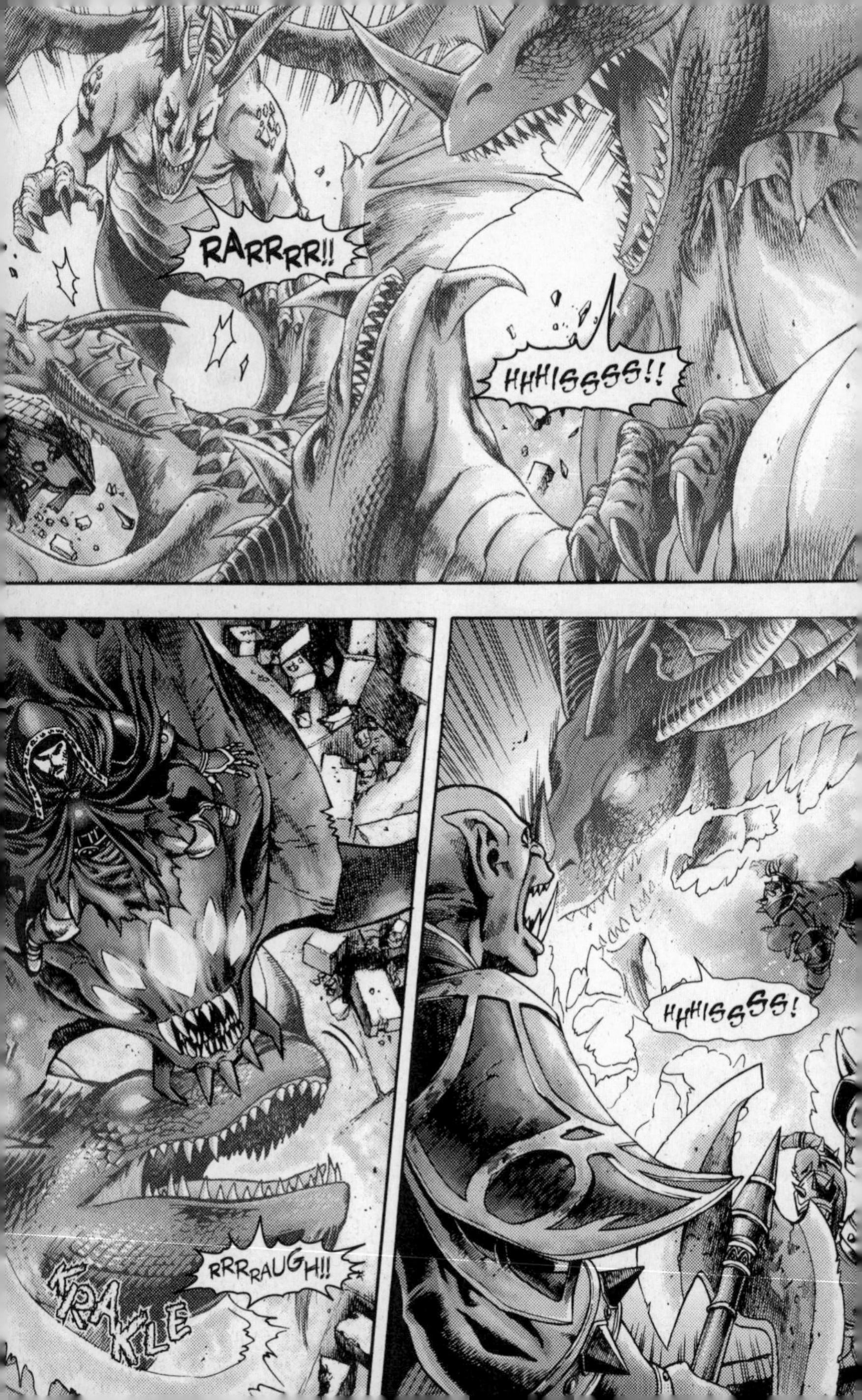
RARRRR!!
HHHISSSS!!
RRRRAUGH!!
KRAKLE
HHHISSSS!

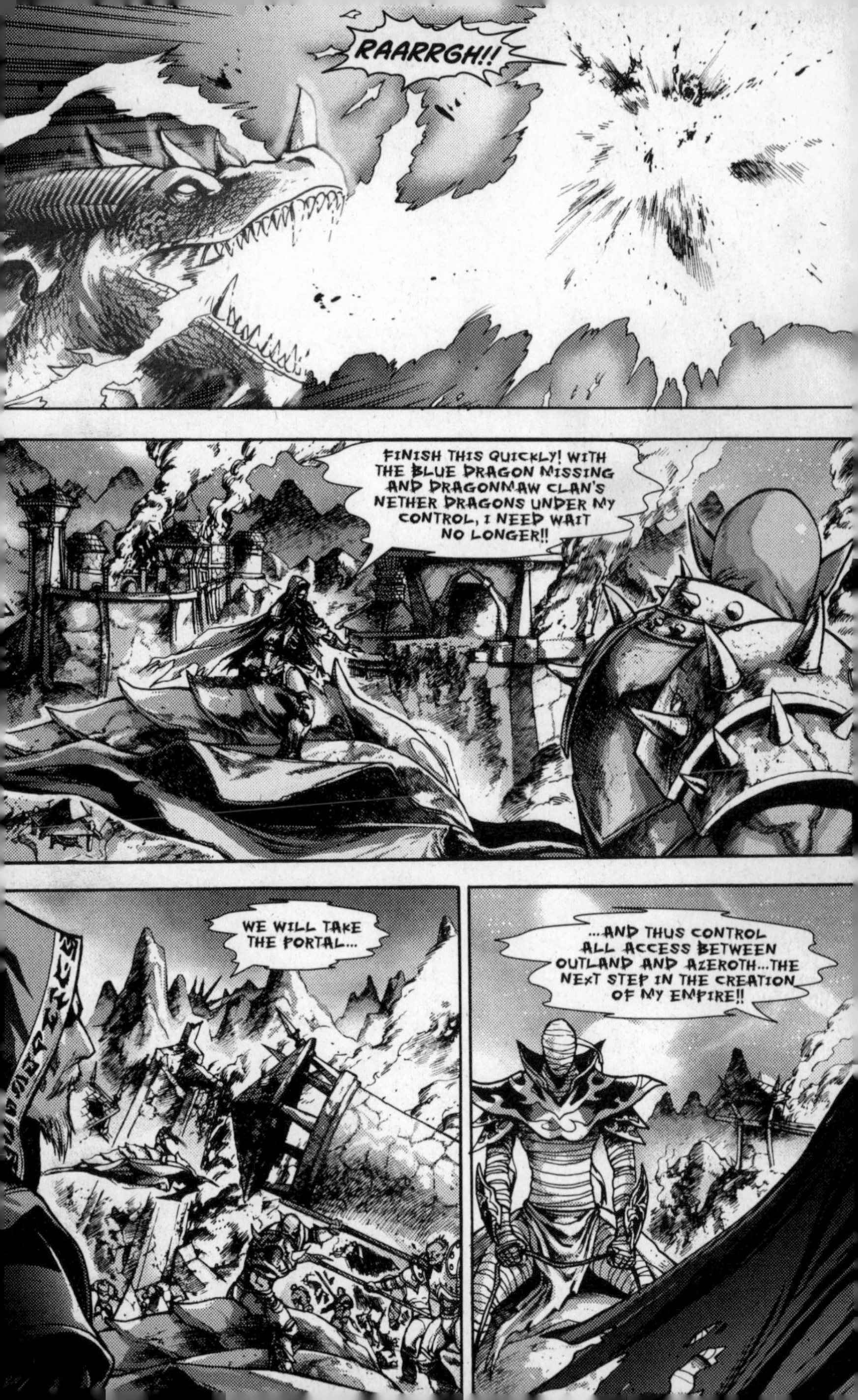
RAARRGH!!
FINISH THIS QUICKLY! WITH THE BLUE DRAGON MISSING AND DRAGONMAW CLAN'S NETHER DRAGONS UNDER MY CONTROL, I NEED WAIT NO LONGER!!
WE WILL TAKE THE PORTAL...
...AND THUS CONTROL ALL ACCESS BETWEEN OUTLAND AND AZEROTH...THE NEXT STEP IN THE CREATION OF MY EMPIRE!!

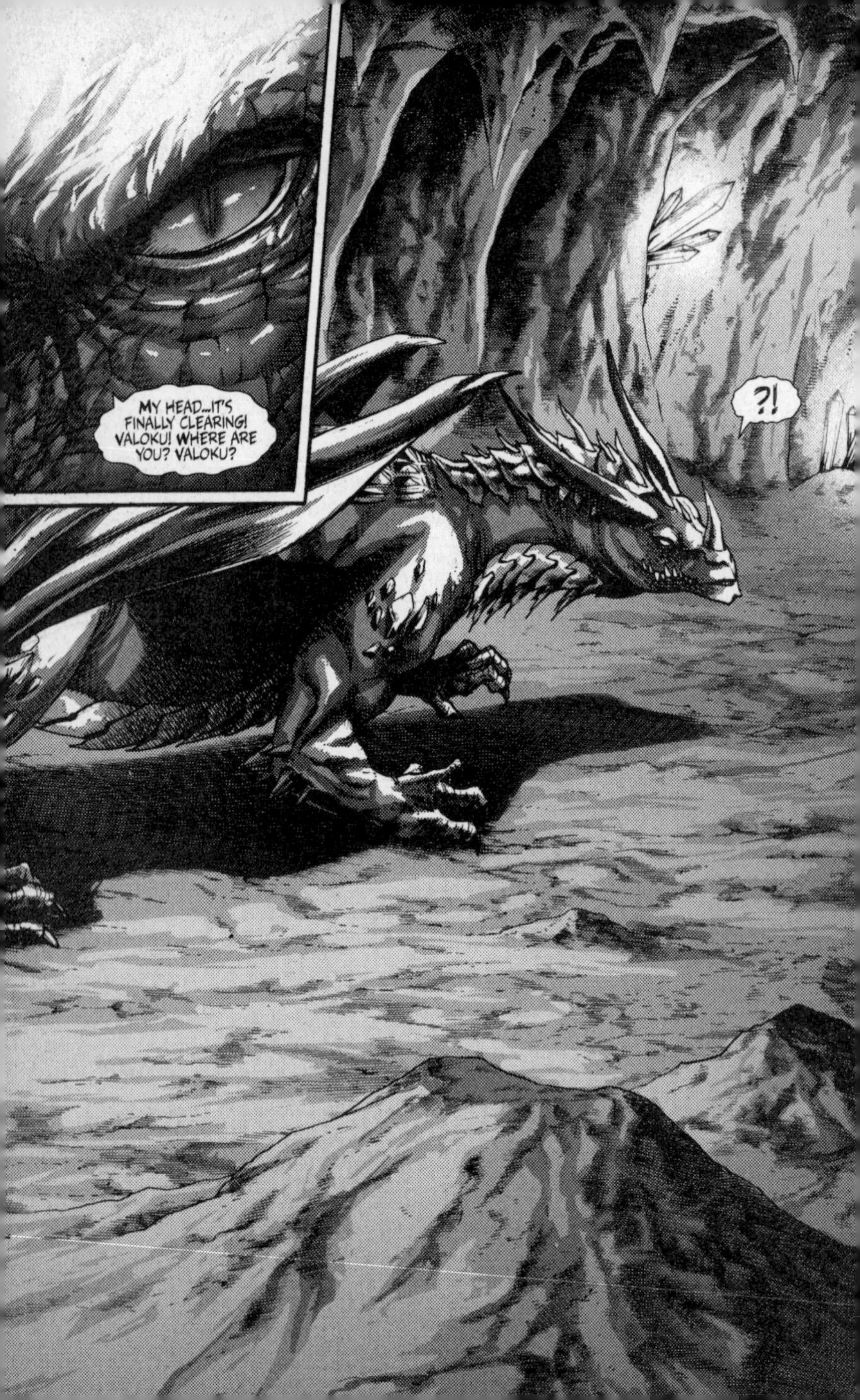
MY HEAD...IT'S FINALLY CLEARING! VALOKU! WHERE ARE YOU? VALOKU?
?!

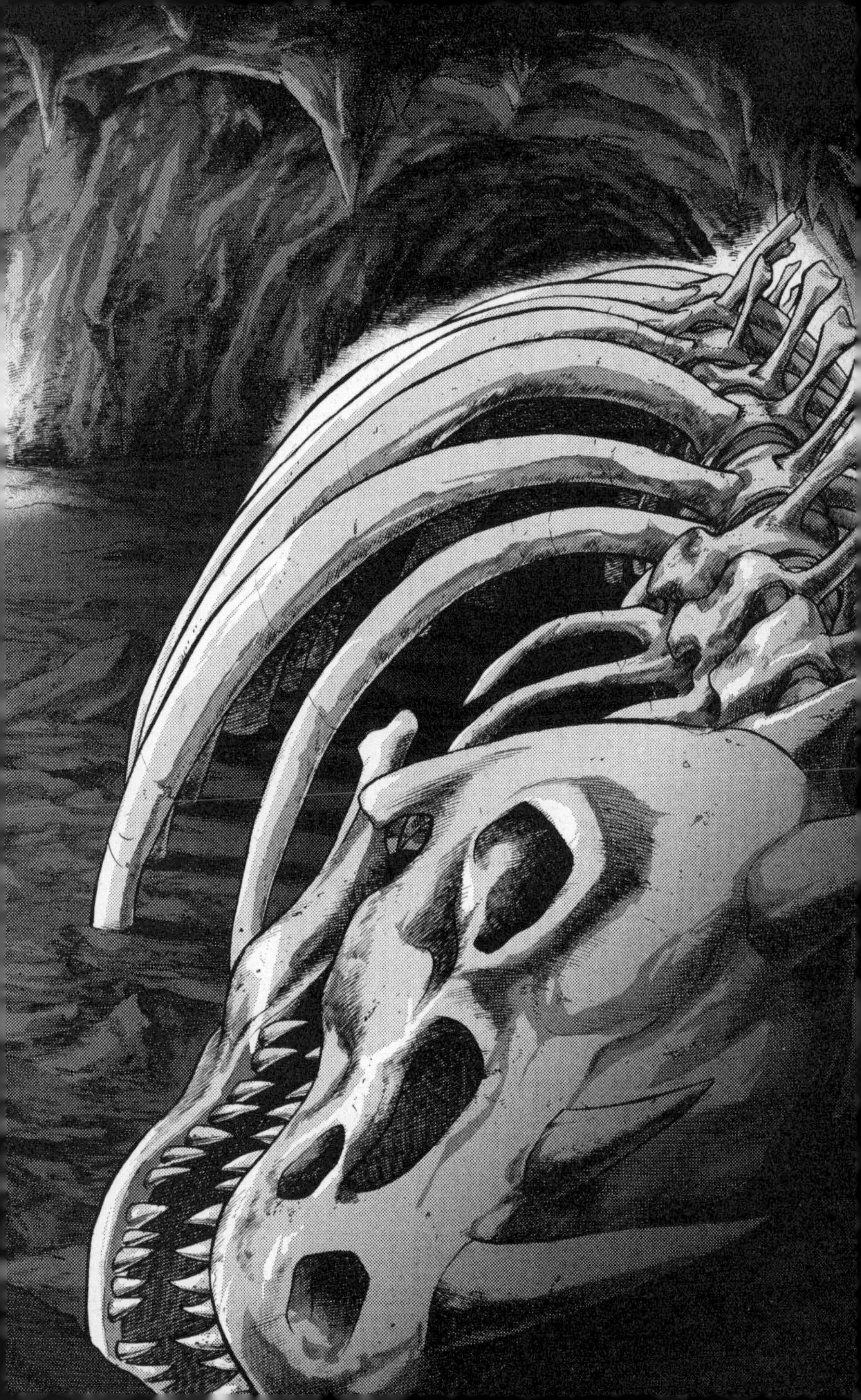

THE MAGICAL TRACES ARE UNMISTAKABLE! THIS CAN ONLY BE ANOTHER OF THE BLACK DRAGONS... LIKE THE ONE IMPALED...ONE OF MONSTROUS *DEATHWING'S* DRAGONFLIGHT...

BUT WHAT WAS *DEATHWING THE DESTROYER* AND HIS ILK DOING HERE? WHAT WERE HIS SERVANTS WILLING TO DIE FOR TO PROTECT?

FOR WHAT REASON WOULD THE MALEVOLENT ONE SPREAD HIS EVIL TO OUTLAND?

HMMM...THIS BLACK DRAGON PERISHED LONG AGO... SO WHATEVER HAPPENED IS LIKELY PAST AND OF NO MORE CONCERN...

BESIDES...I SUPPOSE I SHOULD SEE TO *JORAD*... AND *WARRITH*...THEY MAY NEED HELP...

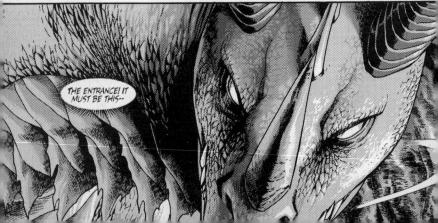

THE ENTRANCE! IT MUST BE THIS--

WHERE IS IT~?

HIDING THE WAY OUT? AS IF AN ILLUSION COULD STAND AGAINST THE MAGIC OF A BLUE DRAGON!

THWWWWWUMMM

SWOOOSH

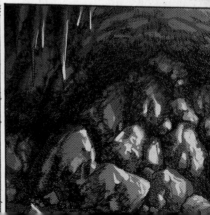

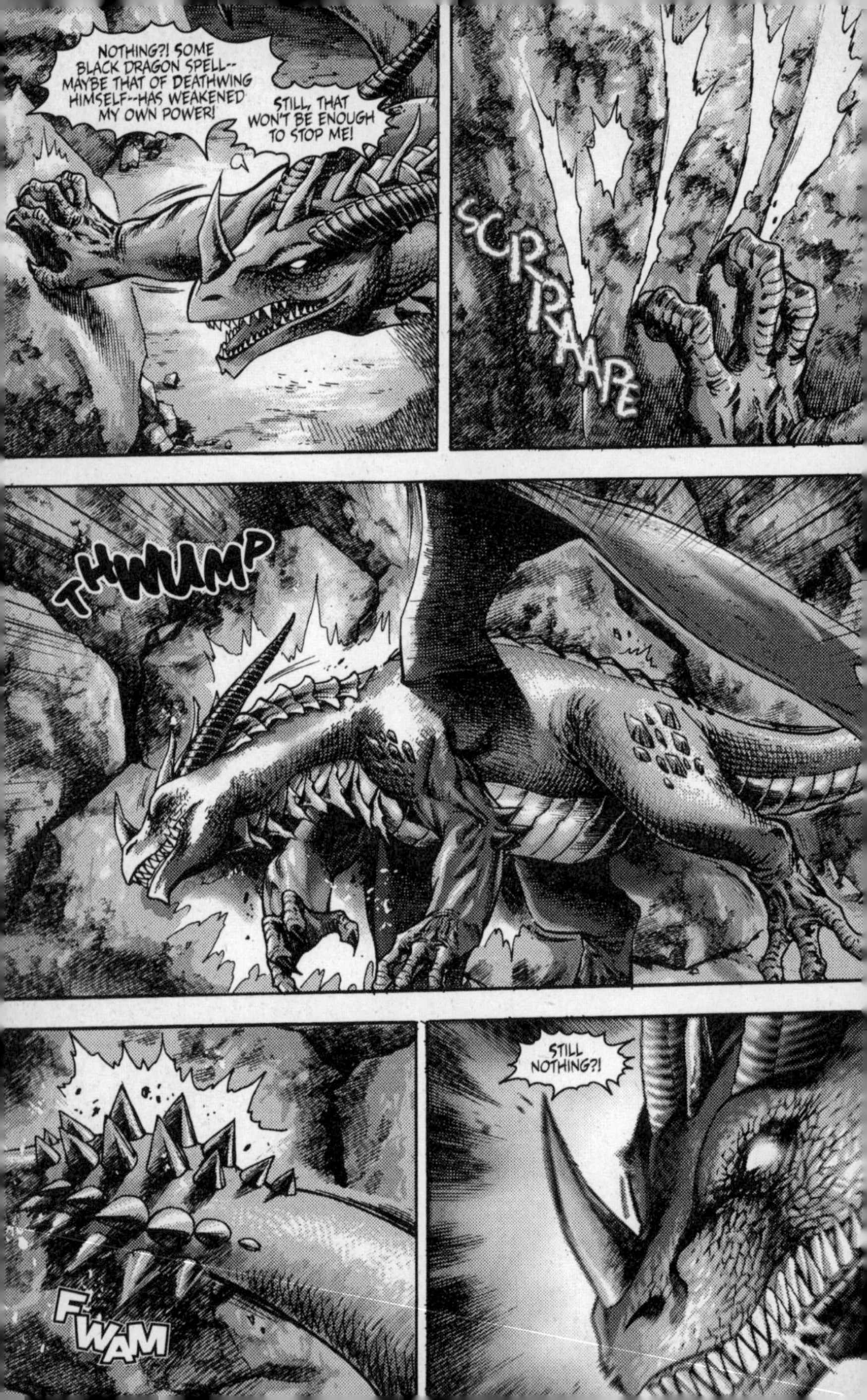
NOTHING?! SOME BLACK DRAGON SPELL--MAYBE THAT OF DEATHWING HIMSELF--HAS WEAKENED MY OWN POWER!
STILL, THAT WON'T BE ENOUGH TO STOP ME!
SCRRAAAPE
THWUMP
FWAM
STILL NOTHING?!

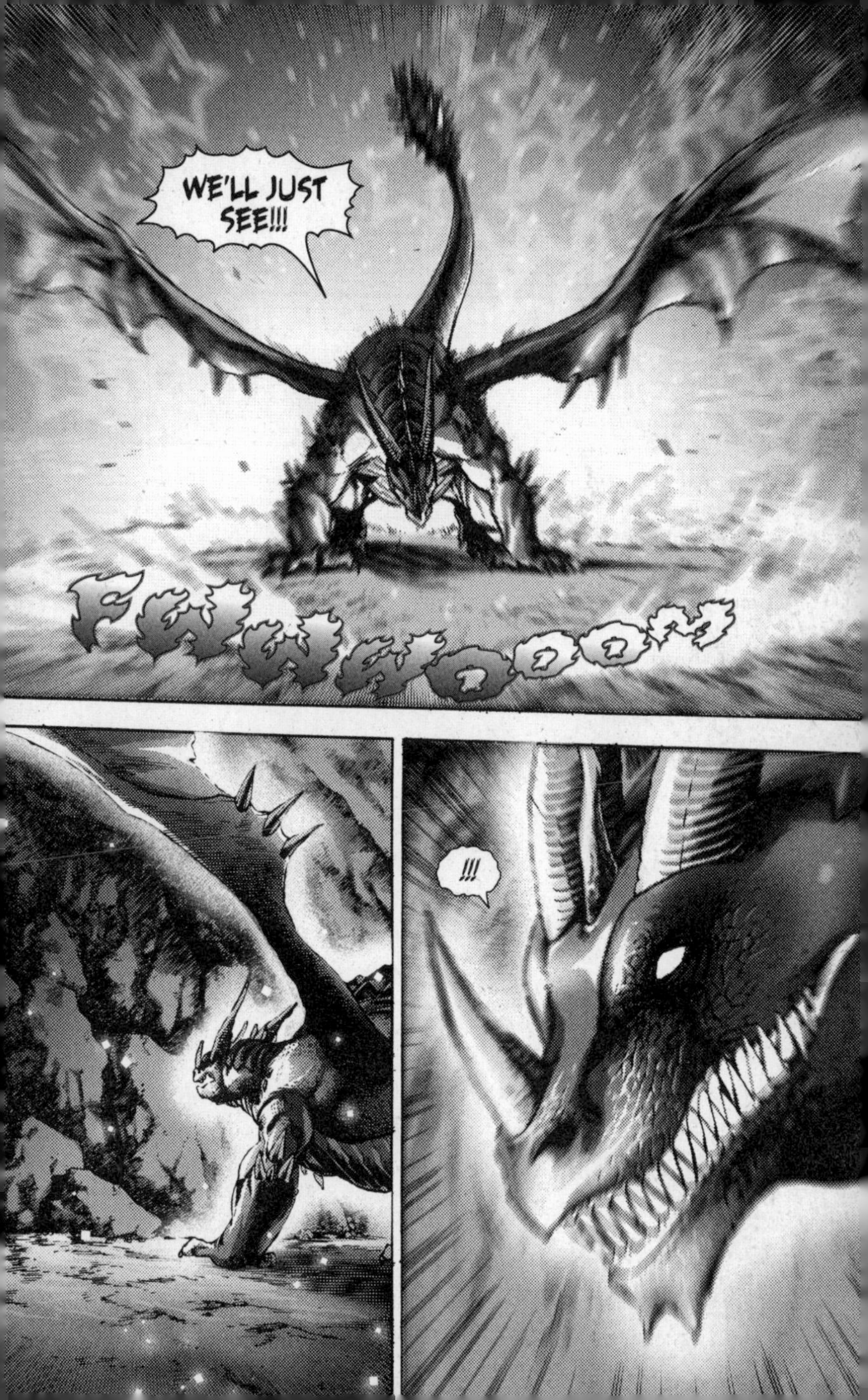
WE'LL JUST SEE!!!
FWWOOOM
!!!

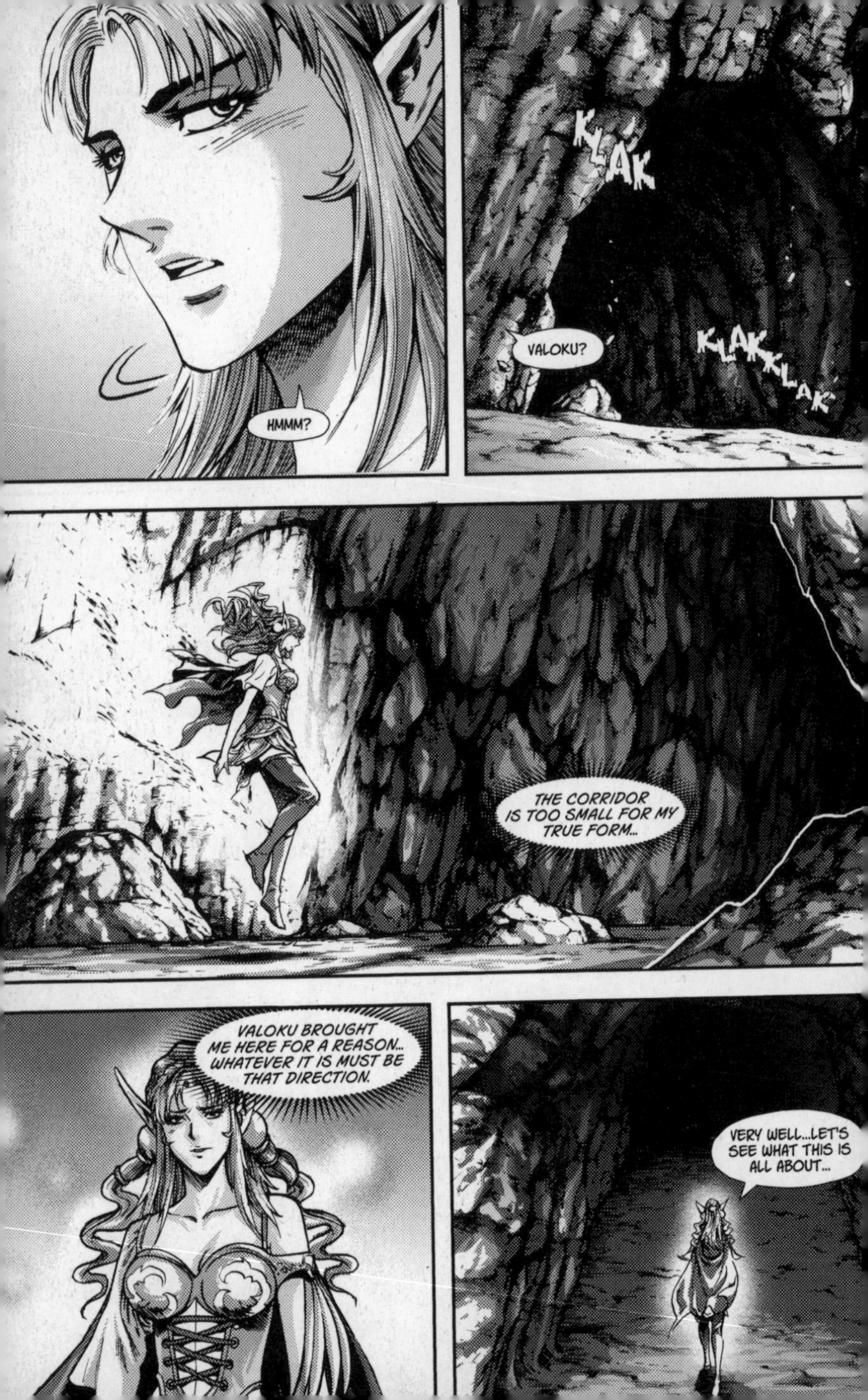
HMMM?
KLAK
VALOKU?
KLAKKLAKKLAK
THE CORRIDOR IS TOO SMALL FOR MY TRUE FORM...
VALOKU BROUGHT ME HERE FOR A REASON... WHATEVER IT IS MUST BE THAT DIRECTION.
VERY WELL...LET'S SEE WHAT THIS IS ALL ABOUT...

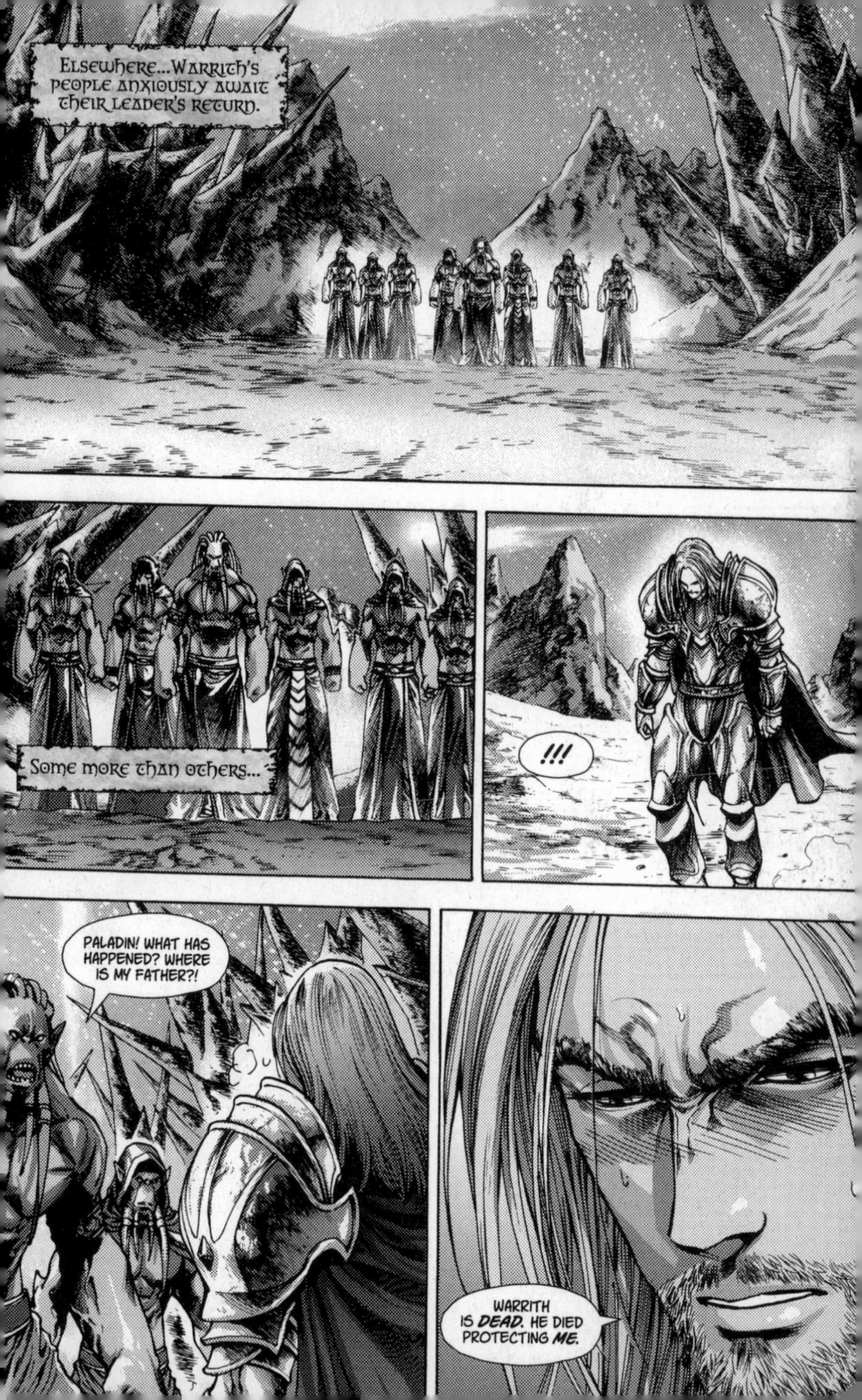
ELSEWHERE...WARRITH'S PEOPLE ANXIOUSLY AWAIT THEIR LEADER'S RETURN.
SOME MORE THAN OTHERS...
!!!
PALADIN! WHAT HAS HAPPENED? WHERE IS MY FATHER?!
WARRITH IS DEAD. HE DIED PROTECTING ME.

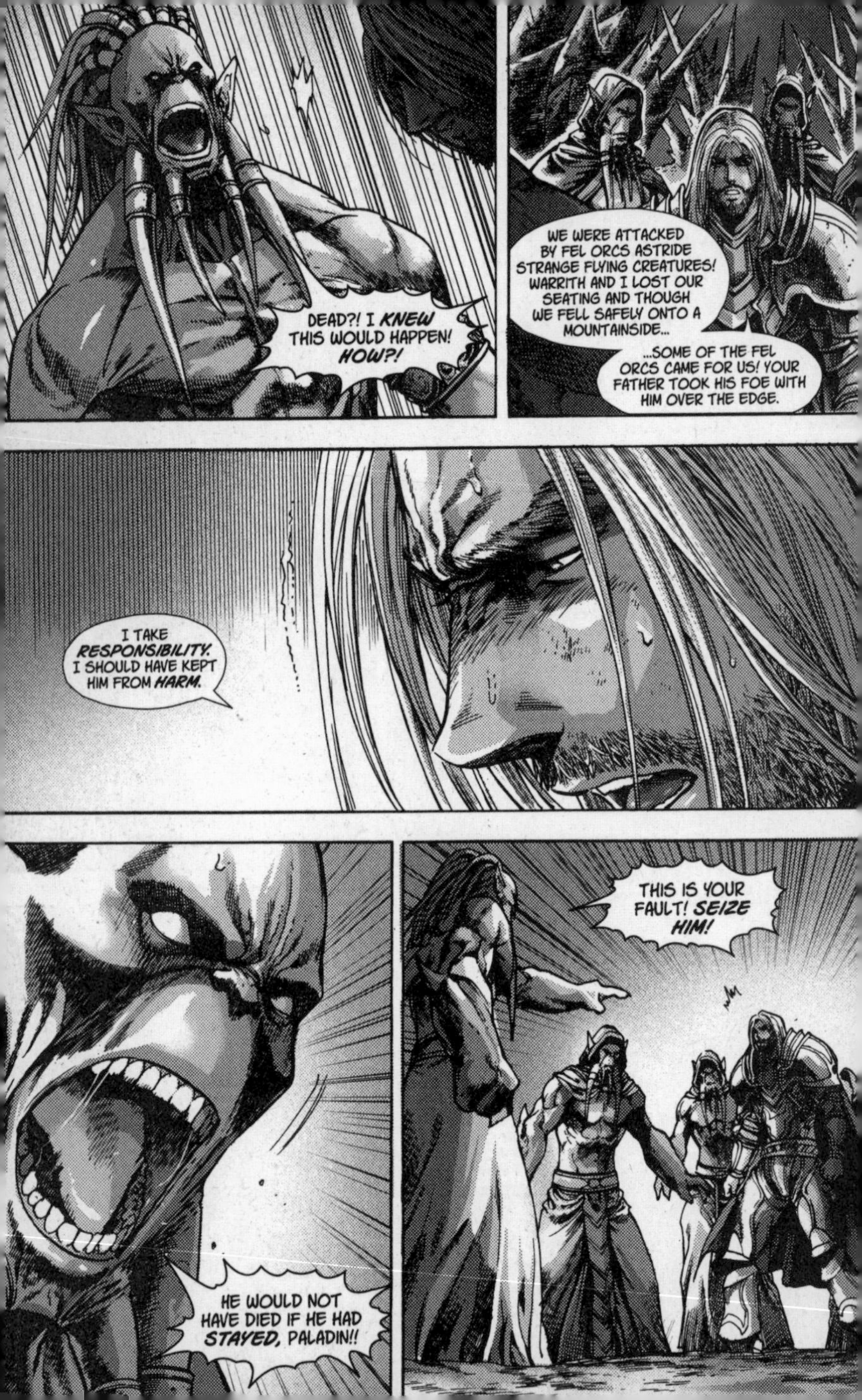

DEAD?! I KNEW THIS WOULD HAPPEN! HOW?!
WE WERE ATTACKED BY FEL ORCS ASTRIDE STRANGE FLYING CREATURES! WARRITH AND I LOST OUR SEATING AND THOUGH WE FELL SAFELY ONTO A MOUNTAINSIDE...
...SOME OF THE FEL ORCS CAME FOR US! YOUR FATHER TOOK HIS FOE WITH HIM OVER THE EDGE.
I TAKE RESPONSIBILITY. I SHOULD HAVE KEPT HIM FROM HARM.
HE WOULD NOT HAVE DIED IF HE HAD STAYED, PALADIN!!
THIS IS YOUR FAULT! SEIZE HIM!

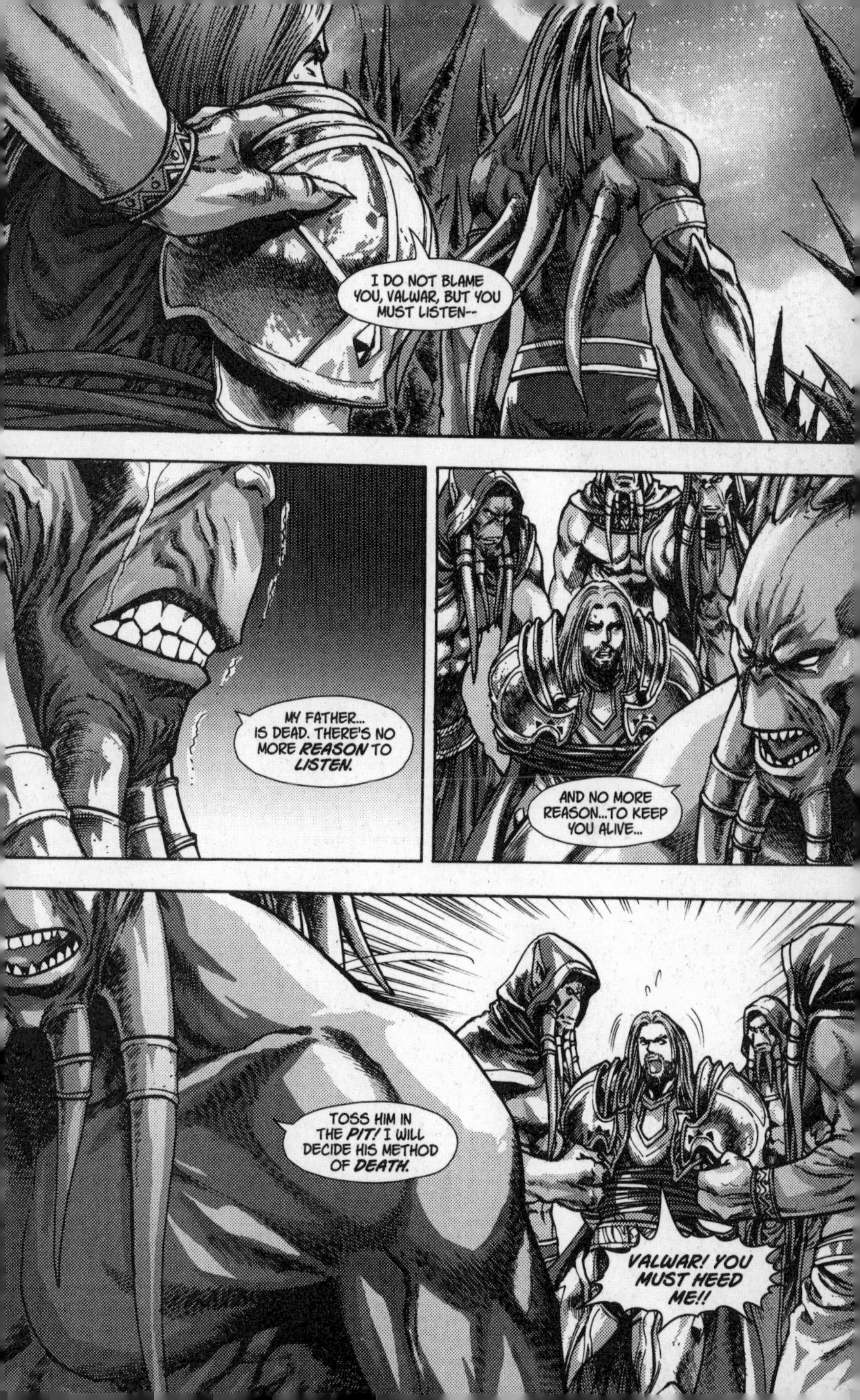
I DO NOT BLAME YOU, VALWAR, BUT YOU MUST LISTEN--
MY FATHER... IS DEAD. THERE'S NO MORE *REASON* TO *LISTEN.*
AND NO MORE REASON...TO KEEP YOU ALIVE...
TOSS HIM IN THE *PIT!* I WILL DECIDE HIS METHOD OF *DEATH.*
VALWAR! YOU MUST HEED ME!!

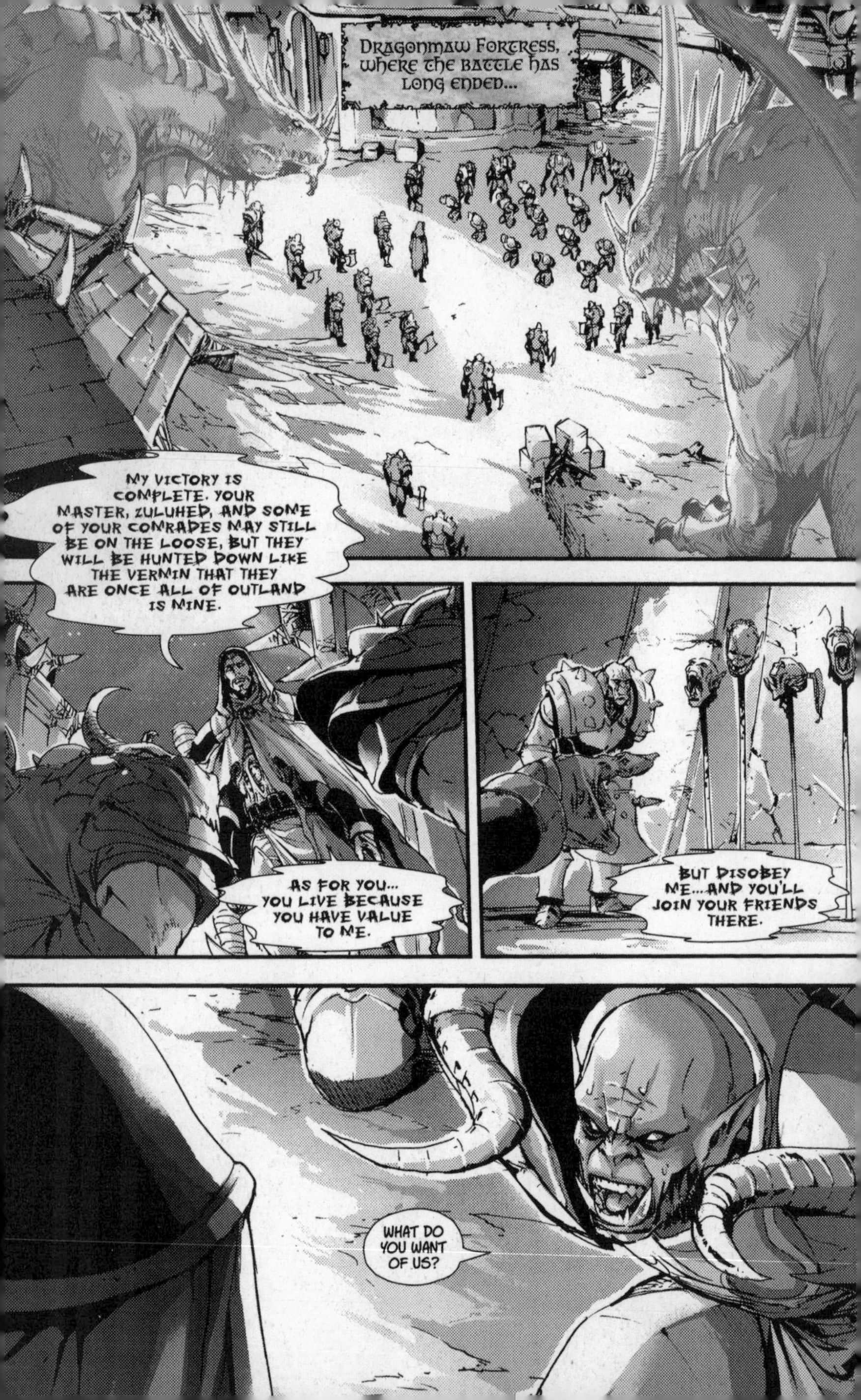

DRAGONMAW FORTRESS, WHERE THE BATTLE HAS LONG ENDED...
MY VICTORY IS COMPLETE. YOUR MASTER, ZULUHED, AND SOME OF YOUR COMRADES MAY STILL BE ON THE LOOSE, BUT THEY WILL BE HUNTED DOWN LIKE THE VERMIN THAT THEY ARE ONCE ALL OF OUTLAND IS MINE.
AS FOR YOU... YOU LIVE BECAUSE YOU HAVE VALUE TO ME.
BUT DISOBEY ME...AND YOU'LL JOIN YOUR FRIENDS THERE.
WHAT DO YOU WANT OF US?

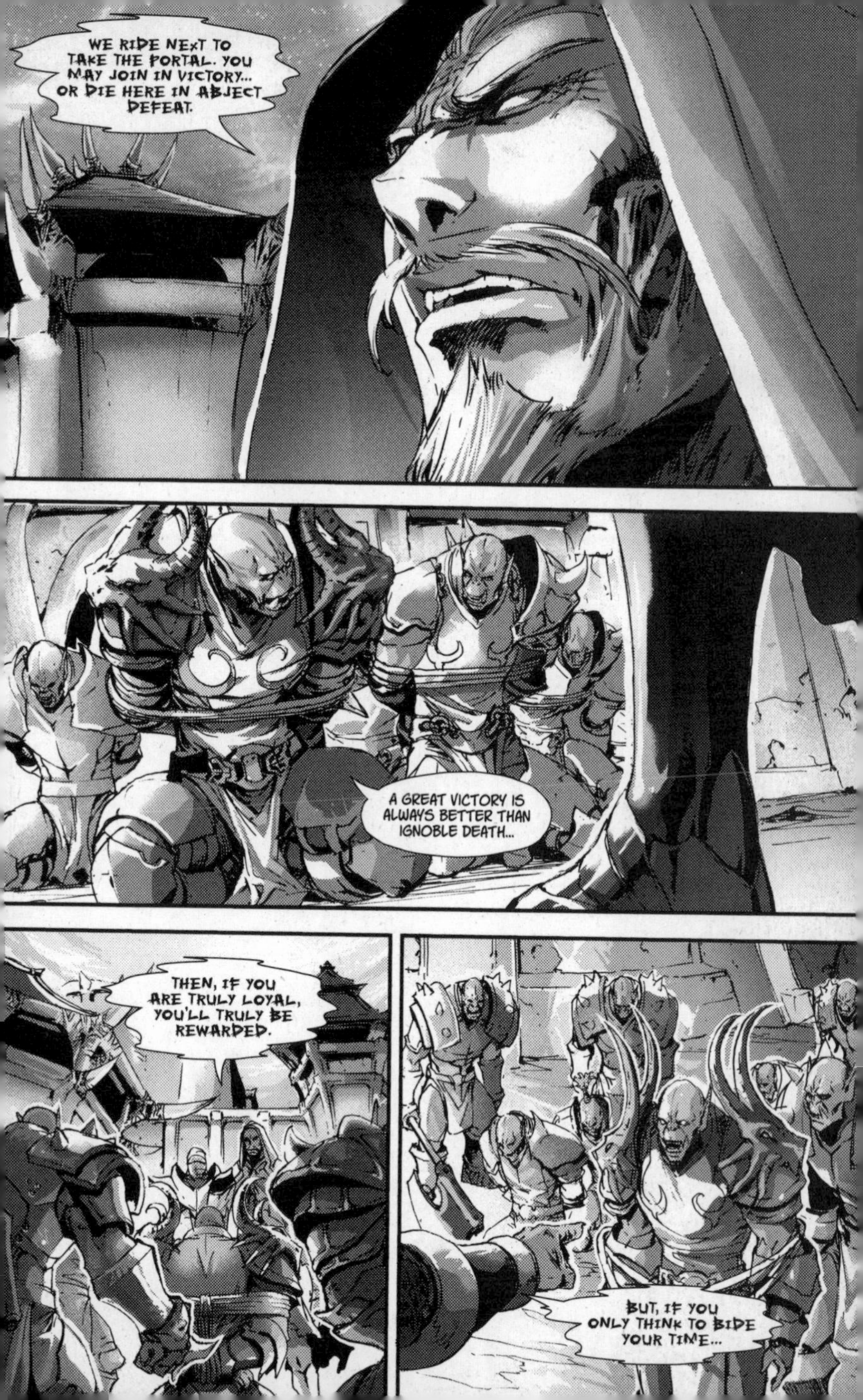
WE RIDE NEXT TO TAKE THE PORTAL. YOU MAY JOIN IN VICTORY... OR DIE HERE IN ABJECT DEFEAT.
A GREAT VICTORY IS ALWAYS BETTER THAN IGNOBLE DEATH...
THEN, IF YOU ARE TRULY LOYAL, YOU'LL TRULY BE REWARDED.
BUT, IF YOU ONLY THINK TO BIDE YOUR TIME...

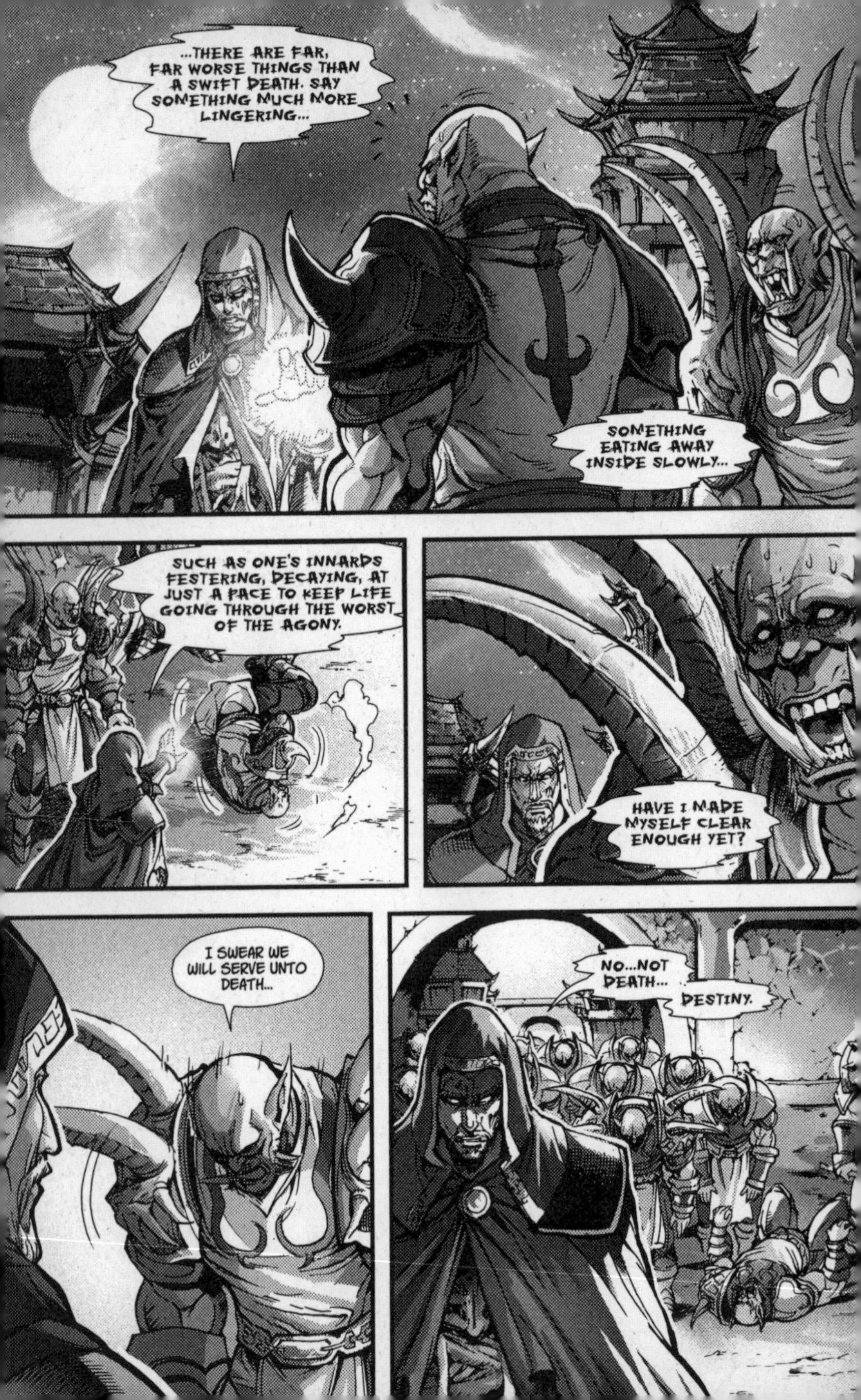

...THERE ARE FAR, FAR WORSE THINGS THAN A SWIFT DEATH. SAY SOMETHING MUCH MORE LINGERING...
SOMETHING EATING AWAY INSIDE SLOWLY...
SUCH AS ONE'S INNARDS FESTERING, DECAYING, AT JUST A PACE TO KEEP LIFE GOING THROUGH THE WORST OF THE AGONY.
HAVE I MADE MYSELF CLEAR ENOUGH YET?
I SWEAR WE WILL SERVE UNTO DEATH...
NO...NOT DEATH...
DESTINY.

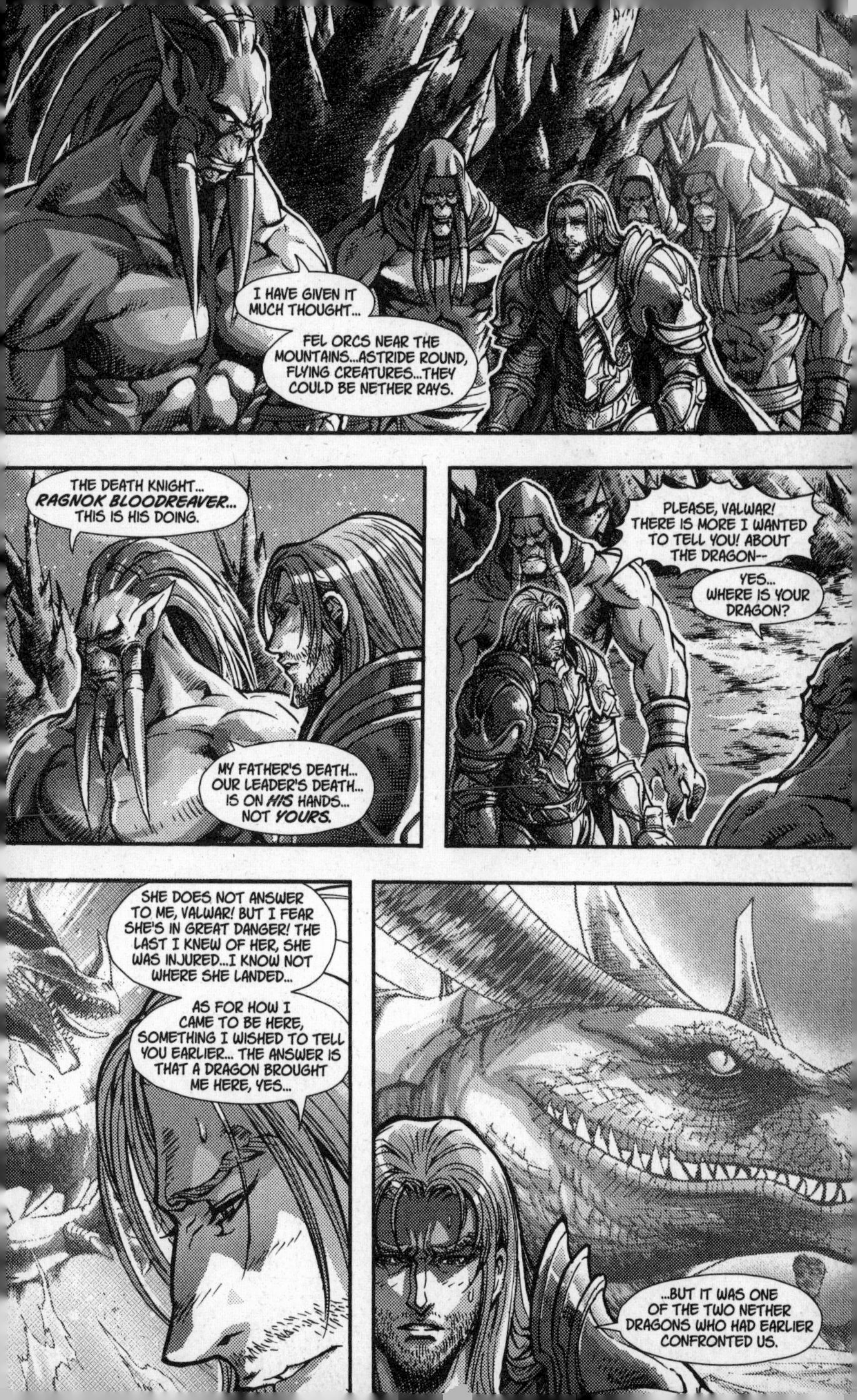
I HAVE GIVEN IT MUCH THOUGHT...
FEL ORCS NEAR THE MOUNTAINS...ASTRIDE ROUND, FLYING CREATURES...THEY COULD BE NETHER RAYS.
THE DEATH KNIGHT... ***RAGNOK BLOODREAVER...*** THIS IS HIS DOING.
MY FATHER'S DEATH... OUR LEADER'S DEATH... IS ON ***HIS*** HANDS... NOT ***YOURS.***
PLEASE, VALWAR! THERE IS MORE I WANTED TO TELL YOU! ABOUT THE DRAGON--
YES... WHERE IS YOUR DRAGON?
SHE DOES NOT ANSWER TO ME, VALWAR! BUT I FEAR SHE'S IN GREAT DANGER! THE LAST I KNEW OF HER, SHE WAS INJURED...I KNOW NOT WHERE SHE LANDED...
AS FOR HOW I CAME TO BE HERE, SOMETHING I WISHED TO TELL YOU EARLIER... THE ANSWER IS THAT A DRAGON BROUGHT ME HERE, YES...
...BUT IT WAS ONE OF THE TWO NETHER DRAGONS WHO HAD EARLIER CONFRONTED US.

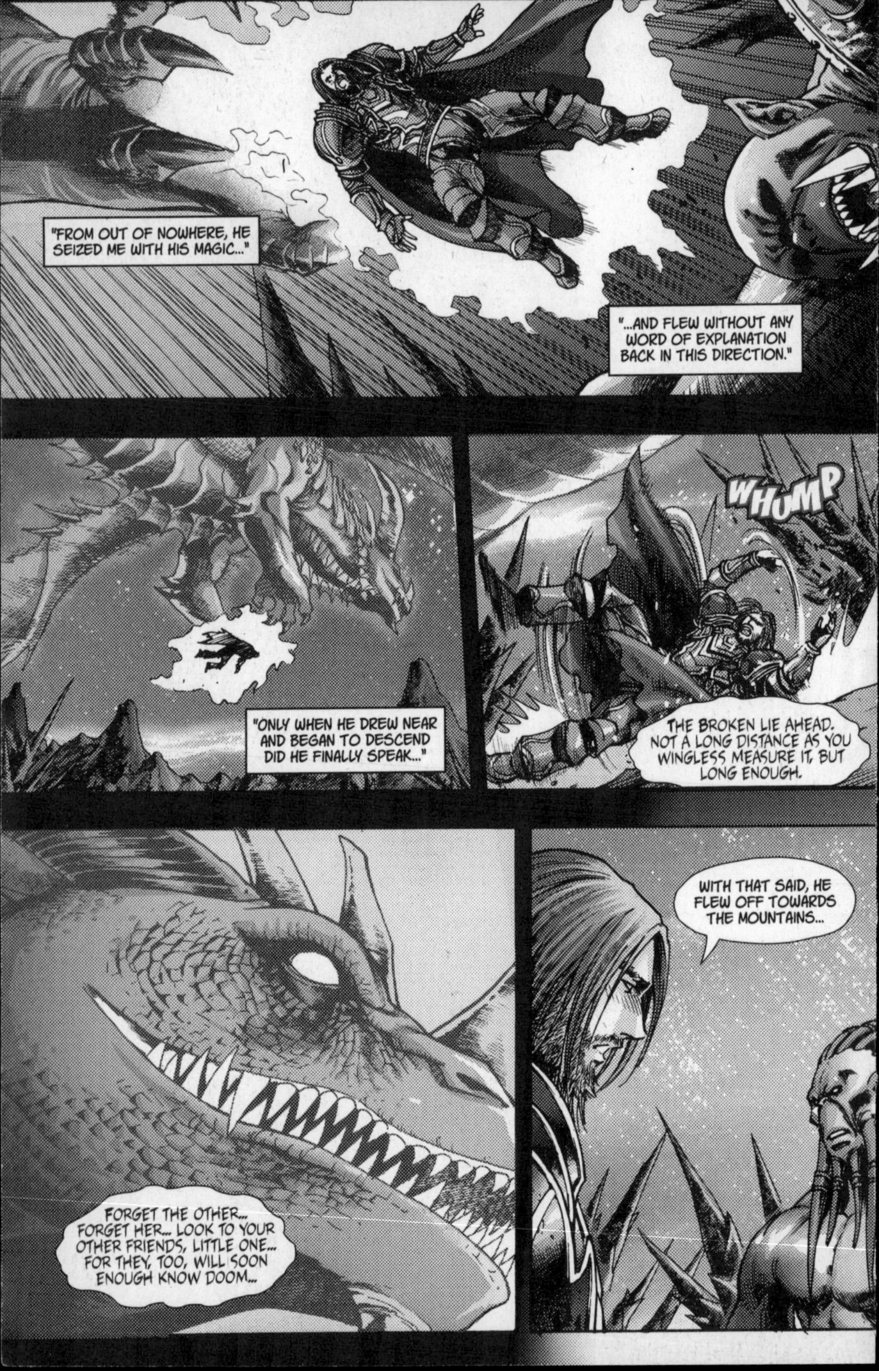
"FROM OUT OF NOWHERE, HE SEIZED ME WITH HIS MAGIC..."
"...AND FLEW WITHOUT ANY WORD OF EXPLANATION BACK IN THIS DIRECTION."
"ONLY WHEN HE DREW NEAR AND BEGAN TO DESCEND DID HE FINALLY SPEAK..."
WHUMP
THE BROKEN LIE AHEAD. NOT A LONG DISTANCE AS YOU WINGLESS MEASURE IT, BUT LONG ENOUGH.
FORGET THE OTHER... FORGET HER... LOOK TO YOUR OTHER FRIENDS, LITTLE ONE... FOR THEY, TOO, WILL SOON ENOUGH KNOW DOOM...
WITH THAT SAID, HE FLEW OFF TOWARDS THE MOUNTAINS...

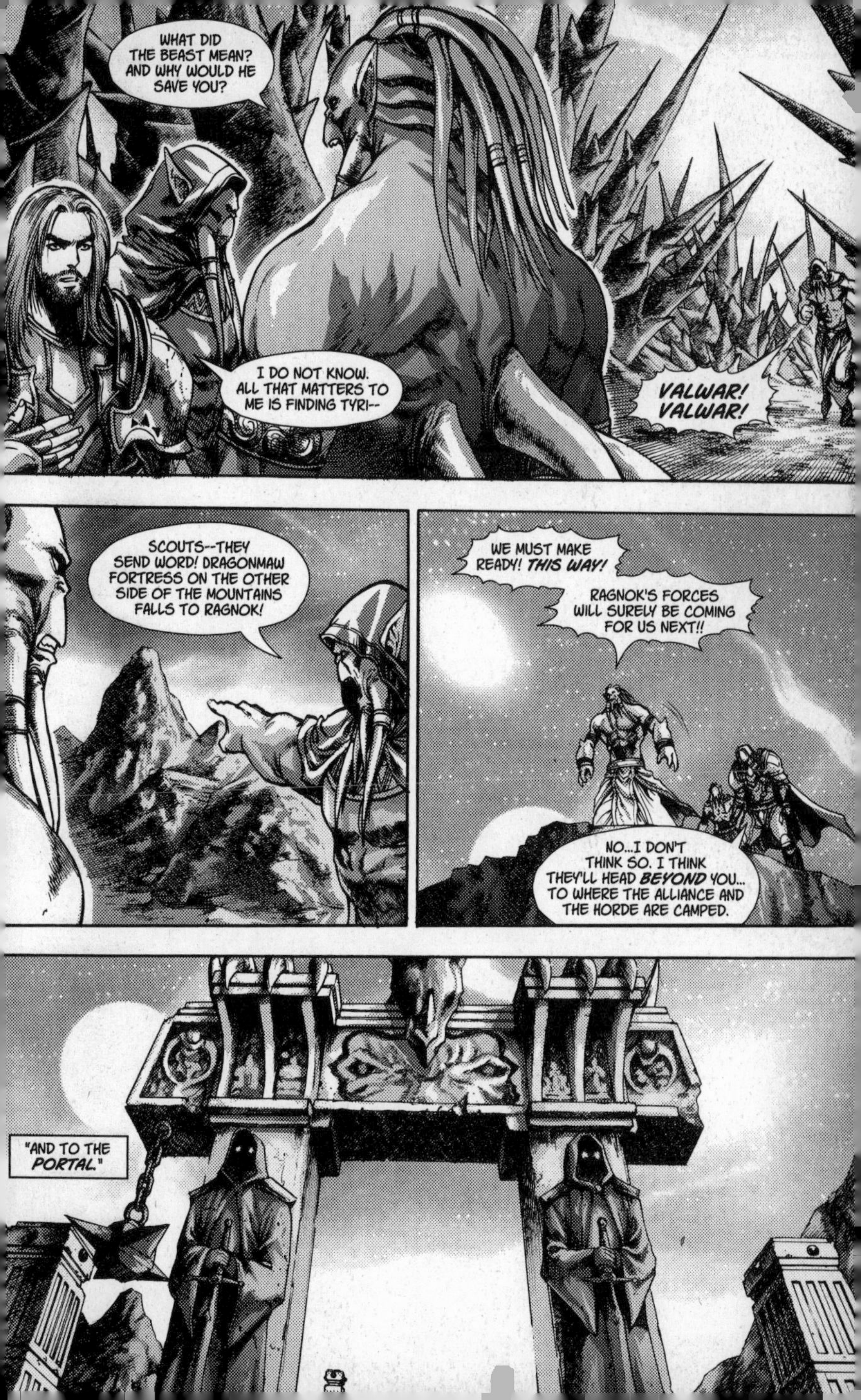
WHAT DID THE BEAST MEAN? AND WHY WOULD HE SAVE YOU?
I DO NOT KNOW. ALL THAT MATTERS TO ME IS FINDING TYRI--
VALWAR! VALWAR!
SCOUTS--THEY SEND WORD! DRAGONMAW FORTRESS ON THE OTHER SIDE OF THE MOUNTAINS FALLS TO RAGNOK!
WE MUST MAKE READY! THIS WAY!
RAGNOK'S FORCES WILL SURELY BE COMING FOR US NEXT!!
NO...I DON'T THINK SO. I THINK THEY'LL HEAD BEYOND YOU... TO WHERE THE ALLIANCE AND THE HORDE ARE CAMPED.
"AND TO THE PORTAL."

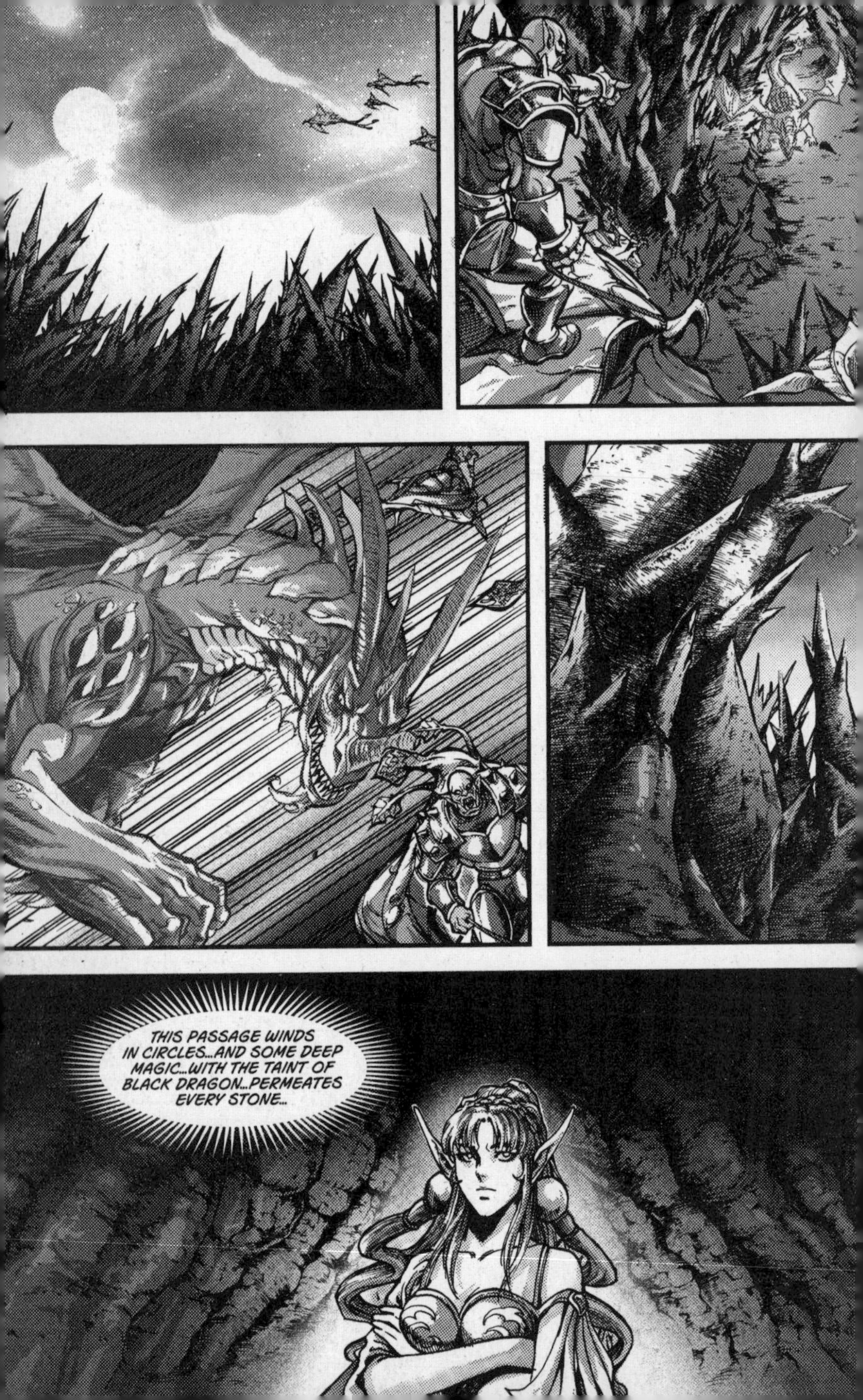
THIS PASSAGE WINDS IN CIRCLES...AND SOME DEEP MAGIC...WITH THE TAINT OF BLACK DRAGON...PERMEATES EVERY STONE...

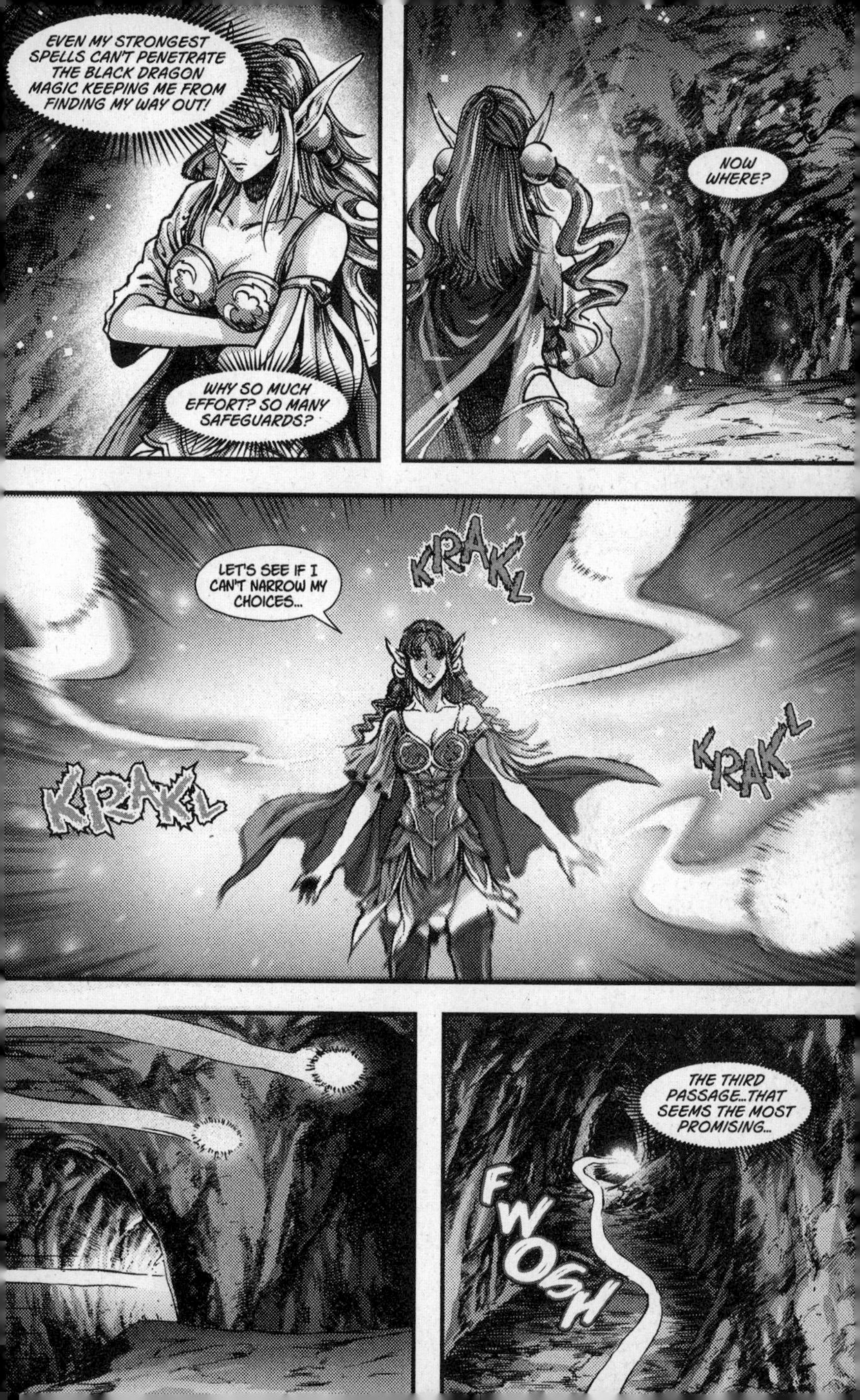
EVEN MY STRONGEST SPELLS CAN'T PENETRATE THE BLACK DRAGON MAGIC KEEPING ME FROM FINDING MY WAY OUT!
WHY SO MUCH EFFORT? SO MANY SAFEGUARDS?
NOW WHERE?
LET'S SEE IF I CAN'T NARROW MY CHOICES...
KRAKL
KRAKL
KRAKL
THE THIRD PASSAGE...THAT SEEMS THE MOST PROMISING...
FWOSH

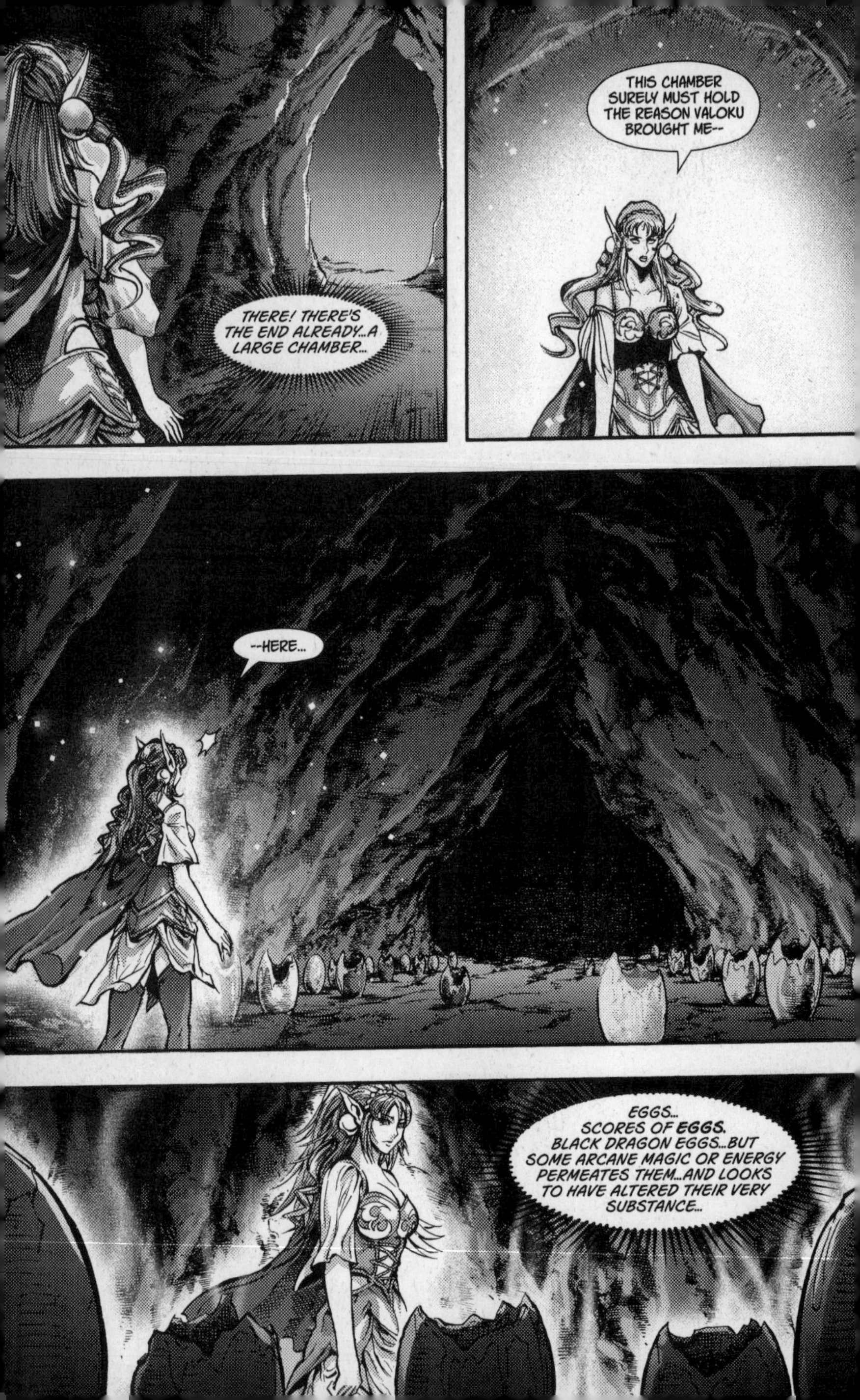
THERE! THERE'S THE END ALREADY...A LARGE CHAMBER...
THIS CHAMBER SURELY MUST HOLD THE REASON VALOKU BROUGHT ME--
--HERE...
EGGS... SCORES OF **EGGS**. BLACK DRAGON EGGS...BUT SOME ARCANE MAGIC OR ENERGY PERMEATES THEM...AND LOOKS TO HAVE ALTERED THEIR VERY SUBSTANCE...

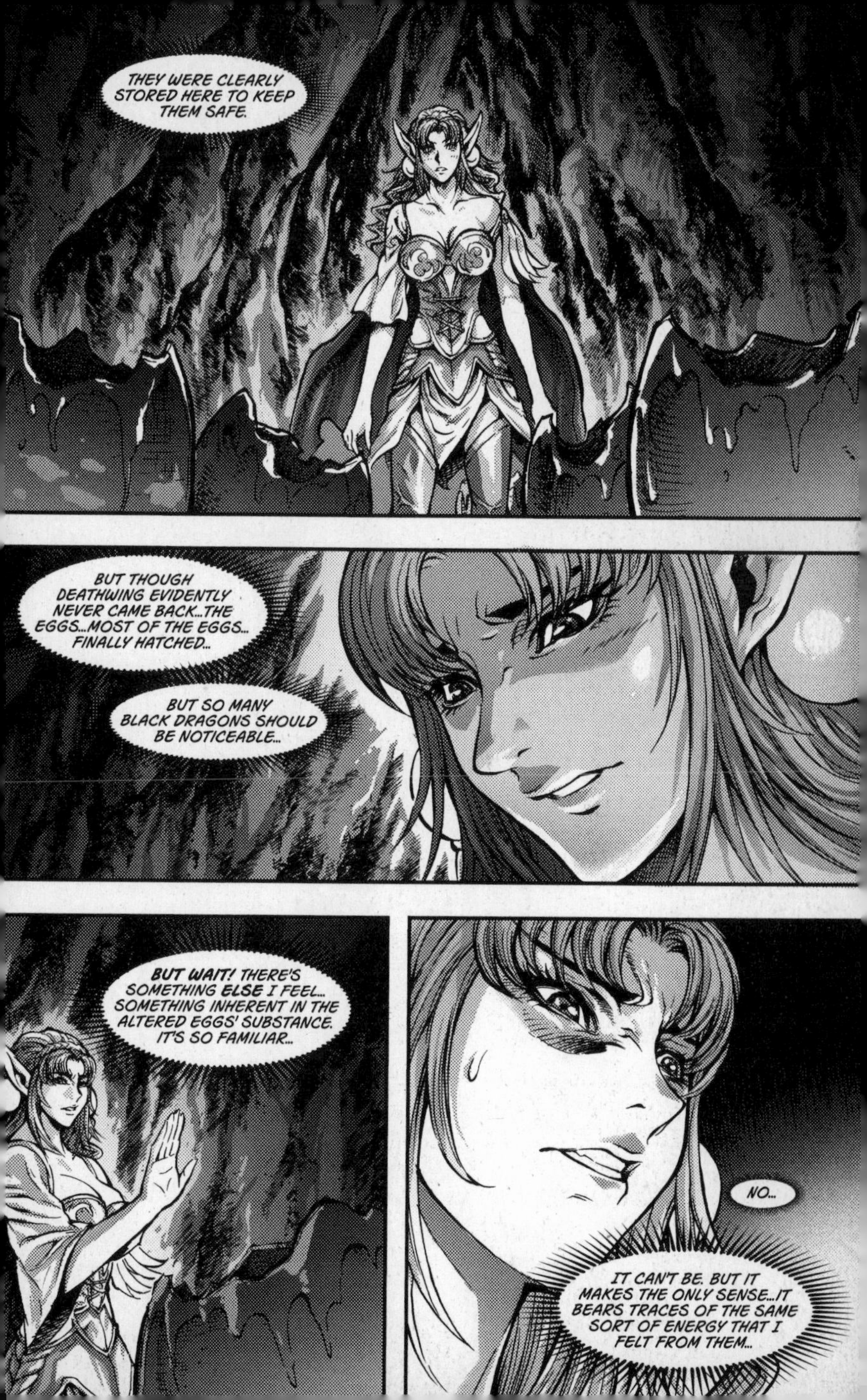
THEY WERE CLEARLY STORED HERE TO KEEP THEM SAFE.
BUT THOUGH DEATHWING EVIDENTLY NEVER CAME BACK...THE EGGS...MOST OF THE EGGS... FINALLY HATCHED...
BUT SO MANY BLACK DRAGONS SHOULD BE NOTICEABLE...
BUT WAIT! THERE'S SOMETHING ELSE I FEEL... SOMETHING INHERENT IN THE ALTERED EGGS' SUBSTANCE. IT'S SO FAMILIAR...
NO...
IT CAN'T BE. BUT IT MAKES THE ONLY SENSE...IT BEARS TRACES OF THE SAME SORT OF ENERGY THAT I FELT FROM THEM...

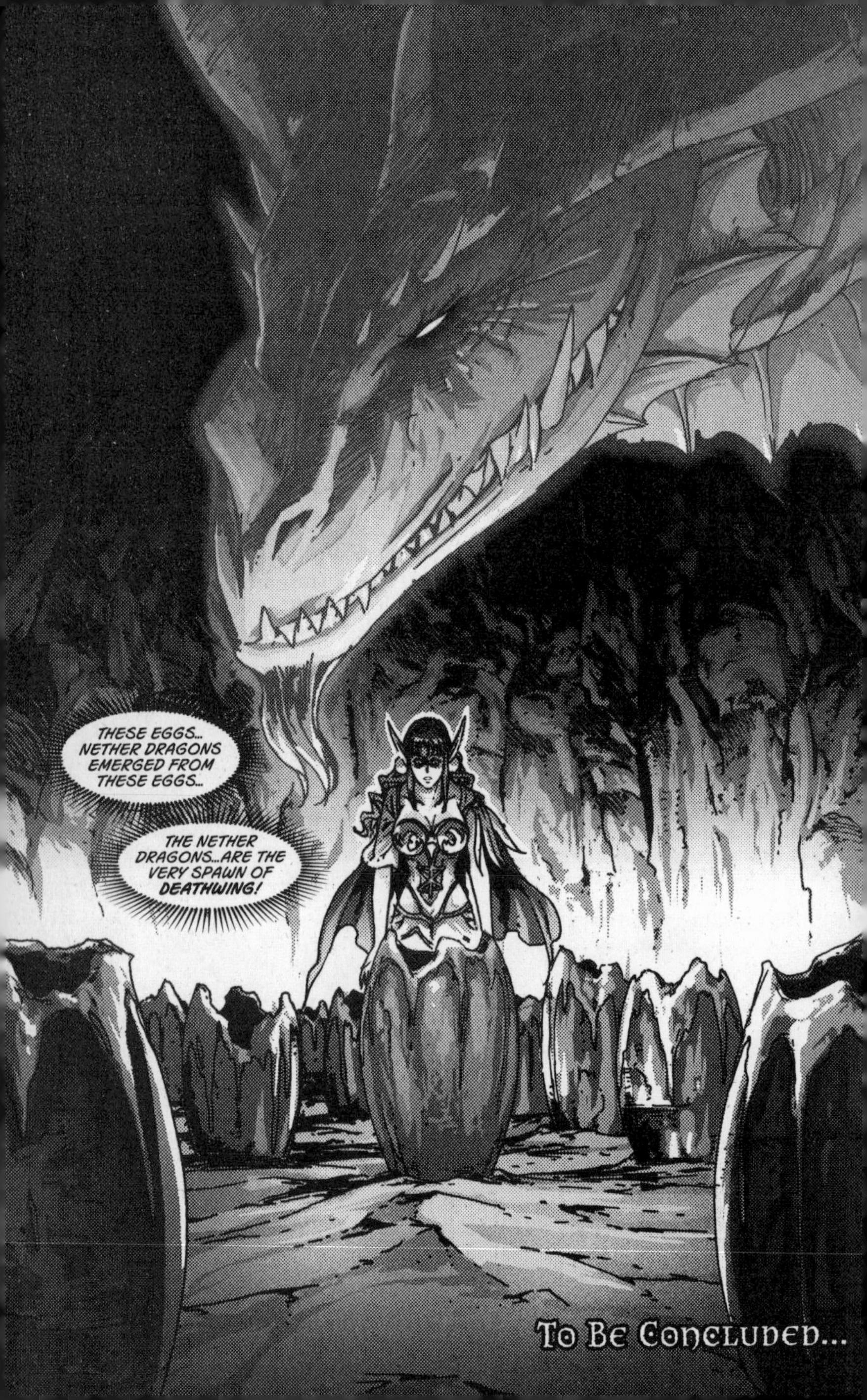
THESE EGGS... NETHER DRAGONS EMERGED FROM THESE EGGS...
THE NETHER DRAGONS...ARE THE VERY SPAWN OF DEATHWING!
To Be Concluded...

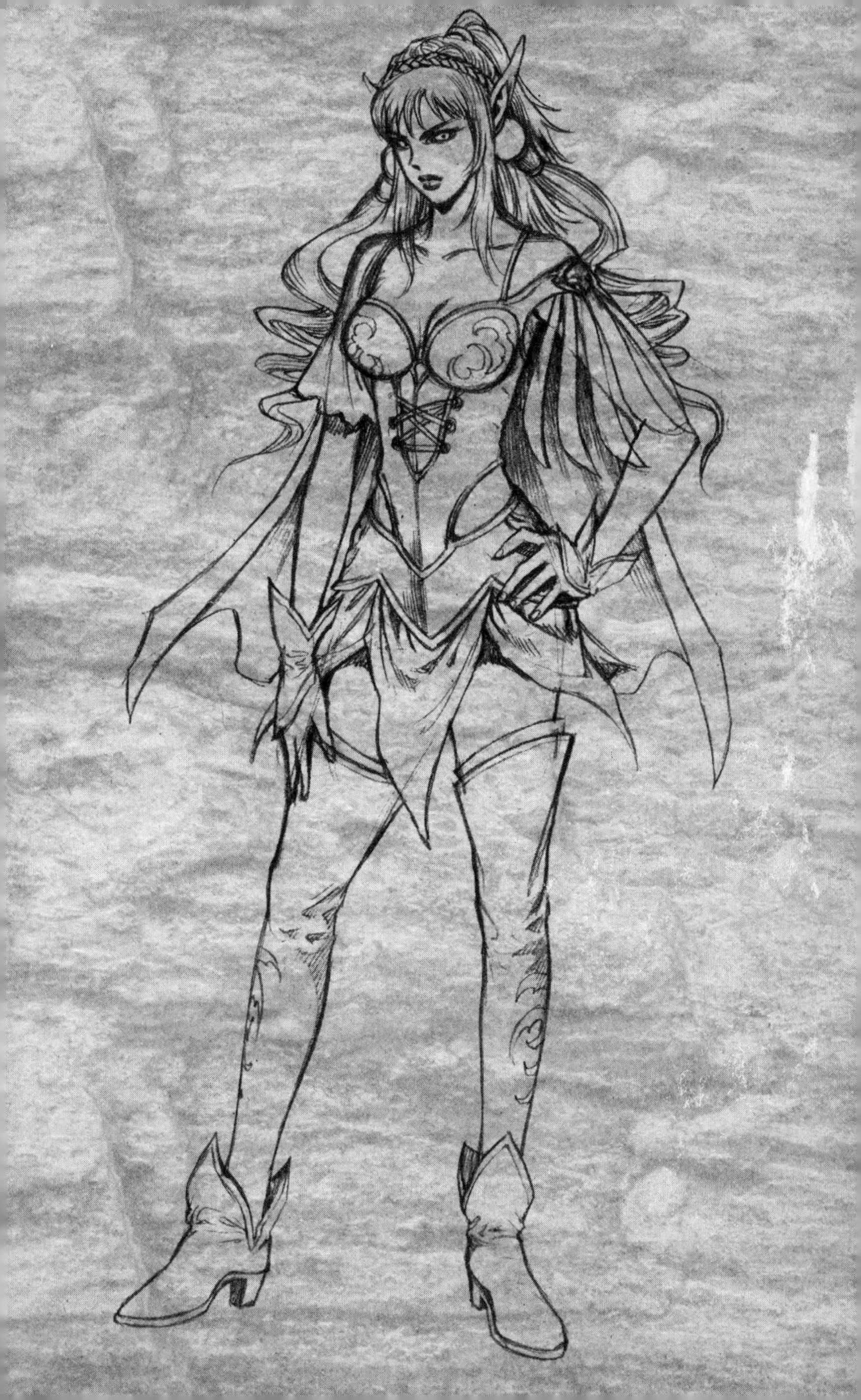

SPECIAL THANKS

At long last, WORLD OF WARCRAFT: SHADOW WING, volume one of the sequel series to the international bestseller *Warcraft: The Sunwell Trilogy*--made it into your eager hands! On behalf of TOKYOPOP and Blizzard Entertainment, we hope it was worth the wait! Luckily, the second volume of the *Shadow Wing* series--*Nexus Point*--will hit stores in November 2010--so you don't have long to wait! In the meantime, make sure to pick up our new class-based manga, *World of Warcraft: Mage,* on shelves now! And in October 2010, *World of Warcraft: Shaman* will be throwing its totems down, so be on watch for that exciting new addition to the class-based series. To further whet your appetite, check out the world exclusive sneak peek at *World of Warcraft: Shaman* inside the pages of this very book!

Of course, we wouldn't be able to bring you so many thrilling *Warcraft* titles without the talented folks at Blizzard. Their expert guidance makes them not just a partner, but true comrades in the ever-intense deadline war. Many thanks to Jason Bischoff, Joshua Horst, James Waugh, Micky Neilson, Evelyn Fredericksen, Samwise Didier, Tommy Newcomer, Cameron Dayton and Chris Metzen!

He's no stranger to the *World of Warcraft,* and by now, he should be no stranger to praise--the peerless Richard A. Knaak! Thanks for delivering a fantastic story, Richard! We wonder how many **words** of **Warcraft** you've written by now? You should take a count!

Jae-Hwan Kim has set the bar very high when it comes to art in TOKYOPOP's *World of Warcraft* manga--and he does not disappoint in *Shadow Wing.* Many thanks to Jae-Hwan and his entire team!

Janice Kwon is an unsung hero, and she played a major role in making this book a reality. She's not an artist. She's not a writer. She's not an editor. Janice is a translator! As our Korean translator, Janice maintained the lines of communication between Jae-Hwan and team TOKYOPOP. Without her immense help, this project would not have run as smoothly as it did! Janice Kwon, take a well-deserved bow!

We'd like to also thank TOKYOPOP's secret weapon...and his name is Michael Paolilli. Michael is incredibly talented. He can letter a book, he can make art fixes and he has an encyclopedic knowledge of the *Warcraft* universe. Thanks for all your assistance, Michael!

Lastly, we want to express our gratitude to all of the fans. Without you, these books wouldn't exist. So, do us a favor and buy a *ton* of copies so we can keep making awesome *Warcraft* stories. After all, we're doing it for you!

- Paul Morrissey and Troy Lewter
Editors

CREATOR BIO'S

RICHARD A. KNAAK

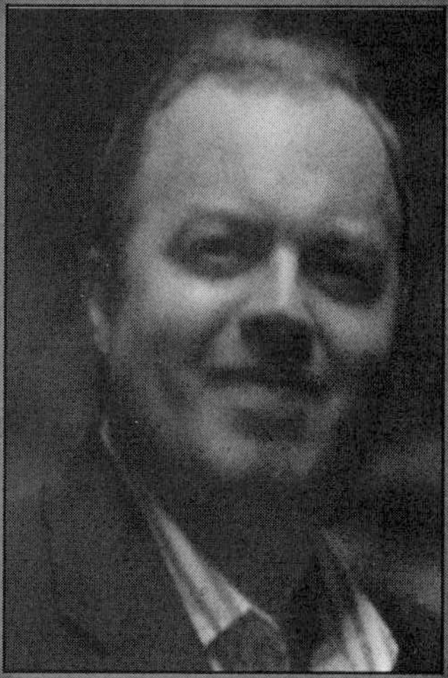

Richard A. Knaak is the New York Times and USA Today bestselling fantasy author of 40 novels and over a dozen short stories, including most recently the national bestseller, *World of Warcraft: Stormrage.* He is also well known for such favorites as *The Legend of Huma* & *The Minotaur Wars* for Dragonlance, the *War of the Ancients* trilogy for *Warcraft,* and his own *Dragonrealm* series. In addition to the TOKYOPOP series *Warcraft: The Sunwell Trilogy,* he is the author of five short stories featured in *Warcraft: Legends* Volumes 1-5. He also recently released *The Gargoyle King,* the third in his *Ogre Titans* saga for Dragonlance and *Legends of the Dragonrealm,* which combines the first three novels of his world. A second volume will be released in October. To find out more about Richard's projects, visit his website at www.richardaknaak.com.

JAE-HWAN KIM

Born in 1971 in Korea, Jae-Hwan Kim's best-known manga works include *Rainbow*, *Combat Metal HeMoSoo* and *King of Hell,* a series published by TOKYOPOP. Along with being the creator of *War Angels* for TOKYOPOP, Jae-Hwan is the artist for TOKYOPOP's *Warcraft: The Sunwell Trilogy,* as well as Richard Knaak's four-part short story featured in *Warcraft: Legends* Volumes 1-4.

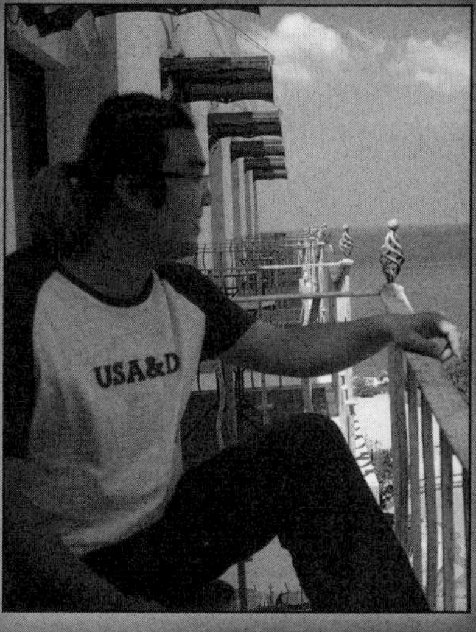
USA&D

EXCLUSIVE INTERVIEW WITH PAUL BENJAMIN—WRITER OF *WORLD OF WARCRAFT: SHAMAN*

You've worn many hats throughout your career. Tell us a little bit about your background.

Fedora, baseball, fez, yarmulke... oh, you didn't mean hats I've *literally* worn? My business card says, "Writer, Editor, Supermodel" which comprises having been a development executive for film and television, an editor for comics and graphic novels, and a video game producer. As a writer I've worked on video games featuring characters like Wolverine, G.I. JOE, Hulk and Spider-Man. A few of my comic book writing highlights include MARVEL ADVENTURES HULK and SPIDER-MAN, MONSTERS, INC., STARCRAFT and now, I'm excited to say, SHAMAN. As a supermodel I've walked the runways of Paris and Milan as well as... oh, never mind. You've all seen the billboards...

So, you are clearly an avid role-playing gamer. Is it safe to assume that you've played a fair amount of WARCRAFT? Do you have a favorite class to play?

My main is a pally retadin. That's a paladin built to do lots of damage for any noobs reading this (Hi, Mom!). I tend to do a fair amount of solo play because if I play with a group I'm on for too long and wouldn't make any of my Warcraft writing deadlines! The pally is great for soloing because I can heal myself and do plenty of damage. That said, I do have a lot of fun playing with guildies or doing random heroics when I've got the time. And, of course, since writing SHAMAN I've really been digging my new shammy character as well.

Give the fans the inside scoop on WORLD OF WARCRAFT: SHAMAN. What's the story about? Is it true that it will tie into the upcoming CATACLYSM expansion?

SHAMAN is the tale of a group many players have seen around Azeroth and beyond: the Earthen Ring. The main characters are Muln, the tauren High Shaman of the Earthen Ring, and his orc apprentice, Kettara. The focus is on them and the elder council of the Earthen Ring, so I've gotten to write draenei and trolls as well as a few very important (and well known) orcs from Orgrimmar. The secrets of CATACLYSM are quite closely guarded at the time of this writing, but there's a lot of connection between this book and the upcoming expansion. I *can* tell you that the elements are in upheaval and that's wreaking chaos with the powers of Muln and the Earthen Ring. SHAMAN is a story about tradition versus change and choosing which one is more important. It's also full of shaman calling down lightning, summoning elementals and manifesting totems to help them smack down any monsters stupid enough to threaten the shaman way of life. And it's all beautifully illustrated by DEATH KNIGHT artist Rocio Zucchi, so I imagine fans will be as excited to read the book as I have been to see those pages coming in as she works!

You've also written several STARCRAFT: FRONTLINE stories. Tell us a bit about those stories and how they came about.

Those were a lot of fun. I co-wrote them with my game designer friend, Dave Shramek. It all started with a story in the first STARCRAFT: FRONTLINE book in which we introduced Colin Phash, the psionic son of a senator. The two of them were trapped in a mine with zerg and hilarity ensued. The folks at Blizzard dug the story and had us write a follow up in volume three. Then we wrote another story in volume four that was a lead in to STARCRAFT: GHOST ACADEMY where Colin and Senator Phash are important characters in their own subtle ways. It's been fantastic to work in the worlds of STARCRAFT and WARCRAFT. I'm hoping that I'll even get to see some of the characters I've written show up in the games!

A SNEAK PEEK AT THE NEXT THRILLING CLASS-BASED MANGA FROM TOKYOPOP AND BLIZZARD...

WORLD OF WARCRAFT: SHAMAN

Earthquakes. Fires. Floods. Tornados. The elements of Azeroth are out of control, unleashing devastating natural disasters that threaten to tear Azeroth asunder. All hope rests with the shaman, who are able to commune with the elements. Muln Earthfury, the shaman leader of the secretive Earthen Ring, attempts to pacify the elements--but his pleas fall on deaf ears. The elements are unresponsive, full of confusion and chaos. The Earthen Ring is riddled with doubt. Have the shaman lost their ability to corral and guide the elements?

Mysteriously, Shotoa arrives. This Tauren shaman doesn't just merely tend to the elements--he **forces** them to do his bidding. Shotoa promises to lead the Earthen Ring into a new era of Shamanism... As the world crumbles around them, Muln and the Earthen Ring must decide if Shotoa is a hero or a heretic...

Written by Paul Benjamin (*StarCraft: Frontline*) and drawn by Rocio Zucchi (*World of Warcraft: Death Knight*), *WORLD OF WARCRAFT: SHAMAN* ties into the upcoming *World of Warcraft: Cataclysm* expansion in stunning ways!

Available October 2010!

-COMMUNING WITH A COVER-

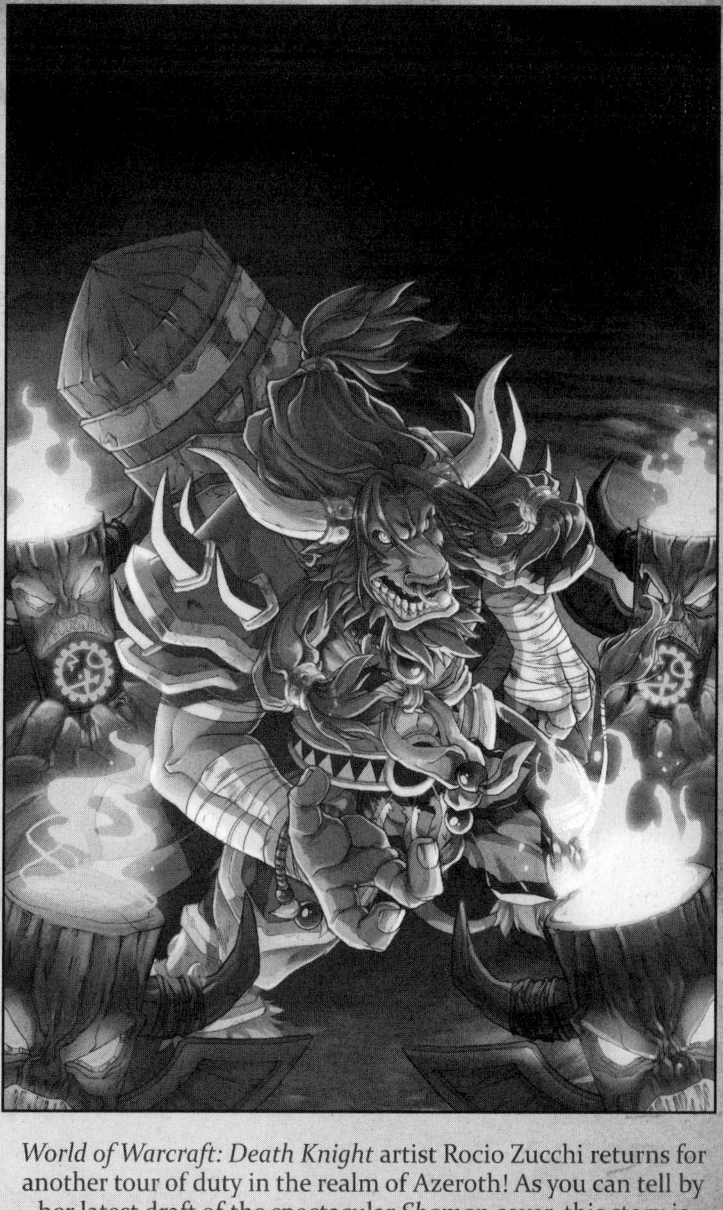

World of Warcraft: Death Knight artist Rocio Zucchi returns for another tour of duty in the realm of Azeroth! As you can tell by her latest draft of the spectacular *Shaman* cover, this story is going to be intense!

-COMMUNING WITH A CAST-

MULN EARTHFURY

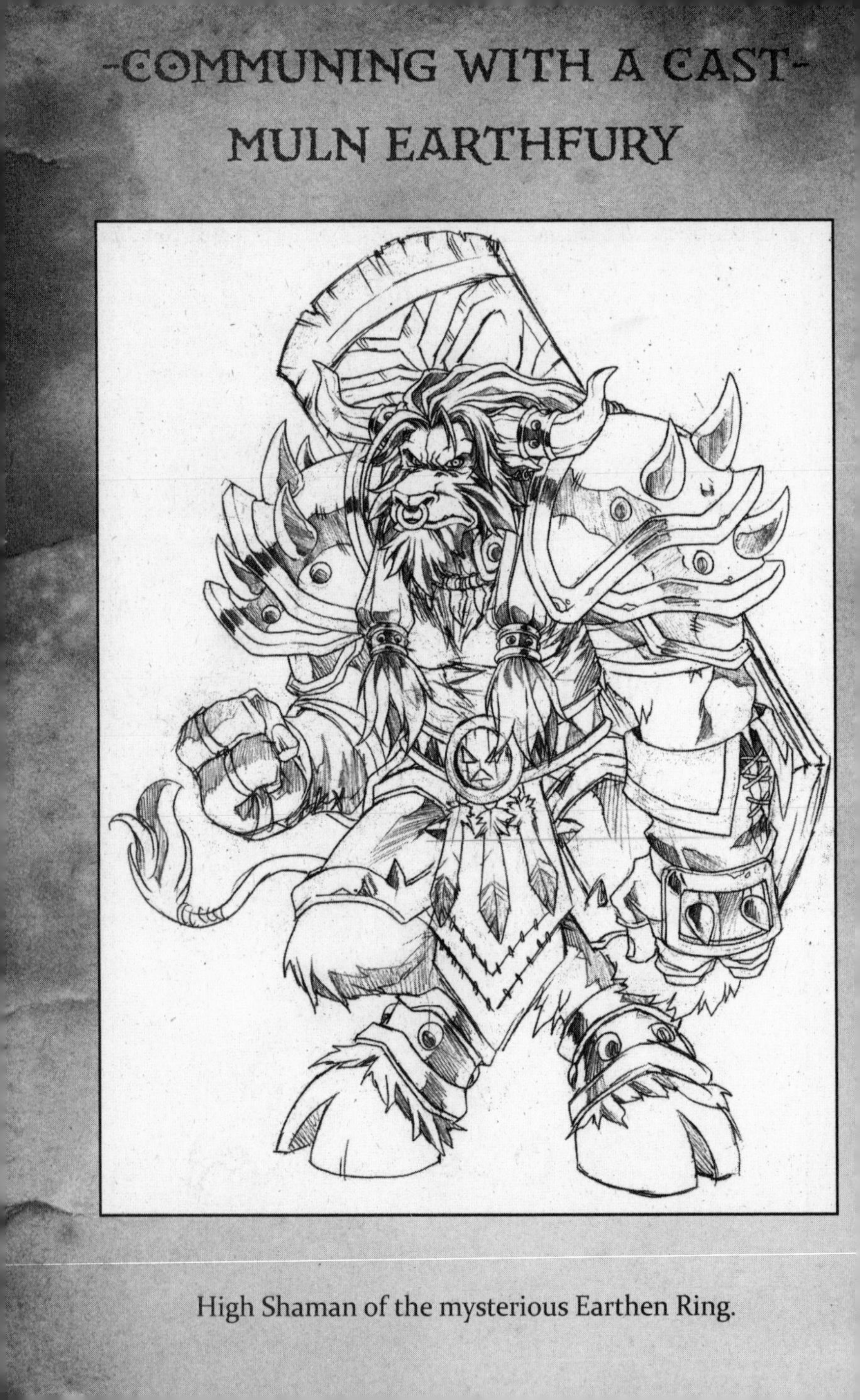

High Shaman of the mysterious Earthen Ring.

KETTARA BLOODTHIRST

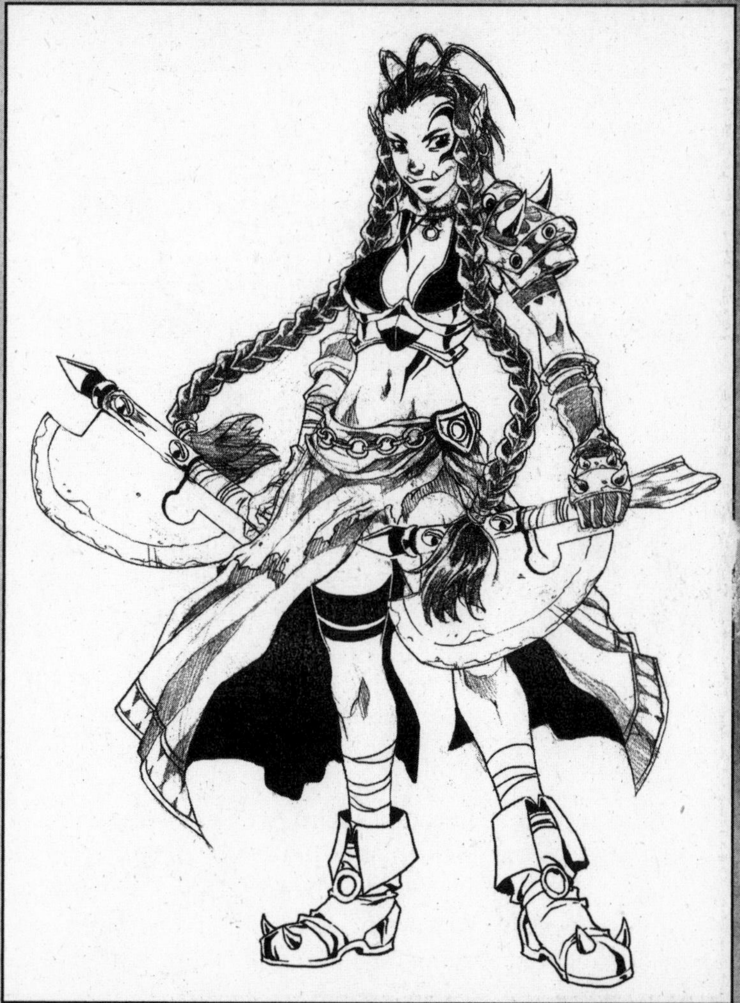

The most gorgeous orc you've ever seen, Kettara Bloodthirst is Muln's apprentice.

PREVIEW

TOKYOPOP and BLIZZARD ENTERTAINMENT proudly present an exciting new volume in *World of Warcraft's* ongoing class series: *Mage!*

Aodhan comes from a lineage that includes some of Azeroth's most heroic paladins and warriors, but the whip-smart young man is not built for physical combat. He's thin, bookish, and he desperately wants to be a mage. After his controlling father forbids him to practice magic, Aodhan flees to study the arcane arts in the city of Dalaran.

Yet Aodhan's dream of becoming a powerful spellcaster is violently interrupted when a host of blue dragons lays siege to Dalaran.

Written by acclaimed author Richard A. Knaak (*World of Warcraft: Shadow Wing*) and drawn by fan favorite Ryo Kawakami (*Warcraft: Legends*), *World of Warcraft: Mage* is an action-packed tale of temptation, power and heroics that will leave *World of Warcraft* fans spellbound!

Available now!

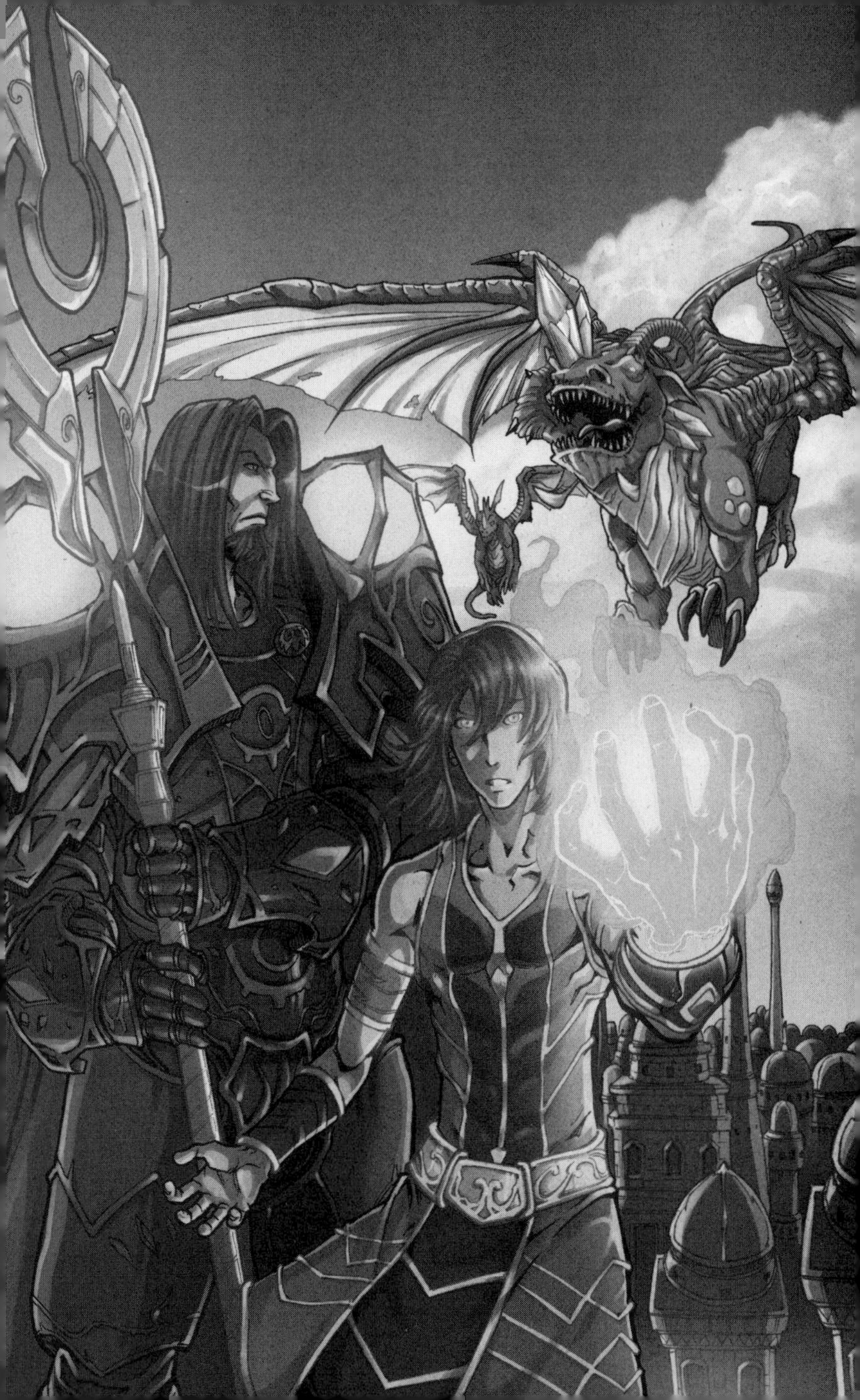

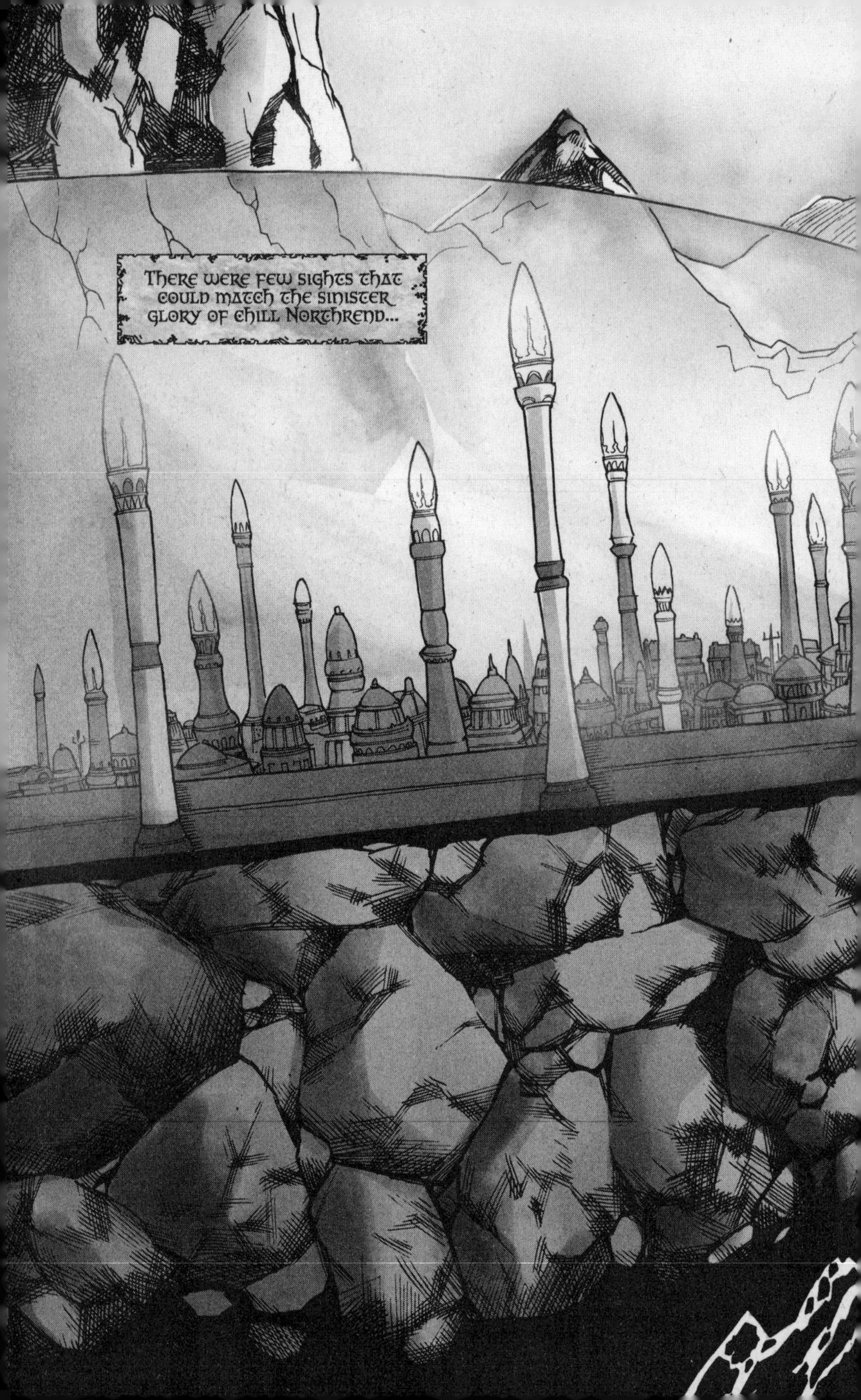
THERE WERE FEW SIGHTS THAT COULD MATCH THE SINISTER GLORY OF CHILL NORTHREND...

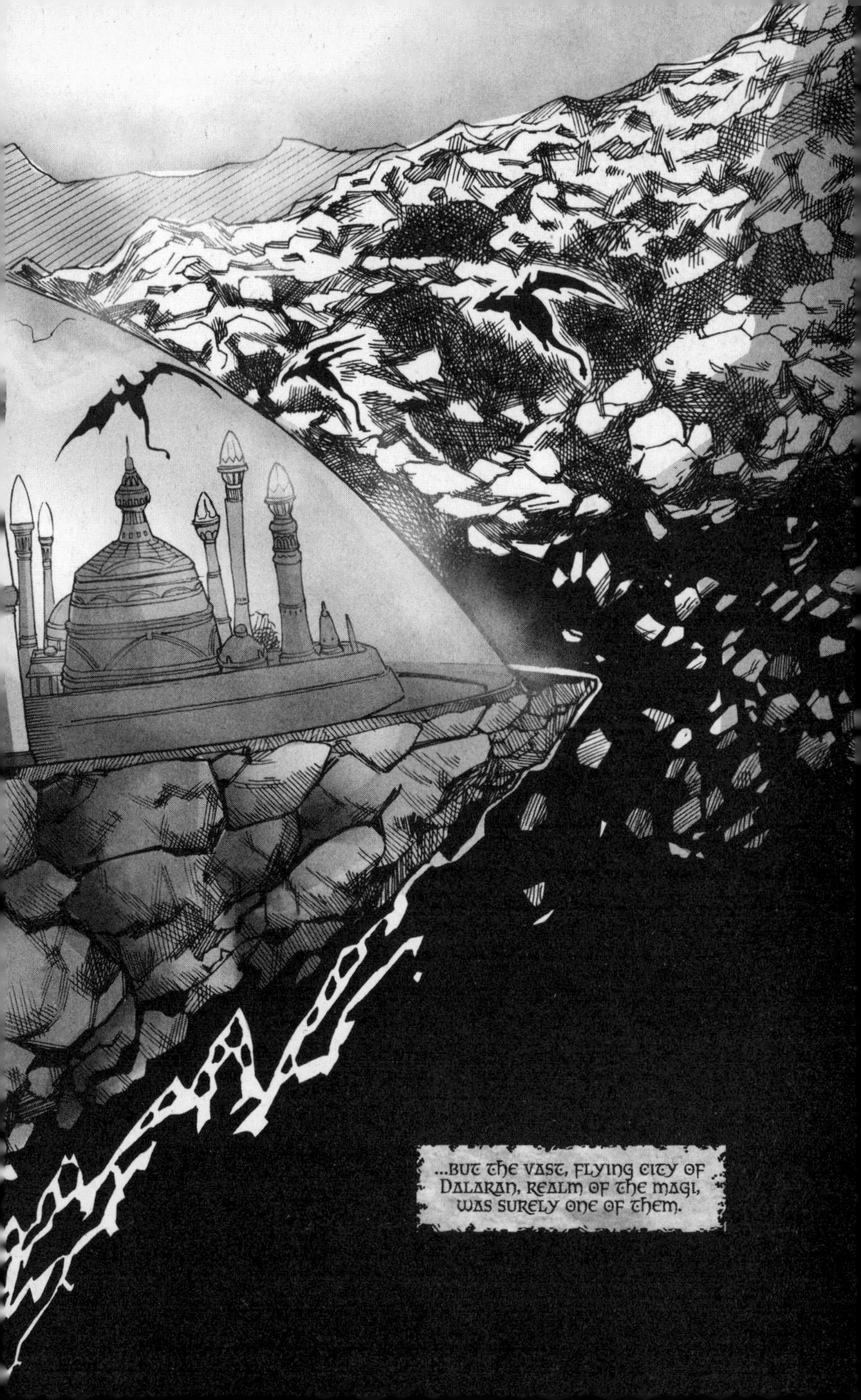
...BUT THE VAST, FLYING CITY OF DALARAN, REALM OF THE MAGI, WAS SURELY ONE OF THEM.

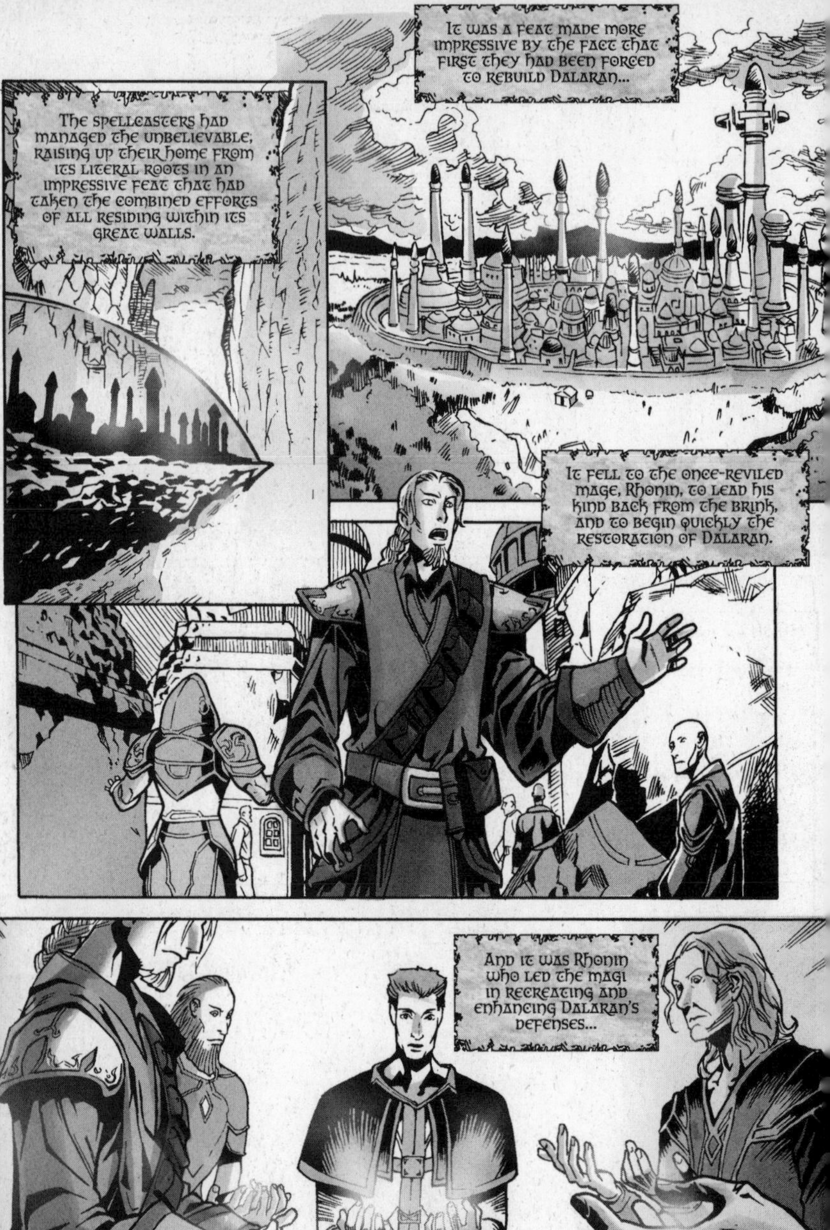
The spellcasters had managed the unbelievable; raising up their home from its literal roots in an impressive feat that had taken the combined efforts of all residing within its great walls.
It was a feat made more impressive by the fact that first they had been forced to rebuild Dalaran...
It fell to the once-reviled mage, Rhonin, to lead his kind back from the brink, and to begin quickly the restoration of Dalaran.
And it was Rhonin who led the magi in recreating and enhancing Dalaran's defenses...

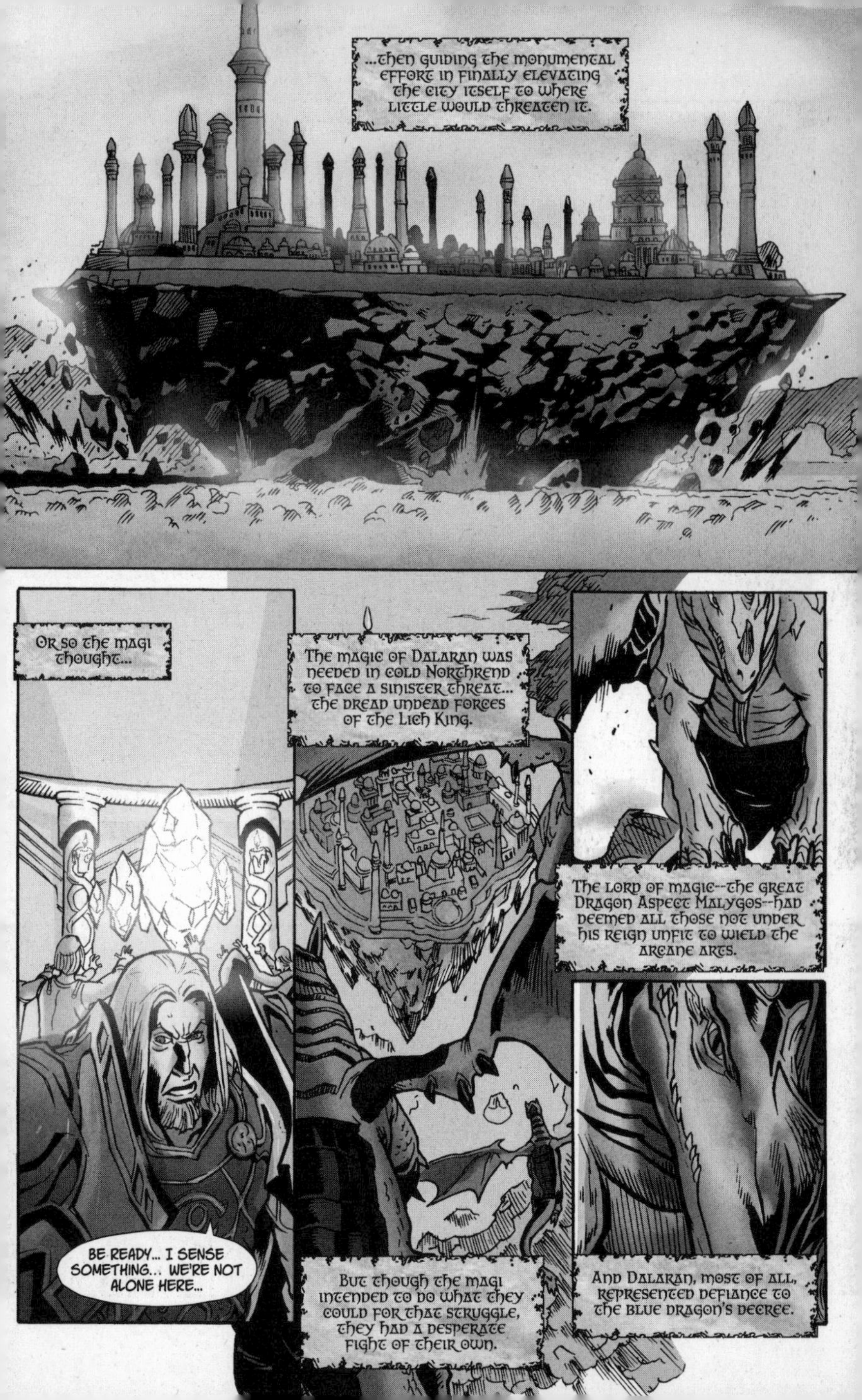
...then guiding the monumental effort in finally elevating the city itself to where little would threaten it.
Or so the magi thought...
Be ready... I sense something... we're not alone here...
The magic of Dalaran was needed in cold Northrend to face a sinister threat... the dread undead forces of the Lich King.
But though the magi intended to do what they could for that struggle, they had a desperate fight of their own.
The lord of magic--the great Dragon Aspect Malygos--had deemed all those not under his reign unfit to wield the arcane arts.
And Dalaran, most of all, represented defiance to the blue dragon's decree.

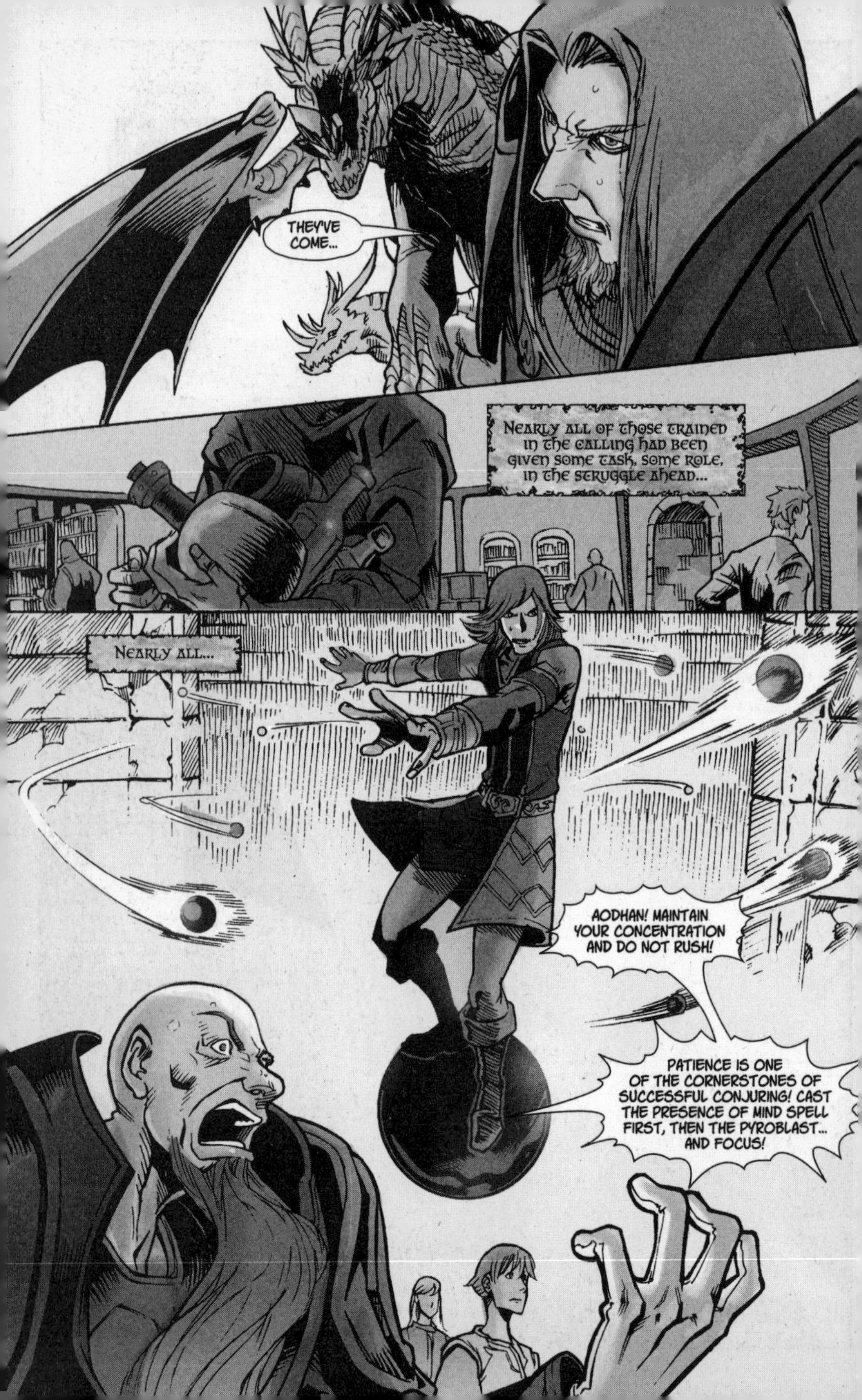
THEY'VE COME...
NEARLY ALL OF THOSE TRAINED IN THE CALLING HAD BEEN GIVEN SOME TASK, SOME ROLE, IN THE STRUGGLE AHEAD...
NEARLY ALL...
AODHAN! MAINTAIN YOUR CONCENTRATION AND DO NOT RUSH!
PATIENCE IS ONE OF THE CORNERSTONES OF SUCCESSFUL CONJURING! CAST THE PRESENCE OF MIND SPELL FIRST, THEN THE PYROBLAST... AND FOCUS!

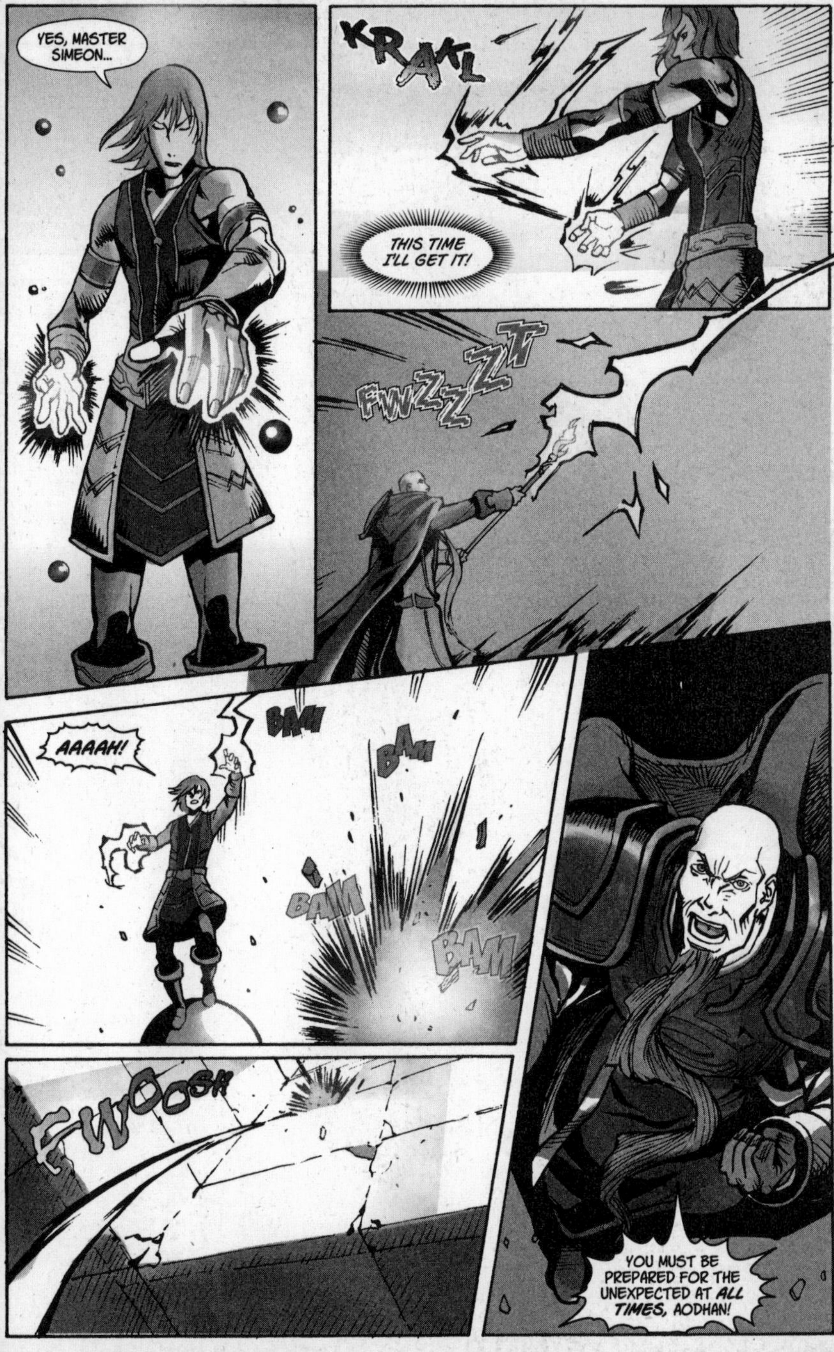
YES, MASTER SIMEON...
KRAKL
THIS TIME I'LL GET IT!
FWZZZZT
AAAAH!
BAM
BAM
BAM
BAM
FWOOSH
YOU MUST BE PREPARED FOR THE UNEXPECTED AT ALL TIMES, AODHAN!

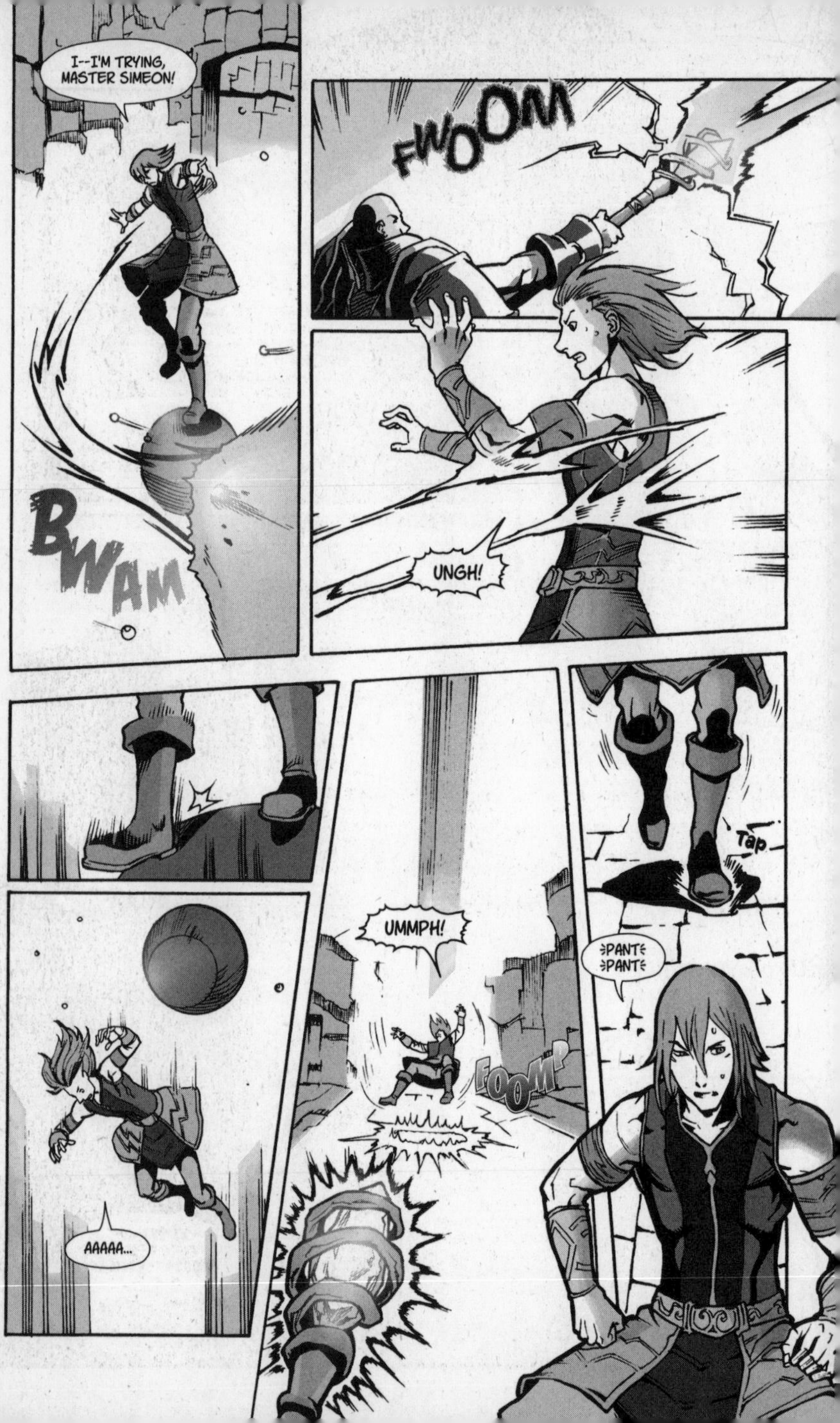
I--I'M TRYING, MASTER SIMEON!
BWAM
FWOOM
UNGH!
AAAAA...
UMMPH!
FOOMP
Tap
PANT PANT

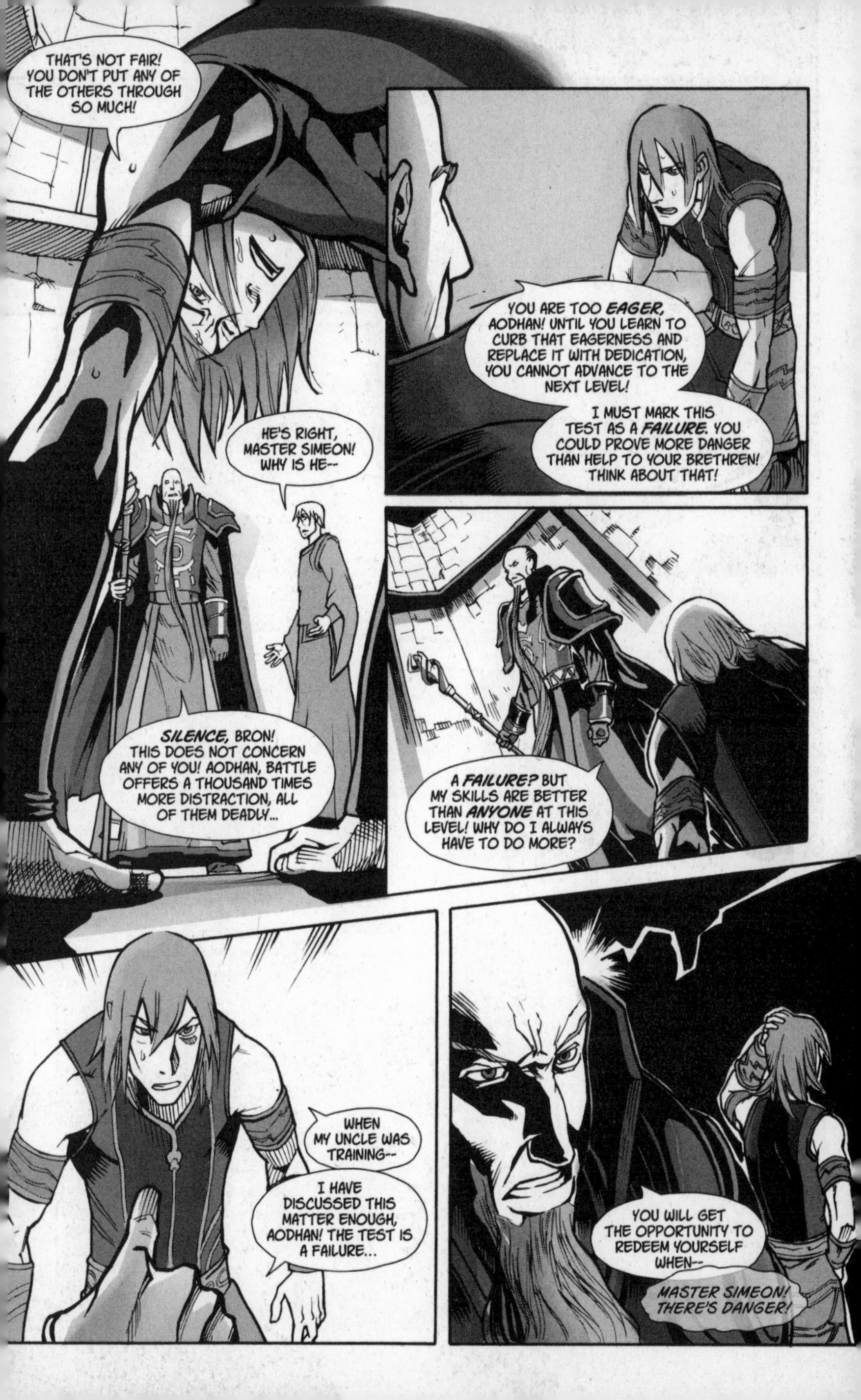
THAT'S NOT FAIR! YOU DON'T PUT ANY OF THE OTHERS THROUGH SO MUCH!
YOU ARE TOO EAGER, AODHAN! UNTIL YOU LEARN TO CURB THAT EAGERNESS AND REPLACE IT WITH DEDICATION, YOU CANNOT ADVANCE TO THE NEXT LEVEL!
I MUST MARK THIS TEST AS A FAILURE. YOU COULD PROVE MORE DANGER THAN HELP TO YOUR BRETHREN! THINK ABOUT THAT!
HE'S RIGHT, MASTER SIMEON! WHY IS HE--
SILENCE, BRON! THIS DOES NOT CONCERN ANY OF YOU! AODHAN, BATTLE OFFERS A THOUSAND TIMES MORE DISTRACTION, ALL OF THEM DEADLY...
A FAILURE? BUT MY SKILLS ARE BETTER THAN ANYONE AT THIS LEVEL! WHY DO I ALWAYS HAVE TO DO MORE?
WHEN MY UNCLE WAS TRAINING--
I HAVE DISCUSSED THIS MATTER ENOUGH, AODHAN! THE TEST IS A FAILURE...
YOU WILL GET THE OPPORTUNITY TO REDEEM YOURSELF WHEN--
MASTER SIMEON! THERE'S DANGER!

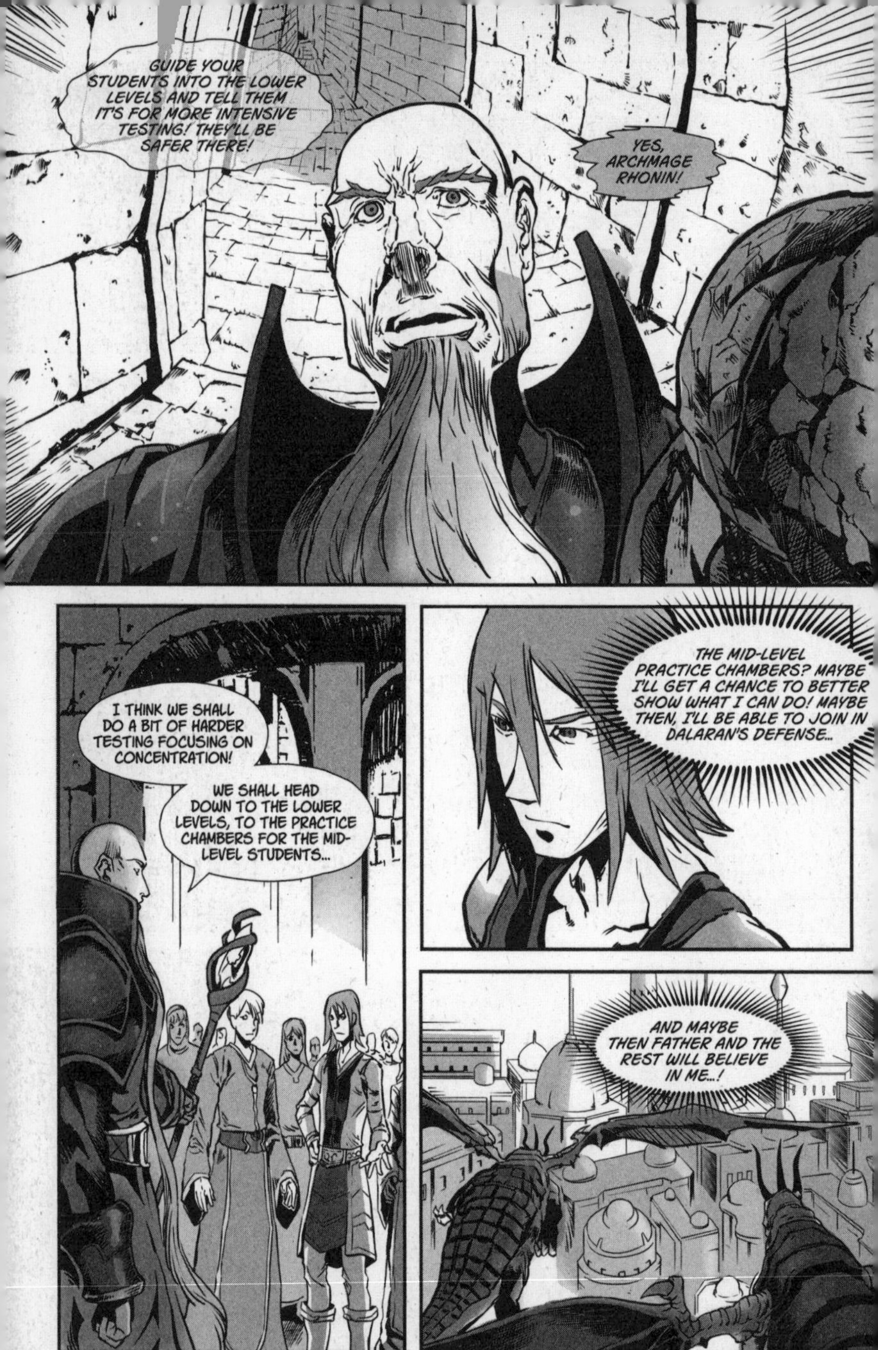
GUIDE YOUR STUDENTS INTO THE LOWER LEVELS AND TELL THEM IT'S FOR MORE INTENSIVE TESTING! THEY'LL BE SAFER THERE!
YES, ARCHMAGE RHONIN!
I THINK WE SHALL DO A BIT OF HARDER TESTING FOCUSING ON CONCENTRATION!
WE SHALL HEAD DOWN TO THE LOWER LEVELS, TO THE PRACTICE CHAMBERS FOR THE MID-LEVEL STUDENTS...
THE MID-LEVEL PRACTICE CHAMBERS? MAYBE I'LL GET A CHANCE TO BETTER SHOW WHAT I CAN DO! MAYBE THEN, I'LL BE ABLE TO JOIN IN DALARAN'S DEFENSE...
AND MAYBE THEN FATHER AND THE REST WILL BELIEVE IN ME...!

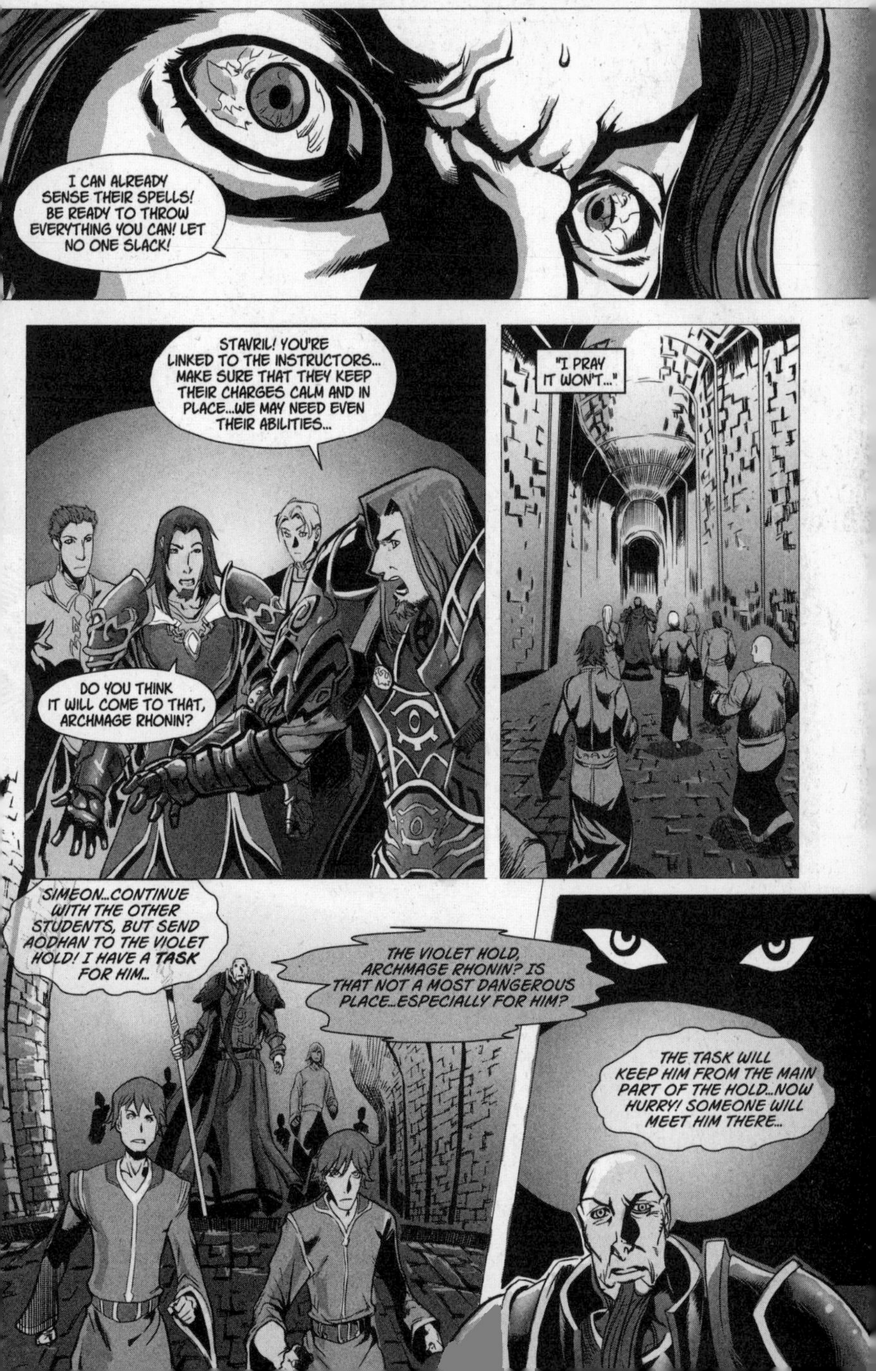
I CAN ALREADY SENSE THEIR SPELLS! BE READY TO THROW EVERYTHING YOU CAN! LET NO ONE SLACK!
STAVRIL! YOU'RE LINKED TO THE INSTRUCTORS... MAKE SURE THAT THEY KEEP THEIR CHARGES CALM AND IN PLACE...WE MAY NEED EVEN THEIR ABILITIES...
DO YOU THINK IT WILL COME TO THAT, ARCHMAGE RHONIN?
"I PRAY IT WON'T..."
SIMEON...CONTINUE WITH THE OTHER STUDENTS, BUT SEND AODHAN TO THE VIOLET HOLD! I HAVE A TASK FOR HIM...
THE VIOLET HOLD, ARCHMAGE RHONIN? IS THAT NOT A MOST DANGEROUS PLACE...ESPECIALLY FOR HIM?
THE TASK WILL KEEP HIM FROM THE MAIN PART OF THE HOLD...NOW HURRY! SOMEONE WILL MEET HIM THERE...

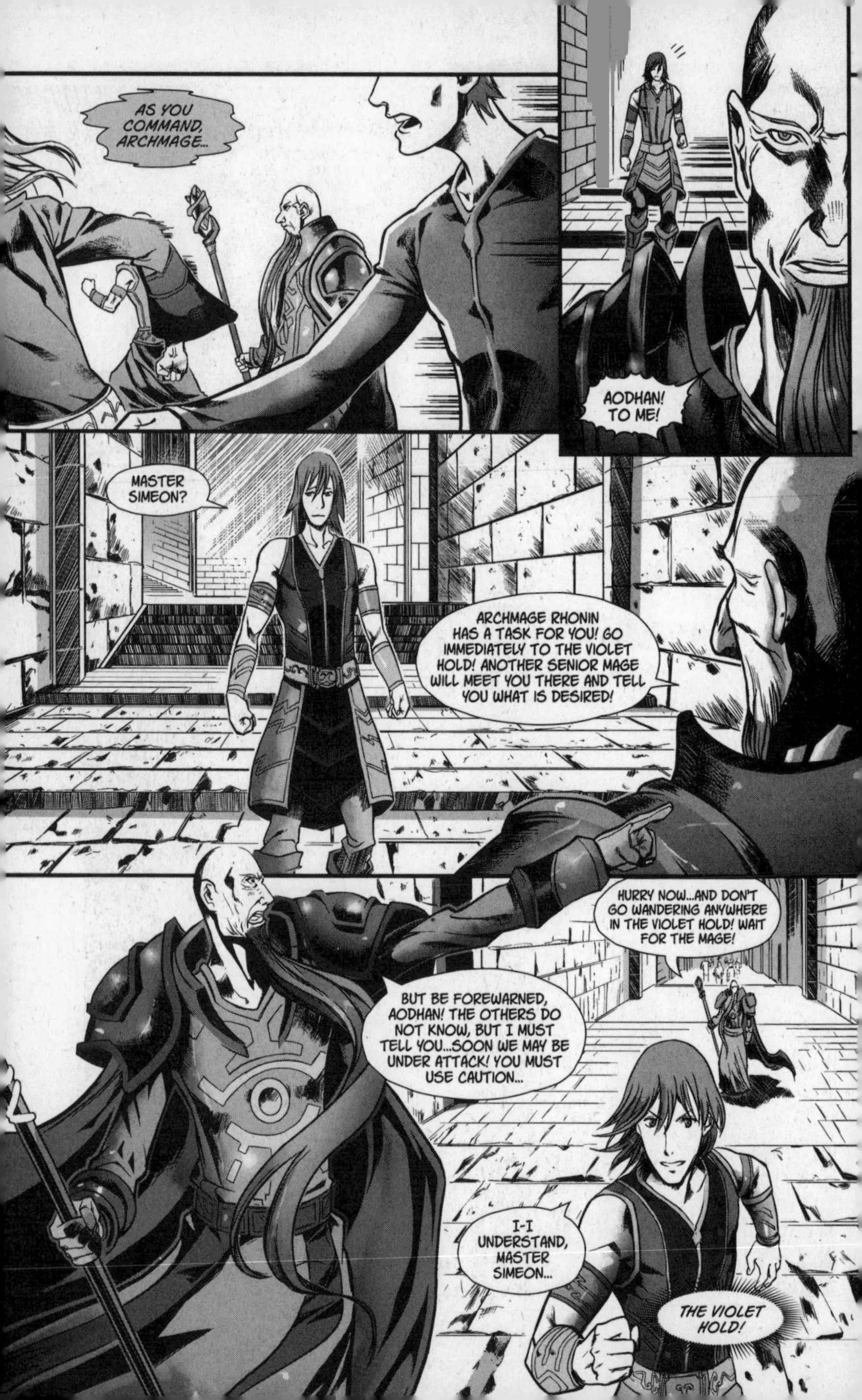

AS YOU COMMAND, ARCHMAGE...
AODHAN! TO ME!
MASTER SIMEON?
ARCHMAGE RHONIN HAS A TASK FOR YOU! GO IMMEDIATELY TO THE VIOLET HOLD! ANOTHER SENIOR MAGE WILL MEET YOU THERE AND TELL YOU WHAT IS DESIRED!
BUT BE FOREWARNED, AODHAN! THE OTHERS DO NOT KNOW, BUT I MUST TELL YOU...SOON WE MAY BE UNDER ATTACK! YOU MUST USE CAUTION...
I-I UNDERSTAND, MASTER SIMEON...
HURRY NOW...AND DON'T GO WANDERING ANYWHERE IN THE VIOLET HOLD! WAIT FOR THE MAGE!
THE VIOLET HOLD!

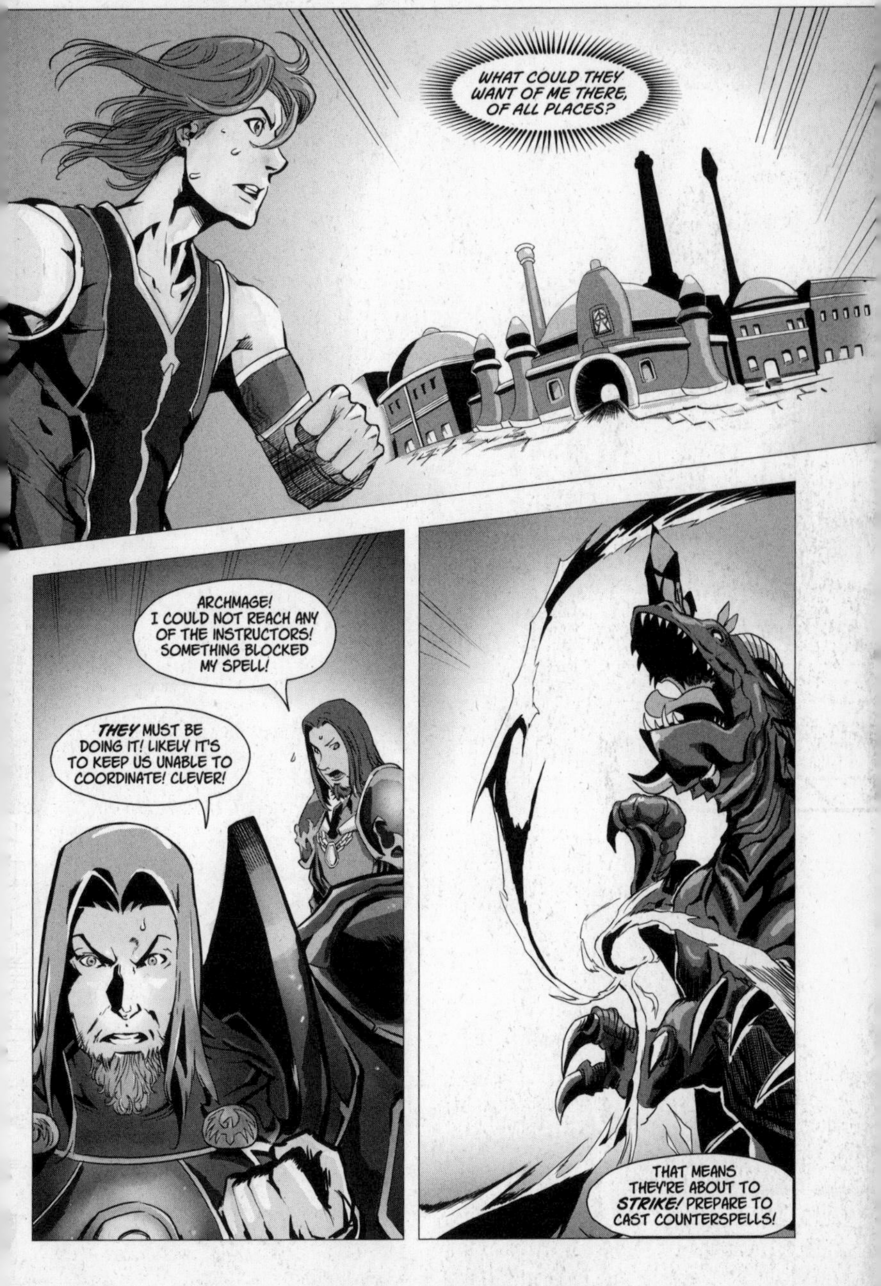
WHAT COULD THEY WANT OF ME THERE, OF ALL PLACES?
ARCHMAGE! I COULD NOT REACH ANY OF THE INSTRUCTORS! SOMETHING BLOCKED MY SPELL!
THEY MUST BE DOING IT! LIKELY IT'S TO KEEP US UNABLE TO COORDINATE! CLEVER!
THAT MEANS THEY'RE ABOUT TO STRIKE! PREPARE TO CAST COUNTERSPELLS!

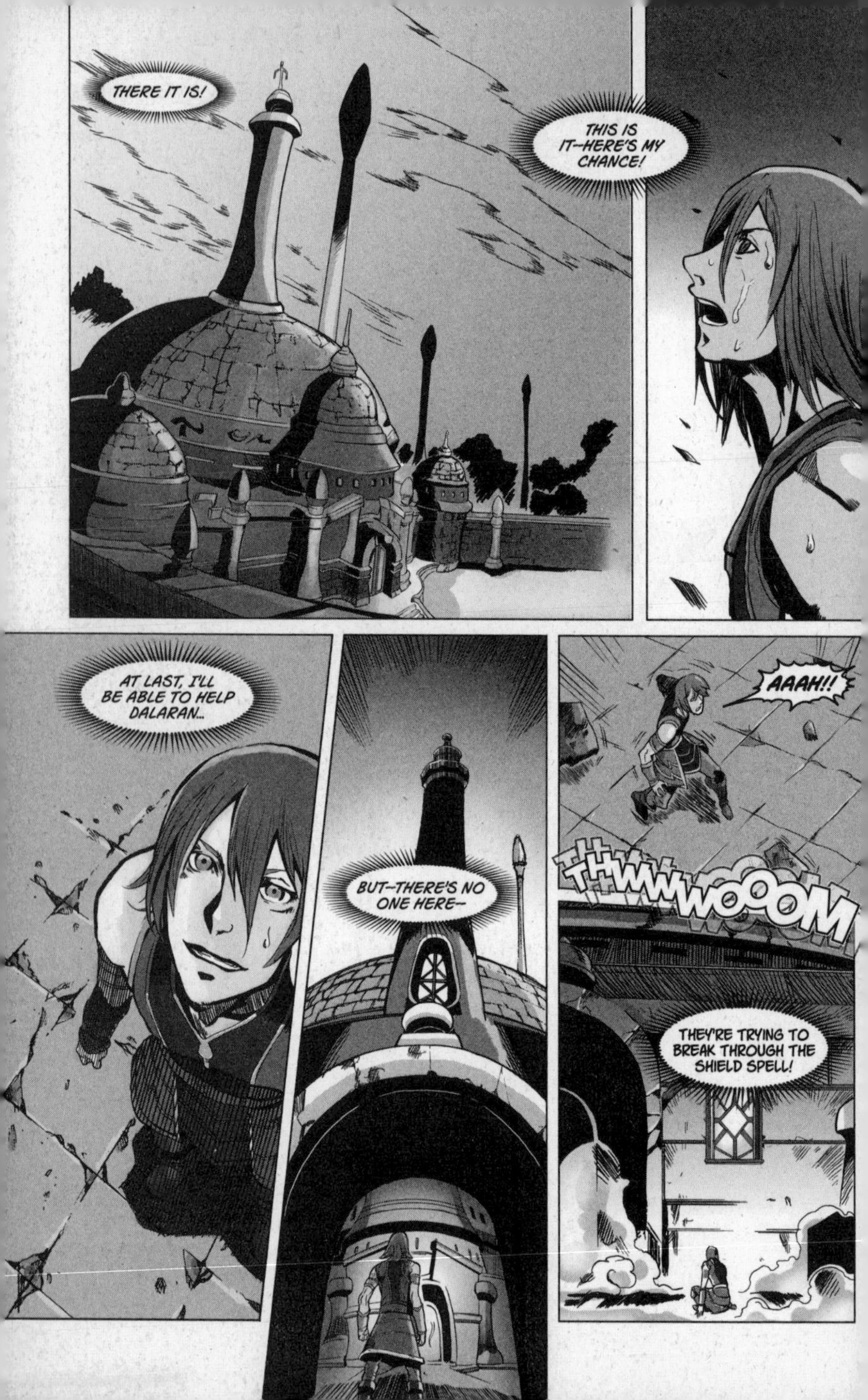
THERE IT IS!
THIS IS IT--HERE'S MY CHANCE!
AT LAST, I'LL BE ABLE TO HELP DALARAN...
BUT--THERE'S NO ONE HERE--
AAAH!!
THHWWWOOOOM
THEY'RE TRYING TO BREAK THROUGH THE SHIELD SPELL!

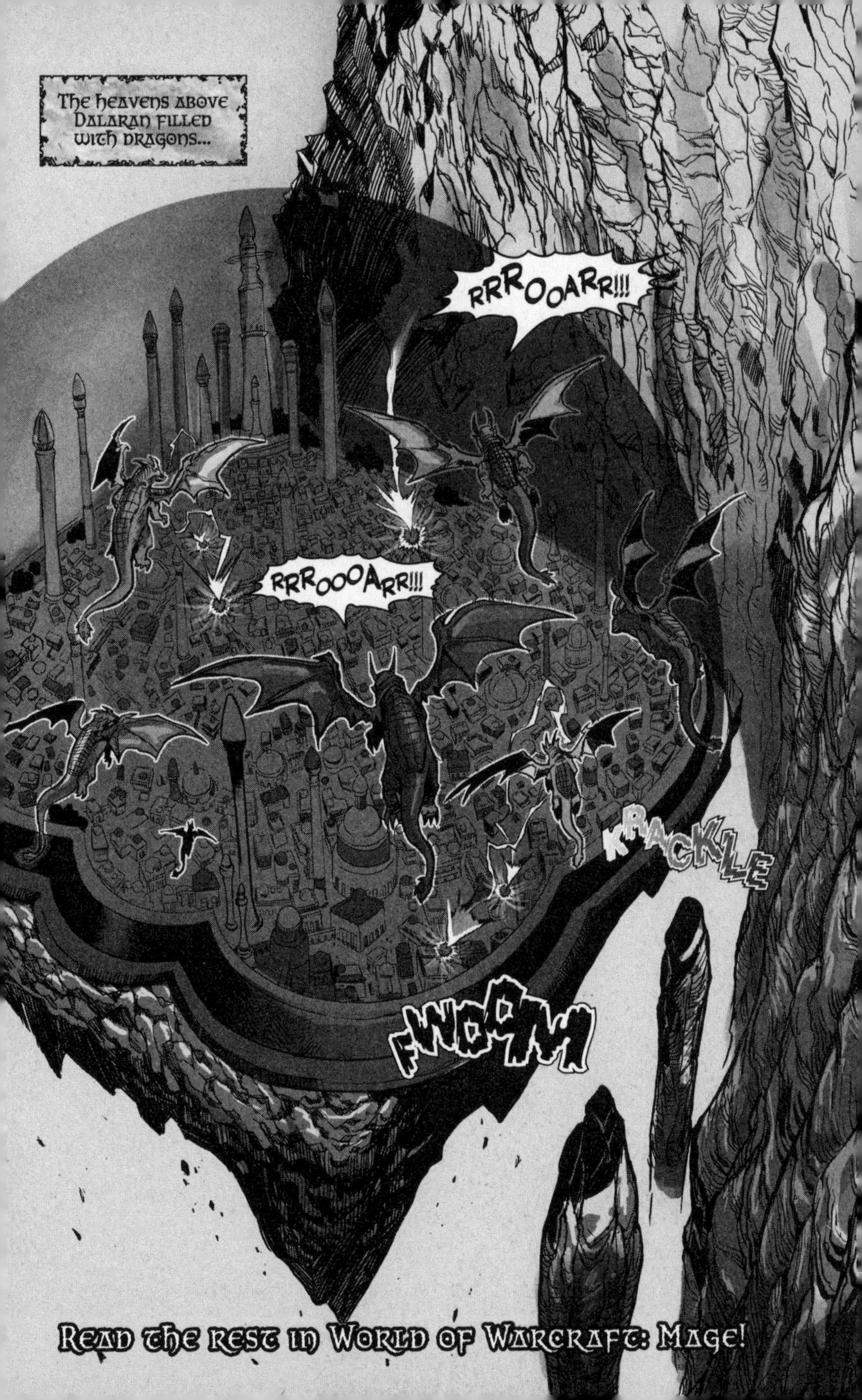
The heavens above Dalaran filled with dragons...
RRROOARR!!!
RRROOOARR!!!
KRACKLE
FWOOM
Read the rest in World of Warcraft: Mage!